The Art of Nutritional Cooking

Second Edition

Michael Baskette, C.E.C., C.C.E., A.A.C.
Eleanor Mainella, R.D.

Photographs by Spencer Tucker
Drawings by Jessica Delfino

Prentice Hall, Upper Saddle River, New Jersey 07458

Library of Congress Cataloging-in-Publication Data

Baskette, Michael.
    The art of nutritional cooking / Michael Baskette, Eleanor
Mainella; photographs by Spencer Tucker.—2nd ed.
        p.   cm.
    Includes index.
    ISBN 0-13-754417-0
    1. Cookery. 2. Nutrition. I. Mainella, Eleanor M. II. Title.
TX714.B373 1999
641.5—dc21   98-18834
                                                           CIP

Acquisition Editor: Neil Marquardt
Development Editor: Judy Casillo
Editorial Assistant: Jean Auman
Managing Editor: Mary Canis
Project Manager: Linda B. Pawelchak
Prepress and Manufacturing Buyer: Ed O'Dougherty
Design Director: Marianne Frasco
Interior Design: Jill Little
Cover Design: Ruta Fiorino
Cover Art: Steven Salerno/Lingren & Smith
Marketing Manager: Frank Mortimer Jr.

This book was set in 9/11 Bookman
by Pine Tree Composition and was printed
and bound by Banta Company.
The cover was printed by Banta Company

 © 1999 by Prentice-Hall, Inc.
Simon & Schuster / A Viacom Company
Upper Saddle River, New Jersey 07458

Earlier edition copyright © 1992
by Van Nostrand Reinhold

Printed in the United States of America
10 9 8 7 6 5 4 3 2

ISBN 0-13-754417-0

Prentice-Hall International (UK) Limited, *London*
Prentice-Hall of Australia Pty, Limited, *Sydney*
Prentice-Hall Canada Inc., *Toronto*
Prentice-Hall Hispanoamericana, S.A., *Mexico*
Prentice-Hall of India Private Limited, *New Delhi*
Prentice-Hall of Japan, Inc., *Tokyo*
Simon & Schuster Asia Pte. Ltd., *Singapore*
Editora Prentice-Hall do Brasil, Ltda., *Rio de Janeiro*

Contents

Preface   vii

1. *Nutritional Awareness* / 1
    Nutrition: knowledge or best guess   4
    The pleasures of taste   4

2. *Exploring the Past* / 7
    Food preservation   8
    Discriminating tastes   11
    Historical awareness of the nutritional value of food   12
    Properties of food   13

3. *Nutritional Guidelines* / 15
    Dietary guidelines for Americans   17
    Food guide pyramid   18
    Carbohydrates   18
    Proteins   32
    Fats and oils   44
    Vitamins   53
    Phytochemicals   70
    Minerals   71

4. *Health and Diet* / 97
    Diet and skin care   98
    Diet and aging   98
    Osteoporosis   99
    Diabetes   99
    Heart disease   100
    Cancer   101

Arthritis 101
Blood pressure 101

5. *Smell and Taste* / *103*

6. *Taste with Herbs and Spices* / *111*
History of spices 112
History of herbs 113
Availability and use of spices and herbs today 114
The flavors and smells of herbs and spices 116
An anthology of the most generally used herbs
and spices 117

7. *Natural Flavorings* / *127*
Flavoring vegetables 129
Oils and fats for flavor 140
Acid products 142
Flavored vinegars 142

8. *Flavoring with Wines and Spirits* / *145*
Nutritional components 146
Wines 147
Beers and ales 151
Brandy 152
Liqueurs 152

9. *Cooking for Nutrition* / *155*
Proper cooking techniques 157
Substituting fats in cooking 159
Reducing natural saturated fats in cooking 160
Substituting meats in cooking 161
Portioning 162

10. *Weight Control* / *165*
Nondiet approaches 166
Nutrition and weight control 169
The causes of chronic obesity 175
Appetite suppressants 176
Exercise and weight control 177

11. *The Food Label, Daily Values, and Goals 2000* / *179*

12. *The Vegetarian Diet* / *183*
Vegetarian classifications 184
Cooking for vegetarians 185
Seasonal menus 186
Balanced vegetarian items 187

13. *Menu Planning* / *189*
Nutrition: fad or trend? 190
The chef's role 191

Menu construction   191
The recipe   193
Substituting for fats   193
Substituting meats   194
Substituting protein alternatives   195
Staff development   195

14. *Marketing Nutritional Menus* / *197*
Federal guidelines   198
Building a reputation   200
Giving samples   200
Staff development   200
Food allergies and intolerances   201

15. *Breakfast Foods* / *209*

16. *Appetizers* / *227*

17. *Soups* / *247*

18. *Salads and Entremets* / *261*

19. *Vegetables, Legumes, Potatoes, and Grains* / *281*

20. *Meat* / *301*

21. *Poultry* / *323*

22. *Seafood* / *339*

24. *Vegetarian Entrees* / *357*

25. *Desserts* / *371*

Bibliography   385

Index   393

Preface

The science of nutrition, born out of our need to survive and our humanistic thirst for knowledge, has finally taken ground in the modern American kitchen. Whether food is professionally prepared or prepared for home use, the pairing of good cuisine with good nutritional value is a growing concept.

The Art of Nutritional Cooking, 2nd edition, is both a guide and a tool for those interested in preparing healthy food. It is more than a recipe book and much more than a nutrition text. It combines the science of nutrition with the art of cooking to illustrate the infinite possibilities for healthy foods that also satisfy hunger and taste and have eye appeal. We have taken the tenets of nutrition, combined them with the theories of cooking, and built a model for modern cuisine.

Good nutrition does not only help heal the sick, protect the aged, or build the young; it is what we should all strive to achieve in our quest for long and healthy lives. *The Art of Nutritional Cooking* does not deal solely with restrictive diets or stringent nutritional guidelines, but it proposes a change in the philosophy of cooking for all kitchens everywhere. The focus is on the natural flavors and textures of foods; the recipes rely on simple preparations and the world's larder of flavoring ingredients to heighten natural flavors and provide substance within nutritional guidelines.

We would like to acknowledge the support of the entire Prentice Hall staff for making this text a reality. In particular, we thank Robin Balizewski and our good friend Alice Barr, who encouraged us to write a second edition; and Neil Marquardt and Judy Casillo, who guided the writing of the manuscript and gave untiring advice and criticism along the way. A special thanks to a young Baltimore chef, Todd Pitera, who helped proofread the manuscript and who gave innumerable insights into making it user friendly as a reference, accurate in its premises, and fun to read as well.

Mike Baskette
Eleanor Mainella

Nutritional Awareness

People are becoming increasingly aware that what they eat has a direct effect on their standard of life and on their longevity. Yet the overabundance of food in the Western world has set the stage for gluttony and gourmandism. Nutritional science affirms that restraint and balance are necessary for good health. Americans, however, are leading hectic, busy lives—lives that often include meals eaten away from home, at fast food establishments, in workplace cafeterias, and in restaurants of a seemingly endless variety. Food service executives, therefore, must provide foods that not only meet standard nutritional guidelines but that cater to the dietary needs of specialized consumer groups, such as vegetarians. Thus in today's world nutritional awareness is necessary not just for consumers but for providers as well.

After completing this chapter, the student will be able to

▪ describe consumer perceptions of nutritionally prepared foods

▪ explain why nutritional guidelines do not take away from the chef's ability to create exciting and tasty meals

▪ discuss the trend that nutritional choices now appear on fast food, family dining, catering, and fine dining menus across the nation

▪ describe the three undeniable truths about nutrition

▪ describe taste as a complex sense

▪ discuss the notion of pleasure of taste as a well-founded psychological human attribute

Nutritional cooking is a philosophy of cooking that considers dietary guidelines of low fat, low cholesterol, and controlled sodium intake when prescribing cooking or baking techniques for the preparation of traditional and nontraditional foods. The art of nutritional cooking involves making foods that not only look and taste good but that promote good health.

This philosophy does not dictate abstinence, but the measurement and control of nutrient intake (including fats, cholesterol, vitamins, minerals, proteins, and carbohydrates). In most cases it is not necessary to eliminate fats or salt for a healthy diet, but instead to measure their amounts in foods and control how much of them you eat. The Department of Agriculture and the Department of Health and Human Services propose seven dietary guidelines for the promotion of good health. With the Food Guide Pyramid as a model, these seven guidelines, combined with nutritional cooking, a balanced diet, and exercise, are a prescription for good health.

The seven dietary guidelines for Americans include (1) balancing the food you eat and your level of physical activity to maintain or improve your weight; (2) choosing a diet rich in grain products, vegetables, and fruits; (3) choosing a diet low in fat, saturated fat, and cholesterol; (4) eating a variety of foods; (5) following a diet with a moderate intake of salt and sodium; (6) restraining your intake of sugar; and (7) using alcohol in moderation, if at all.

Each person's genetics, current health, and level of physical activity place different demands on nutrients and calories. Nutritionists determine general guidelines, but only a dietician can study each case, prescribe specific measurements of foods, and recommend specific cooking procedures for each need or goal. Whether weight control is doctor prescribed or an individual's personal goal, a dietician can prescribe daily, weekly, and monthly menus that, if followed, will foster healthy results. When the dietician joins with a chef in planning those menus, then nutritionally prepared foods can taste good, too.

Convincing the modern consumer that the health benefits of nutritionally prepared foods outweigh dining traditions and habits will be a difficult task. Nutritional guidelines seem to change from study to study, and many chefs do not appear committed to making nutritionally prepared foods taste good. It is no wonder that people often do not choose heart healthy or light fare unless it is medically necessary for them to do so—and even then such choices seem like a sacrifice, not a pleasing option.

It will be equally difficult to teach practicing chefs that good cooking does not depend on fats and salt for flavor. Chefs have been taught traditionally that fat equals flavor and that salt enhances taste. Dieticians may tell chefs to cut back on fat and salt in the meals they prepare, but what do dieticians know about cooking?!

The art of nutritional cooking can entice dieticians and chefs to work together to create great-tasting foods based on nutritional guidelines of low fat, low cholesterol, controlled sodium, high fiber, and high nutrient values while still satisfying the discriminating tastes of customers. Nutritional cooking is a move toward the natural flavors of foods through simple preparations.

It will be especially difficult to convince American diners to follow the principles of nutritional cooking in their fast-paced lives. The craze for fast, convenient food swept the United States in the mid-1950s and will likely continue unabated into the twenty-first century.

Food has become a convenience store item. Hot dogs, nachos, hamburgers, and pizza are available at a myriad of convenience stores alongside newspapers, cigarettes, coffee, and sodas. These foods can be grabbed and eaten quickly before work, at lunchtime, or after work or school.

With busy schedules, complicated family structures, and both parents working to support the family, who has time to plan and cook balanced meals every day?

The effects of poor nutrition often are not manifested in the young and strong. Often it is not until middle age and later in life that such ailments as heart disease, high blood pressure, and cancer take hold—all of which can be related to long-term poor nutritional habits. It is easy to forget the warnings of nutrition experts and worry about nutrition and health later in life. The easy accessibility of fast and convenient foods makes poor nutrition the easy choice for thousands of people every day.

The perception that foods must contain fats and salts for flavor is based on centuries of tradition and lore and a lifetime of personal experience and practice. It is difficult to change traditions in diet and cooking that have endured the passage of time. Diet and cooking are linked with the evolution of human civilization and are woven into the fabric of the human psyche. The lack of empirical evidence that poor nutrition affects everyone will cause most people to feel immune to the health risks associated with poor nutrition. "It will never happen to me" or "I'll worry about it later" become common attitudes. In the United States, "life, liberty, and the pursuit of happiness" translates into candies, ice cream, hamburgers, and fries—we are free to have them anytime we want them.

Spurred on by television, movies, and advertisements, "thin" is portrayed as beautiful and sexy, "overweight" as unhealthy, and "obese" as grotesque. Because most people want to be considered beautiful and to be accepted by others, there is a trend toward the fad diets and exercise videos that people hope will transform them into the models and actors they admire. Thus begins a new outcry for alternatives to traditional foods and eating habits.

Heart Healthy and light fare menu items in restaurants around the country are gaining market share every day. Consumer advocates won the battle for nutritional labeling on convenience foods in grocery stores. Vegetarianism is on the rise, and diet books of all descriptions become best sellers and daily topics of conversation.

Consumers who are aware of the health and life benefits of good nutrition are putting the burden on restaurants and food manufacturers to present good nutritional choices. If consumers don't have time to plan and cook in a nutritional way, it becomes the chef's problem and the store's responsibility to offer good-tasting foods that are nutritionally prepared and balanced.

The foundation for food service in the 1990s and beyond is comprised of nutritionally prepared menus in which taste and good nutrition go hand in hand, convenience and ease of preparation, and a wide variety of healthful choices. Nutrition is fast becoming a concern for all types of people: young, old, active, and sedentary.

Handwritten margin notes: Instant Gratification.

MSG- Chinese rest. Syndrom- head aches, Bad stuff etc.

Nutrition: knowledge or best guess

Scientific knowledge, based on the study of nutrition and health, strengthens the arguments of dieticians who lead the cause for nutritional awareness. It can take many years, however, to validate theories with measurable observations. Furthermore, the average person sees a dietician only when hospitalized. (Dieticians don't make house calls . . . yet.) If you are in the hospital, your main concern is getting well, not developing nutritional awareness. You have accepted that hospital food tastes bad, and your visitors smuggle in ice cream or potato chips. If you have been hospitalized for health problems caused by diet, you accept nutritional guidance and nutritionally selected and prepared foods as medicine—something you *must* take if you want to recover good health.

Consumers are expected to sift through mounds of inconsistent and fluctuating information regarding nutrition, diet, and health (information that the experts cannot even agree on). How can cholesterol be bad if our bodies generate their own source of cholesterol? What is the difference between "good" and "bad" cholesterol? What are the real concerns about salt? How can salt be bad and necessary for human health at the same time? Chocolate is bad for you one day, and good the next. In all cases the most important underlying questions still remain: How do you measure what is good and what is bad? Which "experts" do you believe?

The proper amounts of nutrients needed for good health are still being verified. Theories are proposed and studies made to prove or disprove those theories. Then more theories and more proof. It will take years to add verifiable knowledge to the study of nutrition. It may take even longer to change perceptions on health and diet.

Awareness and understanding of the basic tenets of nutrition can improve the quality of life as we know it. This knowledge will fuel continued studies and the fight to change perceptions. The human quest for healthier and longer lives may give the study of nutrition its strongest champion ever.

One reaction to the ever-changing information regarding nutrition and health may be to accept the three undeniable nutrition guidelines, the rules that everyone can agree on: (1) All fats need to be controlled in the diet, (2) salt should be used only for specific purposes, and (3) balance of foods consumed is the most important rule.

The pleasures of taste

Body and mind interact as our physical sense of taste, excited through outside stimuli, is interpreted by memory and perception. Although taste is a purely physical sense, centered on the mechanism of the tongue with its thousands of interpretive taste buds, it takes smell, touch (the texture of food in the mouth), traditions, religion, personality, and even genetics to turn an involuntary physical impulse into an interpretation of flavor. Flavor is, therefore, the quintessential collaboration of taste, smell, textures, genetics, and personal favoritism. Enjoyment of the flavor of foods is one of life's greatest pleasures.

The sense of taste is as complicated as any of the other natural senses. It is complex, refined, primal, and personal. Its indulgence is rewarded by sustenance and satisfaction.

Taste is a complex sense because it can be influenced by all of the other senses: sight, sound, smell, and touch. Foods that look good usually taste good. The sound of biting into a crisp apple speaks highly of a fresh, ripe taste. The feel of crispy, fried foods or smooth mashed potatoes on the palate helps build the level of flavors within a single meal.

Taste is a refined sense. It is in the harmony of flavors that cooks create the greatest tastes. Discord of flavors creates confusion in the mouth. Overly pronounced flavors in any single dish or accompanying dish will affect the overall ability to taste the foods on other plates. Flavors that are delicate need delicate accompaniments, and those that are pronounced need balance.

Taste is a primal sense. It was perhaps the first mechanism available to humans to help them discriminate between wholesome and poisonous foods. Taste creates involuntary repulsive impulses when something bad is placed in the mouth. It stimulates saliva production, in anticipation of eating, when something tastes good.

Taste is personal. It is a sensation guided by past experiences, family traditions, and personal commitment. There are some people who actually like the taste of soybean byproducts just because soybean is considered healthier than meat. Others like the taste of chitterlings, boiled okra, and Limburger cheese; others do not.

Anticipation for the taste of foods encourages us to eat when we're hungry and satisfies us when we're full. Akin to both art and science, taste combines the chemical elements and physical attributes of food and beverage with emotion to create individual boundaries of discrimination and appreciation.

We frequently use the pleasure of taste to escape from the many inconsistencies of life. We eat when we are happy, and overeat when we are depressed. The eighteenth-century gourmet Brillat-Savarin said, "It [taste] invites us, by means of pleasure, to make good the losses which we suffer through the action of life."* There are many reasons to eat for the sake of self-counseling.

In anticipation of a hard day's work we allow ourselves an extra portion of this or that to fuel our physical machines. At the end of the day or week, chiffon pie becomes a prize for hard work and peach cobbler a reward for honesty.

It is not easy, therefore, to accept a scientist who says we must give up taste and food preferences in light of better nutrition. After all, scientists are only looking at the issue of nutrition from the purely physical side of the equation. People who have major health or diet problems that require rigid dietary guidelines believe that they are bound to this scientific advice. For them, the perception is that nutritional cooking and the total absence of fats and salts are their medicine. They also know that medicine is not meant to be pleasurable, so they don't complain about the lack of flavor in their food. They do complain about the lack of choices.

Good nutrition is not just for the weak and the old but for all people who want to strive for a longer and healthier life. The design for nutritional cooking is no longer in the hands of scientists and dieticians alone. Educated chefs are offering their expertise and helping to turn tasteless, good-for-you food into food that is a feast for the senses as well as a boon for the body.

Review Questions

1. What are some of the problems in overcoming public opinion about the value and flavor of nutritionally prepared foods?

---

*Jean Anthelme Brillat-Savarin, *The Philosopher in the Kitchen* (New York: Penguin Books, 1984), p. 45.

2. How do the convenience food and fast food crazes affect the consumer's ability to obtain balanced meals and seek nutritional alternatives?

3. What does it mean for a science, like nutrition, to be verifiable?

4. What are some of the problems affecting the verifiability of nutritional science?

5. What are three generally accepted beliefs about nutrition and health?

6. Explain why taste is a complex sense.

7. Explain why taste is a refined sense.

8. Explain why taste is a primal sense.

9. Explain why taste is a personalized sense.

10. Who benefits from knowledge of nutrition and health?

Exploring the Past

For thousands of years, people across the globe have been dependent on fat and salt for survival. Then, in the middle of the twentieth century, people have been told that those same ingredients are bad for their health. No wonder there is so much skepticism and concern about the values of nutritional cooking.

By examining why, for centuries, people depended on fat and salt and by discussing why fat and salt are no longer of paramount importance, we can begin to foster acceptance of the tenets of nutritional cooking.

After completing this chapter, the student will be able to

- discuss why humans became dependent on fat for warmth and the preservation of foods
- describe how fat is still used today as a food preservative
- discuss why salt was depended on as a food preservative
- describe other forms of food preservation than those that require salt or fat as a major ingredient
- discuss the development of culinary art during the European Renaissance
- discuss the discoveries that linked food and nutrition to good health
- describe the one tenet of nutritional science that most people agree is the most important

A brief look at the history of food and cooking will help us understand why there is such a dependence on salts and fats in European, Asian, Baltic, and American diets. If we also consider the physiological and psychological associations with the taste of salt and the flavor of fat, we can conjecture why there is a reluctance to give them up for the sake of better nutrition.

As we discuss in this chapter, cooking with less fat and salt does not mean forfeiting taste for nutrition. There are ways to enhance the natural flavors of foods to the point that fats and salts are not required for great taste. In this chapter we suggest putting aside prejudice and questioning tradition when making decisions in cooking and baking.

Food preservation

Fats

Humans learn through observation and experimentation what to eat and how to survive. Often experiments would lead to a better way of life or other food sources; sometimes experiments led to disaster and death. Humans lived, experimented, remembered, and recorded their findings on safe and dangerous foods over several thousand years and long before written records.

A lot is left to conjecture on how humans first realized that there was a natural need for fat and salt in their diets, but there is little doubt that this fact was learned early on. Most members of the animal kingdom demonstrate the same basic needs. Perhaps it is from them that early humans took their first lessons.

Animals use fat for warmth and for reserves of energy when foods are scarce. Humans evolving on the colder continents would have been able to witness this occurrence in many instances. For example, black, Kodiac, brown, grizzly, and even polar bears are able to survive in extremely cold climates and winters when food becomes scarce by fattening themselves during the spring and summer months when food is plentiful. Their annual cycle begins when they emerge from their winter hibernation, drawn by the scent of spring flowers and berries. Then they spend the greater part of their waking days satisfying their voracious appetites.

Ducks, geese, beaver, muskrats, and other birds and animals that survive cold, barren winters wear great coats of fur or feathers over thick layers of fat.

Early humans stole the coats and consumed the flesh of these creatures. Similar to bears, these animals, which seemed to prefer cold climates, were always larger and fuller in the winter months. Early humans must have wondered if they, too, could survive winter's severe cold and shortage of fresh food by overeating during the plentiful months.

It would not take long to realize the advantages of eating animals high in fat. Such animals supplied clothing, shoes, and food—all from a single source. The humans who evolved in regions affected by cold weather were deeply concerned about keeping warm and struggled to keep from starving to death during long, barren winters. Copying the habits of other warm-blooded animals and birds that managed to survive cold climates and shortages of food was a natural progression and laid the groundwork for human adaptation.

In addition, fat is highly palatable. Scientists at Monell Chemical Senses Center in Philadelphia claim that the palatability of fat is partly due to its physiological properties. Fats, which contain twice as many calories as proteins and carbohydrates, provide the richest energy source for the human body. One of humankind's earliest fears, that of starving to death, was assuaged by the consumption of fatty animals and birds.

The feel of fat in the mouth contributes flavor to foods. "Mouthfeel," which describes the effect of textures and moisture on flavor, is an important aspect of fat. Fats tend to stay in the mouth longer than other foods do. Human body temperature is high enough to soften but not fully melt most animal fats. Just as fats and oils are hard to clean off exposed skin, they remain on the tongue with equal perseverance. The heavier, or more saturated, the fat, the longer it stays on the tongue. The length of exposure to flavor coupled with fat's innate property of supplying energy and warmth made fatty foods appear as great food sources for health, energy, and protection.

After many thousands of years of experimentation and observation, a discovery was made in the Nile Valley of Egypt that incorporated fat as a food preservation medium: Cooking animals that are naturally high in fat, like ducks and geese, and storing the cooked meats and cooking juices in the same baked clay jar they were cooked in would preserve those meats for long periods of time. Duck confit (duck cooked and served in its own fat and natural juices) is an example of this early cooking and preservation method, which provided food in times when fresh meats were not readily available. The Egyptians did not understand that fat rendered from cooking fatty birds and animals and allowed to float to the top of the cooking vessel and congeal sealed out the oxygen necessary for most bacteria to grow (these bacteria are the main cause of food deterioration), but this simple procedure did work. The association between the presence of fats and preserved foods was firmly established.

By the time of the European Renaissance (A.D. 1150–1500), it was a sign of opulence if a person could afford enough food during the winter months to maintain a plump physique year-round. Obesity eventually became fashionable, even a sign of beauty, for the wealthy.

A heavy, fatty taste was a sign of foods being well preserved. Fats were also used to give moisture to dried foods like sausages and meat puddings. It was this ancient practice that predicated the recipe for an American Indian food called *pemmican*, which was used for survival during North American winters. When Alexander MacKenzie became the first European to cross the North American continent in 1793, he carried with him this powerfully sustaining food. Traveling unsettled lands was treacherous, and fresh game and wild vegetables were often scarce. Pemmican was a portable food supply that provided high-energy proteins and insulating fats.

The recipe for pemmican had been handed down for thousands of years as a sustaining meal for travelers and hunters. Pemmican was a mix of dried lean meat and equal amounts of animal fat pounded into a thick paste. The technique of drying thin strips of meat in the sun and the wind had been used for centuries; the addition of fat lent pemmican its palatability. The paste was then wrapped in animal skins and sealed with tallow (a blend of beeswax and rendered animal fat). The Cree Indians, who aided MacKenzie's expedition, would have included chopped berries or nuts for variety and flavor. Along with its amazing holding properties, pemmican could also taste good.

Pemmican was one of the first products to benefit from a new invention: the canning process, developed by Nicholas Appert in France and Bryan Donkin in England at the beginning of the nineteenth century. Canning increased the holding qualities of foods like pemmican and placed them in easily portable containers at the same time. Even today, in a world of science and nutrition, pemmican is still used by explorers. William Steger and his five companions—Jean-Louis Etienne, Victor Boyarsky, Geoff Somers, Keizo Funatsu, and Qin Dahe—depended on the nutritional properties of pemmican when they crossed Antarctica by dog sled in a seven-month journey between August 1989 and March 1990.

For thousands of cultures throughout history, the use of animal fat as a preservative kept wholesome food from spoiling; its use as an insulator protected people from the cold; and fat gave moisture to otherwise unpalatable foods. In addition to salts and smoking techniques, "well-fatted meats" became a symbol of properly preserved and expensive food. In situations like MacKenzie's, foods rich in fats and salts were necessary to sustain life.

Salt

The use of salt as a preservative dates back many thousands of years. Egyptians used salt as part of the mummification process for their pharaohs in an attempt to preserve the flesh for the resurrection of the body (in line with Egyptian religious beliefs). The Egyptians understood that heavily salted flesh could be preserved almost indefinitely. Salted fish became one of Egypt's earliest exported foods.

Another religious tradition fostered the prevalence of salted foods. The tradition of Lent in Christianity required, under penalty of death, that only fish be eaten during the forty days culminating with the Passion of Christ at Easter. Whereas fish was available only to people living near water, salted fish became a source of salvation to many inland Christians.

By the seventh century A.D., salted fish, poultry, and meat became a steady food supply where and when fresh meat was not available. Fresh meat was hard for the average person to obtain. The dependence on hunting dwindled as population centers grew too large to be supplied by the occasional kill, and hunting lands grew ever distant as civilization spread into cities and towns. Few people could afford to slaughter an animal every time they wanted meat, so when they did slaughter, they had to preserve most of the meat for later consumption. Even farmers who raised livestock could not afford the fields needed to raise hay or straw for winter cattle feed; these fields were needed to grow grain and legumes for the dinner table. The farmers' practice was to slaughter the majority of the livestock in the fall of the year, sell what little fresh meat they could, make sausage and salamis out of the fatter animals, and salt and cure the rest.

The earliest cooking method simply placed fresh meats directly onto hot coals. This method had the unpleasant side effect of coating the meat with ashes and grit. With the invention of iron, great spits were forged to hold meats over smoldering coals, improving the results tremendously. As the development of ironworks continued, great cauldrons were produced and were used to cook fresh, salted, and dried meats along with root vegetables and herbs for a type of soup that became the daily meal. Cooking in a cauldron with large amounts of water returned some of the moisture to dried meat and removed some of the salt from salted meats. Dried legumes and root vegetables were added for sustenance and helped absorb some of the saltiness, producing a more palatable meal. There were no recipes for these cauldron meals, but time and experience turned soup making into staple meals for millions of people worldwide.

Smoking and drying

Smoking and drying are two additional ancient food preservation techniques. Juices were first forced out of thin strips of meat by pounding and crushing the flesh with large stones. In dry climates, the meat strips were then hung outside in the sun and wind to finish drying. In moist climates, houses had to be built in which meat could be hung to dry. A fire would be built to dry the flesh quickly.

Smokehouse fires provided additional benefits. Smoke kills the bacteria that cause meat deterioration, and it adds flavor depending on the type of wood used. Even though bacteria were not discovered until the second half of the nineteenth century (by Louis Pasteur), people knew that smoked meat had enormous holding properties. The different types of wood used to fuel the fires produced a wide variety of flavors. The woods that produced pleasant tastes were used, and the ones that produced unpleasant tastes were abandoned.

Smoking became so popular a trend that it crossed the boundaries of food preservation into food flavoring. It would be used to flavor any number of foods, including wines and cheeses. A hearty red wine stored in a charred oak barrel or a piece of smoked aged cheese became great accompaniments to the most ornate meals.

Many types of sausages and salamis, including chorizo, andouilles, and pepperoni, resulted from early experiments in smoking and drying cured meat products. Meats that are finely ground, originally by hand, along with almost equal parts of fat are then mixed with herbs, spices, and a significant amount of salt. The resulting product, when smoked slowly over a hardwood fire, lasts for several months without the aid of refrigeration. Variety in these products is achieved through the use of different kinds of meats and different combinations of herbs, flavored seeds, and spices. Other foods that incorporate fats or salt as preserving ingredients include almost all processed meats, hams, bacon, caviar, sardines, anchovies, pickles, and olives.

Discriminating tastes

The European Renaissance thrived between the twelfth and sixteenth centuries and was a time when art and music were raised to new heights of excellence. Culinary art was no exception. (Culinary art may be defined as taking food beyond what is required for sustenance into a realm of appreciation and discrimination.)

In the Renaissance, people (especially royalty and wealthy people) were willing to experiment with combinations of various food flavors and ingredients for the sake of creation rather than for mere food. Food was no longer scarce. Exotic foods from other parts of the world could be bought with a price that wealthy individuals were willing to pay. They were not afraid to experiment and even sought different and new preparations and presentations of their foods. Europeans became so enthralled by the introduction of spices and seasonings from the Eastern countries that wars were fought over their procurement and great prices paid for their delivery.

Over thousands of years, humans became so consumed with the indulgence of the physical senses that society placed restrictions on such extravagance. Sex and alcohol were the main articles of offense. Taste, a reasonably private sense, could be defended as a reward for controlling the other expressive senses. Overeating was an acceptable indulgence of the flesh. Overeating became so popular over the centuries that taste and pleasure became synonymous. According to the French gourmet Jean Anthelme Brillat-Savarin, "And yet of all our senses, taste, such as Nature has created it, remains one which, on the whole, gives us the maximum of delight."* This serves as testament that food was no longer used solely for nourishment but for mere joy.

Understanding the history of fat and salt in our diets gives us the strength to abandon them in search of new taste discoveries. They are no longer required as food preservatives, and bodily fat reserves are no longer needed since food has become available year round due to reliable and fast transportation, efficient planting and harvesting machines, refrigeration, freezing, and improved canning.

New sensations in taste can be created using only the natural flavors of foods and modern cooking techniques to stimulate our senses. Salt and fat will never have to dominate over other natural flavors. They will now take their proper place as equals to the other flavors of the world's food supply.

Historical awareness of the nutritional value of food

For centuries people accorded certain healthful properties to food. Their reasoning was usually guesswork and was often laced with legend and superstition. For example, garlic was used to ward off demons (the belief that garlic could dispel demons arose from evidence that garlic and other herbs relieved people of common ailments, which were thought to be based on demonic possession). As the centuries progressed, humankind's information regarding health and disease became more scientific. Evidence began to show a direct connection between diet and good health. There still wasn't enough evidence, however, to affirm any specific relationship between the two.

By the turn of the seventeenth century, sea captains had learned that sailors would be less likely to contract scurvy if they received rationed citrus juice as part of their daily food allotment. Scurvy affected the gums and the healing of sores. It still wasn't known why citrus must be taken daily, nor why other cheaper fruits would not produce the same results. Scurvy is a disease caused by a deficiency of vitamin C. We now know that vitamin C is water soluble and therefore needs to be consumed daily. The concept of vitamins was unknown in earlier days, let alone the concept of water and fat solubility.

By the beginning of the eighteenth century, people were beginning to realize that it was not merely the quantity of food, but the types, varieties, and wholesomeness of food that was important for a healthy diet. The science of nutrition, the precise discrimination of the composition of foods and their effect on human development, was born in the early nineteenth century.

---

*Jean Anthelme Brillat-Savarin, *The Philosopher in the Kitchen* (New York: Penguin Books, 1984), p. 45.

Properties of food

In 1840, Justus von Liebig was the first scientist to describe human and animal tissue, including food, as being composed of carbohydrates, fats, and "albuminoids," later called proteins. He hypothesized that these, together with liquids, would be the "parts of foods" needed to sustain human life. Together with other nineteenth-century theorists, Liebig linked the mechanisms of the human body to the principles of fuel-burning engines. Leibig conjectured that there existed a precise connection between the specific types of foods consumed and good health. These initial discoveries lent support to the benefits of eating meats, fats, and starches. Fruits and vegetables were still considered supplemental foods.

During the same period, Louis Pasteur was perfecting his theories on the existence of microorganisms. He believed it was the "high" smell of rotten foods that identified them as unfit for consumption. The process of fermentation also intrigued Pasteur. Evidence of fermentation was thousands of years old, but no one could explain the process. Pasteur believed something came from the air itself that triggered the transformation of malt grains and grape juice into ale, beer, and wine. Thus began the search for living particles too small to be seen with the human eye. Pasteur identified and studied these microorganisms. He raised theories that would later be used to perfect the process of canning and would lead to the discovery of pasteurization and the use of controlled fermentation.

Vitamins were not discovered until the beginning of the twentieth century, when Dutch scientists began research into the causes for certain diseases like beri-beri. It is no wonder, then, that controversies and disagreements persist about the importance of certain components of food in maintaining good health.

There is only one premise of nutrition that everyone seems willing to accept: A healthy diet requires a balance of foods and a balance of ingredients. Overconsumption is now considered unhealthy. The new science of nutrition grows more exact every day, threatening thousands of years of traditional food habits. No wonder it is often met with such skepticism.

Review Questions

1. How does the history of food preservation affect the acceptance of nutritional information and guidelines in today's market?

2. How does a study of habits of bears, ducks, and geese explain the dependence on fat in the early human diets?

3. What classical duck preparation has its origin in ancient cooking traditions?

4. How is fat used today as a food preservative and to add moisture to dried and smoked food products?

5. What are two of the earliest known uses for salt in religious and food preservation practices?

6. Why was cauldron cooking an early development in cooking techniques during the Middle Ages?

7. Name two ancient food preservation techniques, in addition to fats and salts, that are still practiced in the modern world.

8. Name food products used in modern kitchens that use fats or salt for their preservation qualities as well as for taste.

9. What influences in both trade and economics influenced the development of culinary art during the European Renaissance?

10. How did English sea captains accidentally discover the cure for scurvy, a deadly disease?

11. In 1846, what scientist first identified carbohydrates, fats, and proteins as components of food necessary for health?

12. What food preservation technique that does not rely on heavy amounts of salt or fat came as a result of Louis Pasteur's studies of bacteria and other microorganisms?

13. What major nutrition component was discovered by Dutch scientists in the early twentieth century?

14. What is one premise of nutrition that has gained overwhelming support from scientists, nutritionists, and doctors?

Nutritional Guidelines

It is critical that practicing cooks and chefs understand the basic concepts and theories of nutritional science. This knowledge will help them promote good nutrition by selecting the proper ingredients and cooking techniques. Nutritional science is a complex field, and in this text we can discuss only the basics of the ever-evolving science of food and health. Nonetheless, knowledge of the basics will go a long way toward promoting good health.

After completing this chapter, the student will be able to
- describe the importance of carbohydrates as an energy source
- list the enzymes needed for the digestion of carbohydrates
- discuss the problem of lactose intolerance
- describe the roles of fiber in maintaining good health
- describe the features of insoluble and soluble fiber
- discuss how glycogen acts as a stored energy source
- describe the hormone regulation of blood sugar
- explain the protein requirements for cell renewal and other functions
- determine a person's protein requirement based on standard formulas
- describe the value of plant protein in the diet
- discuss special concerns of vegetarians regarding protein intake
- describe net protein utilization, protein effectiveness rating, and nitrogen balance
- discuss the role of cholesterol in health
- discuss the importance of fat in the diet
- list food sources of saturated and unsaturated fat
- describe health considerations when selecting fats and oils
- develop a plan for moderate cholesterol intake
- describe how hydrogenated and trans fats are formed, and discuss current concerns about both
- plan a low-fat diet
- define and describe fat soluble vitamins and their relationship to health
- define and describe water soluble vitamins and their relationship to health
- list recommended dietary amounts for each vitamin
- list which vitamins are toxic when taken in excess
- discuss the role of each vitamin in supporting health
- discuss the health problems associated with inadequate amounts of each vitamin
- list the major food sources of each vitamin
- describe phytochemicals and their protective function
- list and describe the macrominerals and recommended intakes
- list and describe the microminerals and recommended intakes
- discuss the role of each mineral in health
- discuss the problems associated with excess intake of minerals
- select foods based on their mineral content

The natural foods we eat possess health-giving nutrients required for the growth and support of all body functions. The human body is a marvelous machine capable of processing and utilizing these life-sustaining nutrients, but the nutrients must first be consumed, digested, absorbed, and then metabolized before any benefits can be gained.

There are two categories of nutrients: macronutrients (carbohydrate, protein, and fat) and micronutrients (vitamins and minerals). The designations *macro* and *micro* refer to the amounts needed for normal health. Macronutrients are needed in larger amounts and make up the greatest mass in foods. Micronutrients are needed in lesser amounts but are equally important.

The U.S. Department of Agriculture and the U.S. Department of Health and Human Services define a healthy diet as one that "contains the amounts of essential nutrients and calories needed to prevent nutritional deficiencies and excesses. . . . Healthful diets also provide the right balance of carbohydrate, fat, and protein to reduce risks for chronic diseases, and are a part of a full and productive lifestyle."* This chapter deals with those nutrients, their requirements, and their benefits.

Beginning with a discussion of the *Dietary Guidelines for Americans* and the Food Guide Pyramid, we explore the world of nutrients, their role in promoting life, and the foods they come from. We discuss the presence and purpose of carbohydrate, which should make up the major part of our food intake, as well as protein, fat, vitamins, and minerals. Separate sections cover starches, naturally occurring sugars, and dietary fiber.

Nutritional information continues to be tested and may change in light of future findings. Once the basics of nutrition have been learned, however, it is easy to incorporate new findings about food requirements.

Dietary guidelines for Americans

The U.S. Department of Agriculture and the U.S. Department of Health and Human Services jointly published a document on nutrition and diet therapy entitled *Dietary Guidelines for Americans* (DGA). This document is available by writing to the U.S. Department of Agriculture and is summarized here. The seven primary guidelines are as follows:

- Balance the food you eat with physical activity; maintain or improve your weight.
- Choose a diet with plenty of grain products, vegetables, and fruits.
- Choose a diet low in fat, saturated fat, and cholesterol.
- Eat a variety of foods.
- Choose a diet moderate in salt and sodium.
- Choose a diet moderate in sugars.
- If you drink alcoholic beverages, do so in moderation.

People require essential nutrients for growth, health, and energy that the body cannot produce itself and must obtain from food. Recommended dietary allowances have been established for each essential nutrient and can best be obtained through the consumption of a variety of foods.

---

*U.S. Department of Agriculture and U.S. Department of Health and Human Services, *Dietary Guidelines for Americans*, 4th ed. (Washington, D.C.: Government Printing Office, 1995), pp. 1–48.

Physical activity is also required for good health. Calorie needs vary depending on age and health, and they increase or decrease in direct relationship to physical activity and exercise. According to the DGA, sedentary people, including may older adults, need fewer calories relative to younger, more active individuals. People who severely restrict their calorie intake to lose weight jeopardize their ability to consume the proper amounts of nutrient-rich foods. Care, exercise, and a prescribed plan must be followed to guarantee good health.

Food Guide Pyramid

The Food Guide Pyramid is a model that describes the proper selection of foods to promote good health. It is a prescription to consume a variety of foods.

The United States Department of Agriculture (USDA) has identified five food groups from which to choose. Previously there were four such groups, but the fruit and vegetable group has been split into two separate categories. The five groups are grain products (breads, cereals, rice, and pasta); vegetables; fruits; milk, yogurt, and cheese; and the meat group, which includes meat, poultry, fish, dry beans, eggs, and nuts.

The Food Guide Pyramid offers these simple guidelines:

- Choose most of your daily foods from the grain products group (six to eleven servings), the vegetable group (three to five servings), and the fruit group (two to four servings).
- Eat moderate amounts of foods from the milk group (two to three servings), and the meat group (two to three servings).
- Choose sparingly foods that provide few nutrients and are high in fat, salt, and sugars.

The smaller number of servings is recommended for people who should take in about 1600 calories daily (e.g., those who are sedentary). The larger number of servings is for those who consume 2800 calories per day, such as more active people.* The average person requires about 2000 calories per day and needs to consume a number of servings between the low and the high numbers.

Portions are defined in the DGA. Portions of grain products include 1 slice of bread; 1 ounce of ready-to-eat cereal; or 1/2 cup cooked cereal, rice, or pasta. For the vegetable group, 1 cup raw leafy vegetables, 1/2 cup of other vegetables (cooked or chopped raw), or 3/4 cup of vegetable juice equals one portion. For the fruit group, 1 medium apple, banana, or orange; 1/2 cup chopped, cooked, or canned fruit; or 3/4 cup of fruit juice equals a single portion. A single portion of the milk group includes 1 cup of milk or yogurt, 1½ ounces of natural cheese, or 2 ounces of processed cheese. For the meat group, a single portion is 2 to 3 ounces of cooked, lean meat, poultry, or fish; 1/2 cup cooked dried beans; 1 egg; 2 tablespoons of peanut butter; or 1/3 cup nuts.

Carbohydrate

The main function of carbohydrate is to supply energy for normal bodily functions and levels of physical activity. Each gram of carbohydrate supplies 4 calories of energy.

---

*DGA, 1995, p. 6.

The major energy-yielding carbohydrates are starches and sugars. These are represented by a whole range of foods, including cane, beet, and fruit sugar; molasses; honey; flour; corn starch; rice; and potatoes. Refer to Figure 3–1 for the carbohydrate content of foods.

Although it is not digested by humans, fiber can contribute small amounts of energy when bacteria ferment it to produce short-chain fatty acids (which can be metabolized to energy).

Carbohydrate's role is to combine with protein to form various compounds in the body. If there is not enough carbohydrate present in the diet, then protein must be used for energy, before it can be used for building and renewing body cells. Therefore it is said that carbohydrate "spares" protein. A high-carbohydrate meal also increases the release of serotonin, a neurotransmitter. Serotonin has a calming effect on the body.

	Starch	Sugar	Fiber
Milk, 1 cup	—	Lactose, 12 grams	—
Meat, poultry, and fish	—	—	—
Eggs	—	—	—
Seeds, 1/2 cup	30 grams	—	2–6 grams
Beans, 1/2 cup	20 grams	—	5–8 grams
Nuts, 1/2 cup	20 grams	—	2–5 grams
Fruits, 1/2 cup	—	Mainly fructose, 15 grams	1.5–3 grams
Vegetables, 1/2 cup	5 grams	Some vegetables have small amounts	1.5 grams
Bread, 1 slice, and cooked grains, 1/2 cup	15 grams	—	Whole grains (2.5 grams) are a better source of fiber than processed flour products (1.0 grams, refined)
Sugar, 1 teaspoon	—	Sucrose, 5 grams	—
Fat	—	—	—

Figure 3–1 Carbohydrate Content of Foods *(Source: The amount of starch and sugar is based on the Exchange Lists for Meal Planning, The American Diabetes Association, Inc., and The American Dietetic Association, 1995; fiber figures are estimated by the author.)*

Starches and sugars

Examples of starch-containing foods are those made from grains (such as bread, crackers, pasta, and cereal) and beans, potatoes, other tubers, nuts, and seeds. Well-known grains include wheat, rye, oats, rice, barley, and corn. Less commonly used grains are millet, spelt, quinoa, and amaranth.

Examples of sugar-containing foods are milk, fruit, juices, some vegetables, honey, and products made with sugar (beet sugar, corn syrup, and/or sugar cane) such as candy, cakes, and sweet chocolate.

Over half of an individual's daily calorie intake should come from carbohydrates. If the proper amount of carbohydrate is lacking in the diet, the liver will convert fatty acids and amino acids to carbohydrate to supply energy. If fewer than 15% of a person's total daily calories come from carbohydrate foods, the brain will not be supplied with nourishment quickly enough. Therefore, eating a high-protein diet that is low in carbohydrate often leads to headache, dizziness, and fatigue.

Digestion of Starches

All carbohydrate must be converted into glucose before the body can use it for energy. Starches, called complex carbohydrates or polysaccharides, have many glucose units that must be broken apart in the process of digestion.

Starch is composed of two kinds of molecules, amylose and amylopectin. Amylose consists of glucose units joined to form linear chains. Amylopectin consists of many short chains of glucose units that form branches. Starch is 16 to 20% amylose and the remainder amylopectin. In the dry starch granule molecules of linear amylose twist and intertwine around the branches of amylopectin.

Starch digestion begins in the mouth with an enzyme called salivary amylase or ptyalin. This process hydrolyzes cooked starch into dextrin and shorter-chain sugars. (Raw starch, such as uncooked macaroni, cannot be digested.)

Food does not remain in the mouth long enough for much digestion to take place. The salivary amylase that mixes with the food continues to work in the stomach so that as much as 50% of the starch can be broken down there. When the stomach acids become mixed with the food, starch digestion halts.

Starch digestion continues when the chyme (liquefied food) enters the duodenum. There, an enzyme called pancreatic amylase, which is secreted from the pancreas, breaks the unbranched starches into maltose, a disaccharide (a two-unit sugar). Branched starches, which can contain up to 2000 units of glucose, are broken down into dextrin, which has six units of glucose. Dextrin is then further broken down into the disaccharide maltose.

Finally, maltose is broken down into two units of glucose, which can be used for energy. The breakdown process is called hydrolysis because it is literally a splitting of the bond by the addition of water.

Digestion of Sugars

Disaccharides are two-unit sugars. Maltose, sucrose, and lactose are the disaccharides. Maltose comes from the breakdown of starch. It is also found in sprouting grain, malted cereals, malted milk, and corn syrup. Sucrose is associated with table sugar, but it is also found in some fruits and vegetables. Lactose is milk sugar.

Specific enzymes in the intestine digest the disaccharides. Maltose is acted on by the enzyme maltase, sucrose by sucrase, and lactose by lactase. The end results are monosaccharides, also called simple sugars.

The monosaccharides are glucose, fructose, and galactose. Maltose yields two units of glucose, sucrose yields glucose and fructose, and lactose yields glucose and galactose.

disaccharide	+	enzyme	=	monosaccharides
maltose	+	maltase	=	glucose + glucose
sucrose	+	sucrase	=	glucose + fructose
lactose	+	lactase	=	glucose + galactose

Only glucose can be used as an energy source. Fructose and galactose are converted into glucose in the liver. The chemical formula for all three monosaccharides is $C_6H_{12}O_6$.

Another name for glucose is *dextrose* or *grape sugar*. Glucose is widely distributed in nature and is found in fruit, vegetables, and tree sap. *Levulose* is an old name for fructose.

Fructose is often called fruit sugar. It is the sweetest tasting of the monosaccharides and is found in fruits and vegetables, in the nectar of flowers, in honey, and in molasses.

Galactose is primarily found in lactose (milk sugar). When milk is digested, the lactose is broken down into glucose and galactose.

Small amounts of galactose are found in apples, bananas, pears, carrots, peas, sweet potatoes, and some other fruits and vegetables. Legumes, organ meats (although high in cholesterol), and cereals contain small amounts of galactose.

Dietitians need to plan a galactose-restricted diet for infants born with galactosemia, a defect in galactose metabolism. Low galactose infant formulas are now available.*

Absorption of Sugar

Some glucose can be absorbed through the lining of the mouth, but it is primarily absorbed in the small intestine and is taken up by the cells that need it. The absorbed glucose that is not needed for energy is carried to the liver to be stored as glycogen.

Fructose and galactose go to the liver and can be converted into glucose. Glucose is carried to all parts of the body via the bloodstream. It passes into the tissues and cells by way of fluids surrounding the cells. Glucose is oxidized in the cell in a long series of chemical processes that culminate in the production of energy, carbon dioxide, and water. Carbon dioxide is excreted by the lungs. Excess carbohydrate can be converted and stored as fat, or it can assist in the formation of amino acids.

Glycogen

The liver converts some glucose into a starch called glycogen (glucose can also be converted into amino acids or fatty acids). Glycogen can be converted to glucose and released when needed by the body. Muscle cells can also store glucose as glycogen, for use during physical activity. The process of converting glucose to glycogen is called glycogenesis.

One-third of the body's glycogen is stored in the liver. Two-thirds is stored in the muscles as an emergency energy supply, which can last two to three hours.

---

*Gropper S., Gross, K., and Olds, J., "Galactose Content of Selected Fruit and Vegetable Baby Foods: Implications for Infants on Galactose Restricted Diets." *Journal of the American Dietetic Association*, Volume 93, number 3, March 1993, pp. 328–329.

Hormone Regulation of Glucose

Hormones regulate blood glucose levels. After a meal, glucose in the blood stimulates the pancreas to release the hormone insulin, which causes the entry of glucose into the cells. Insulin also triggers the liver to produce glycogen from glucose and to remove glucose from the blood if glucose levels are high. If there is not enough insulin, the blood sugar will be too high (as in type I diabetes).

The classic early symptoms of diabetes are excessive thirst and frequent urination. Non-insulin-dependent diabetes is the result of inadequate insulin receptors on the cells. Obesity is a risk factor for this type of diabetes.

A normal fasting blood sugar level is 70 to 100 milligrams per 100 milliliters of blood. It takes one to one and a half hours after a meal for the blood sugar to return to fasting levels.

Too much insulin results in hypoglycemia (too little sugar in the blood). There are a number of medical factors that could be responsible for hypoglycemia. Symptoms of hypoglycemia are irritability, nervousness, and shakiness. Severe hypoglycemia can lead to unconsciousness. A nutritional plan that includes six small meals per day (low in refined sugar and high in protein) is prescribed for hypoglycemic individuals. A sample 6 meal plan might include fruit, egg, cereal or bread, and low-fat milk for breakfast; yogurt or cheese as a mid-morning snack; fish, salad, fresh fruit, and low-fat milk for lunch; 1/2 sandwich or nuts or cold chicken for an afternoon snack; meat, two vegetables, and a potato for dinner; and an evening snack of 1/2 meat sandwich.

Glucagon, another hormone produced by the pancreas, is involved in releasing glucose from the liver's glycogen when blood glucose levels are low.

Adrenaline, also called epinephrine, is a hormone produced by the adrenal glands. Adrenaline can stimulate the breakdown of liver glycogen into glucose, which can then pass to the tissues for use. Adrenaline also changes muscle glycogen into glucose, but lactic acid is formed in the process. Part of the lactic acid can be reconverted to glycogen and stored in the liver for later use. Stress is one of the signals that releases adrenaline. This stress trigger ensures that energy is available in the case of emergencies.

Excessive stress can cause rushes of adrenaline. These adrenaline rushes, in turn, release glucose and elicit insulin. The adrenal gland can become exhausted with repeated stress, and hypoglycemia can result. This type of hypoglycemia can have the following symptoms: fatigue, headache, irritability, visual disturbances, shortness of breath, dizziness, rheumatoid-type pains, backache, digestive disturbances, shakiness, and numbness in the arms and legs.

Waiting too many hours between meals can also bring on hypoglycemic symptoms.

Enzyme Deficiency: Lactose Intolerance

Sugars can be digested only when the proper disaccharide enzyme is present. Diseases that damage the intestinal lining, such as celiac disease, are associated with enzyme deficiency. Celiac disease is an inherited intolerance to gluten, a protein in wheat, rye, barley, and oats. Aging is also accompanied by a decrease in enzyme abundance. This is one reason why the elderly may experience gas when eating too much sugar.

The disaccharide lactose, found in milk, may cause problems such as bloating, cramps, gas, and diarrhea in some individuals. People who live in parts of the world where milk is not a safe food, or where it is not available, show a diminished amount of the enzyme lactase. Lactose intolerance then becomes a genetic condition and passes to future generations. Much of the world's population is lactose intolerant.

Lactose intolerance can easily be verified by a hydrogen breath test. Milk is given to the patient and the breath is then tested for hydrogen; its presence (not usually found in the breath) indicates lactose intolerance. The flatulence (gas), nausea, bloating, diarrhea, and cramps associated with lactose intolerance are partly due to osmotic activity (water entering the intestine to dilute the sugar) and partly due to bacterial fermentation. Intestinal bacteria form lactic acid, fatty acids, and hydrogen gas. The fatty acids are absorbed by the intestine and are an energy source. When the lactose concentration of the small intestine exceeds the bacteria's ability to digest it, osmotic pressure results in increased motility, pain, and diarrhea.

Most lactose intolerant people do not develop symptoms before ingesting the amount of lactose in two glasses of milk, about 24 grams. The lactose intolerance test, when it is given, uses the amount of lactose in about a quart of milk.

Lactose is mostly found in whey (the liquid part of milk). Therefore, hard cheeses made from milk curd have little lactose if aged for 60 days and can be eaten with relative safety. Cream, ice cream, and milk chocolate, on the other hand, contain large amounts of lactose. Although whole milk is better tolerated than skim milk, milk in general causes fewer problems if it is taken with a meal. Yogurt is well tolerated if it contains active cultures. Freezing yogurt, however, destroys the *Lactobacillus* bacteria, which would otherwise ferment the lactose to lactic acid. Frozen yogurt, therefore, is not recommended for those with lactose intolerance.

The culture used in acidophilus milk also does not help those with lactose intolerance. This culture does not grow in the milk but is added after being grown in a medium. Thus it does not ferment the lactose to lactic acid.

Although calcium absorption is not influenced by lactose intolerance, milk products are usually avoided by those who develop symptoms. Fortunately, calcium can be obtained from other natural sources. Calcium-rich foods other than milk include collard greens, turnip greens, mustard greens, kale, small fish with bones (sardines, for example), salmon, beans (particularly soybeans), and tofu (soybean curd).

The lactose enzyme lactase, in the form of a liquid or pill, can be added to milk or ingested along with it to help people who are lactose intolerant enjoy milk and milk products.

Carbohydrate Loading for Sports

Athletes engaging in endurance sports know the importance of carbohydrate foods for energy. They have learned to manipulate their diets to increase the glycogen content of their muscles, in this way ensuring that they have extra energy available when they need it.

Research shows that stripping the muscles of glycogen allows them to be replenished with an increased amount of glycogen. There are various methods to achieve this glycogen loading. One two-phase method is as follows:

Phase I	*Phase II*
1. Increased exercise	1. Rest
2. Low-carbohydrate meal plan	2. High-carbohydrate meal plan

Each phase is three days long and should be started one week prior to the activity or sport. The total number of calories consumed in each phase should be equal.

A sample daily diet containing approximately 4000 calories might contain as many as 16 servings of starchy food (8 cups) during the loading phase, whereas the stripping phase would feature as much as 18 ounces of animal protein and 12 tablespoons of fat. Both phases would include moderate servings of fruits and vegetables and adequate liquids. It is easy to see why Phase I of this diet, which may be high in cholesterol and saturated fat, is subject to criticism. Several precautions must be taken if the diet is used at all. The stripping phase should contain at least 100 grams of carbohydrates to prevent hypoglycemic symptoms. The loading phase should not contain candy and sweet sodas, which may cause stomach bloating.

There is controversy concerning the merits of glycogen loading for athletes, who are better able than most to turn fatty acids into energy. It must be remembered that glycogen will hold water, and this reserve in the muscle will cause a tight, stiff feeling. The athlete might need this reserve of water, however, so this could be considered an advantage as well as a disadvantage.

Sweets for Energy

There is a fallacy about using sweets, often in the form of candy, to increase energy before exercise or sporting activities. An overload of simple sugar in the gastrointestinal tract will cause bloating and diarrhea, which will detract from any energy gain. The bloating and diarrhea are due to excessive water drawn into the intestines to decrease the unnaturally high concentration of sugar. Sugar (which is the disaccharide sucrose) and honey both break down into the simple sugars glucose and fructose. Therefore, excessive amounts of sweets should not be taken before participation in sports events. Refined sugar is a source of energy, but it has no other nutritional advantage. It is without vitamins and minerals and contributes to tooth decay, a major health problem in children. Honey also has few nutrients.

Weight Reduction Gone Wrong

A weight reduction diet that promoted fruit as the main food resulted in death from osmotic diarrhea (osmotic diarrhea is caused when too much water drains into the intestines). The major nutrient in fruit is the carbohydrate fructose—a simple sugar. Too much fruit sugar draws excessive amounts of water into the intestine and can cause osmotic diarrhea. Too much diarrhea can lead to dehydration, which can cause death. Although fruit contains vitamins, minerals, and valuable fiber, it should be eaten in moderation, not as the sole food source in the diet.

Fiber

Although fiber is carbohydrate, it is not digested by humans. Consequently, fiber is not a source of energy. The human intestine does not have the capacity to digest fiber that cows, sheep, and some other animals possess. It is true, however, that small amounts of energy are released when the intestine's bacteria produce short-chained fatty acids from fiber.

The fact that fiber is basically not digested by human intestinal enzymes is its main advantage. The indigestible substances help carry harmful wastes from the body.

Dietary fiber is categorized into two types, soluble and insoluble. The insoluble fibers are lignin and the celluloses (both cellulose and most of the hemicelluloses). The soluble fibers are some of the hemicelluloses, pectin, gums, and mucilages.

Fiber is found in varying amounts in all plants. Cellulose, hemicelluloses, pectin, and lignin are components of the plant cell wall. The fiber within the plant cells is sometimes referred to as storage polysaccharides and includes gums, algal polysaccharides (such as alginate, carrageenan), and mucilages. There is a synthetic fiber called methylcellulose, which is a gummy product resulting from the introduction of the methyl group into cellulose.

All plants have more than one type of fiber. The amounts of soluble and insoluble fiber vary from plant to plant. More insoluble fiber is found in whole wheat, corn bran, vegetables, and the skins of fruit. More soluble fiber is found in dried beans, oats, barley, sweet potatoes, carrots, citrus fruits, and apples.

The following are types of fiber and their functions in the plant:

Type of Fiber	Plant Function
Cellulose	Cell wall
Hemicelluloses	Cell wall
Lignins	Woody part of plants
Pectins	Intercellular cement
Gums and mucilages	Secretions

Animal Fiber

For all practical purposes, animal products do not contain fiber. Meat, poultry, fish, eggs, and milk products are considered fiber-free foods. Of some interest, however, are indigestible polysaccharides, of animal origin, called chitin and chitosan. These are found in the skeletons of insects and in aged beef as well as in tempeh and shellfish. Chitosan can also be produced synthetically. These viscous polysaccharide substances could, in the future, be used as thickeners and stabilizers in processed food.

Properties of Soluble and Insoluble Fiber

Soluble fibers dissolve in water and thicken liquids. Pectin is an example and is used in pie fillings, jams, and jelly. Commercial pectin is usually extracted from citrus products for use as a thickening agent. Natural sources of pectin include orange pulp, sweet potatoes, apples and other fruits, and vegetables.

Purified pectin is not palatable and causes nausea if taken in large amounts. It is used to thicken yogurt.

Gums are used extensively in the food industry to affect food texture. Oat gum is extracted from oat bran, and guar gum comes from the Indian cluster bean.

Mucilage is also viscous and gummy. It is one of the water soluble fibers found in plants such as seaweeds.

Insoluble fiber absorbs water and swells like a sponge. (Think of a cellulose sponge.) Insoluble fibers increase the bulk and softness of the stool and are important for regular bowel movements.

Selecting High-Fiber Foods

Removing the peels from fruits and vegetables reduces the amount of fiber eaten. Juices contain only a small fraction of the fiber found in the fruit or vegetable. Dates, figs, prunes, and raisins are very high in fiber. Melons and berries also have a high fiber content, but they have less sugar and are lower in calories than dates, figs, prunes, and raisins.

The lowest-calorie fiber foods are vegetables such as celery, cucumber, mushrooms, zucchini, and string beans. Iceberg lettuce is mostly water and has very little fiber content.

It can be confusing to choose high-fiber grains because a brown color does not always reflect the presence of bran. In some products caramel is added to deepen the brown color. There are excellent high-fiber whole wheat breads, cereals, and crackers available. Read the ingredient list to make sure that whole wheat, not just wheat, is mentioned. Also check the percentage of the recommended daily values for fiber. In some breads, the percentage can range from 5 to 10%. Rye bread and rye crackers usually contain very little whole rye flour.

In the beginning, whole grain breads may be enjoyed by toasting them or even adding jam to lessen the effect of the whole grain taste. A choice of a partial whole grain product is also a good way to start including whole grains in the diet.

Whole grain flour can replace some of the refined flour in baking, thus adding nutrients without completely changing the taste. Whole grain pastry flour makes a softer crumb for cakes and pies than regular whole wheat flour.

The bran contains most of the fiber in grain. The germ contains some fiber as well. Adding either of these to refined flour helps increase fiber, vitamins, and minerals.

A high-fiber diet can be palatable and tasty—it goes far beyond a bowl of bran cereal for breakfast, as shown in Figure 3–2.

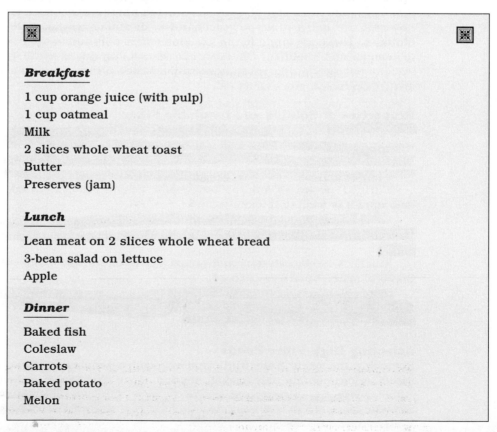

Breakfast

1 cup orange juice (with pulp)
1 cup oatmeal
Milk
2 slices whole wheat toast
Butter
Preserves (jam)

Lunch

Lean meat on 2 slices whole wheat bread
3-bean salad on lettuce
Apple

Dinner

Baked fish
Coleslaw
Carrots
Baked potato
Melon

Figure 3–2 Sample High-Fiber Diet

A Problem with Wheat Fiber

A much discussed disadvantage of wheat fiber is in the phytates that it contains. Phytates are necessary for the synthesis of the cell wall starch during the plant's germination and are, therefore, a necessary part of plant's life cycle. The problem is that in humans phytates bind minerals and keep the body from reaping their nutritional benefits.

In countries where the diet is marginal for adequate nutrition, phytates are a problem, but in healthy diets, mineral intake often exceeds the amounts bound by phytates or phytic acid.

The problem of phytates is solved in whole grain breads by the addition of yeast, which inactivates the phytates. There is no phytate problem with sprouted grains. Phytates in unleavened whole wheat bread may decrease vitamin D metabolism as well. This is another reason to choose yeast-raised varieties. Whole grains are important because they contain the B vitamins that are needed for the chemical processes to turn carbohydrates into energy. Enrichment puts back only vitamins B_1, B_2, and B_3, but not vitamin B_6 or pantothenic acid, another important B vitamin.

Healthy but Problematic Beans

Beans of many varieties provide water soluble fiber, protein, minerals, and the important vitamin folic acid. Many people, however, are concerned about the flatulence, or intestinal gases, that beans produce. Gas discomfort from beans can be prevented by taking a commercial enzyme available in pill or liquid form. Soaking beans, changing the water before cooking, and rinsing off canned beans also help to prevent this gas. One type of bean may cause gas whereas another may not. It is worth discovering individual tolerances in deference to beans' nutritional values. Beans are also low in fat, come in many varieties, and are generally inexpensive food choices. Soups and salads are a good way to introduce beans into the diet for people who won't eat them in whole portions.

Other Fiber-Containing Foods

Rice bran has half the soluble fiber of oat bran and can be found in some cakes and cereals. Corn and barley also contain soluble dietary fiber.

Nuts also contain fiber but have a high oil content and should be eaten in moderation. They are a good source of protein, vitamins, and minerals. A nut butter spread on whole wheat bread packs a lot of fiber.

No RDA for Fiber

There is not RDA for fiber, but health experts recommend 25 to 35 grams per day for a healthy diet. Most Americans, however, eat only half of that amount because of a high dependence on processed foods. The American Cancer Institute recommends 25 to 40 grams of fiber per day. Over 50 grams of fiber per day may decrease zinc, iron, magnesium, and calcium absorption and should be avoided.

The new food labels define high fiber as being 5 grams or more per serving, and a good fiber source as 2.5 to 4.9 grams per serving. Products claiming "more fiber" indicate an extra 2.5 grams per serving.

Psyllium

Psyllium is an herb high in soluble fiber. Psyllium seed husk is used as a laxative. It is produced from a plant, plantago, that grows in India and the Mediterranean. Psyllium seed husk is usually made into a powder and used as a medicine to regulate the bowels. Plenty of water must be taken with psyllium medication; otherwise, an impaction of the stool could occur. For healthy people, it is better to eat a balanced diet with high-fiber foods than to take psyllium seed products. A balanced diet will provide necessary nutrients along with the fiber.

There are reports of some allergies to psyllium. One psyllium-containing cereal was removed from the market for this reason.

It may be the other components in fruits, vegetables, and grains besides fiber that protect against disease. This is another reason to eat a normal diet rather than to take psyllium seed medication.

Locust Bean Gum

Locust bean gum comes from the endosperm of the locust bean, also called carob. Locust bean gum is not from the same part of the plant from which the chocolate substitute, carob, is obtained. (That comes from the husk.) Carob, however, is high in pectin and in lignin. It comes from trees grown in the Middle East, Spain, Morocco, Greece, and Cyprus, as well as in southern regions of the United States. It takes 15 years before the trees bear the carob fruit, which is a glossy, brown pod 4 to 12 inches in length and 1 to 2 inches wide. Each pod contains numerous hard seeds in a sticky, sweet membrane. This sticky part dries and resembles peanut brittle and is enjoyed by some ethnic groups.

In research studies, locust bean gum has been reported to decrease low-density lipoprotein (LDL) and very-low-density lipoprotein (VLDL) cholesterol by binding bile acids, but it has no effect on glucose. In large amounts, it causes temporary flatulence and increased stool bulk. In ancient times it was used as a laxative. The other gums do not seem to have this water-holding capacity. Locust bean gum is used as a food additive and helps the texture of commercial products by making them thicker. An example is ice cream, which may have gum agents added.

Flaxseed

A report on ground flaxseed used in the preparation of banana nut muffins and oatmeal cookies appeared in the *American Dietetics Association Journal.** Replacing the flour with 30 to 50% ground flaxseed produced an acceptable product. The fat in the recipe was also reduced by 35% to allow for the flaxseed's own oil.

Flaxseed is a source of soluble (mucilage) and insoluble (lignins) dietary fiber. Omega 3 fatty acid in flaxseed provides another benefit.

Whole flaxseed keeps well in a cool, dry place. Ground flaxseed should be kept frozen to prevent rancidity.

Flaxseed can also be used as an egg replacer in baking (it acts as a binder). This makes it possible for people who are allergic to eggs to continue to enjoy their favorite desserts. The flaxseed is boiled in water and then simmered until the water becomes viscous and resembles raw egg white (about five minutes). To replace one egg, use 1 tablespoon of flaxseed to 1/3 cup water.

Health Aspects of Fiber

Lignin comes from the woody part of plants. Although classified as fiber, lignin is described by some as a monocarbohydrate with no known role in human nutrition. Lignin may protect against diarrhea. On the other hand, cellulose, found in the plant cell walls, and hemicellulose, found in both the cell wall and cell contents, bind water and thereby increase stool bulk and decrease transit time. This gives them laxative characteristics.

Frequent evacuation of waste from the colon may help in preventing colon cancer. Water soluble fibers do not increase stool bulk, but they help in moving

---

*Alpers, L., Sawyer-Morse, M., "Eating Quality of Banana Nut Muffins and Oatmeal Cookies Made with Ground Flaxseed. *Journal of the American Dietetic Association*, Volume 96, number 8, August 1996, pp. 794–796.

waste out of the body faster. Wheat bran is the best food source for cellulose. A bran flakes breakfast cereal is, therefore, a good laxative. Avoiding constipation also helps prevent hemorrhoids, a painful swelling of the veins near the anus.

Cholesterol-Lowering Properties of Fiber

The pectins, gums, and mucilages carry away some bile salts and some fatty acids. Bile salts contain cholesterol, which is usually recycled back to the liver. Removal of cholesterol by fiber can aid in controlling cholesterol levels. (See the section on cholesterol on page 44.)

The water soluble fiber in oats and beans lowers high-density lipoproteins (HDLs) and LDLs in a favorable proportion. Pectin, guar gum, and oat gum have these unique cholesterol-lowering properties.

Neither cellulose nor hemicellulose has significant cholesterol-lowering effects. It is the high viscosity of the gums that is responsible for lowering cholesterol in the blood (known as hypocholesterolemic action). Pectin and guar gum, however, are five times less effective than the medicine cholestryamine in binding bile salts. Therefore, medication in addition to diet may be necessary to reduce blood cholesterol levels.

It is possible that dietary fiber imparts another mechanism to lower cholesterol other than bile excretion. It may increase clearance of LDL (the bad cholesterol).

The *Nutrition Action Health Letter* reported that a Harvard male health professional study of 43,000 men showed that a fiber intake of 29 grams per day led to a 41% lower risk of heart attack over men who ingested only 12 grams of fiber per day.* Fiber from grains appears to be the most helpful (see Figure 3–3). The usual American intake is about 16 grams of fiber per day.

The cholesterol protection of fiber may come from antioxidants in the bran; from the minerals selenium, copper, and manganese; or from the vitamin E from the germ. Phytic acid and phenolic acids in whole grains might also be beneficial.

Other studies found that the rate of heart disease decreases with an increase in fiber, but adjustments for fat removed the association. Contrary to this finding, a 12-year follow-up study showed a decrease in death from heart disease associated with a 6-gram increase in daily fiber from cereal. The effect was independent of any other dietary variables.[†]

Blood Sugar Control

There are studies that link fiber to the control of blood sugar in diabetes. A highly processed diet is rapidly absorbed in the upper small intestine, creating a rapid rise in blood sugar. The presence of fiber in the diet delays sugar absorption. All types of fiber impede the outward passage of sugar from the intestine, but the most effective are the viscous fibers guar gum and traguncanth.

Pectin and methylcellulose (a gummy product resulting from the introduction of the methyl group into cellulose) are also viscous, but in research studies the use of a special crisp bread made with guar provided the best results. In tests done with natural foods, beans were found to lower blood sugar better than breads and grain products. Diabetics on a diet of high-fiber foods such as

---

*Liebman, Bonnie, "The Whole Grain Guide." *Nutrition Action Health Letter*, Volume 24, number 2, March 1997, p. 9.
†Committee on Diet and Health, Food and Nutrition Board, Commission on Life Sciences, National Research Council, *Diet and Health: Implications for Reducing Chronic Disease Risks.* Washington, DC: National Academy Press, 1989, pp. 294–295.

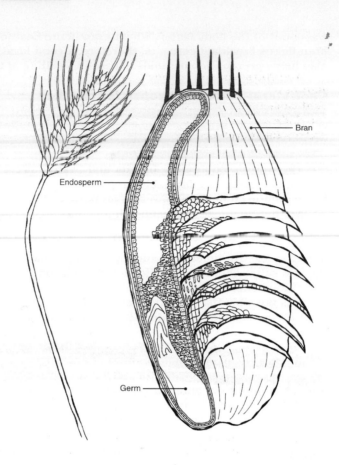

Vitamins	Bran	Germ	Endosperm
B$_1$	33%	64%	3%
B$_2$	42%	26%	32%
B$_3$	86%	2%	12%
B$_6$	73%	21%	6%
Pantothenic acid	50%	7%	43%

Note: Most of the protein (70 to 75%) is in the endosperm, but the quality of this protein is less than the quality of the protein found in the germ (8%).

Figure 3–3 **Grain of Wheat** (Source: *Drawing by Geraldine Mintz. The Wheat Flour Institute, "Kernel of Wheat." Millers National Federation: 600 Maryland Avenue, S.W., Suite 305 West Wing, Washington, DC 20024.*)

whole grain cereals, vegetables, and legumes are able to reduce their intake of insulin. Whole grains are not processed to remove the fiber that is in the bran, whereas white flour has most of the fiber removed.

The Nurses Health Study has followed 80,000 women (nurses) since 1986. Part of the study involved participants filling out diet questionnaires. It appears that women who eat the most sugar, white bread, and pasta are at higher risk for diabetes than women who reported eating a high-fiber diet. By 1992, 915 nurses had developed non-insulin-dependent diabetes.[*]

Diverticulosis

There is evidence that fiber helps prevent diverticulosis, a condition in which pockets are formed in the wall of the colon. These diverticuli, little herniations, may become inflamed and can rupture. Fiber increases the stool volume, which expands the colon. The filled, expanded colon is better able to withstand pressure from outside the colon, which can be the cause of the diverticuli. Close to half the U.S. population over age 50 have diverticuli, and most are asymptomatic. Not all cases improve with increased fiber intake. Rupture of the diverticuli can lead to possible death from sepsis.

Weight Control and Fiber

Fiber is often used to put bulk into weight reduction diets since it is filling and contributes few calories overall. Intestinal bacteria ferment some of the fiber into gas and short-chain fatty acids, which do provide calories in varying amounts, but the calorie amounts are insignificant in comparison to other foods. Fiber, however, also replaces foods containing other needed nutrients. When a person is counting calories as a way to diet, his or her food choices have already been restricted. Adding large quantities of fiber-rich foods restricts the diet even further.

There are pros and cons on the benefits of fiber-rich, low-calorie diets. More study is needed to examine closely the relationship of fiber to satiety and, ultimately, satiety to weight loss.

Protection Against Cancer

In a number of studies, colon cancer rates did not correlate with fiber intake after controlling for fat intake.[†] The National Research Council reported inconsistent findings with regard to colon and rectal cancer and fiber. Animal studies indicate an enhancing effect or no effect of dietary fiber on colon cancer. Fiber can produce intestinal cell changes that may modify risk. Wheat bran may increase the excretion of bile acids and fecal mutagens, which are believed to promote colon cancer.

Some of the soluble fibers found in oat bran, pectin, and guar gum also stimulate excretion of bile acids. Although the findings are inconsistent, there seems to be a protective effect of fiber-rich foods. The phytochemicals in vegetables, fruits, and grains may help provide the protection against cancer. Phytochemicals are natural plant chemicals that include carotenoids, flavonoids, indoles, isoflavones, capsaicin, and protease inhibitors. Much research is being carried out today to test the disease protection afforded by these plant constituents.

In the future, results of the National Cancer Institute study, now under way, will report on the effect of a high-fiber, low-fat diet on polyps. A Canadian study is examining the effect of lignins and phytoestrogens in breast cancer risk.[§]

---

[*]Liebman, "The Whole Grain Guide," p. 8.
[†]Duyff, R., *The American Dietetic Association's Complete Food and Nutrition Guide*, Minneapolis, MN: Cronimed Publishing, 1996.
[§]Liebman, "The Whole Grain Guide," pp. 9–10.

Proteins

Proteins are those nutrients needed for building body tissue and renewing body cells. Except for sugar, fat, and alcohol, most foods contain some protein.

Protein is essential to growing infants, children, adolescents, and pregnant and lactating women. It is also needed for new tissue growth during the healing of fractures, surgery, and burns. Protein is needed to support the growth of hair, nails, and skin, as well as for the renewal of blood cells, intestinal cells, and other body cells.

Foods that contain the largest amounts of protein are meat, poultry, fish, shellfish, eggs, milk products, and legumes. Second to these are grains and vegetables. Fruits also contain small amounts of protein.

The number of grams of protein in the sample meal plan (Figure 3–4) is based in part on the exchange system defined by the American Diabetes Association and

Food Eaten	Amount	Grams of Protein
Breakfast		
Egg	1	7
Toast	2 slices	6
Margarine	2 teaspoons	0
Skim milk	8 ounces	8
Cooked cereal	1/2 cup	3
Orange juice	8 ounces	1
		25 total for breakfast
Lunch		
Bread	2 slices	6
Tuna	2 ounces	14
Mayonnaise	1 tablespoon	0
Medium peach	1	0.5
Tossed salad	1 cup	2
Cola beverage	8 ounces	0
		22.5 total for lunch
Dinner		
Sautéed chicken	4 ounces	28
Potato	1 medium	3
Broccoli	1/2 cup	2
Rice	1 cup	9
Watermelon	1 cup	1
Tea	1 cup	0
Sugar	1 teaspoon	0
		43 total for dinner
Snack		
Skim milk	1 cup	8
		98.5 day's total

Figure 3–4 Sample Daily Protein Total

the American Dietetic Association. The food composition tables in the *USDA Home and Garden Bulletin* (no. 72, 1989) can used to locate specific foods to determine the amount of protein in each. Nuts, for example, may range from 2 to 6 grams of protein per ounce, depending on the nut chosen. Almonds have more protein than pistachio nuts. The same principle applies to each category of protein foods. It is not important to use individual calculations when you eat a variety of food; the numbers will balance out. If, however, a particular food is eaten often, then it would be more prudent to look up the particular food using "The Nutritive Value of Foods" (*USDA Home and Garden Bulletin*, no. 72, 1989).

Choosing protein foods

The best protein foods to use are ones that are low in fat, salt, and sugar. Skim milk, lean meat, fish, skinless chicken, beans, and tofu are good choices. These help the consumer avoid cardiovascular disease, cancer, and obesity. Individuals who avoid obesity can lower their chances of getting diabetes, gout, and arthritis. Fresh protein foods are less salty than processed protein foods. Canned meats, fish, and beans and processed cheese are saltier than fresh meat, fish, beans, and natural cheese. Examples of protein foods that contain sugar are ice cream, custards, flavored yogurts, some sausages, cold cuts, and cured ham.

Examples of lean meat cuts are the shank, first cut brisket, flank steak, and top round. Because they are lean, these cuts are also tougher than fatty ones. They can be tenderized before or during cooking by grinding, pounding, slow cooking, braising, and marinating. Marinades contain an acid product, such as wine, vinegar, molasses, tomato, or some varieties of fruits, that helps to break down protein strands and partially tenderize the food.

The U.S. Dietary Goals for protein are 12 to 15% of one's daily calorie intake. Because it is known that each gram of protein has 4 calories, protein intake can be calculated easily. Table 3–1 lists the protein calorie calculations for some common food groups.

> **Example:** *Recommended daily protein intake, given an intake of 2500 calories per day*
>
> 2500 calories/day
> × 15% (recommended percentage of protein)
> 375 calories of protein recommended
> divided by 4 calories per gram of protein =
> 93.75 grams of protein recommended

One method of calculating the minimum daily protein requirement is to use the formula 0.8 × adult body weight in kilograms. The following example calculates this protein requirement for a person who weighs 150 pounds, or 68 kilograms. Divide the weight, in pounds, by 2.2 to determine the number of kilograms.

> **Example:** *Minimum daily protein intake for a 150-pound individual*
>
> Step 1. $\dfrac{150 \text{ pounds}}{2.2}$ = 68.2 kilograms
>
> Step 2. 68.2 kilograms
> × 0.8
> 54.6 grams protein

Calculations for protein intake

Table 3-1 *Protein Calories per Portion for Various Food Items*

Food Type	Portion Size	Grams of Protein per Portion	(x 4 Calories per Gram of Protein =)	Protein Calories per Portion
Meat, poultry, fish, eggs	1 oz	7		28
Legumes	1/2 cup	7		28
Milk (whole, skim)	8 oz	8		32
Bread	1 slice	3		12
Starchy food, such as rice, pasta	1/2 cup	3		12
Vegetable, cooked	1/2 cup	2		8
Vegetable raw	1 cup	2		8
Fruit	1/2 cup	0.5		2
Nuts	1 oz	2–6		8–24

The method in the preceding example is based on the recommended dietary allowances of the Food and Nutrition Board, National Academy of Sciences, and National Research Council. The RDA charts show the protein requirement for the "reference woman" who is 5 feet 4 inches tall and weighs 128 pounds. It tends to yield a lower figure than the 15%-of-calories formula. One should not intake less than this lower recommendation.

Amounts in excess of the 15% recommendation would not be harmful to healthy individuals. Eating too much protein, however, could affect carbohydrate and fiber intake and create an opportunity for a high-fat diet (especially if the protein choices are meats, nuts, or whole milk dairy products).

There are times when an increased protein intake is necessary. Pregnancy and lactation require an additional 20 and 30 grams, respectively, of protein daily. Infants, children, and teenagers need proportionately more protein than adults to allow for growing bones and muscles. For example, a baby needs 2.2 grams of protein per kilogram of body weight in the first six months of life, and 2 grams of protein per kilogram of body weight for the second half of the first year. A baby will have tripled his or her body weight by the first birthday.

Protein does not account for all of a food's calories. Flesh foods, even lean meats, contain fat. Fat can also be found in whole and partially skimmed milk. Carbohydrates are found in bread, vegetables, and fruits. All types of fat contain 9 calories per gram; carbohydrates contain 4 calories per gram.

Nuts are plentiful sources of protein but contain large amounts of fat. Beans are also good sources of protein, yet they have virtually no fat. Beans, however, contain large amounts of carbohydrates.

Sugars, jellies, syrups, honey, and sweet drinks contain no protein; neither do fats and oils. Alcoholic beverages do not contribute to protein intake.

Digestion and absorption of protein

Protein foods are digested in the stomach and the small intestine. When food reaches the stomach, a hormone called gastrin stimulates the production of hydrochloric acid, which activates an enzyme called pepsinogen. Pepsinogen converts into pepsin, which, in turn, breaks down the protein into smaller parts called polypeptides. Some of the still-intact proteins, some polypeptides, and a small amount of amino acids leave the stomach and enter the upper portion of the small intestine, the duodenum. Duodenal hormones stimulate the release of pancreatic hormones, which break down the proteins that are still intact. Hormones in the duodenum stimulate the release of pancreatic juice. The enzymes trypsin and chymotrypsin, which come from the pancreas, break down proteoses and peptones to form polypeptides. Other intestinal juice enzymes break down the polypeptides into amino acids, the final protein breakdown. Magnesium, zinc, copper, and manganese are all essential for this enzyme activity. These minerals can be found in foods such as meats, grains, and vegetables.

The enzyme rennin, found naturally in the stomach, coagulates milk and begins to digest the milk protein casein. There is a question as to whether rennin exists in adults, but it is definitely the milk-digesting enzyme for young children. Rennin obtained from calves' stomachs is used in the cheese-making process to curdle milk. Another stomach enzyme, gelatinase, liquifies gelatin, an animal byproduct.

Amino acids are absorbed through the lining of the small intestine into the bloodstream. These acids then enter the portal vein, go into the liver, and from the liver disperse to body tissues.

Amino acids: the building blocks

Amino acids are white and crystalline and are tasteless, sweet, or bitter. They are the building blocks of protein. Most proteins are composed of 12 to 20 amino acids locked together in one large molecule. Some proteins contain up to 280 amino acids.

The human body needs 20 amino acids for proper nutrition. Some of these can be generated through the digestion of dietary nitrogen from various protein sources. Others cannot be made in the body and must be ingested directly from the appropriate food sources. These are called essential amino acids. The ones that the body can make are known as nonessential amino acids (Figure 3–5). It was once believed that foods containing the essential amino acids had to be consumed in the same meal in order for the body to use them for building tissue. That meant that combinations of grains, nuts, beans, and seeds were recommended for all vegetarian meals, and often in the same dish. It is known today that this is not necessary as long as adequate amounts of the essential amino acids are eaten in the course of a day.

The right amounts of all the essential amino acids needed to support growth are present in animal foods such as pork, beef, lamb, veal, chicken, fish, eggs, and milk. The exception is gelatin, an animal food product that has a poor balance of the essential amino acids. Plant foods, with the exception of soybeans, tofu, and soy milk, do not contain a good balance of the essential amino acids. Almonds, Brazil nuts, buckwheat, and wheat germ contain a better balance of these acids than do most plants.

A limiting amino acid is one that is provided in an insufficient amount, thereby causing the food to be categorized as less than complete. Adding the limiting amino acid to a deficient food will put the essential amino acids in a proportion that will foster optimal growth. However, if two foods having the same limiting amino acid are eaten together, the resulting complete protein value is less than that for either food alone.

Buckwheat has an amino acid composition that is nutritionally superior to that of other cereals. It is high in lysine, the limiting amino acid in wheat and rice. Buckwheat grows in cool-weather areas, and its flour is commonly used as

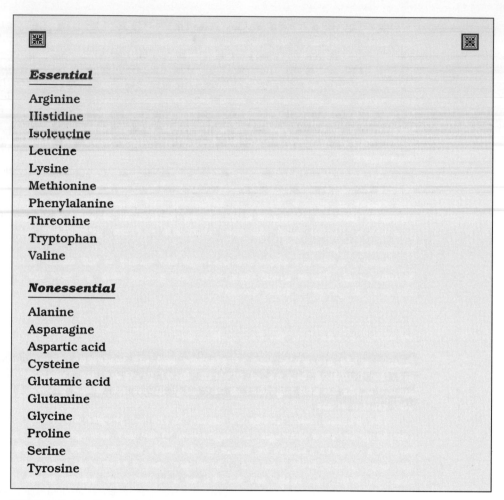

Figure 3–5 Essential and Nonessential Amino Acids

a pancake ingredient. It is even more delicious when used in the groat form (the hulled grain). Buckwheat comes in coarse, medium, and fine groats.

Nonessential amino acids are as important as the essential amino acids (Figure 3–5). They make up 40% of tissue-building proteins and supply nitrogen for the synthesis of body compounds such as enzymes, hormones, and antibodies.

All proteins contain the elements carbon, hydrogen, oxygen, and nitrogen. Carbohydrates and fats do not contain nitrogen. Nitrogen, the distinguishing element in protein, can be used to make nonessential amino acids.

Some proteins contain sulfur or other minerals, such as iron, iodine, and cobalt. The human body uses these mineral-rich proteins to make DNA, RNA, antibodies, enzymes, hemoglobin, and certain hormones (insulin, thyroxine, and adrenaline). Protein is also necessary for regulating the water balance and for balancing the acid base.

Proteins can be used to supply energy as well as muscle building. In order for protein to be used as energy, it must be converted to glucose or fatty acids that contain carbon, hydrogen, and oxygen. The nitrogen that is removed from

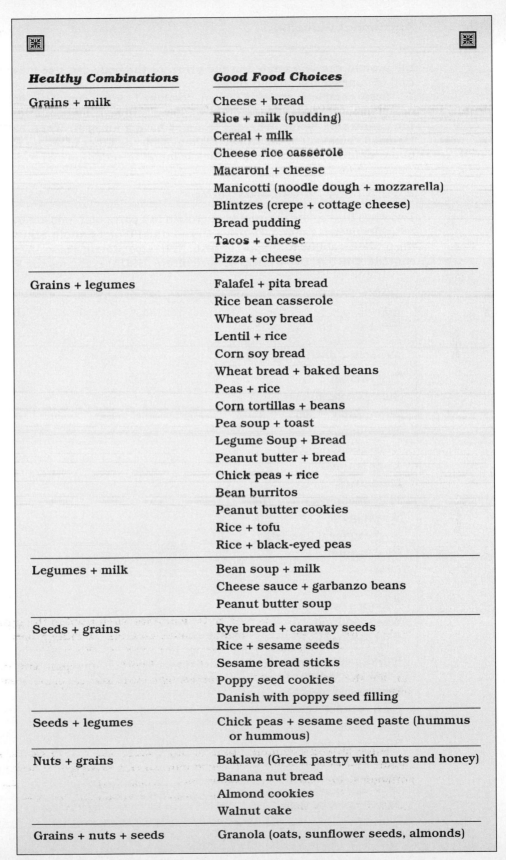

Healthy Combinations	Good Food Choices
Grains + milk	Cheese + bread
	Rice + milk (pudding)
	Cereal + milk
	Cheese rice casserole
	Macaroni + cheese
	Manicotti (noodle dough + mozzarella)
	Blintzes (crepe + cottage cheese)
	Bread pudding
	Tacos + cheese
	Pizza + cheese
Grains + legumes	Falafel + pita bread
	Rice bean casserole
	Wheat soy bread
	Lentil + rice
	Corn soy bread
	Wheat bread + baked beans
	Peas + rice
	Corn tortillas + beans
	Pea soup + toast
	Legume Soup + Bread
	Peanut butter + bread
	Chick peas + rice
	Bean burritos
	Peanut butter cookies
	Rice + tofu
	Rice + black-eyed peas
Legumes + milk	Bean soup + milk
	Cheese sauce + garbanzo beans
	Peanut butter soup
Seeds + grains	Rye bread + caraway seeds
	Rice + sesame seeds
	Sesame bread sticks
	Poppy seed cookies
	Danish with poppy seed filling
Seeds + legumes	Chick peas + sesame seed paste (hummus or hummous)
Nuts + grains	Baklava (Greek pastry with nuts and honey)
	Banana nut bread
	Almond cookies
	Walnut cake
Grains + nuts + seeds	Granola (oats, sunflower seeds, almonds)

Figure 3–6 Complementary Protein Chart: Some Examples

the protein can be excreted in the urine, or the body can use it for the production of nonessential amino acids.

Less complete proteins, when combined, form complete proteins called complementary proteins (Figure 3–6). For example, wheat contains very little of the amino acid lysine, whereas legumes have a lot of it. When eaten together, legumes complement the wheat. Legumes, on the other hand, do not have much of the amino acid methionine, which is found in generous quantities in wheat.

Evaluating protein nutrition

Two ways to evaluate the quality of protein in a particular food are by its PER (protein effectiveness rating; Figure 3–7) and its NPU (net protein utilization). PER is the protein's ability to support growth; NPU rates protein according to its nitrogen content. The U.S. Department of Agriculture (USDA) evaluates the PER of food.

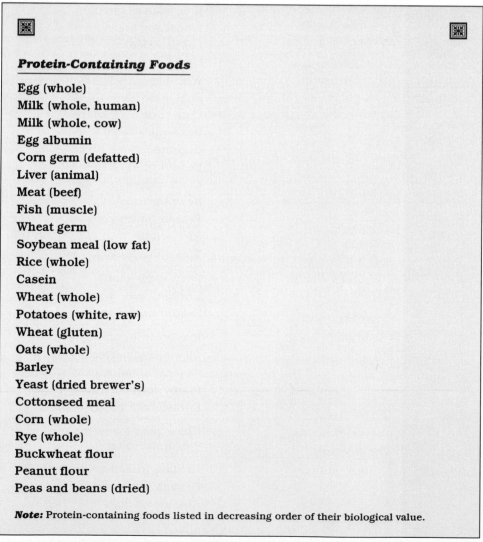

Protein-Containing Foods

Egg (whole)
Milk (whole, human)
Milk (whole, cow)
Egg albumin
Corn germ (defatted)
Liver (animal)
Meat (beef)
Fish (muscle)
Wheat germ
Soybean meal (low fat)
Rice (whole)
Casein
Wheat (whole)
Potatoes (white, raw)
Wheat (gluten)
Oats (whole)
Barley
Yeast (dried brewer's)
Cottonseed meal
Corn (whole)
Rye (whole)
Buckwheat flour
Peanut flour
Peas and beans (dried)

Note: Protein-containing foods listed in decreasing order of their biological value.

Figure 3–7 Protein Efficiency Rating

Nitrogen balance and excess dietary protein

Nitrogen balance occurs when the nitrogen obtained from the daily food intake equals the nitrogen output in the urine. This is the ideal state of protein nutrition. If the body is not getting enough protein, then muscle tissue is broken down to supply the nitrogen the body needs. When the body uses its own tissue because of a lack of adequate protein intake, the result is negative nitrogen balance. More nitrogen will be excreted in the urine than is taken in.

On the other hand, if more nitrogen is retained than is excreted, there is a positive nitrogen balance. Positive nitrogen balance can occur during growth, pregnancy, lactation, and the healing of wounds and burns. These conditions require extra dietary protein so the nitrogen balance can be sustained.

If the body takes in too much protein on a regular basis, there is a good possibility that dehydration will result. During the digestive process, water is required to split amino acids that are joined together. This is called hydrolysis. If protein intake increases and water intake remains the same, dehydration may occur. Therefore, fad diets promoting excessive amounts of protein are not recommended.

Athletes may consume extra protein in the belief that it is needed for strengthening or building muscle. Muscle, however, is about 75% water and only about 25% protein. Consequently, if a weight lifter were trying to increase his muscles by 4.4 pounds per month, he would need only one extra ounce of protein a day. If the weight lifter eats more protein than is necessary for muscle growth, the protein is wasted. The body will simply turn the protein into carbohydrates by removing the nitrogen. The nitrogen is excreted in the urine, and the carbohydrates will be used for energy. Natural carbohydrates would have been a more efficient source of energy in the first place.

Insufficient dietary protein

Protein deficiency disease is not often seen in the Western world because of the availability and variety of protein foods. The symptoms of a mild protein deficiency include lackluster hair and nails. More severe protein deficiency leads to thin, easily pluckable and dyspigmented hair. The parotid glands, located below and in front of each ear, become enlarged. Moderate protein deficiency may also cause the liver to become enlarged.

Kwashiorkor is the protein deficiency disease usually encountered in underdeveloped parts of Africa, where the diet consists primarily of plant proteins. This disease is characterized by retarded growth, edema, peeling skin, anemia, and susceptibility to infection. The mortality rate is very high. Delivering skim milk powder to underdeveloped countries, to provide protein, alleviates the deficiency; help should also include lessons in the farming of soybeans and education about combining plant proteins for better nutrition.

Protein cookery

Eggs, milk, and flesh foods, the major sources of protein, need to be cooked properly for maximum nutritional value, taste, and dining satisfaction. A general rule for cooking protein is to use low to moderate heat whenever possible. Too high a heat will make eggs rubbery, milk curdle, and meat tough.

High heat draws water out of the protein and leaves a dry, tough product. The exceptions are broiling and grilling, in which naturally tender cuts of meat, poultry, and fish are subjected to very high heat but for short periods of time.

Other meats cooked at high heat will not only be tough but will also lose a great deal of volume. Their excreted juices collect in the bottom of the pan and evaporate. Custard cooked at a high temperature will weep, a classic example of overheated protein.

Tender meat cuts, such as the tenderloin, rib roast, and sirloin, contain a high amount of collagen. Collagen and elastin are the two types of connective tissues in muscles. Collagen takes on water (hydrolyzes) when cooked and changes to gelatin, which has a tenderizing effect on meat. Elastin does not react with water and must be ground or chopped to soften. Meat in which the collagen dominates can be cooked at higher temperatures, but only for a brief time (such as in grilling and broiling).

Vegetarian versus nonvegetarian protein choices

Many believe that avoiding the flesh of meat, poultry, and fish is a healthful choice to make. Some extend this belief to all animal products, including eggs, milk, and milk products. For others, the vegetarian choice is based on religion, ethics, economics, or ecology. Whatever the basis of the decision, deciding not to indulge in animal products does not automatically produce a low-cost, healthful diet. Much care must be taken in planning a well-rounded vegetarian menu to ensure proper nutrient levels in the foods that are consumed.

The term *vegetarianism* is an umbrella that covers different styles of eating. All vegetarians avoid animal products to some degree, some more than others. The pure vegetarian does not eat meat, poultry, fish, eggs, or milk products and may even avoid preservatives derived from these foods. The appropriate term for the strict vegetarian is *vegan*. Within the vegan camp are subcategories of vegetarians, some of whom restrict themselves to uncooked raw food. A fruitarian will eat fruits, nuts, olive oil, and honey but not vegetables.

Macrobiotic vegetarians follow a plan based on an ancient Eastern religious culture, which emphasizes the use of whole grains and legumes in the diet. Certain foods are thought to be bad combinations (yin and yang). Some stages of the Zen macrobiotic diet feature stringent deprivations because of the lack of balance with other foods.

Slightly more liberal than the vegans are the lacto vegetarians. Adherents of the Hindu faith, for example, eat a diet that includes milk products such as yogurt and butter along with plant foods, but no meats. Eggs are also not acceptable. The lacto-ovo vegetarian includes eggs as well as milk in the diet.

The lacto-ovo diet poses no threat of nutritional deficiencies when planned well. As long as nonmeat diets include a variety of plants, protein-rich foods, and a sensible level of fat, they can easily sustain healthy and active lifestyles.

The term *pesco-vegetarian* means that one follows a vegetarian diet but allows fish. Meat and poultry are excluded. The semivegetarian eats poultry or fish but not red meat, veal, or pork.

Meat, however, is one of our best sources of complete protein and is an especially good source of the B vitamins thiamin, riboflavin, niacin, pyridoxine, and vitamin B_{12}. Cobalamin, or active vitamin B_{12} as it is commonly called, is not found in plants. It is produced by microorganisms present in the gastrointestinal tracts of animals. B vitamins are necessary for metabolic reactions in the body. Liver is a potent source of vitamin A as well.

Meat is also an excellent source of some minerals, which are more readily absorbed from meat than from plant foods. Meat contains zinc, manganese, selenium, copper, and, of course, iron. Poultry and fish are second to meat in providing these nutrients. The iron in meat is in both the heme and nonheme forms. The heme form of iron is more usable than the nonheme form and is not found in plants. The heme iron in meat helps the absorption of the nonheme iron in plants eaten at the same meal. Heme is a red pigment. The heme iron in meat comes from hemoglobin, which is found in red blood cells, and from myoglobin, which is found in muscle cells in animal tissues. Both hemoglobin and myoglobin function to carry oxygen throughout the body.

Iron deficiency is a health concern for growing infants, children, adolescents, and women in their reproductive years. For non-meat-eating populations, the concern can become critical.

There is the less frequently seen disease of iron overload. Those having the condition would do well to eat less meat. Iron-overloading diseases appear mostly in men over the age of 40. Symptoms include shortness of breath and fatigue. The danger exists when excess iron is deposited in the heart. Large amounts of red wine, which contains iron, could also contribute to the problem.

Eggs contain the less available nonheme source of iron. A vitamin-C-containing food eaten with eggs will help enhance iron absorption. It is now known that eggs do not increase blood cholesterol levels, as originally thought. The 300-milligram daily recommended dietary cholesterol intake does not have to be followed on a day-to-day basis, and people watching their cholesterol can distribute their cholesterol intake over a one-week period. Removing the skin from chicken takes away half the cholesterol.

People who abstain from eating all meat products could develop a vitamin B_{12} deficiency. Eggs contain vitamin B_{12}, and so does milk. The lacto-ovo vegetarian can rely on these for their vitamin B_{12} needs.

Spirulina, seaweed, tempeh, and other fermented foods are not reliable sources of vitamin B_{12}. As much as 80 to 94% of the so-called vitamin B_{12} in these foods may be an inactive form. Vitamin supplements, fortified soy beverages, fortified breakfast cereals, and some brands of nutritional yeast contain the active form of vitamin B_{12} and should be included in the diet of pure vegans.

Choosing to eat fish helps increase the omega 3 fatty acid content of the diet. Omega 3 fatty acids are beneficial in preventing cardiovascular disease and some types of inflammation. Although these fatty acids can be found in certain plants, fatty fish, like salmon, tuna, and mackerel, contain the most (more on this later in the section entitled "Fats and Oils").

Avoidance of milk makes it difficult to get enough calcium, vitamin D, zinc, and vitamin B_2 (riboflavin) in the diet. These nutrients are of particular importance for growing children, adolescents, and pregnant women. Children who are allergic to milk protein should stay on fortified infant soy formulas to ensure adequate intake of these nutrients. Some studies have shown, however, that vegetarians absorb and retain more calcium from foods than do nonvegetarians. Calcium intake recommendations for Americans are set high to compensate for the urinary calcium losses that accompany a high intake of animal protein.

The strict vegetarian who eats no flesh, eggs, or dairy products should take vitamin B_{12} and vitamin D supplements. Other nutrients can be obtained through careful selection of beans, nuts, dried peas, and soy products eaten with generous amounts of dark green leafy vegetables, fruits, and whole grains.

Less cardiovascular disease, cancer of the gastrointestinal tract, and cancer of the colon is found among vegetarians. This could be attributed to other lifestyle habits, such as regular exercise, not smoking cigarettes, and maintaining lean body weight. Those who are not vegetarians should try to develop these habits and include lots of fruits, vegetables, and whole grains in their diets. Legumes can be a healthful part of both the vegetarian and nonvegetarian lifestyle. Fruits and vegetables contain antioxidants, phytochemicals, and laxative fiber that are beneficial in the prevention of cardiovascular disease and cancer. The vitamins C and E and the mineral selenium are antioxidants. The phytochemicals are non-nutrients, such as plant pigments, that are currently being researched. Some of the phytochemicals are the carotenoids, indoles, isothiocyanates, flavonoids, phenols, and limones.

Many vegetarians choose their diet because they are concerned about food additives, pesticides, hormones, antibiotics, and the humane treatment of livestock. Articles have been written about the treatment of milking cows and egg-producing chickens, which is less than idyllic.* These concerns should be important to all of the population, and abuses should be corrected through legislation. Consumer groups and government agencies can take a leading role in dealing with such issues.

Nutritional balance is necessary for both the vegetarian and the nonvegetarian. Neither is guaranteed an automatic low-fat, moderate-sodium, high-fiber diet, safely prepared, with the proper number of calories; achieving such a diet requires nutritional awareness. A nonvegetarian eating freshly sliced skinned turkey breast with lettuce and tomato on plain whole wheat bread would be getting less fat, less sodium, and more fiber than a vegetarian eating a peanut butter sandwich on salted white crackers made with shortening. Likewise, a nonvegetarian could be eating water-packed salt-free sardines, a salad of fresh greens sprinkled with lemon juice, a crust of French bread with a little olive oil and garlic, a cup of nonfat yogurt and fresh fruit; whereas, the vegetarian could be eating refried beans, French fries, salad with bleu cheese dressing, and apple pie. The latter is higher in fat than the carefully chosen nonvegetarian meal.

The vegetarian can make wholesome, delicious meals that are nutritious in every way. Such meals must be planned, however. The menu for all, vegetarians and nonvegetarians alike, should be low in fats and oils, salad dressings, fried foods, high-fat desserts, and whole milk products. Calories must be sufficient to meet energy needs.

The Food Guide Pyramid provides recommendations that can be used by both vegetarians and nonvegetarians, with the exception that for vegans the milk group would be replaced with soy milk or almond milk. The soy milk can be fortified with vitamin B_{12}, or a B_{12} supplement can be taken. Today soy milk with extra calcium is available.

For vegetarians, legumes, nuts, and meat analogues replace flesh foods in the meat group. Legumes work well in soups, casseroles, and salads.

Tofu (a soy product) and other soy products, such as texturized vegetable protein, soy grits, and fermented soy products (such as miso), can also be used. Meat analogues are usually made with soy protein and sometimes with grains. They are made to resemble meat products, such as hamburgers, sausages, cold cuts, and cheese. Brands that are not high in salt should be selected. Recipes made from scratch usually are more acceptable, but they take time to prepare. The results are worth the effort, however.

It is difficult to tell which food additives contain or are derived from animals or insects and which are totally vegetarian. Here is a partial list of food additives and their sources. These were excerpted from V*egetarian Journal's Guide to Food Ingredients* by Jeanne-Marie Bartas.[†]

---

*Raymond, Jennifer, "Free Range Eggs." *Vegetarian Journal Reports*, 1990, pp. 64, 65, 78–80.
[†]Bartas, Jeanne Marie, *Vegetarian Journal's Guide to Food Ingredients.* Used with permission. Full journal available from the Vegetarian Resource Group, P.O. Box 1463, Baltimore, Maryland 21203 (vrg@vrg.org;www.vrg.org).

Vegetarian status of some commercial food ingredients

Contains Dairy

calcium caseinate: Commercial source: mineral-animal. Used in imitation cheese, creamed cottage cheese, diet foods and beverages, frozen desserts, vegetable whipped toppings. Definition: An additive that is used as a source of protein and as a replacement for sodium caseinate in low-sodium foods.

simplesse: Commercial source: animal (milk and egg). Used in margarine, ice cream, salad dressings, yogurt. Definition: A fat substitute.

sodium caseinate: Also known as casein. Commercial source: mineral-animal (milk). Used in processed meats, ice cream, sherbet, frozen desserts, nondairy whipped toppings, coffee whiteners, egg substitutes, desserts, imitation sausage, soups, stews, diet foods. Definition: A common food additive with many foods uses including whitening, whipping, and binding.

casein: Commercial source: animal (milk). Used in cereals, breads, imitation cheeses, ice cream, fruit sherbets, special diet preparations. Definition: The principal protein in milk.

whey: Commercial source: animal (milk). Used in baked goods, ice cream, dry mixes, processed foods. Definition: The watery material that remains after most of the protein and fat have been removed from milk.

Contains Animal or Insect Products

carmine: Commercial source: animal (insect). Used in confections, juices, "New Age" beverages, pharmaceuticals, dairy products, baked goods, yogurt, ice cream, fruit fillings, puddings. Definition: A food coloring derived from the dried bodies of female beetles.

cochineal: Commercial source: animal (insect). Used in confections, juices, yogurt, ice cream, fruit fillings, puddings. Definition: A coloring derived from the dried bodies of female beetles.

gelatin: Commercial source: animal (cow or hog derived). Vegetable or synthetic "gelatins" are found in some foods on the market. Used in puddings, yogurt, ham coatings, marshmallows, sour cream, frozen desserts, cheese spreads, soft drinks, pill capsules, wine, and juice. Definition: An animal protein used especially for its thickening and gelling properties.

Usually Contains Animal Products

calcium stearate: Commercial source: typically animal (cow or hog derived), mineral, or vegetable-mineral. Used in garlic salt, dry molasses, vanilla, vanilla powder, salad dressing mix, meat tenderizers. Definition: An additive that helps make ingredients blend well together. It also may function as an additive that prevents dry ingredients from sticking together.

Production Involves Animal Products

sucrose: Also known as sugar, cane sugar, beet sugar, refined sugar. Commercial source: vegetable. Sucrose derived from sugar cane may have been processed through a cow bone filter. Sucrose derived from beets has not been produced through a cow bone filter. Used in confections, baked goods, processed foods, condiments, beverages, breakfast cereals. Definition: The major component of refined sugar. Typically nonvegetarian.

Fats and oils

There is a great deal of emphasis today on monitoring the quality and quantity of fat in the diet. There is no question, however, that fat plays a very important role in regular bodily functions. Fats are needed for cushioning the body's organs, insulating against the cold, transporting the fat soluble vitamins, and providing a source of stored energy. Fats also provide a sense of satiety because they are digested slowly, which means that we feel full for longer after we eat fats than we would after eating nonfat or low-fat foods.

The chemical composition of fat combines glycerol with one, two, or three fatty acid chains of various lengths. The chains can be saturated, monounsaturated, or polyunsaturated. The degree of saturation has to do with the amount of hydrogen in the carbon chain. For example, a monounsaturated fat is missing one hydrogen pair on its carbon chain. This is indicated by a double bond.

Example diagram of a monounsaturated fat (Missing one hydrogen pair)

```
H H H H H H H          H H H H H H H
C–C–C–C–C–C–C–C–C = C–C–C–C–C–C–C–C–C–C
H H H H H H H H H    H H H H H H H H H H
```

(H = hydrogen; C = carbon)

Saturated fatty acids do not have double bonds, monounsaturated fatty acids have one double bond, and polyunsaturated fatty acids have more than one double bond. The higher the number of double bonds, the greater the degree of polyunsaturation. Polyunsaturated fat is essential for humans. It is needed for healthy skin, normal liver function, membrane fluidity, prostaglandin production (prostaglandin is a regulatory substance), and eicosanoid synthesis (for immune function).

Most of the fat in our diet consists of triglyceride, a glycerol attached to three fatty acid chains that do not have to have the same saturation. The fatty foods that we eat are made up of a combination of saturated, monounsaturated, and polyunsaturated fatty acids. The particular fatty acids that predominate in a food are important because certain fatty acids are implicated as contributory agents in cardiovascular disease. Figure 3–8 shows the fatty acid composition of common fats and oils.

Cholesterol

Cholesterol is one of the substances found in the plaque that produces arteriosclerosis (hardening and thickening of the arterial walls). Cholesterol is a fat-like, waxy substance that is not broken down and yields no calories, as do other fats. It is classified as a sterol and is made by our liver. It is not necessary to get cholesterol from food.

The liver makes much more cholesterol (over 1000 milligrams per day) than the body gets from food. Food sources very high in cholesterol are fish eggs

Figure 3-8 Grams of Fatty Acids in Oils and Fats/100-Gram Portion (*Source: Adapted from USDA Nutrient Database for Standard Reference, Release II [September 1996] http://www.nal.usda.gov/fnic/cgi-bin/list_nut.pl*)

Oil or fat	Saturated													Monounsatured				Polyunsatured							Cholesterol
	Acetic 2:0	Butyric 4:0	Caproic 6:0	Caprylic 8:0	Capric 10:0	Lauric 12:0	Myristic 14:0	Palmitic 16:0	Stearic 18:0	Arachidic 20:0	Behenic 22:0	Tetracosanoic 24:0	Docosanoic 22:0	Palmitoleic 16:1	Oleic 18:1	Gadoleic 20:1	Erucic 22:1	Linoleic 18:2	Linolenic 18:3	Morotic 18:4	Arachidonic 20:4	Timnodonic (EPA) 20:5	Clupanodonic 22:5	Docosahexaenoic (DHA) 22:6	
Soybean oil								10.300	3.800					.200	22.800	.200		51.0	6.800						
Corn oil								10.900	1.800						24.200			58	.700						
Cottonseed oil							.800	22.700	2.300					.800	17.0			51.500	.200		.100				
Palm oil						.100	1.000	43.500	4.300					.300	36.600	.100		9.100	.200						
Peanut oil							.100	9.500	2.200	1.400	2.800	.900		.100	44.800	1.300		32.0							
Olive oil								11.0	2.200					.800	72.500	.300		7.900	.600						
Canola oil								4.000	1.800	.700	.400	.200		.200	56.100	1.700	.600	20.300	9.300						
Safflower—high oleic								4.800	1.300					.400	75.300			14.200							
Safflower oil							.100	6.200	2.200						11.700			74.100	.400						
Sunflower oil								5.900	4.500						19.500			65.700							
Coconut oil			.600	7.500	6.000	44.600	16.800	8.200	2.800						5.800			1.800							
Palm kernel oil			.200	3.300	3.700	47.00	16.400	8.100	2.800						11.400			1.600							
Cocoa butter							.100	25.400	33.200					.200	32.600			2.800	.100						
Butterfat		2.630	1.560	.906	2.030	2.280	8.160	21.300	9.830					1.820	20.400			1.830	1.180						218.900
Beef tallow						.900	3.700	24.900	18.900					4.200	36.000	.300		3.100	.600						109.00
Chicken fat					.100	.100	.900	21.600	6.0					5.700	37.30	.100		19.500	1.0		.100				85.00
Lard						.100	1.600	23.000	15.200					3.100	40.9			9.700	1.100						56.00
Fish oil—cod-liver							3.568	10.630	2.799					8.309	20.653	10.422	7.328	.935	.935	.935	.935	6.898	.935	10.96	570.000
Fish oil—menhaden							7.958	15.146	3.775					10.482	14.527	1.332	.352	2.154	1.490	2.739	1.169	13.160	4.915	8.562	521.000
Wheat germ oil							.100	16.600	.500					.500	14.600	.400		54.800	6.900						
Walnut oil								7.0	2.0					.100	22.200	.400		52.900	10.400						
Sesame oil								8.900	4.800					.200	39.300	.200		41.300	.300						

(such as caviar and shad roe), brains, and liver. Egg yolks, shrimp, sardines, and poultry skin are also high in dietary cholesterol.

Milk contains a small amount of cholesterol, most of it in its butterfat. Foods made with large amounts of this fat, such as cheeses and ice cream, are high in cholesterol if eaten in generous amounts.

All meats, poultry, and fish contain cholesterol regardless of how lean they may be. Cholesterol is part of the cell membrane of all animal tissue.

No plants produce cholesterol. Fatty foods of plant origin, such as avocados, olives, nuts, and all plant oils, do not contain cholesterol.

Although much is said about the health risks associated with high cholesterol counts, cholesterol has many positive functions. It is necessary for hormone production, for completing the active form of vitamin D, and for making bile. The liver produces about 700 milligrams of cholesterol daily for this purpose alone. Bile functions as an emulsifier in fat digestion. Cholesterol is also found in human breast milk (this demonstrates cholesterol's importance in infant development).

Some individuals can eat liberally foods that contain a high level of cholesterol and will not develop the health problems associated with a high cholesterol intake; others may develop such problems. It is a good idea to have blood cholesterol levels tested, particularly if there is a positive family history of cardiovascular disease and stroke.

One must differentiate between exogenous (dietary) cholesterol and endogenous cholesterol (that produced within the body). Some fatty foods that are completely free of cholesterol will increase the body's cholesterol production. The type of endogenous cholesterol that health professionals are concerned about is found in LDLs.

LDLs are a byproduct of VLDLs, which are made in the liver. The liver makes VLDLs from fatty acids that come from the food we eat and digest. The VLDL from the liver enters the blood, is broken down into IDLs (intermediary-density lipoproteins), and then is broken down into LDLs. LDLs are 50% cholesterol and are associated with coronary disease. Less LDLs result when the diet is high in polyunsaturated fat.

Not all of the saturated fats elevate plasma cholesterol. Myristic acid is considered the most potent plasma cholesterol-raising saturated fatty acid. It is found in large amounts in coconut oil. Palmitic and lauric acid are also positively associated with plasma cholesterol. Figure 3–8 shows the percentages of fatty acids in oils.

In a recent study using special test diets with a total fat intake of 40% of total calorie intake both lauric and palmitic acids were hypercholesterolemic. Lauric acid raised total serum cholesterol more than palmitic acid. This is partly due to a greater increase in HDL cholesterol (the good cholesterol). Lauric also raised LDL levels more than did palmitic acid.* (All fats and oils listed in Figure 3–8 contain some palmitic acid.)

In some patients, high LDLs are caused by genetically produced faulty proteins that carry LDL in the blood. The problem in these cases is not dietary.

The food industry is responding to concerns about tropical oils and is replacing coconut and palm oil with more desirable fats. Palm kernel oil is much more saturated than palm oil. Palm oil is similar in composition to human breast milk fat and in some studies did not raise cholesterol levels. In some parts of the world coconut oil and palm oil are the main oils used, but there is less incidence of car-

---

*"Effects of Specific Saturated Fatty Acids on Serum Lipids and Lipoproteins." *Close Up*, Volume 14, number 1. Washington, DC: Egg Nutrition Center, Spring 1997, p. 5.

diovascular disease in those areas than in the United States. Obviously, there are factors other than fat intake that affect cardiovascular health.

Stearic acid, another saturated fatty acid found in meat and chocolate, does not raise LDL levels. This is not the only fatty acid in meat or chocolate, however. Chocolate contains from 15 to 35% cocoa butter as fat.

No food has just one type of fatty acid. Stearic acid comprises about 88% of the saturated fatty acids in beef, pork, and poultry; 34% of the fatty acids in cocoa butter; and about 20% of the fatty acids in fish.

The liver also makes HDLs. Small amounts of HDLs are made in the intestines as well. HDLs act as receptor cells for clearing cholesterol from the blood. They cycle the cholesterol from LDLs back to the liver. Thus HDLs are important in the prevention of cardiovascular disease. People at risk for coronary heart disease may have inadequate amounts of HDLs (less than 35 milligrams per deciliter). Aerobic exercise, such as running, biking, dancing, swimming, and walking, will increase levels of HDLs. Cessation of smoking and maintenance of a healthy body weight help raise the HDLs to healthy levels. Low HDL levels are the most serious lipoprotein risk factor for women.

Polyunsaturated and monounsaturated fats

It has been discovered that omega 6 polyunsaturated fatty acids (linoleic acids) lower HDL levels as well as LDL levels. Programs promoting the ingestion of large amounts of oils containing linoleic fatty acid led to other problems, however, such as weight gain and gallbladder problems. The omega 6 polyunsaturated oils display a strong promoting effect on tumor growth.[*]

Animal feed that is high in grains is also high in omega 6 fatty acids. Grain-fattened animals have much higher levels of saturated fat than animals eaten years ago (those animals were fed mostly by grazing).

A recent study showed that monounsaturated fat intake results in a non-significant decrease in LDL levels, whereas plasma HDL cholesterol is increased.[†]

The main monounsaturated fatty acid is oleic acid, which is found in all fats. The body produces oleic from acetic acid. Animal fats vary in oleic content from 20 to 40%. Vegetable fats range from 12 to 75% oleic. The richest source of oleic acid is olive oil, followed by canola oil and then peanut oil. No health problems have yet been associated with oleic acid. Olive oil is recommended as a replacement for corn oil, which was traditionally the recommended fat. A light, tasteless, odorless form of olive oil is now available for baking and other uses in which a pronounced flavor is not wanted. Canola oil is also being promoted as a good choice, particularly because it has a mild odor and flavor. Not much has been publicized to confirm or refute any possible benefits from peanut oil. Although olive oil is promoted as a good fat, a recent study shows that too much of any of the fatty acids is associated with a risk of new atherosclerotic lesions. Total fat should be kept at 30% of calorie intake.[§]

---

[*]Weisburger, J. H., "Dietary Fat and Risk of Chronic Disease: Mechanistic Insights from Experiment Studies." *Journal of the American Dietetic Association*, Supplement, July 1997, p. 16.
[†]"Dietary Lipids and Plasma Lipoprotein Levels: A Meta-Analysis. *Close Up*, Volume 14, number 1. Washington, DC: Egg Nutrition Center.
[§]Blankenhorn, D., Johnson, R., Mack, W. J., Hafey, A., Elzein, M.D., and Vailias, L., "The Influence of Diet on the Appearance of New Lesions in Human Coronary Arteries." *Journal of the American Medical Association*, Volume 263, number 12, March 23, 1990.

Two other beneficial fatty acids are found in fish oil. They are omega 3 fatty acids and are commonly referred to as EPA and DHA (eicosapentaeoic and docosahexaenoic). Epidemiological evidence shows that Eskimos, who eat a generous amount of salmon, have little heart disease. The omega 3 fatty acids in fatty fish may prevent the development of coronary heart disease by competing with omega 6 polyunsaturated fatty acids (linoleic and arachidonic, an essential fat produced in the body from linoleic acid) in the cell membrane. The result is to decrease platelet aggregation, which may cause blood clotting, and increase dilation of the blood vessels. Figure 3–9 shows the pathways taken by omega 6 and omega 3 fatty acids to produce the substances that cause blood vessels to dilate and constrict and platelets to help in normal blood clotting. These substances work in harmony to regulate blood flow. Fatty acids are also the precursors for immune substances. Diet impacts the symptoms, with the omega 3 fatty acids producing a more gentle set of regulators. DHA is needed for the development of the brain and central nervous system. It is a component of human milk as well as of fish.

Fish such as salmon, mackerel, herring, albacore tuna, lake trout, bluefish, Atlantic halibut, sardines, and anchovies contain omega 3 fatty acids and are good food choices. Continued research is needed, however, to verify the facts about omega 3 fatty acids.

For the present, it is best not to take supplements of fish oil in the form of liquids and tablets. One study found that non-insulin-dependent diabetics developed impaired insulin secretion and increased glucose output after one month of taking 18 grams per day of fish oil concentrate.*

Another problem is the risk of cancer associated with fatty fish, which pick up more pollutants from the waters in which they live than do leaner fish. (Cautions on contaminated fish are issued by state health departments.)

Plant sources of omega 3

There is a plant source of omega 3 fatty acid: alpha linolenic acid. Linolenic acid converts in the body to EPA, which also converts into DHA (EPA and DHA are abbreviated names for the long-chain polyunsaturated fatty acids found in fish). Walnuts are a plentiful source of linolenic fatty acid. Four teaspoons of chopped walnuts or 1¼ teaspoons of walnut oil gives the equivalent of 300 milligrams of omega 3 fatty acid. Walnuts do, however, contain omega 6 fatty acids.

Canola oil, which is made from rapeseed (a relative of the mustard family grown in Canada and the northwestern United States, with similar large yellow flowers and small, round, black, oil-rich seeds), contains 60% oleic, 24% linoleic, and 10% linolenic fatty acids. The predominance of monounsaturated fat and the benefit of linolenic acids make canola oil a good choice. In the past, rapeseed oil was banned by the Food and Drug Administration because it contained erucic acid. Rapeseed oil once contained 30 to 60% of its fatty acids as erucic acid. Today, erucic acid makes up only 2% of rapeseed oil.

Another plant source of linolenic acid is wheat germ oil, an oil that has culinary limitations. Soybean oil also contains linolenic fatty acid, in addition to generous amounts of linoleic acid. Because linolenic fatty acid has three double bonds, it can become rancid easily. Oxygen reacts with the double bonds in unsaturated fatty acids to form peroxides, which break down into ketones and aldehydes, causing objectionable tastes and odors. Heat and light accelerate this process.

---

*"Adverse Effects of Omega 3 Fatty Acids on Type II Diabetes." *Nutrition and the M.D.*, Volume 16, number 1, January 1990, p. 6.

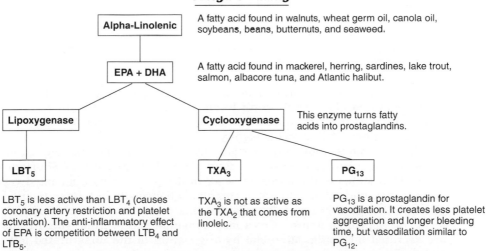

Omega 6 Family

Linoleic — An essential fatty acid found in most foods with fat. Especially rich sources are sunflower oil, safflower oil, corn oil, cottonseed oil, and sesame seed oil.

* Enzymes

Arachidonic — An essential fatty acid formed from linoleic. Found in lard. Arachidonic acid is acylated in membrane phospholipids and then released.

Lipoxygenase ——— **Cyclooxygenase** — An enzyme. This enzyme oxygenates and turns arachidonic acid into prostaglandins.

This enzyme produces leukotrienes.

LTB_4

TXA_2

PG_{12}

LTB_4 is formed in the leukocytes. It causes coronary artery constriction and platelet activation. LTB_4 brings the agents of the immune system to the site of an injury. It is associated with inflammation. LTB_4 makes LTC_4 and LTE_4, which react in bronchopulmonary functions and asthma.

TXA_2 causes vasoconstriction and increases platelet activity. The platelets make more TXA_2.

PG_{12} is a prostaglandin or prostanoid that is synthesized in the endothelial cells. It causes vasodilation and platelet activity (antiaggretory).

Omega 3 Family

Alpha-Linolenic — A fatty acid found in walnuts, wheat germ oil, canola oil, soybeans, beans, butternuts, and seaweed.

EPA + DHA — A fatty acid found in mackerel, herring, sardines, lake trout, salmon, albacore tuna, and Atlantic halibut.

Lipoxygenase

Cyclooxygenase — This enzyme turns fatty acids into prostaglandins.

LBT_5

TXA_3

PG_{13}

LBT_5 is less active than LBT_4 (causes coronary artery restriction and platelet activation). The anti-inflammatory effect of EPA is competition between LTB_4 and LTB_5.

TXA_3 is not as active as the TXA_2 that comes from linoleic.

PG_{13} is a prostaglandin for vasodilation. It creates less platelet aggregation and longer bleeding time, but vasodilation similar to PG_{12}.

The prostanoids and the leukotrienes are called eicosanoids. In normal health, at normal concentrations, they work in harmony for good heart health and immune function. In excessive amounts they are involved in atherogenesis, thrombosis, arthritis, inflammation, tumor growth, asthma, and psoriasis.

*This is where EPA competes with linoleic acid.

Figure 3–9 **Polyunsaturated Fatty Acids** (*Adapted from Kris-Etherton et al., "The effect of diet on plasma lipids, lipoproteins, and coronary heart disease." Copyright The American Dietetic Association. Reprinted by permission from* Journal of the American Dietetic Association *88 [1988] 1373.*)

The food production industry partially hydrogenates soybean oil when it is processed (see the following subsection). Such fats have a higher smoking point and last longer under high production cooking. Hydrogenation also prevents the fats from spoiling. Because hydrogenation removes most of the linolenic acid from soybean oil, the nutritional benefits of the linolenic acid are lost in shortenings and margarines made from this oil. An ounce of cooked soybean sprouts gives a generous amount of linolenic fatty acid and avoids the hydrogenation issue.

Hydrogenation

Unsaturated fat can be hardened and thereby partially saturated through a manufacturing process called hydrogenation. An example is margarine, which is partially hydrogenated to allow vegetable oil to gain the spreading consistency of butter. Another example is shortening. Changing a liquid oil into a semisolid gives the product a higher melting point and better keeping qualities.

The hydrogenation issue is a cause of some concern, however. The negative point of view fears that transisomers, which are formed during hydrogenation, do not act in the same manner as normal fatty acids, which occur in the cis form. (If the hydrogen atoms are on the same side of the carbon chain at the double bond, the arrangement is called cis; if the hydrogen atoms are on opposite sides of the carbon chain at the double bond, the arrangement is called trans.)

It is feared that mistakes can be made by the body when it is presented with these abnormal fats. The body tries to incorporate the new trans fat, with its different spatial arrangement, but then discovers that it is in the wrong shape. Pigs given hydrogenated fat with 50% trans fatty acids developed lesions of the aorta.

Some stick margarines contain 25 to 35% trans fatty acids. Tub margarines contain 13 to 20% and hydrogenated oil contains 10 to 20% trans fatty acids. There are a few margarines on the market that do not contain trans fat. Those that are without trans fat advertise this fact and are therefore recognizable. Those with trans fat do not advertise this on the label. Including trans fat in the list of product ingredients is not yet a requirement of the NLEA (Nutrition Labeling and Education Act of 1990). A major recent meta-analysis reports that trans monounsaturated fat had an effect comparable to saturated fat, a risk factor for elevated blood cholesterol levels.[*] In the Nurses Health Study, women who consumed the largest amounts of trans fatty acids had the highest risk of heart attack over the following eight years.

Food products containing partially hydrogenated vegetable oils continue to be important sources of essential fatty acids. The Institute of Shortening and Edible Oils states that studies show all of the partially hydrogenated vegetable oils are metabolized and do not accumulate abnormally in human tissue.[†] In addition, although it is generally regarded that transisomers are unnatural, these forms do appear in nature. Cows may consume plants from which trans acids are secreted into milk. Microbial hydrogenation of the unsaturated fatty acids within the cow also contributes a share of trans acids to butter. Representatives from the shortening industry point out that trans fats merely replace some of the saturated fat in the diet and are no worse. When a person controls the total fat in the diet, the problem with trans fats is minimized. There is no scientific recommendation to return to butter from margarine.

---

[*]Kwiterovich, P., Jr.,"The Effect of Dietary Fat, Antioxidants, and Pro-Oxidants on Blood Lipids, Lipoproteins, and Atherosclerosis." *Journal of the American Dietetic Association*, Supplement, July 1997, p. 39.

[†]"Food Fats and Oils." Institute of Shortening and Edible Oils, January 1988, pp. 9–10. 1750 New York Avenue, N.W., Washington, DC, 20006.

Oxidation

Many experiments confirm that cholesterol is not a problem unless it is oxygenated. Cholesterol can be oxidized in food and in our bodies. Oxidation is a process that occurs normally in all body tissues. In food, cholesterol is oxidized when heat and air are mixed in during the processing of some items such as powdered eggs, powdered milk, and whey. Many commercially prepared products contain these ingredients. The high heat used in making evaporated milk and smoked fish and meat can cause oxidation. Oxidation also occurs in oils used for deep frying.

Fresh eggs probably do not contain oxidized cholesterol, but cooking methods that incorporate air together with heat, such as making hollandaise sauces and soufflés, can cause oxidation. The cholesterol in scrambled eggs, for example, is more likely to become oxidized than the cholesterol in boiled eggs. Most food, however, has not been analyzed for oxidized cholesterol.

There is no certain way to prevent oxidation. Antioxidants, natural and artificial, are possible future interventions. EDTA, BHA, and BHT are some of the artificial antioxidants. Vitamin E, betacarotene, vitamin C (ascorbic acid), and selenium are some natural antioxidants. (See the sections on vitamins and minerals in this chapter regarding cautions on the use of these nutrients as dietary supplements.)

Prostaglandins

Prostaglandins are yet another factor in the diet/heart issue. They are produced every few seconds in the body. Enzymes help convert linoleic acid (omega 6) into arachidonic acid, a precursor for various prostaglandins.

In heart tissue, prostaglandins work in harmony—one dilating (PG_{12}) and the other constricting (TXA_2) vessels. When the latter is produced in excessive amounts, too much constricting of an atherosclerotic vessel can diminish blood flow. Other prostaglandins create normal platelet aggregation, which keeps blood from becoming too thin. Too much linoleic acid can enhance this process and lead to the formation of blood clots, a risk for heart attack and stroke.

It appears that fish oil (omega 3) can decrease the production of prostaglandins produced from arachidonic acid by competing for an enzyme. This, in turn, produces similar prostaglandins with a gentler action.

The fatty acids also produce leukotrienes that regulate the functioning of the immune system. These leukotrienes cause inflammation at the site of injuries. Precise dietary recommendations for those with inflammatory diseases, such as arthritis, asthma, and psoriasis, are not yet available.

The omega 6 fatty acids, linoleic and arachidonic, produce a strong immune response. The omega 3 fatty acids linolenic, EPA, and DHA produce responses with a gentler action. It might be helpful for those with inflammatory conditions to avoid too much intake of safflower, sunflower, and corn oil and to use canola oil instead.

Tips about fatty acids

Most current research focuses on the role of fatty acids in heart disease and their effect on the immune system. Not enough information is available on how much of each fatty acid should be part of the diet of healthy individuals. Translating this meager information into specific dietary recommendations is a difficult task.

More research needs to be done before pronouncements can be made concerning the correct amounts of certain fats in the diet. It may be prudent, however, to replace some of the omega 6 fatty acids with monounsaturated fatty acids and omega 3 fatty acids (that is, more olive oil, canola oil, walnuts, and fish in place of corn oil, safflower oil, and sunflower oils). Supplemental doses of omega 3 oils may lead to prolonged bleeding and bruising. Decreased immunity to disease could also result, especially from fish oil supplements.

Another important consideration is that food contains a mixture of several fatty acids, and all fatty acids are high in calories. Excess calories can contribute to weight gain. Obesity is an independent risk factor for some of the same conditions that fatty acids are used to alleviate. Fat should comprise no more than 30% of the total daily calorie intake, with saturated, monounsaturated, and polyunsaturated fat each contributing 10%.

For example, a person needing 2000 calories daily would multiply 2000 by 0.30, which equals 600 calories. There are 9 calories in each gram of fat. Dividing the 600 by 9 equals 67 grams of fat (the answer is rounded off). The new food labels list the grams of fat, so it is possible to determine how much fat one gets from these products. The fat grams in fresh foods are as follows (average numbers):

Food	*Fat*
Milk (whole)	8 grams per 8 ounces
Milk (2% fat)	4 grams per 8 ounces
Milk (skim)	0 grams per 8 ounces
High-fat meat	8 grams per ounce
Meat (medium fat)	5 grams per ounce
Lean meats, poultry, fish	3 grams per ounce
Vegetables	0 grams per serving
Fruits	0 grams per serving
Butter, margarine, oil, or nuts	5 grams per teaspoon
Breads and starches without added fat	1 gram per slice or 1/2-cup serving

Diet is not the entire answer to the heart health issue. The predicted response from cholesterol feeding studies is 2.5 milligrams per deciliter of plasma per 100 milligrams daily of dietary cholesterol. Some of this increase is HDL, the good cholesterol, along with LDL.*

In a seven countries study, 20 milligram per deciliter change in the plasma cholesterol level is associated with a 17% change in CHD (cardiovascular heart disease) risk. The editors of *Close Up* believe that using this data and figuring on an 11 milligram per deciliter decrease in total cholesterol levels, CHD risk is lowered by 9%. This is a relatively small effect in the U.S. population, whose risk is high compared to other industrialized countries. *Close Up* editors believe that there is more to CHD risk than merely reducing dietary fat and cholesterol.[†]

---

*"Effects of Shrimp and Egg Consumption on Plasma Lipoproteins." *Close Up*, Volume 14, number 1, Spring 1997, p. 3.
[†]"Lowering Blood Cholesterol Levels Alone Isn't Enough to Combat Heart Disease." *Nutrition Close Up*, Volume 12, number 3, 1995, p. 5.

Fat replacers

The FDA has approved several fat replacers in processed foods. "Simplese" contains 1 to 2 calories per gram compared to 9 calories per gram for fat. It is made from microparticulated protein and is derived from egg whites or skim milk. It does not lend itself to cooking but is used in cheeses and ice cream. "Olestra" has no calories. It is made with sugar and a chemically altered fat that passes unabsorbed through the digestive system. Olestra also carries out the fat soluble vitamins A, E, D, and K, however, and it can cause diarrhea if too much is ingested. Olestra lends itself to frying and is used in potato chip production. (The brand name is "Olean.") "Salatrin" contains 5 calories per gram and is only partially absorbed. It is used in baked goods.

Modified food starches, dextrins, cellulose, and gums behave as thickeners in fat-free salad dressings. These are also used as texturizers in many other foods, giving the mouth the feel of fat, but with many fewer calories.

The food manufacturing industry has responded to the call for lower-fat foods that resemble those foods that many people enjoy. There are several issues to think about concerning these trends. The first is the nutritional merit of most of these types of foods. Generally, they are high in salt, sugar, or corn syrup and low in fruits, vegetables, and whole grains. Second, one may rationalize indulging in larger portions of the reduced fat items and crowd out the basic foods. Third, the art of cooking delicious, tasty, wholesome food is getting lost in the craze for low-fat and fat-free foods. Children are growing up without ever knowing the taste of home-cooked food. How many nuts or raisins does a commercial cookie have? How much tofu or fruit does a commercial frozen dessert have? Artificial flavors and sugars predominate in such foods. Low-fat and fat-free salad dressings can be made at home with low-fat yogurts, cottage cheese, tofu with herbs, or tomato juice with lemon and spices (See Figure 3–10.)

Vitamins

Vitamins are organic compounds that are necessary for good health and are obtained from food sources. Without vitamins, symptoms and sicknesses appear, leading to poor health, physical deformities, and, in some cases, death. In proper amounts, vitamins are essential for growth and life. The word *vitamin* comes from *vita*, which means life, and *amine*, which indicates chemical structure.

The discovery of vitamins was a slow process beginning in the early eighteenth century, when it was discovered accidentally that oranges and lemons prevented the disease called scurvy in sailors. In addition, it was found that sailors in the Far East needed foods other than white rice to prevent the disease beriberi. It was not known that vitamins were the substances responsible for preventing and curing these diseases, but the groundwork for the discovery of vitamins was being laid.

Various European studies were conducted in 1905, 1906, and 1907 using animals that were fed purified diets of carbohydrates, protein, fat, and minerals. These were all the known food components at the time. Evidence suggested, however, that some other food element was missing. An unknown food factor was apparently necessary for the maintenance of good health. Slowly, between 1925 and 1955, each of the vitamins was isolated and discovered.

The body's need for a specific vitamin to prevent health problems does not in itself establish the function of that vitamin. Studies of vitamins' functions still continue. Vitamins are specific and work as cofactors with enzymes in many different capacities and in each cell. Not all animal species need the same

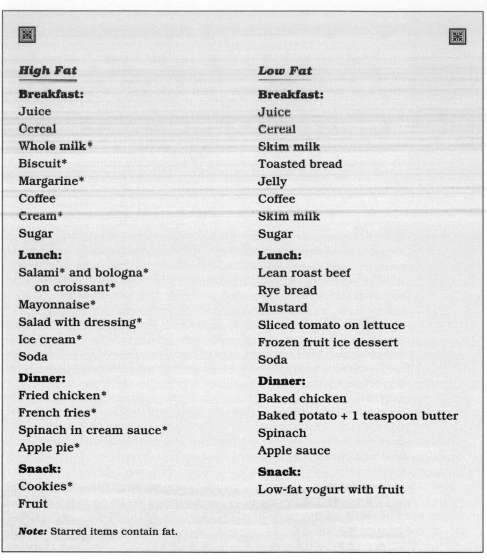

High Fat	Low Fat
Breakfast:	**Breakfast:**
Juice	Juice
Cereal	Cereal
Whole milk*	Skim milk
Biscuit*	Toasted bread
Margarine*	Jelly
Coffee	Coffee
Cream*	Skim milk
Sugar	Sugar
Lunch:	**Lunch:**
Salami* and bologna* on croissant*	Lean roast beef
	Rye bread
Mayonnaise*	Mustard
Salad with dressing*	Sliced tomato on lettuce
Ice cream*	Frozen fruit ice dessert
Soda	Soda
Dinner:	**Dinner:**
Fried chicken*	Baked chicken
French fries*	Baked potato + 1 teaspoon butter
Spinach in cream sauce*	Spinach
Apple pie*	Apple sauce
Snack:	**Snack:**
Cookies*	Low-fat yogurt with fruit
Fruit	

Note: Starred items contain fat.

Figure 3–10 Comparison of High-Fat and Low-Fat Meals

vitamins, however. For example, dogs do not need vitamin C. Their bodies can manufacture it, whereas human bodies cannot.

Vitamins are classified into two categories—fat soluble and water soluble. Fat soluble vitamins require dietary fat for absorption. Excess amounts of fat soluble vitamins are stored in fat tissues or in the liver. Water soluble vitamins are excreted in the urine when body tissues are saturated. The fat soluble vitamins are A, E, D, and K. The water soluble vitamins are C and the B group (there are eight B vitamins).

A problem with vitamin supplements

Some people rely on vitamin supplements rather than on natural foods for their vitamin intake. Too much of certain vitamins can be problematic, however.

High intakes of both types of vitamins can create imbalances, and excesses of certain vitamins can cause toxicity. Excess intake of the fat soluble vitamins

A and D creates the most serious problems. Fat soluble vitamin E is not toxic but too much can interfere with vitamin K's clotting function. Excess vitamin K would not be a problem, except in its synthetic form, which is available only through prescription. Vitamins B_3 and B_6 are the two water soluble vitamins that cause toxicity if taken in excessive amounts.

Fat soluble vitamins

Vitamin A

Vitamin A is fat soluble and is needed for growth. Taking supplements (in a range of 25,000 to 50,000 international units [IUs]) of vitamin A could lead to toxicity and cause severe headaches, nausea, lethargy, skin rash, and hair loss. Vitamin A is destroyed by oxygen, and proper care in preparing and storing food is needed to prevent its loss. Air-tight storage containers, lids on pots, and quick preparation can help. Vitamin E helps prevent oxidation of vitamin A in the body.

Vitamin A is more stable than most vitamins when heated. A vitamin A deficiency in the body may occur if the nutrients that help metabolize and transport vitamin A—zinc, protein, and fat—are not included in the diet.

Vitamin A is necessary for a chemical reaction that allows day vision to switch to night vision. Night blindness is one of the symptoms of inadequate vitamin A intake.

Vitamin A is also necessary for keeping our epithelial tissue moist (this is the tissue that lines the body—the skin on the outside of the body and the mucous membrane on the inside). A moist mucous membrane helps prevent respiratory infections. If the lining of the lung is not moist mucus, the tiny hairlike structures that sweep out bacteria cannot do their job.

There is a theory that some types of tumors begin when epithelial tissue dries out and becomes abnormal. In the past tests done on animals, using large doses of detoxified vitamin A, indicated that the vitamin was effective in combating these types of tumors.

Vitamin A from food sources comes in two types: preformed and provitamin. The preformed type comes in liver, egg yolks, whole milk, milk fat products (such as butter, cream, cheeses, and ice cream) and cod liver oil. Ingestion of bear liver should be avoided since it has been reported to cause acute toxicity.* Neither muscle meats nor grain foods are considered good sources of preformed vitamin A. Fortification with vitamin A is required for all skim milk and margarine.

Fruits and vegetables, on the other hand, are often a good source of the second type of vitamin A: the provitamin, a precursor called beta carotene. Beta carotene is a yellowish-orange pigment. Generally, chlorophyll masks carotene, and green as well as orange-colored fruits and vegetables are rich in carotene. Such foods include sweet potatoes, winter squash, pumpkin, carrots, cantaloupes, spinach, collard greens, turnip greens, romaine lettuce, and all other produce that is colored all the way through. Fruits and vegetables that have color only on the peel, such as cucumbers, or in the outer leaves, such as cabbage, are not good sources of vitamin A.

In the United States, vitamin A deficiency is rare, but deficiency is found in other parts of the world. Many children are blind because of vitamin A defi-

---

*"Diet and Health Implications for Reducing Chronic Disease Risk: A Publication of the National Research Council of the National Academy Press." Washington, DC: Committee on Diet and Health, Food and Nutrition Board, Commission on Life Science, National Research Council, 1989.

ciency. In certain parts of China, children are given vitamin A injections every six months to prevent blindness.

As a rule, nutritionists do not recommend vitamins as cures for medical problems unrelated to nutrition, but vitamin A derivatives have been used for years to fight acne. A topical form of vitamin A is being used as a short-term treatment to lessen wrinkles in middle-aged people's skin.

Vitamin A was formerly measured in IUs. The recent and more accurate measurement is in retinol equivalents (REs). One IU of vitamin A equals 0.3 micrograms of retinol or 0.6 micrograms of beta carotene.

The U.S. RDA for vitamin A is 1000 REs per day for adult men. The allowance for women is less (800 REs). The measurement used in the past was 5000 IUs for men and 4000 IUs for women. The 1989 edition of the Recommended Dietary Allowances established by the Food and Nutrition Board, National Academy of Science began listing vitamin A in retinal equivalents. Some nutritionists still refer to the IU measurements.

Although supplements of beta carotene function as a weak antioxidant, they should not be used because beta carotene can interfere with vitamin E metabolism. One study on beta carotene was discontinued when it was discovered that smokers who were subjected to beta carotene supplements also had increased incidents of lung cancer.*

Vitamin E

Vitamin E, a fat soluble antioxidant, is actually a family of vitamins called tocopherols. Alpha tocopherol is the most effective vitamin E and is sometimes included in the ingredient list of processed foods containing fat. In this capacity it acts as a food preservative rather than as a vitamin. The antioxidant properties of vitamin E prevent fat from becoming rancid.

In the body, vitamin E prevents oxygen from destroying vitamins C and A. Nearly all foods contain some vitamin E.

The U.S. RDA for vitamin E (12 to 15 milligrams) is based on the average intake of polyunsaturated fat in the diet. Oils in the form of salad dressings, cooking oils, and margarine supply most of the polyunsaturated fats in our diets. They are also the richest sources of vitamin E.

Wheat germ oil is another potent source of vitamin E, but the oil (and thus the vitamin E) has been removed from some brands of wheat germ. Other oil-containing foods that are also good sources of vitamin E include seeds and nuts. Green, leafy vegetables are also high in vitamin E. Whole grains contain vitamin E, whereas their refined counterparts do not.

Vitamin E has been the subject of many claims, especially those promoting disease cures and athletic performance, but to date there has not been any proof to support such claims. There may, however, be a connection between vitamin E and preventing the formation of nitrosamines (carcinogens formed from nitrites and amines). Nitrites are normally found in the soil, in plants, in saliva, and in foods containing nitrite preservatives. (Sodium nitrite is effective against botulism formation in anaerobically packaged foods, such as vacuum-packed cold cuts and canned meats.) Nitrites can combine with amines, which occur naturally in our bodies and in food. Vitamin E may also help prevent muscular dystrophy and infertility in some animals, but not in humans.

Vitamin E has been used in large doses (from 100 to 800 IU) to treat fibrocystic breast disease. Not all women with fibrocystic breast disease, however,

---

*"The Alpha-Tocopherol, Beta-Carotene Cancer Prevention Study in Finland." *Nutrition Reviews*, Volume 52, number 7, July 1994, pp. 242–246; found under Health Reference Center's CD-ROM Infotrak, 1996.

improve when they take vitamin E. Vitamin E also is currently being used in the treatment of ulcers, wounds, scar tissue, and circulatory problems of the legs. Again, the usefulness of this treatment has not been proven.

Large doses of vitamin E can upset the stomach, but there have been no cases of vitamin E toxicity. Too much vitamin E can compete with vitamin K's vital clotting activity, however.

Vitamin E is routinely given to premature infants, who are born in a relative state of vitamin E deficiency. Without this vitamin E treatment, these infants, when exposed to oxygen, may develop an opaque membrane on the posterior surface of the lens of the eye. This condition, which is known as retrolentive fibroplasia, can cause blindness in premature babies.

The most recent wave of interest in vitamin E concerns its role as an antioxidant in the prevention of heart disease and cancer.

Vitamin K

Vitamin K is a fat soluble vitamin produced by plants and bacteria and synthetically in laboratories. It is the only vitamin that cannot be bought over the counter. The bacteria that produce vitamin K in the intestines supply 50% of the body's daily requirement. Excellent food sources of vitamin K include pork liver, soybeans, brussels sprouts, cabbage, broccoli, cauliflower, and dark green leafy vegetables such as kale. Vitamin K is needed by the liver for the synthesis of blood-clotting proteins.

Injections of vitamin K may be given before surgery to prevent hemorrhage. Vitamin K is also given to infants immediately after birth for the same purpose. The baby's gut is sterile in the first few days after birth, and there are no bacteria to produce vitamin K until the fourth day of life.

Oral supplementation of vitamin K may be necessary if a person has been on a long-term antibiotic that may have killed the good vitamin-K-producing bacteria in the colon. People on blood-thinning medication (anticoagulants) may need to avoid eating large amounts of foods high in vitamin K.

Vitamin K is necessary for maintaining a healthy skeleton and a healthy immune system.

Mineral oil and cholestyramine (a cholesterol-lowering drug) may interfere with vitamin K absorption, as may diseases of the liver or gallbladder that interfere with bile secretion.

Vitamin K is stable to heat but unstable to alkalies and strong acids, oxidation, and light. Therefore, cooks should never prepare green vegetables with baking soda, which is very alkaline. Although this custom preserves the green color of the vegetables, it destroys vitamins. Putting a lid on a pot during cooking helps prevent vitamin loss from air (oxidation) and light but also has a negative effect on color. The best strategy is to cook green vegetables as quickly as possible to help preserve important vitamins.

There are two naturally occurring forms of vitamin K, phylloquinone and menaquinone. Phylloquinone (K_1) comes from plants. Menaquinone (K_2) is produced by bacteria in the intestinal tract. A synthetic form of vitamin K is called menadione. Menadione has twice the biological activity as the natural forms. Toxicity from excessive doses can occur only with the synthetic form. Hemolytic anemia, an accelerated breakdown of red blood cells, jaundice, and brain damage could result.

Vitamin D

Vitamin D is another fat soluble vitamin. The RDA for vitamin D is 400 IUs for children and 200 IUs for adults. A newer measurement is 10 micrograms for children and 5 micrograms for adults. The 5 micrograms is equivalent to 200

IUs. People could get sufficient vitamin D if their hands, face, and arms were exposed to the sun's rays for 15 minutes a few times a week. Dark-skinned people would require about three hours of sun exposure per week to get the same amount of vitamin D from the sun. (These time recommendations are based on sun exposure in the midaltitudes on a clear summer day.) There's a good chance that people are not getting enough vitamin D from the sun for at least a month or two out of every year if they live as far north as an imaginary line connecting Baltimore, Cincinnati, Topeka, Denver, and Sacramento. Chances are that people are not getting enough vitamin D at all from the sun if they live on or above a line drawn from Boston to Milwaukee, Minneapolis, and Boise.* This exposure should be spread out, of course, to avoid overexposure and the danger of skin cancer. Heavy clouds, smoke, or smog block the ultraviolet rays of the sun that contain the vitamin. Dark-skinned people living in northern smoggy cities are more prone to rickets, caused by vitamin D deficiency, than are light-skinned people.[†]

Ultraviolet rays from tanning lamps also stimulate vitamin D synthesis. However, the FDA warns that if the lamps are not properly filtered, people risk skin cancer, burns, and damage to the eyes and blood vessels.[§]

Small amounts of vitamin D are found in eggs, butter, and fatty fish. Liver is also a source of vitamin D. In the United States, where all milk is fortified with vitamin D (to a level of 400 IUs per quart), milk is an excellent source. Milk was chosen for fortification because vitamin D helps metabolize calcium, the mineral that builds bones and teeth. Milk is the best source of calcium.

Inadequate intake of vitamin D in children can lead to rickets, which causes bones to soften at the ends and flare out. This condition produces bowed legs, knock-knees, and a distorted rib cage. Vitamin D deficiency in adults can lead to osteomalacia, a softening of the bones.

Toxic doses of vitamin D can cause headaches, weakness, weight loss, constipation, and calcification of soft tissue. Cod-liver oil provides the RDA for vitamin D in 1 teaspoon. Amounts higher than 1 teaspoon should be avoided because 1 teaspoon contains 400 IUs and too much vitamin D is toxic.

The liver and the kidneys each play a role in the formation of vitamin D in its active form. Disease of these organs can cause vitamin D deficiency.

Vitamin D synthesis begins with 7-dehydrocholesterol, which is made in the liver from cholesterol. This precursor for vitamin D is found in the skin. When irradiated by the sun's ultraviolet rays, 7-dehydrocholesterol becomes previtamin D_3 (cholecalciferol). Cholecalciferol enters the blood and travels to the liver, where it is converted to the form 25-hydroxy vitamin D_3. It must then go to the kidneys to be converted to the active form 1,25-dihydroxy vitamin D_3.

Vitamin D_3, cholecalciferol, is also found in fish oils and eggs. Vitamin D_2, ergocalciferol, is found in plants. Irradiation of ergocalciferol produces synthetic vitamin D.

Vitamin D obtained from food must also be transformed into the active form by the liver and kidneys. Dairy products are fortified with D_2 or D_3. Bile is needed for normal absorption of the vitamin from the intestines.

Vitamin D is stable to heat, oxygen, and alkaline substances. Opinions differ whether storage, processing, and cooking have any effect on vitamin D.

Calcitrol, a chemical cousin of vitamin D that raises calcium levels in the body, is given to women to help prevent osteoporosis.

Tufts University Diet and Nutrition Letter, Volume 13, number 5, July 1995, p. 1. Academic Data Base Baltimore City Community College Library Infotrac.
[†]Ibid.
[§]Whitney, E., Rolfes, S., *Understanding Nutrition* (7th ed.). Minneapolis, St. Paul, New York, Los Angeles, San Francisco: West Publishing Company, 1996, p. 410.

Some antacids and some anticonvulsant drugs may lead to vitamin D deficiency.

Water soluble vitamins

The B Vitamins

The water soluble B vitamins all function as coenzymes. Indirectly, they are necessary for normal functioning of the nervous system. Early symptoms of vitamin B deficiency are irritability, grumpiness, and nervousness.

The B vitamins are spread throughout the basic five food groups (Figure 3–11). Unfortunately, some of them have been processed out of refined grain products like white flour and white rice. Some flour products that have been enriched will contain vitamins B_1, B_2, and B_3. Enrichment also returns B_1 and B_3 to white rice (B_2 causes a yellowish color and is not used). These are the major B vitamins needed for metabolizing carbohydrates. Folic acid is added to prevent birth defects.

Vitamin B_6 and folacin, or pantothenic acid—a B vitamin found in all natural foods—are not put back through enrichment. Vitamin B_6 is needed for metabolizing protein as well as carbohydrates, and all of the protein foods are good sources of this vitamin.

The effectiveness of vitamin B_6 in providing relief from premenstrual syndrome (PMS) has not been proven. Because toxic levels of B_6, which cause nerve damage, are possible, it is questionable whether the vitamin should be recommended for relief of PMS. Use of the birth control pill, however, does increase the need for vitamin B_6.

In the belief that vitamin B_6 enhances athletic performance, some athletes have ingested toxic amounts of the vitamin.

Vitamin B_6 is required for cellular multiplication, protein synthesis, and antibody formation. It is also used as a part of the therapy for counteracting carpal tunnel syndrome, a disorder of the hands and wrists caused by repetitive motion. Higher levels of vitamin B_6 were related to better performance on two measures of memory in 70 men aged 54 to 81 years old who completed a battery of cognitive tests.[*]

Vitamin B_{12}, also called cobalamin, is needed to prevent anemia. Absorption of B_{12} requires intrinsic factor, a protein synthesized by the stomach. Vitamin B_{12} is made by bacteria that are found in animal products—meat, fish, poultry, milk, and eggs. Strict vegetarians could develop a deterioration of the spinal cord if they do not take B_{12} supplements. This deterioration begins with numbness in the extremities and progresses to a loss of muscle coordination and paralysis. More than 70% of older people who are deficient in B_{12} also have Alzheimer's. It is unknown whether the deficiency is a cause or a result of the disease.[†]

Biotin, another B vitamin, is produced by intestinal bacteria and is not a dietary concern. Antibiotics, however, may kill these bacteria. Some other medications have caused deficiencies of biotin. Avidin, found in raw egg whites, binds biotin and could cause a biotin deficiency if taken in large amounts.

All of the B vitamins are soluble in water, and thus care should be taken in preparing food. Minimal amounts of water or waterless cooking methods should

---

[*]Riggs, K., Spiro, A. III, Tucker, K., and Rush, D., "Relations of Vitamin B_{12}, Vitamin B_6, Folate, and Homoupteine to Cognitive Performance in the Normative Aging Study." *The American Journal of Clinical Nutrition*, Volume 63, March 1996, pp. 306–314.
[†]Garrison, R., Jr., and Somer, E., *The Nutrition Desk Reference*. New Canaan, CT: Keats Publishing, Inc., 1990.

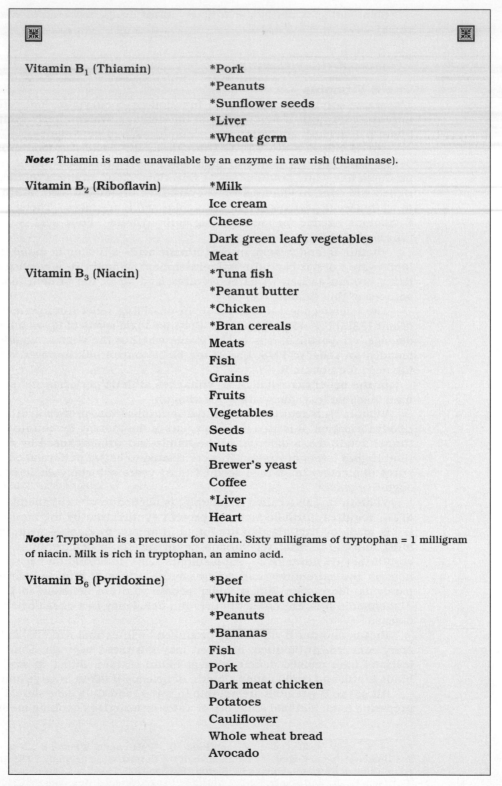

Vitamin B$_1$ (Thiamin)
*Pork
*Peanuts
*Sunflower seeds
*Liver
*Wheat germ

Note: Thiamin is made unavailable by an enzyme in raw rish (thiaminase).

Vitamin B$_2$ (Riboflavin)
*Milk
Ice cream
Cheese
Dark green leafy vegetables
Meat

Vitamin B$_3$ (Niacin)
*Tuna fish
*Peanut butter
*Chicken
*Bran cereals
Meats
Fish
Grains
Fruits
Vegetables
Seeds
Nuts
Brewer's yeast
Coffee
*Liver
Heart

Note: Tryptophan is a precursor for niacin. Sixty milligrams of tryptophan = 1 milligram of niacin. Milk is rich in tryptophan, an amino acid.

Vitamin B$_6$ (Pyridoxine)
*Beef
*White meat chicken
*Peanuts
*Bananas
Fish
Pork
Dark meat chicken
Potatoes
Cauliflower
Whole wheat bread
Avocado

Figure 3–11 Excellent Food Sources of the B Vitamins

Sunflower seeds
Yeast
Liver

Note 1: Pyridoxine is found in plant foods. Related pyridoxal and pyridoxamine compounds are found in animal foods.

Note 2: Canning causes 50% losses of this vitamin.

Note 3: Starred items contain the highest amount of the vitamin.

Vitamin B$_{12}$ (Cobalamin)	*Organ meats
	*Clams
	*Oysters
	(All other flesh and dairy products)

Note: Cobalamin refers to cobalt-containing carrinoids that have biological activity for humans.

Folacin	*Green leafy vegetables
	*Organ meats
	*Bananas (excellent availability)
	*Lima beans
	Oranges

Note: There are 213 different forms of folacin (polyglutamates).

Pantothenic acid	*Egg
(widespread in foods)	*Liver
	Beef
	Pork
	Bran
	Most foods from the basic food groups (grains, meats, fish, poultry, eggs, milk, fruits, vegetables)

Note: Lost in canning.

Biotin	*Liver and organ meats
	*Yeast
	*Egg yolk
	*Soybeans
	Muscle meats
	Dairy
	Grains
	Nuts
	Fruits
	Vegetable

Figure 3–11 (continued)

be used, the cooking liquids should be saved, and soaking should be avoided. Saved cooking liquids can be used again to make soups, gravies, and sauces. Vegetables should be washed quickly and not left in a pan of water, as is sometimes done with lettuce and potatoes. The B vitamins are destroyed by baking soda, so baking soda should not be added to the water when cooking vegetables (as mentioned earlier, this is a trick often used to maintain the green color of vegetables).

Two vitamin B deficiency diseases, beriberi (a disease of the nerves, digestive system, and heart) and pellagra (which affects the skin, stomach, and central nervous system), have been prevented in the United States by the enrichment of breads and cereals. Beriberi is caused by a deficiency of thiamin (B_1) and pellagra by a deficiency of niacin (B_3). Both beriberi and pellagra, if left untreated, can lead to death.

Thiamin, B_1

Thiamin is the most unstable of all of the B vitamins. A synthetic version of B_1 is more stable, however. Early thiamin deficiency symptoms involve the mouth and tongue. The mouth is sore and the tongue is bright red and swollen. Other symptoms include fatigue, muscle weakness, and nerve damage. Because thiamin is the most important vitamin in carbohydrate metabolism, a deficiency will result in decreased appetite and weight loss. Beriberi is triggered by thiamin deficiency.

Thiamin deficiency is common in alcoholics. Vitamin B therapy is a necessary part of an alcohol recovery program; however, it is not always effective. Alcohol interferes with mechanisms that regulate food intake, and the alcoholic then eats poorly. Toxic effects of alcohol interfere with the metabolism and storage of nutrients. Malabsorption of nutrients occurs in response to alcohol ingestion. Alcohol also interferes with thiamin metabolism. The most severe form of thiamin deficiency is Wernicke's encephalopathy, characterized by visual disorders, confusion, and coma.*

The RDA for thiamin is based on total calorie intake: 0.5 milligram per 1000 kilocalories, or one-half milligram for each thousand calories. Major food sources of thiamin are products made with enriched flour, pork, dried beans, and whole grains. In the United States, grain products supply 42% of B_1 in the average diet, whereas meat, poultry, and fish supply close to 25%. The mean thiamin intake of the U.S. population is more than 100% of the RDA. Excess vitamin B_1 is excreted in the urine.

Riboflavin, B_2

Milk is the best source of B_2 and provides the highest proportion of B_2 in the American diet. Enriched and whole grain products, meat, liver, poultry, fish, and dark leafy green vegetables provide most of the remaining riboflavin in the diet.

Vitamin B_2 is lost when exposed to light. Therefore, opaque containers for milk, lids on pots during cooking, and quick preparation help conserve B_2.

Vitamin B_2 is involved in cell respiration and the health of tissues such as the esophagus lining. It also helps change the amino acid tryptophan in food into niacin (B_3).

Riboflavin deficiency begins with fissures, or cracks, that radiate from the corners of the mouth onto the skin and can extend into the mucous membrane. This symptom is called angular stomatitis and is followed by cheilosis (painful cracks on the upper and lower lips). Another classic symptom of vitamin B_2 defi-

---

*Zeman, Frances, J., *Clinical Nutrition and Dietetics.* Lexington, MA: The Collamore Press, 1983, p. 459.

ciency is magenta tongue, a purplish-red, sore, swollen, and glossy tongue. Other body areas affected by vitamin B_2 deficiency are the eyes, which feel gritty and burn or itch; the nostrils, which develop weepy, crusty lesions; and the genitalia, which develop an itchy, scaly dermatitis on the vulva of the female and the scrotum of the male. B_2 is also needed for growth and healthy vision. Cataracts are an eye disorder that may be caused by a deficiency of B_2.

The RDA for riboflavin is also based on total calorie intake: 0.6 milligram per 1000 kilocalories, or six-tenths of a milligram for each thousand calories.

Niacin, B_3

Niacin is a coenzyme that helps produce energy in all body cells. Its precursor is the amino acid tryptophan. Sixty milligrams of tryptophan convert to one milligram of niacin. Milk, which has little niacin, has enough tryptophan to prevent a niacin deficiency when taken on a regular basis. Recommendations for niacin intake are given in niacin equivalents, (NEs), which take into account tryptophan conversion and natural niacin.

The RDA for niacin, as for thiamin and riboflavin, is based on total calorie intake. Generally, the allowance is 6.6 milligrams NE per 1000 kilocalories, or six and six-tenths milligrams NE per thousand calories.

The highest proportion of niacin in the diet comes from meat, poultry, fish, and grain products. Legumes, seeds, and peanut butter are also good sources. The dietary intake of Americans appears to be adequate because of the use of enriched flours and cereal products.

Niacin has been used pharmacologically (and effectively) to reduce VLDL cholesterol synthesis. However, high doses of niacin are accompanied by the unpleasant side effects of flushing and itching. Niacin as medicine, in the large doses needed to lower cholesterol, is not a good choice for those with diabetes or gout. Niacin must be monitored by a physician and should not be self-prescribed.

Pantothenic Acid, B_5

Pantothenic acid gets its name from the Greek word *panthos*, which means "everywhere." Pantothenic acid is found in all natural foods, both plant and animal.

Fifty percent of the pantothenic acid in wheat is found in the bran. Liver, kidney, yeast, egg yolk, salmon, and milk are the best sources. Meats, poultry, and legumes provide good amounts, whereas lesser amounts are found in fruits and vegetables. Eating a healthful diet will supply adequate amounts of B_5, and deficiency is uncommon. The author has observed, however, that many college students' daily diets are lacking in wholesome foods, and thus their intake of B_5 is less than the estimated RDA of 4 to 7 milligrams.

In the body, B_5 is found in all tissues. There are high concentrations of B_5 in the liver and kidney and lesser amounts in the adrenal glands. These glands are important in the stress response and require adequate B_5 to function properly.

Pantothenic acid functions as an important part of coenzymes, which play a role in producing energy from carbohydrates and fats. Coenzymes are also needed for chemical reactions that produce antibodies, fatty acids, cholesterol, sterols, and acetylcholine, which regulates nerve tissue.

Experimentally induced deficiencies of B_5 have caused irritability, restlessness, fatigue following mild exertion, alternating insomnia and sleepiness, vomiting, stomach distress, staggering gait, and tenderness of the heels and feet.

The "burning feet syndrome" seen in malnourished people is alleviated by pantothenic acid treatments.

Taking supplements of B_5 over the estimated requirement, even by as little as 10 to 20 milligrams, can cause diarrhea.

Cooking of food causes some B_5 loss because the vitamin is readily destroyed by heat. Much B_5 is lost in the canning process because canned foods are overly heated as a preservation technique.

Pyridoxine, B_6

Vitamin B_6 is a family of compounds that includes pyridoxine, pyridoxal, and pyridoxamine. All three forms are found in foods. Pyridoxine functions as a coenzyme in at least 50 different enzyme reactions. The most important of these reactions maintains nerve tissues and forms some of the neurotransmitters that allow nerve cells to communicate with each other. Pyridoxine also helps metabolize fatty acids.

B_6 is needed for enzymes involved in the synthesis and catabolism of all amino acids. It is involved in the transformation of the amino acid tryptophan to the vitamin niacin (B_3). It is involved in the regeneration of red blood cells, antibody production, insulin production, and absorption of vitamin B_{12}.

The highest proportion of B_6 intake in the American diet comes from meat, poultry, and fish; followed by fruits and vegetables; and finally by grain products. The National Research Council of the National Academy of Sciences, which produces the Recommended Dietary Allowances, assumes that the usual daily protein intake is 100 grams for women and 110 grams for men, which is the basis for the RDA for B_6: 2.2 milligrams for men and 2.0 milligrams for women (B_6 is necessary for protein metabolism). Excellent sources of B_6 are red meat, poultry, fish, liver, kidney, peanuts, legumes, whole grains, milk products, bananas, potatoes, avocado, sunflower seeds, wheat germ, and bran. Egg is a moderate source.

B_6 deficiency is uncommon in the United States because of liberal intake of proteins. Deficiency is seen when drugs are used that antagonize B_6. Examples are alcohol, hydrazine drugs, isoniazid, anti-Parkinson drugs (levodopa), and anti-Wilson drugs (penicillamine). Depression, irritability, nausea, greasy flaky skin, and hypochromic anemia (characterized by red blood cells with a small amount of pigment) are symptoms of B_6 deficiency.

In the 1950s, an infant formula containing insufficient B_6 caused convulsions and some cases of permanent brain damage.

Neurological problems develop with intakes of 2 to 6 grams of B_6 per day. The symptoms are numbness and tingling in the hands and feet, difficulty walking, and sharp pains in the spine and other bones. Large doses of B_6 can cause irreversible nerve damage.

Isoniazid, a drug used to prevent and treat tuberculosis, interferes with vitamin B_6 metabolism. For patients on this drug, 5 milligrams per day of B_6 is given to prevent peripheral neuropathy. Oral contraceptives increase the need for B_6. Other medications that interfere with B_6 nutrition include dopamine, cycloserine, penicillamine, and hydrazine.

There is evidence that B_6 helps in treating some cases of carpal tunnel syndrome.

Folate

Folate is also known as folic acid. Formerly it was known as folacin, a term no longer used. The chemical name for folate is pteroylglutamic acid (PGA). There are many forms of folate in food.

Folate functions as a coenzyme in reactions involving the transfer of one carbon fragment. This makes folate important in the synthesis of nucleoproteins and in blood cell production. Folate plays an essential role in making new body cells by helping to produce DNA and RNA (the cell's master plan for cell reproduction). Folate is also needed in the metabolism of amino acids, and it supplies carbon and hydrogen for methyl groups needed in the metabolic process.

Folate works with vitamin B_{12} to form hemoglobin in red blood cells. Folate also helps convert vitamin B_{12} to one of its coenzyme forms. B_{12} is needed to convert folate to its active form.

The first symptoms of folate deficiency are fatigue, weakness, and a smooth, sore tongue, and it culminates in anemia. Folate deficiency impairs cell division and protein synthesis. If replacement of intestinal cells falters, gastrointestinal deterioration results. This state slows down DNA synthesis, and cells lose their ability to divide, which, of course, impairs growth.

The large-cell anemia of folate deficiency is known as macrocytic or megaloblastic anemia. In this condition, the blood cells are large, malformed, and few in number. They carry insufficient hemoglobin, the substance that carries oxygen to body tissues.

The RDA for folate is 200 micrograms for men and 180 micrograms for women. Pregnant women, and those who may become pregnant, need 400 micrograms daily. Women who are breast feeding should take 280 micrograms daily to ensure that both they and their baby get enough folate.

Legumes are considered a good practical source of folate. Leafy green vegetables provide folate (e.g., spinach). Asparagus also contains appreciable amounts.

Organ meats, liver, kidney, and brewer's yeast are potent sources of folate but are less likely to be ingested. Lettuce, cabbage, soybeans, and wheat germ contain a form of folate which is not well absorbed by the body. Although orange juice has a less available form of folate (a form not well used by the body), it is commonly ingested and contributes an important share of folate in the U.S. diet. Some fruits, such as avocados and bananas, contain folate. The amount of folate in bananas is not great, but its form is of good availability. Meats and milk are poor sources of folate. Children on goat's milk formula have developed folate deficiencies.

It is difficult to analyze the folate content in foods. A high percentage of folate values in the USDA database are estimated rather than measured.

The fortification of enriched flour products makes folic acid more available. The FDA announced plans in February 1996 for folic acid fortification of enriched flour by January 1, 1998. Fortification with 140 micrograms of a readily absorbed form of folic acid supplies four times that available in whole grain flour. This fortification program covers foods such as breakfast cereals, cornmeal, hominy grits, breads, and macaroni and noodles. The purpose of fortification is to prevent neural tube defects in infants.

Foods contain a form of folic acid that must be acted on by an intestinal enzyme before absorption.

The folate percentages of the daily values cited on food labels are based on RDIs (reference daily intakes) rather than the RDAs (recommended daily allowances). The RDI is 400 micrograms or four-tenths of a milligram, the amount needed by pregnant women and those planning a pregnancy. (Men need 200 micrograms and women who are not pregnant need 180 micrograms. The RDI is based on the group with the greatest need.)

Folic acid and birth defects.   Every year 2500 infants are born with spina bifida (an open spine) and anencephaly (no brain). Another 1500 fetuses with these defects are aborted. Many women do not know that they are expecting in the early weeks of pregnancy, when the neural tube is closing. This tube becomes the spinal cord—it closes 18 to 26 days after conception. If an error occurs at the top of the tube, the child will have no brain and dies at birth. If an error occurs further down the tube, the spinal cord does not close. Children who survive will lack bladder and bowel control and may be paralyzed from the waist down or suffer from mental retardation.

Women need 400 micrograms of folate daily to prevent these defects. Folic acid should be taken in this amount beginning one month before pregnancy and should be taken throughout the first trimester. A woman can get 400 micrograms of folate from food if she selects a healthful diet. She would be assured of obtaining other nutrients also. Five fruits and vegetables a day could give 400 micrograms of folate. Most women do not eat well enough, and the fortification program mentioned previously is the result of this acknowledgment. Studies show that only 25% of women of childbearing age regularly consume enriched cereal or supplements containing 400 micrograms of folate. With the new fortification of enriched bread, four servings of bread, one serving of cereal, and one serving of pasta total 320 micrograms of folate, 80% of the RDI.[*]

Folic acid and heart disease. Improved folate status protects against mildly elevated homocysteine levels and cardiovascular disease. Homocysteine is a normal result of human chemistry. After eating protein food, the digestive process breaks down protein into amino acids, one of which is methionine. When methionine is metabolized for use in the body, homocysteine is released into the bloodstream. Homocysteine is an amino acid used to make protein. Folic acid is needed to convert the homocysteine back to methionine. If folic acid is unavailable, too much homocysteine will be in the bloodstream. Excess homocysteine is linked to an increased risk of coronary artery disease and stroke. Homocysteine causes oxidation, which is responsible for injury to blood vessels. Injured blood vessels attract a buildup of cholesterol-containing plaque. Homocysteine also aids in clot formation and restriction of blood flow. It has not been proven yet that lowering homocysteine helps.[†]

Folic acid and the elderly. Folate fortification of enriched bread and grains should increase mean folate intake in the U.S. population by 16.5%. Fortification began in January 1998. The new folate fortification laws could be a risk for the elderly, however, because excess folate intake can mask vitamin B_{12} deficiency. Vitamin B_{12} absorption problems are prevalent among the elderly. Lack of B_{12} can cause irreversible neurological damage. Accurate laboratory tests are available to screen for B_{12} deficiency by obtaining blood concentrations of the metabolite methylmalonic acid. This test does not confuse B_{12} deficiency with folate deficiency. (If folate is given when B_{12} is needed, folate cures the blood symptoms but the B_{12} deficiency goes undiagnosed, and nerve symptoms progress.) Those responsible for care of the elderly need to be aware of this screening method to detect B_{12} deficiency.

Folate losses through cooking. Folate losses in cooking and canning can be very high due to heat destruction. Steaming and frying food results in 90% folate losses, whereas the boiling of food results in 80% losses.

---

[*]Hine, Jean R., "What Practitioners Need to Know About Folic Acid." *Journal of the American Dietetic Association*, Volume 96, number 5, pp. 451–452.
[†]Margolas, Simeon, "Coronary Artery Disease in Diabetes." Continuing Education Lecture for Dietitians at Johns Hopkins University, March 18, 1998.

A study was carried out in the food services industry using a cook/chill system to determine the effect of cooking and chilling on folate retention.* Thirty percent of folate was lost when the food was reheated after being chilled for only 24 hours at 30°C. Vitamin retention is better in conventional cooking, when foods are cooked and served immediately. If foods have to be chilled, they should be cooled adequately within a two-hour time frame. Longer cooling periods result in even greater folate losses.

When vegetables containing folate are blanched for later use, they should be cooled as quickly as possible. Long cooling periods may result in greater folate loss.

Folate interaction with drugs.   Folate is the vitamin that is most vulnerable to interactions with many medications, such as anticancer drugs, anticonvulsive medications, antacids, aspirin, prednisone, phenytoin sulfasalazine, and birth control pills. Alcohol ingestion and smoking also interfere with folate nutrition. Smokers need 685 micrograms of folate daily to achieve a plasma folate level comparable with that of a nonsmoker consuming the RDA of 200 micrograms of folate.

Cobalamin, B_{12}

Vitamin B_{12} is needed to prevent anemia. It works with folic acid to make red blood cells. The absorption of B_{12} requires intrinsic factor, a protein which is made in the stomach. Intrinsic factor is a glycoprotein found in gastric juice. It facilitates the absorption of vitamin B_{12} from food. Lack of this intrinsic factor causes pernicious anemia.

Vitamin B_{12} is made by bacteria that are found in animal products like meat, poultry, fish, and eggs. Strict vegetarians could develop a deterioration of the spinal cord if they do not take B_{12} supplements. This deterioration begins with numbness in the extremities and progresses to a loss of muscle coordination and paralysis. Memory problems caused by B_{12} deficiency reverse when the deficiency is corrected. A deficiency of B_{12} can be masked if high doses of folic acid are taken.

Biotin

Biotin, another B vitamin, is produced by intestinal bacteria and is not a dietary concern. Antibiotics, however, may kill these bacteria. Avidin, which is found in raw egg whites, binds biotin and could cause a deficiency if taken in large doses. Biotin is needed for the metabolism of protein, fat, and carbohydrate.

There are no reports of excess biotin consumption, and there is no RDA for biotin intake. The safe and adequate amount established by the Food and Nutrition Board, National Academy of Sciences, National Research Council is 30 to 100 milligrams daily.

Pseudovitamins

Vitamin B_{17}, also known as laetrile, is not a true vitamin. It is a drug derived from apricot pits and is 6% cyanide. Laetrile has been used to treat cancer but, unfortunately, usually kills patients before the cancer.[†]

Vitamin B_{15}, or pangamic acid, also is not a true vitamin. It is extracted from apricot kernels and was once widely used and promoted by enthusiasts as a physical fitness enhancer. There is no valid scientific evidence, however, that

*Williams, Peter G., "Vitamin Retention in Cook/Chill and Cook/Hot Hold for Hospital Foodservice." *Journal of the American Dietetic Association,* Volume 96, number 5, pp. 490–496.
†Herbert, V., "Nutrition Myths and Misconceptions," open lecture. Medical School Teaching Facility, University of Maryland, February, 1982.

B_{15} improves oxygen uptake in the cells or removes lactic acid from the muscles. Any improvement in physical performance is the result of training.

Choline is included in a class of nutrients called lypotropes. It is made by the body and does not need to be obtained from food. Lypotropes are essential for metabolic processes involved in cell proliferation and for the maintenance of tissue integrity.

Less Commonly Eaten Foods That Are Rich Sources of the B Vitamins

Liver (B_1, B_2, B_3, B_6, B_{12}, folate, pantothenic acid, biotin)

Yeast (B_2, B_3, B_6, folate, pantothenic acid biotin)

Wheat germ (B_1, B_2, B_3, B_6, folate, pantothenic acid)

Peanuts (B_1, B_3, pantothenic acid)

Soybeans (B_1, B_3, biotin)

Heart (B_2, B_{12}, biotin)

Kidney (B_1, B_{12}, biotin)

Vitamin C

Vitamin C is water soluble. It is destroyed by baking soda, copper, and iron and is unstable at warm temperatures and when exposed to oxygen. Fruit juices rich in vitamin C (Figure 3–12) should be kept in tightly closed jars and refrigerated. Vegetables should be cooked quickly and without water, if possible. Microwave cooking retains most of the vitamin C in foods. (Figure 3–13 lists cooking recommendations for foods rich in vitamin C and other vitamins as well.)

Vitamin C's most important function is the formation of collagen, the intercellular cement. Collagen is necessary in the supporting tissues, particularly in capillaries, the body's smallest blood vessels. Extra vitamin C is needed for the healing of cuts and wounds, particularly after surgery. The RDA for vitamin C (60 milligrams daily) is enough to allow for tissue saturation of 1500 milligrams for a five-month reserve.

Vitamin C is necessary for proper immune system function and for preventing infections. Studies do not support the claims made for vitamin C in the prevention of colds, however. Very large doses of vitamin C decrease the duration of the common cold.*

Mild deficiency of vitamin C causes fleeting joint pains, irritability, poor wound healing, susceptibility to infection, and easy bruising. Severe deficiency results in the deficiency disease called scurvy. Symptoms of scurvy include swollen glands, loosened teeth, anemia, and hemorrhage of the blood vessels of the skin and mucous membranes. Death can result if scurvy is left untreated.

Too much vitamin C causes a rebound scurvy. In other words, the body will be used to the higher dose, and lower doses will cause scurvy even if the lower doses are in the recommended range. This is most likely to happen to a newborn whose mother was taking large doses of vitamin C. After birth, formula provides only normal amounts of the vitamin. The sudden drop in dosage can produce scurvy in the infant. Taking over 250 milligrams of vitamin C daily leads to dependence on a high dose, even though the bloodstream levels are the

---

*Hemila, H., and Herman, Z. S., "Vitamin C and the Common Cold, A Respective Analysis of Chalmer's Review." *Journal of the American College of Nutrition*, Volume 14, April 1995, pp. 116–123.

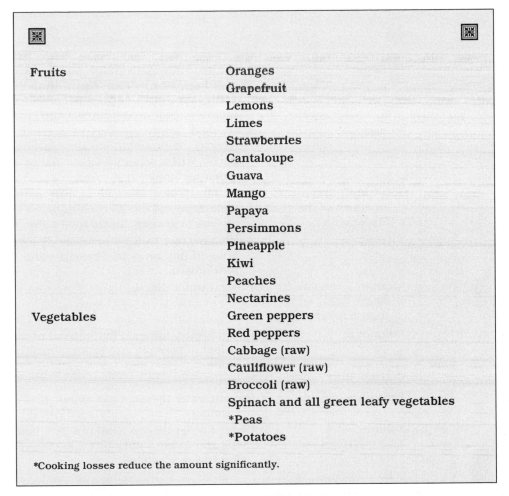

Fruits	Oranges
	Grapefruit
	Lemons
	Limes
	Strawberries
	Cantaloupe
	Guava
	Mango
	Papaya
	Persimmons
	Pineapple
	Kiwi
	Peaches
	Nectarines
Vegetables	Green peppers
	Red peppers
	Cabbage (raw)
	Cauliflower (raw)
	Broccoli (raw)
	Spinach and all green leafy vegetables
	*Peas
	*Potatoes

*Cooking losses reduce the amount significantly.

Figure 3-12 Excellent Food Sources of Vitamin C

same as on a normal dose. Too much vitamin C may also cause inaccurate blood glucose tests and blood in the stool, which may lead to false diagnosis of medical problems. There are reports that too much vitamin C leads to kidney stones and diarrhea. People who smoke need about twice as much vitamin C as nonsmokers.

Orange juice is the most popular food associated with vitamin C. Kept frozen, it retains its vitamin C for up to one year. Pasteurized orange juice in a waxed container keeps well for a month. Freshly squeezed juice, kept tightly bottled, keeps for about three weeks. Flavor retention is a good indicator of vitamin content.*

It is a good practice to consume a food rich in vitamin C every day because water soluble vitamins leave the body more quickly than fat soluble ones. Studies have found that it is not necessary to take vitamin C every day, at every meal, or every four hours. The absorption of nonheme iron from eggs and from plant foods is an issue related to vitamin C intake. This form of iron is better utilized by the body when vitamin C is present in the same meal.

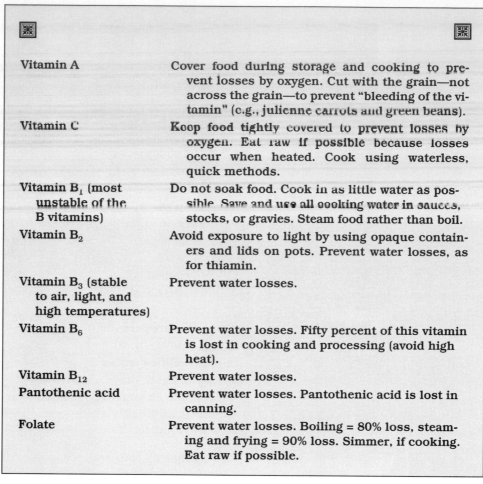

Vitamin A	Cover food during storage and cooking to prevent losses by oxygen. Cut with the grain—not across the grain—to prevent "bleeding of the vitamin" (e.g., julienne carrots and green beans).
Vitamin C	Keep food tightly covered to prevent losses by oxygen. Eat raw if possible because losses occur when heated. Cook using waterless, quick methods.
Vitamin B_1 (most unstable of the B vitamins)	Do not soak food. Cook in as little water as possible. Save and use all cooking water in sauces, stocks, or gravies. Steam food rather than boil.
Vitamin B_2	Avoid exposure to light by using opaque containers and lids on pots. Prevent water losses, as for thiamin.
Vitamin B_3 (stable to air, light, and high temperatures)	Prevent water losses.
Vitamin B_6	Prevent water losses. Fifty percent of this vitamin is lost in cooking and processing (avoid high heat).
Vitamin B_{12}	Prevent water losses.
Pantothenic acid	Prevent water losses. Pantothenic acid is lost in canning.
Folate	Prevent water losses. Boiling = 80% loss, steaming and frying = 90% loss. Simmer, if cooking. Eat raw if possible.

Figure 3-13 Special Considerations in Food Preparation

Phytochemicals

Phytochemicals are the newest substances found in food that appear to be important for good health (Figure 3–14). Much research remains to be done, however.

Phytochemicals cannot yet be labeled nutrients because human requirements for them have not been established. It is premature to buy individual phytochemicals in supplement form. It is not known if phytochemicals, taken by themselves, have the same health benefits as when they are ingested with food and other food nutrients. It *is* known that eating plants that contain phytochemicals can help in the prevention of heart disease, cancer, and osteoporosis.

Some of the phytochemicals that are potential cancer fighters are the isothiocyanates, phenolic compounds, flavonoids, indoles, monoterpenes, organosulfides, isoflavones, and carotenoids. (Carotenoids are responsible for the colors found in carrots, tomatoes, beets, grapefruits, and other fruits and vegetables.) Each of these has many subcategories as well. For example, genistein and daidzein are two isoflavones found in soybeans.

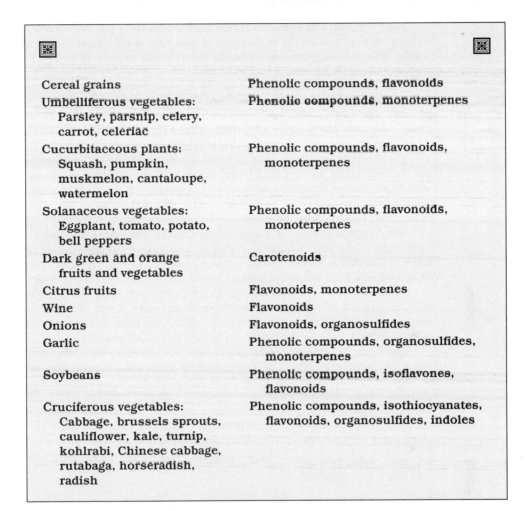

Cereal grains	Phenolic compounds, flavonoids
Umbelliferous vegetables: Parsley, parsnip, celery, carrot, celeriac	Phenolic compounds, monoterpenes
Cucurbitaceous plants: Squash, pumpkin, muskmelon, cantaloupe, watermelon	Phenolic compounds, flavonoids, monoterpenes
Solanaceous vegetables: Eggplant, tomato, potato, bell peppers	Phenolic compounds, flavonoids, monoterpenes
Dark green and orange fruits and vegetables	Carotenoids
Citrus fruits	Flavonoids, monoterpenes
Wine	Flavonoids
Onions	Flavonoids, organosulfides
Garlic	Phenolic compounds, organosulfides, monoterpenes
Soybeans	Phenolic compounds, isoflavones, flavonoids
Cruciferous vegetables: Cabbage, brussels sprouts, cauliflower, kale, turnip, kohlrabi, Chinese cabbage, rutabaga, horseradish, radish	Phenolic compounds, isothiocyanates, flavonoids, organosulfides, indoles

Figure 3–14 Partial List of Foods with Phytochemicals

Phytochemicals work to prevent either the initiation or progression of certain cancers. Soybeans contain phytochemicals that have been found to help in the prevention of heart disease and breast cancer, to control glucose levels in diabetics and to relieve symptoms of menopause.

Minerals

Minerals are inorganic elements that play an important role in maintaining good health. Minerals help regulate body processes and provide structure for body tissues.

Minerals can be obtained from food sources. They are absorbed in the stomach and through the intestines, where many pass directly into the bloodstream and are transported directly to the cells. Excess amounts of minerals are excreted in the urine, in the stool, and in sweat. Some minerals attach to body proteins and are stored for later use.

High amounts of some minerals taken over long periods can be harmful. Excess intake is not likely to happen if one eats a balanced diet and a variety of foods. Mineral supplements should be avoided unless they are recommended and monitored by a health professional.

The minerals that the body needs in the greatest amounts (more than 250 milligrams a day) are called macrominerals, or major minerals. Calcium, phosphorus, magnesium, sulfur, potassium, sodium, and chloride are the macrominerals. The last three are electrolytes that regulate fluid in and out of all cells. They also transmit nerve or electrical impulses.

Microminerals are needed in trace amounts (under 20 milligrams a day) and are essential as well. Chromium, copper, fluoride, iodine, iron, manganese, molybdenum, selenium, and zinc are considered microminerals. These have been evaluated for their health benefits, and RDAs have been determined for iron, zinc, iodine, and selenium.

Scientists have set a range of estimated safe and adequate amounts for chromium, copper, fluoride, manganese, and molybdenum. Not enough is known about the role of vanadium and boron in human health, but these can be obtained in a well-balanced diet of whole foods (not overly processed).

Nickel deficiencies are known to harm the liver and other organs. Although silicon and tin have known functions in animals, more work is needed before human needs are identified. Mercury, silver, barium, cadmium, and arsenic are elements that may be dealt with in future nutrition research.

Food preparation and cooking losses are less for minerals than for vitamins because minerals cannot be destroyed by heat, air, or acid. Losses of minerals in food preparation occur when minerals dissolve in water and the water is discarded. Cooks should wash food quickly without soaking and cook in minimal amounts of water. Leftover liquids in which the foods were cooked can be incorporated into soups, sauces, or gravies. Blanched vegetables should be removed from their ice bath as soon as they are cooled.

Major minerals

Calcium

Calcium's main function in the body is the making, repairing, and maintaining of the bones and teeth. This process is called mineralization. Mineralization involves the combining of calcium and phosphorus to make calcium phosphate, which is deposited in the bones' protein matrix. The skeleton contains 99% of the body's calcium. Calcium also binds with protein for other vital functions, such as blood clotting and muscle contraction. Calcium also helps release neurotransmitters in the brain and activate digestive enzymes. Too much calcium in the blood leads to respiratory or cardiac failure. Too little calcium results in tetany, a condition marked by muscle spasms. Proper muscle contraction of the heart depends on calcium contained in the fluid around the heart cells.

The body regulates calcium so that when calcium levels are too low, a hormone called parathyroid is released and causes the body to take calcium from the bones. When serum calcium level is high, a different hormone, calcitonin, causes calcium to be deposited in the bones.

The richest food sources of calcium are milk and milk products, such as cheese and yogurt. In areas of the world where milk is not a prominent food, calcium is provided by soy products (such as tofu), miso, edible seaweeds, oysters, and small fish with soft, edible bones (e.g., sardines). Soybeans and other legumes and dark green leafy vegetables (particularly collard greens, turnip greens, mustard greens, and kale) are high in calcium. Vegetable calcium is less available than calcium from animal sources.

The chemical form of the nutrient and the presence and amounts of other nutrients in a given food source affect the absorption rate of a particular nutrient during digestion. This is referred to as bioavailability. For example, oxalic acid in spinach ties up 95% of calcium so that it cannot be absorbed. Beet greens and chocolate contain oxalic acid, and the calcium in these foods is poorly absorbed. Foods high in dietary fiber, phytic acid (found in wheat bran), and phosphates (found in brown rice) have been found to decrease calcium absorption. Yeast inactivates phytic acid, so baked goods made from whole wheat flour and raised with yeast do not hinder calcium absorption.

The RDA for calcium is 1200 milligrams for the young (ages 11 to adulthood) and 800 milligrams for adults and children ages 1 to 10 years. The elderly may need 1000 to 1500 milligrams daily to prevent osteoporosis, a condition in which the bones become brittle and fragile. Calcium absorption decreases in people over age 60.

The RDA for calcium is set higher than the actual calcium requirement because of the high protein and phosphorus content of the American diet (i.e., prominence of meat in the diet). Urinary excretion of calcium is increased in this type of diet. In countries in which meat is not a primary part of the diet and the phosphorus content of the diet is low compared to the U.S. diet, daily calcium intakes of between 400 and 500 milligrams do not lead to calcium deficiencies.

The National Institutes of Health recommends 1000 milligrams of calcium daily for women age 25 to 50 and for women under age 65 who are taking estrogen, 1200 to 1500 milligrams daily for pregnant or breast-feeding women, and 1500 milligrams daily for postmenopausal women under age 65 who are not taking estrogen. The recommendation for all women over age 65 is 1500 milligrams of calcium per day.

Osteoporosis has become a major problem in recent times. People are living longer, and this has increased the number of cases. Women are more susceptible than men, and Caucasian women more so than African-American women. Women with small bones and fair complexion are at a greater risk for osteoporosis than are bigger boned, darker complexioned women.

Preventive measures, such as good calcium and vitamin D nutrition in early years and exercise, are the ideal approach to avoiding osteoporosis. Estrogen replacement in women is another preventive measure that may be used under medical supervision.

The popularity of calcium supplements has engendered much research. Calcium carbonate, calcium acetate, calcium citrate, calcium gluconate, and calcium lactate are different forms of calcium supplements. There are no significant differences in absorption of these forms. Calcium citrate malate is superior and is absorbed better than others. Taking these supplements with meals does increase absorption. Calcium is absorbed well from milk because of the lactose in milk. An 8-ounce glass of milk provides 290 milligrams of calcium. The calcium citrate in fortified fruit juices also appears to be readily absorbed.

Overdoses of calcium supplements can cause additional difficulties for people with kidney problems. Calcium supplements reduce iron absorption, which could interfere with healthy nutrition. Calcium carbonate, which is the key component of oyster shell supplements and some antacids, may cause constipation.

The calcium content of calcium supplements varies. For example, calcium carbonate is 40% calcium, whereas calcium gluconate is 9% calcium. The amount of calcium in a supplement is listed as elemental calcium on the label.

To be effective, a calcium pill needs to dissolve in the stomach. Not all do. A test to determine if a particular supplement will dissolve is to drop it into a cup containing 6 ounces of vinegar and stir every few minutes. Pills that remain hard and intact should be avoided.* Dolomite and bone meal should never be used as a calcium supplement because they may be contaminated with lead.

It is better to get calcium from foods than from supplements. Calcium-rich foods include the following:

milk

hard cheese

ricotta cheese

custard

ice cream

sardines

salmon

almonds

dark green leafy vegetables

Ricotta cheese contains more calcium than cottage cheese. Cream cheese, butter, and those dairy products made mostly from milk fat are not good sources of calcium.

Phosphorus

All foods contain phosphorus, which is necessary for energy production. Phosphorus is a part of all cells.

Most of the body's phosphorus occurs in the bones and teeth, where it is tied up with magnesium and calcium to provide strength and rigidity. The remaining phosphorus is found in the cells and body fluids.

Phosphorus is needed to convert sugar into energy for the body. The B vitamins that act as enzymes in carbohydrate metabolism are also phosphorylated. RNA and DNA, the carriers of the genetic code, are phosphorylated. Some lipids (fats), such as lecithin, combine with phosphorus and then become part of all cells. Other fats are connected to phosphorus to be transported through the blood. Phosphorus is one of the nutrients that helps regulate the pH levels of the body; pH is a measure of acidity and alkalinity. Blood needs to be at a neutral pH; neither too acid nor too alkaline.

Ideally, phosphorus should be in a 1:1 ratio with calcium. Excessive amounts of phosphorus upset this balance.

Because phosphorus is so abundant, deficiency rarely occurs. If protein intake is adequate, so is phosphorus intake.

It is difficult to recommend a daily allowance of phosphorus because efficiency of absorption varies with the source of phosphorus and the ratio of calcium to phosphorus in the diet. Vitamin D, considered a hormone, also stimulates phosphorus absorption. Other hormones, particularly parathormone, influence the regulation of phosphorus in the blood. The kidneys play a major role in regulating the body's phosphorus levels, so patients with insufficient kidney function can develop phosphorus toxicity (hyperphosphatemia).

Magnesium

Magnesium is necessary for the efficient use of amino acids in the formation of protein. Magnesium is also a cofactor in many enzyme systems, particularly in carbohydrate metabolism.

---

*"Women's Health Watch." *Harvard Health Letter*, March 1995.

About 60% of the magnesium present in the body is contained in the bones. Soft tissues contain more magnesium than calcium. Because little magnesium is held in the blood, a blood test is not a good indicator of body stores of magnesium.

Extracellular magnesium is important in neuromuscular transmission. When the body gets too much magnesium from food, it absorbs less. When it does not get enough, it absorbs more.

Nuts (especially cashews and almonds) are a good source of magnesium (Figure 3–15). Whole grains provide much more magnesium than do refined grain products. Vegetables that contain chlorophyll also contain magnesium in moderate amounts. Protein foods, such as soy beans and other legumes, contribute magnesium. Flesh foods contain smaller amounts, but their contribution is important. In general, dairy products are poor sources of magnesium, as are most fruits. Hard water contains significant amounts of magnesium.

Nuts (small size or chopped)

Milligrams

420	almonds
356	cashews
760	peanuts
253	black walnuts
327	hazelnuts (filberts)
166	pistachios
138	pecans
203	English walnuts
26	fresh coconut
47	chestnuts

Grains (cooked)

Milligrams

239	wheat germ
366	bran
166	whole wheat flour
26	all-purpose flour
42	whole wheat macaroni
25	enriched flour macaroni
56	oatmeal
34	pearl barley
52	wild rice
84	brown rice
25	white rice
106	millet
22	cornmeal

Legumes (cooked)

Milligrams

47	pinto beans
148	soybeans
70	split peas
58	lima beans
72	lentils
79	garbanzo beans

Vegetables

Although green vegetables are a known source of magnesium, there is wide variation in amounts of magnesium depending on whether the vegetable is fresh, frozen, or canned.

Note: Serving size is 1 cup.

Figure 3–15 Dietary Sources of Magnesium

The body needs about 200 milligrams of magnesium daily because the mineral is only 30 to 40% absorbed. The RDAs are 350 milligrams per day for men and 280 milligrams per day for women.

Magnesium deficiency produces vasodilation and hyperirritability, which have led to convulsions and death in experimental animals. In humans, magnesium deficiency is rarely related to poor dietary intake. Diuretic use, alcoholism, and medical conditions that lead to urinary losses are more likely causes of magnesium deficiencies. Severe magnesium deficiency stemming from these conditions also causes calcium deficiency. Calcium deficiency, in turn, creates magnesium deficiency.

Muscle twitching, tremors, numbness, and tingling are early symptoms of magnesium deficiency. These symptoms can be followed by muscle weakness, convulsions, depression, delirium, and irregular heartbeat. Magnesium is important for proper cardiovascular function. There is a greater incidence of heart attacks and stroke in areas with soft water; this may be related to lower amounts of magnesium in the water. Magnesium toxicity is seen in patients with kidney failure.

Recent reports show magnesium to be beneficial in migraine headaches, depression, and chronic fatigue syndrome.*

Sodium

Sodium, which is found in the fluids surrounding the cells, is one of the most important minerals in the body. Along with potassium and chloride, it is known as an electrolyte. It helps regulate the acid/base balance of the body, osmotic pressure, and neuromuscular transmission of nerve impulses, and it facilitates intestinal nutrient absorption.

All natural foods contain sodium, and extra dietary sodium comes from food additives (Figure 3–16). Of the natural foods, fruit and oils have the least amount of sodium, followed by vegetables, grains, flesh foods, and milk. Cheese, a concentrate of milk, has a very high sodium content, and it is also made with the addition of salt. Processed cheese has even more sodium than natural cheese. Some over-the-counter and some prescription drugs contain sodium.

The greatest addition of dietary sodium comes from the use of table salt to season foods. Table salt, chemically called sodium chloride, contains about 40% sodium. Soy sauce also contains a lot of sodium. Monosodium glutamate (MSG) a natural flavor enhancer, contains substantial amounts of sodium. The leavening agents baking soda and baking powder add to the sodium levels of foods (Figure 3–17).

Commercially processed foods are likely to contain high amounts of sodium in the form of preservatives. Preservatives extend the shelf life of a product by preventing spoilage and by protecting color, texture, and flavor. Sodium-containing preservatives include the following:

   sodium acetate
   sodium alginate
   sodium aluminum sulfate
   sodium benzoate
   sodium bicarbonate
   sodium calcium alginate
   sodium citrate

---

*Calcium, Magnesium, and Boron: Their Combined Roles in Maintaining Bone Strength http:www.all.natural.com/bone.html (International Conference on Human Nutrition, 1995).

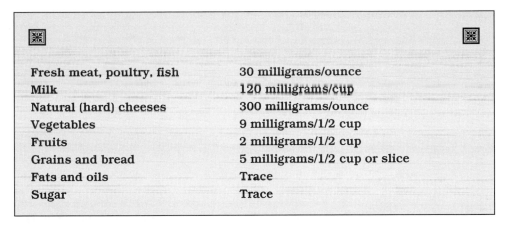

Fresh meat, poultry, fish	30 milligrams/ounce
Milk	120 milligrams/cup
Natural (hard) cheeses	300 milligrams/ounce
Vegetables	9 milligrams/1/2 cup
Fruits	2 milligrams/1/2 cup
Grains and bread	5 milligrams/1/2 cup or slice
Fats and oils	Trace
Sugar	Trace

Figure 3-16   Average Sodium Content of Food Prepared Without Added Salt

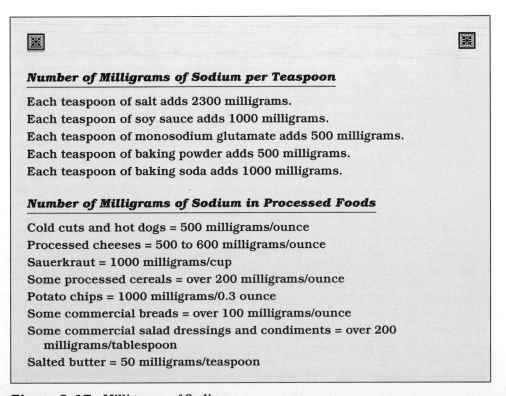

Number of Milligrams of Sodium per Teaspoon

Each teaspoon of salt adds 2300 milligrams.
Each teaspoon of soy sauce adds 1000 milligrams.
Each teaspoon of monosodium glutamate adds 500 milligrams.
Each teaspoon of baking powder adds 500 milligrams.
Each teaspoon of baking soda adds 1000 milligrams.

Number of Milligrams of Sodium in Processed Foods

Cold cuts and hot dogs = 500 milligrams/ounce
Processed cheeses = 500 to 600 milligrams/ounce
Sauerkraut = 1000 milligrams/cup
Some processed cereals = over 200 milligrams/ounce
Potato chips = 1000 milligrams/0.3 ounce
Some commercial breads = over 100 milligrams/ounce
Some commercial salad dressings and condiments = over 200
    milligrams/tablespoon
Salted butter = 50 milligrams/teaspoon

Figure 3-17   Milligrams of Sodium

sodium d-acetate

sodium erythorbate

sodium nitrate

sodium nitrite

sodium propionate

sodium sorbate

sodium stearyl fumarate

dioctyl sodium sulfosuccinate

disodium guanylate

disodium inosinate

MSG

Canned soups and vegetables, factory-made puddings, frozen dinners, bouillons, and dehydrated soups can contain hundreds of milligrams of sodium in a single serving. In general, except for maraschino cherries and some dried fruits, canned fruits are one of the few processed foods that are low in sodium.

The average daily sodium intake in the United States ranges from 6000 to 10,000 milligrams. For good health, a total of 2400 milligrams daily is advised. When heat or exercise leads to a 5- to 10-pound loss of body water, then additional sodium may be required. Circulatory air such as in enclosed spaces (airplanes) and low humidity also cause water loss.

The sodium lost in a 5- to 10-pound water loss can be replaced safely with a quart of water to which 1/3 teaspoon of salt is added. Body water loss can only be measured accurately by weighing before and after exertion. A pickle or a few potato chips with lemonade or fruit juice is the most practical way to recoup sweat losses. Salt tablets can cause dehydration and should not be taken unless prescribed by a doctor.

Sodium deficiency can cause cardiac arrest, convulsions, collapse, and heat exhaustion. In humans with normal kidney and heart functions, 90% of sodium is excreted through the kidneys. Vomiting and diarrhea, especially in children, the frail, and the elderly, can cause huge sodium losses, which must be attended to medically. Dehydration and disturbance of the body's acid/base balance can lead to death.

Sodium toxicity occurs only if large amounts of sodium and insufficient fluids are taken. It also can occur when a person has medical problems that create fluid retention so that sodium is not excreted properly.

The most common health problem linked with sodium is hypertension (high blood pressure), which is a concern for many Americans. High blood pressure has no symptoms at first; years later, a person can become short of breath, develop heart irregularities, suffer a stroke, or have a heart attack with little warning. Epidemiological evidence suggest that in cultures in which there is a low salt intake, hypertension is rare. In cultures with a high salt intake, hypertension is common. There is a genetic component that predisposes a person to hypertension, and not everyone with a high salt intake will be hypertensive.

The events that lead to high blood pressure are as follows (Figure 3–18): A high concentration of salt in the blood increases fluid in the blood (brought in by the salt). This places an increased demand on the kidneys to excrete the salt and the excess fluid. If the kidneys cannot handle the load, the heart works harder to pump the extra fluid; thus hypertension results.

Potassium

Potassium and sodium have interrelated roles and the same function, except that potassium functions inside the cell and sodium functions outside it. They

```
1    ↑ salt intake
2    ↑ salt in blood
3    ↑ fluid in blood (brought in by salt)
4    ↑ demand on kidneys to excrete the salt and excess fluid
5    If the kidney can't handle the load . . .
6    the heart works harder to pump the extra fluid
7    the event leads to high blood pressure
```

Figure 3–18   Events Leading to High Blood Pressure

regulate normal water balance, conduction and transmission of nerve impulses, muscle contractions, heart action, and functions of some enzyme systems. Through excretion and conservation, healthy kidneys help maintain steady levels of potassium and sodium.

The fluid between the cells always has a high concentration of sodium and chloride. The fluid inside the cells always has a high concentration of potassium and phosphate.

All natural foods, except oil, contain potassium (Figure 3–19). Fruits and vegetables provide the most potassium, followed closely by milk and meats. Whole grains contain more potassium than refined grains. Some medications and some salt substitutes also contain potassium. A salt substitute should not be taken without a physician's approval, especially for someone with heart or kidney problems. Potassium is added to processed foods in the form of additives, which help stabilize and preserve commercially produced food products.

The recommended average daily potassium intake is 2 to 6 grams. A few extra grams may be needed by individuals who sweat profusely (e.g., in sports activities or in physical labor in hot places). The kidneys' ability to conserve potassium in these conditions may negate any additional need.

Potassium deficiency is rarely caused by dietary factors, except in cases of starvation. Health problems such as diarrhea, vomiting, burns, injury, and surgery are more likely than diet to create potassium losses. For example, diuretic medications can carry out large amounts of potassium in the urine. Doctors routinely give potassium supplements to patients on diuretics or instruct such patients to take high-potassium foods, usually juices.

Concentrated potassium supplements can injure the intestinal lining unless taken with adequate fluid. Excessive potassium in the blood can lead to death. When the heart does not pump correctly or the kidneys do not excrete properly, potassium may need to be limited in the diet. A dietitian can plan a low-potassium diet when prescribed by a physician.

The treatment for high blood pressure usually involves decreasing dietary sodium. It is less well known that increasing potassium intake also helps control hypertension. The foods with the least sodium and the most potassium are fresh fruits and vegetables, which do not contain preservatives or added salt. Potatoes, oranges, bananas, tomatoes, cantaloupes, and broccoli, eaten in quantity and used to replace higher-calorie foods, will result in weight loss, which will also lower high blood pressure.

600 milligrams

prune juice, 1 cup

500 to 600 milligrams

tomato juice, 1 cup
orange juice, 1 cup
sardines, 8
potato with skin, medium
halibut, 3 ounces
banana, medium large
dates, 10

400 to 500 milligrams

winter squash, 1/2 cup
watermelon, 5 inch × 8 inch wedge
salmon, 1/2 cup
grapefruit juice, 1 cup

300 to 400 milligrams

chicken, 3 ounces
milk, 1 cup
sweet potato, large
bamboo shoots, 1/2 cup
lamb, 3 ounces
orange, medium size

200 to 300 milligrams

apricots, 2 to 3
pork, 3 ounces
lima beans, 1/2 cup
lentils, 1/2 cup
cantaloupe, 1/4
tuna, 3 ounces
avocado, 1/4
raisins, 3 tablespoons
broccoli, 1/2 cup

100 to 200 milligrams

carrots, 1/2 cup
celery, 1/2 cup
mushrooms, 1/2 cup
cauliflower, 1/2 cup
asparagus, 1/2 cup

less than 100 milligrams

oatmeal, 1/2 cup
brown rice, 1/2 cup
whole wheat bread, 1 slice
egg, 1
wheat germ, 1 tablespoon
spaghetti, 1/2 cup
white rice, 1/2 cup
white bread, 1 slice
cheese, 1 ounce

Figure 3–19 Potassium Contents of Natural Foods (listed in order from greatest to least amount)

Cooking potassium-containing foods in large amounts of water leads to potassium loss. The same cooking procedures previously outlined for other minerals and water soluble vitamin retention should be followed.

Chloride

Although the element chlorine is a poisonous gas, chloride is its ionic form and is a required nutrient. Chloride's main function is to maintain the acid/base balance of the body and osmotic pressure (the regulation of fluid in and out of body cells).

Chloride is one of the body's three mineral electrolytes (the other two are sodium and potassium). Electrolytes help transmit nerve impulses and signals.

Chloride binds with both sodium and potassium. It also becomes part of hydrochloric acid in the stomach, which is used for digestion of foods and absorption of nutrients.

The largest dietary source of chloride is table salt, which combines chloride with sodium. One-fourth teaspoon of salt contains 750 milligrams of chloride, which is the estimated minimum requirement for adults. There is no RDA for chloride.

Although sodium is recognized as the mineral most closely related to high blood pressure, one study of hospitalized patients showed that sodium citrate salt did not raise blood pressure in the same way as sodium chloride salt did.* Therefore, it seems that the chloride component of table salt has a role in hypertension. This information is supported by previous studies on rats. More study is needed.

Chloride deficiency is unlikely unless there is dehydration from excessive sweating, diarrhea, or vomiting, which deplete the body of chloride as well as sodium. Normal food and beverage intake will replenish the chloride. Severe dehydration, requiring hospitalization, is treated with intravenous fluids.

Sulfur

Sulfur is important as a constituent of many body tissues and enzyme systems. Most sulfur in the diet comes from organic sources. Sulfur is found in all flesh foods, milk, eggs, and vegetables of the cabbage family (cabbage, cauliflower, broccoli, and brussels sprouts), as well as in legumes and nuts. There is no RDA for sulfur. The sulfur from sulfur dioxide, which is used to keep color in foods such as dried fruit, is unavailable to the body.

Trace minerals

Iron

The main function of iron in the body is the manufacture of hemoglobin in red blood cells. Hemoglobin transports oxygen to every cell and carries carbon dioxide from the cells to the lungs. Normal hemoglobin levels are from 14 to 16 grams per 100 milliliters of blood. The blood contains 55% of the body's iron.

Iron is also an essential component of myoglobin, which is a receptor and storage point for some of the oxygen in the muscles. Iron is stored in the liver, spleen, and bone marrow as ferritin and hemosiderin. Hemoglobin is made in the bone marrow from an iron-containing pigment called hematin and a protein called globin (and some lipid). Copper acts as a catalyst in the process of hemoglobin formation, and cobalt is also necessary.

Iron is part of many enzymes. Too little or too much iron can increase susceptibility to infections. Iron is needed by neutrophils and lymphocytes for good immunity, but large doses of supplemental iron will hasten bacterial growth. Iron supplements can also interfere with copper absorption.

There are two types of dietary iron: heme iron and nonheme iron. Heme iron is obtained from animal sources and is about 15 to 30% assimilated. Half the iron in meat, poultry, and fish is heme iron, which comes from the myoglobin and hemoglobin in these food items. Figure 3–20 lists sources of heme iron. The rest of the iron from these sources is nonheme iron, which is absorbed at the rate of 3 to 8% (some sources state ranges from 2 to 20%).

*Kurtz, T., Hamoudi, A., Al-Bander, S., and Curtis, R. "Salt Sensitive Essential Hypertension in Men—Is the Sodium Ion Alone Important?," *New England Journal of Medicine*, Volume 317, 1987, p. 1043.

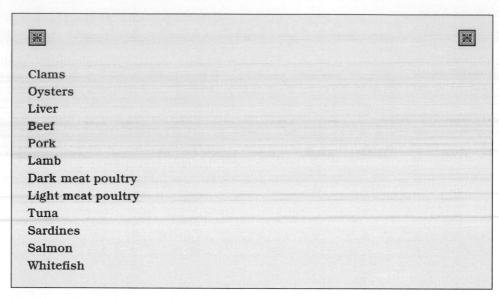

Clams
Oysters
Liver
Beef
Pork
Lamb
Dark meat poultry
Light meat poultry
Tuna
Sardines
Salmon
Whitefish

Figure 3–20   Foods High in Heme Iron

Nonheme iron is also found in eggs and accounts for all of the iron in plant foods. Figure 3–21 lists sources of nonheme iron. It is better absorbed when vitamin C is present at the time of intake or when taken with meat. For example, a meal that contains sweet potatoes, orange juice, and meat will enhance the absorption of iron. Orange juice will also enhance the absorption of the nonheme iron in the meat, and the meat will enhance the absorption of iron from the juice. (Sweet potatoes contain nonheme iron; orange juice contains nonheme iron and vitamin C; meat contains heme iron and nonheme iron).

Tannin in tea inhibits the absorption of iron by binding nonheme iron. Iced tea is a popular American beverage; thus many people are affected by this relationship. Heme iron is absorbed by a different mechanism and is not affected by tea.

Polyphenols in coffee also inhibit iron absorption. Oxalic acid in spinach, rhubarb, and chocolate; phytates in whole grains and soybeans; and phosvitin in egg yolks bind iron. The preservative EDTA and antacids, if consumed in large amounts, also inhibit iron absorption.

The RDA for iron is based on the fact that iron is lost in feces, urine, and sweat at the rate of 1 milligram per day. Because only one-tenth of iron is absorbed, the allowances are set at 10 times the losses for men, or 10 milligrams per day. For women in the reproductive years, the allowance is larger—15 milligrams per day—to cover iron losses in the menstrual flow. After the reproductive years, women need 10 milligrams of iron daily.

Iron deficiency is common in women. The usual symptoms are pallor, weakness, easy fatigability, labored breathing on exertion, headache, palpitations, and persistent tiredness. During pregnancy, iron is very important, and iron supplements are often necessary. Many women are iron deficient even before pregnancy, which creates a greater dilemma. Infants need to get iron from their mothers before birth to accumulate a five-month supply.

Nature prepares for the fact that the infant's early diet is milk, which is low in iron but does contain a type of iron that is five times more efficiently absorbed than that in cow's milk. An infant would have adequate iron nutrition if

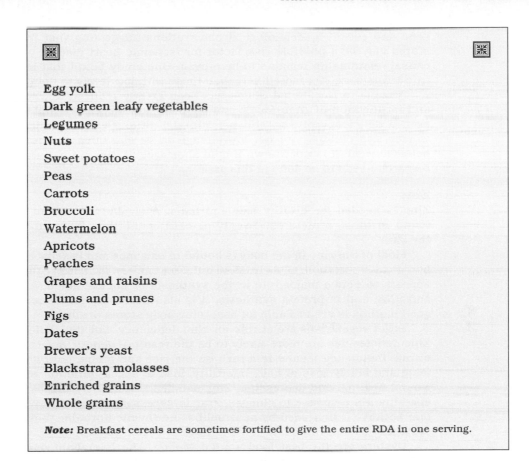

Egg yolk
Dark green leafy vegetables
Legumes
Nuts
Sweet potatoes
Peas
Carrots
Broccoli
Watermelon
Apricots
Peaches
Grapes and raisins
Plums and prunes
Figs
Dates
Brewer's yeast
Blackstrap molasses
Enriched grains
Whole grains

Note: Breakfast cereals are sometimes fortified to give the entire RDA in one serving.

Figure 3–21   Food High in Nonheme Iron

its mother supplied adequate storage iron during pregnancy and followed up with breast feeding. Most baby formulas are fortified with iron to prevent iron deficiency anemia. Many toddlers and school-age children do not get enough iron-rich foods, however. Iron deficiency affects a child's ability to learn and fight off infections.

There are four laboratory tests for iron deficiency anemia: Plasma ferrin estimates iron stores; transferrin saturation estimates iron supply to the tissues; red cell protoporphyrin indicates inadequate iron for the developing red cell; and the hemoglobin test, the test most often performed, measures depletion of the iron stores by measuring the level of hemoglobin.

The hereditary disorder hemochromatosis causes uncontrolled iron absorption, which leads to multiorgan failure and early death.

The *Journal of Clinical Nutrition* raised the topic of specifying a safe upper range for iron intake.* The concerns were for carriers of the hemochromatosis

*Health Reference Center CD-ROM Infotrak, "Deliberations and Evaluations of the Approaches, Endpoints, and Paradigms for Iron Dietary Recommendations" (Workshop on New Approaches, Endpoints and Paradigms for RDA's of Mineral Supplements). *Journal of Clinical Nutrition*, Volume 126, number 9, Summer 1996, pp. 240–246.

gene and recent epidemiological observations suggesting that increased iron stores may be a possible risk factor for ischemic heart disease and cancer. A causal relationship remains to be proven. One study found that men with high iron levels were 37% more likely than those with low levels to develop cancer.*

Anemia in the United States has been greatly reduced due to enrichment and fortification of grain foods, and supplements for women and infants. However, a deficiency of iron still prevails and although the iron levels of many women and children are not low enough to be classified as anemia, they are below normal. It is not known if mild shortages of iron are harmful. Continued research needs to be done in this area.

Zinc

Zinc is needed for healthy hair and nails. A sizable amount of body zinc is found in those structures. Twenty percent of the total body zinc is found in the skin.

Most of the zinc in the body is bound to enzymes and is associated with carbon dioxide metabolism. At least 40 different enzyme systems require zinc. Zinc appears to play a major role in the synthesis of nucleic acids, including DNA and RNA, and in protein synthesis. It is also necessary for wound healing. No good method is yet available for assessing body stores of zinc.

Strict vegetarians are at risk for zinc deficiency, but this deficiency is rare. Zinc deficiencies are more likely to be the result of genetic defects, disease, or burns. Deficiency results in a rash on the face and limbs, poor growth, loss of taste and smell, loss of hair, infertility, loss of sexual function in males, poor wound healing, and depression. Zinc deficiency is also associated with a lessened insulin response to glucose. Zinc is necessary for a healthy immune system because it is needed by neutrophils and thymic hormone, both part of that system.

Oysters are the best food source of zinc. The tale about oysters and sex could stem from this fact because zinc is important in sperm production. Herring is the next highest source of zinc. Other good food sources of zinc are milk, meat, eggs, seeds, whole grains, and brewer's yeast (Figure 3–22). Human milk contains the most bioavailable form of zinc. Cereals lose zinc during the milling process. Zinc bioavailability from beef is about four times greater than that from high-fiber cereals.

The RDA for zinc is 15 milligrams per day for males and pregnant women and 12 milligrams for other women. Zinc absorption averages about 40%. Pregnancy and lactation require extra zinc. Children 1 to 10 years old need about 10 milligrams of zinc daily and may not get enough if they eat refined cereals. In general, zinc intake is proportional to protein intake. Seafood and meat contain the highest amounts of zinc in foods normally eaten.

Zinc toxicity is not common because dietary excess is unlikely. In addition, the body has a very efficient mechanism for regulating zinc levels. Too much zinc (10 times the RDA) could interfere with copper and iron absorption. Excess zinc is also thought to impair the immune response and affects some enzyme activities of the liver in animals.

Populations that eat high amounts of unleavened whole grain bread may develop zinc deficiency because fiber and phytates bind zinc. This deficiency occurs only in areas where nutrition is marginal, however.

---

*Health Reference Center CD-ROM Infotrak, "Too Much Iron May Cause Cancer in Men." Washington, DC: Cancer Researcher Weekly, February 14, 1994, p. 4.

Oysters
Herring
Liver
Beef
Pork
Lamb
Poultry
Fish
Shellfish
Nuts
Sesame seeds
Milk
Hard cheeses
Ricotta cheese
Yogurt
Wheat germ
Wheat bran
Millet
Barley
Buckwheat
Wild rice
Brown rice
Eggs
Many prepared breakfast cereals

Figure 3–22   Zinc-Rich Foods

High calcium and phosphate intake decreases zinc absorption. Zinc in supplement form is absorbed differently and less effectively than when taken in the daily diet. Zinc losses occur mainly in stool, sweat, and menstruation.

Iodine

Iodine is needed to produce thyroxine, a hormone made in the thyroid gland. Nearly all of the body's iodine is located in this gland. Thyroxine regulates body heat, influences protein synthesis, keeps connective tissues healthy, and promotes physical and mental development.

Iodine is found in the ocean, and saltwater fish are excellent sources. Iodine also reaches the soil from rain that comes from evaporated ocean water. Thus, land near the ocean and land once covered by the sea are rich in iodine. Foods grown in these iodine-rich soils and products such as milk from animals feeding on this land are natural sources of iodine.

The U.S. diet may contain extra iodine as a result of the use of iodine sanitizers on utensils and processing equipment in food manufacturing. Certain food colors and dough conditioners also contain iodine. The innovation of iodized salt in 1924 was an important health intervention that eliminated goiter (an enlargement of the thyroid gland caused by a deficiency in iodine) in the United States. Today, salt is available with or without iodine.

The RDA for iodine is set at 150 micrograms per day. Infants and children, however, need less. The average intake is usually well above the requirement because of the liberal use of iodized salt.

Iodine deficiency (less than 50 micrograms daily) causes the thyroid gland to enlarge so it can use what iodine is available. The enlarged goiter protrudes and is visible in the neck. Goiters are common in Africa, Asia, and South America. In certain areas of Africa where iodine deficiency is epidemic, whole populations have massive goiters that hang onto the chest.

An insufficient amount of the thyroid hormone thyroxin causes people to be sluggish, tired, cold, and prone to weight gain. Iodine deficiency during the first three weeks of pregnancy can result in the birth of a child who is a dwarf and mentally deficient. This condition is called cretinism.

Excess amounts of iodine (25 to 70 times the RDA) lead to high levels of thyroxin, thyroid enlargement, impaired glucose tolerance, and heart failure. Excessive intake can also cause hypothyroidism, which will cause a lower metabolic rate and listlessness because the thyroid will stop producing thyroxin.

Allergies to iodine can produce a rash that appears as a raised sore over the skin, nasal congestion, or asthmatic symptoms. People who are allergic to iodine must avoid foods such as kelp, dried seaweed, and shellfish.

Selenium

The main function of selenium is the protection of cell membranes from oxidative damage. Selenium is part of gluthathione peroxidase, an enzyme that neutralizes hydrogen peroxide. Hydrogen peroxide could damage cellular membranes. Selenium binds to a protein that carries selenium through the blood and acts as a defense against oxidant status. Selenium plays a role in electron transfer function and protects against cadmium and mercury toxicity.

Seafood, meat, liver, and kidney are high in selenium. Rice and whole grains contain varying selenium concentrations, depending on the soil concentrations where the plants are grown. Fruits and vegetables are generally considered poor sources of selenium; tomatoes and cabbage have the highest levels among vegetables. Limited data exist regarding the amount of selenium in processed and refined foods. Milling causes loss of selenium in grain foods.

The RDA for selenium is set at 70 micrograms for adult males and 55 micrograms for women. Excesses of selenium are toxic. Cattle grazing in pastures with high concentrations of selenium develop symptoms of hair loss; erosion of the joints of the long bones (which causes lameness); blindness; and liver disease. Animals sometimes die from selenium toxicity. Humans develop problems with only 10 times the maximum intake. A higher incidence of dental cavities occurs in seleniferous areas. Liver failure caused by selenium toxicity can lead to death.

Selenium deficiency is a problem in regions of China where the soil is deficient in selenium. Children ingesting less than 38 micrograms of selenium daily develop Keshan disease. Keshan disease is characterized by heart failure. Kerhan Beck's disease is another regional human disease in China characterized by joint degeneration in the arms and legs. Muscle weakness is a symptom of selenium deficiency seen in hospitalized patients who are unable to eat and in those whose parenteral (other than intestinal) feeding did not contain added selenium.

New research on cancer and selenium has led to conflicting opinions. There are a number of studies that discount the role of selenium deficiency as a cause for cancer. Lower selenium levels are found in cancer patients, possibly as a consequence, not an antecedent, of the cancer. A firm conclusion on the role of cancer risk is not justified at present.*

The FDA has limited trials to 200 micrograms of selenium because of its toxicity. Selenium toxicity is, however, dependent on other factors, even if from dietary sources. For example, some Japanese who are known to consume large amounts of fish ingest 750 micrograms of selenium a day without toxic results. In animal studies, researchers have used 20 to 60 times the nutritional requirement of selenium to demonstrate its effect against cancer. Additional research is needed to determine maximum safety intakes and to prove selenium's effectiveness as an anticancer agent in humans.

Copper

One of the most important functions of copper is its role as a catalyst in hemoglobin formation. Hemoglobin is necessary for carrying oxygen to the body tissues, and a deficiency of copper could be one cause of anemia. Another aspect of copper's relationship to iron is its presence in ceruloplasmin, which transports stored iron. Copper is also necessary for the oxidation of ferrous (FE^{+2}) to ferric (FE^{+3}) iron (which is, in turn, the precursor of transferrin, the form in which iron circulates in the plasma).

Copper influences iron absorption and movement from the liver and other tissue stores. Copper-containing enzymes such as tyrosine (tyrosinase + copper) become dopa, which becomes melanin. Melanin is necessary for color, especially in the hair. Dopa, with copper, becomes norepinephrine, which is vital to central nervous system function.

Copper is a constituent of the elastic connective tissue protein elastin and is involved in the formation of myelin, the material that covers nerve fibers. Copper also acts as part of enzymes that make the crosslinks in bone matrix and in hair and blood vessels. Copper is important in respiration, acts as an antioxidant, and protects cells.

Copper deficiency can cause anemia, osteoporosis, depigmentation of skin and hair, and weakness of elastic tissue in the blood vessels and central nervous system. Central nervous system abnormalities include apnea (difficulty breathing), hypotonia (loss of muscle tone), and psychomotor retardation. Copper deficiency occasionally is seen in children whose diet mainly consists of milk (milk is low in copper).

A rare disease in which an infant is born with an inherited defect in copper absorption does not respond to copper supplements. This disease, called Menkes' syndrome, keeps copper from being absorbed into the tissues. The condition results in death in about four to five years.

The estimated safe and adequate intake for copper is 1.5 to 3 milligrams daily for adults. Excess copper, which can cause restlessness, insomnia, and elevated blood pressure, competes with absorption of other minerals. There is evidence that some psychiatric symptoms result from copper toxicity as well.[†]

Oysters are one of the richest food sources of copper (3623 milligrams in a 100-gram portion). Liver is the next richest source (2450 milligrams of copper per 100 grams) followed by dry beans (960 milligrams per 100 grams). Nuts, peas, whole rye and wheat, and avocados also contain very high levels of copper compared to other foods.

---

*Committee on Diet and Health, Food and Nutrition Board, Commission on Life Sciences, National Research Council, *Diet and Health: Implications for Reducing Chronic Disease Risk.* Washington, DC: National Academy Press, 1989, p. 377.
[†]Bosco, D., *The People's Guide to Vitamins and Minerals From A to Zinc.* Chicago and New York: Contemporary Books, 1989, p. 227.

Manganese

Manganese plays an important role in enzyme functions in the carbohydrate, protein, and lipid metabolism pathways. Therefore, it facilitates energy production.

The average person has 20 milligrams of manganese in the body distributed primarily in the bones and glands. Manganese is an essential ingredient of spinal disks.

The best sources of manganese are whole grains, nuts, and legumes. Tea and cloves also contain manganese. Blueberries are the best source in the fruit and vegetable category. Blueberries can be a moderate source if the manganese content of the soil in which they were grown is good. Dairy, meat, and fish are poor sources.

The estimated safe and adequate daily dietary intake is 2 to 5 milligrams for children over 11 and adults; 1.0 to 1.5 milligrams for children age 1 to 3 years; 1.5 to 2.0 milligrams for children age 4 to 6 years; and 2 to 3 milligrams for children age 7 to 10.

Tests to determine manganese status are not done on blood serum but on tissue that is dried, ashed, and prepared with acid. Manganese deficiency has not been identified in humans. In animals, manganese deficiency causes malformations of the young. Manganese deficiency lowers the immune response in animals.*

Decreased absorption of manganese could result if iron and calcium are taken in excessive amounts. Magnesium toxicity is rare and results only from dust or fumes from industry; magnesium toxicity causes brain disease and nervous system disorders.

Fluoride

The great benefit of fluoride is that it prevents tooth decay. Tooth decay rates have dropped 50% in the last 20 years because of fluoride addition to community water supplies. The National Institute of Dental Research has been pro-fluoridation. One part fluoride per 1 million parts water is ideal to provide protection against dental cavities. Some areas have a naturally high fluoride content in the water, about 2 to 4 parts per million (ppm). Crown calcification occurs between the ages of 8 and 10 (or 12 to 16, if the third molar teeth are considered). The third molar teeth are the wisdom teeth, which come in at age 19 to 22.

The average diet provides 0.25 to 0.32 milligrams of fluoride daily. This increases to 1.0 to 1.5 milligrams of fluoride for adults and 0.4 to 1.1 milligrams of fluoride for children 1 to 12 years of age if water containing 1 ppm fluoride is ingested in adequate quantity of 4 cups per day. The estimated safe intake is 1.5 to 4.0 milligrams daily.

Dentists recommend a 1-milligram daily dietary fluoride supplement if the water supply is not fluoridated. The application of 2% sodium fluoride solution directly to children's teeth is also effective in preventing dental cavities.

Babies need 0.1 to 1.0 milligram of fluoride per day. Breast milk does not provide adequate fluoride to an infant regardless of the mother's intake. An infant taking a cup of water a day in addition to his or her mother's milk will get adequate fluoride if the water supply contains 1 ppm fluoride. Otherwise a supplement prescribed by the doctor is in order for the infant. Fluoride applied directly to the teeth by the dentist should be started at age 3 and continued until age 18. Fluoride application should be done twice a year to prevent tooth decay.

The body contains fluoride in the blood and saliva. Fluoride is excreted in the urine (80%), sweat, and feces.

---

*Bosco, D., *The People's Guide to Vitamins and Minerals From A to Zinc*, p. 250.

Water is the major source of fluoride today. The water used to prepare food will greatly influence the fluoride content of the diet. Fluoride intake can vary from 1 to 4 milligrams per day, depending on the water supply. The water used in commercial food processing can also increase fluoride content. Where food is grown is more important than the type of food in determining fluoride content. Fluoride deficiency does not occur in humans because fluoride is present in all water, plants, and animals.

Some people argue against water fluoridation. There is a fine line between the amount of fluoride that prevents tooth decay and the amount that causes mottling. According to one study, with most fluoridated water supplying 1 ppm, 1% of the population using water at this concentration has at least two mottled teeth.[*] Mottling, which consists of paper white opaque areas of the teeth, is not dangerous but is disfiguring. At fluoride levels of 1.8 ppm, brown stains begin to appear. Mottling is also proportional to temperature and humidity. Allergic reactions, usually hives, from normal fluoride concentrations in fluoridated water and toothpaste are alleviated when the fluoride is discontinued.

The *Journal of Public Health Dentistry* published an article stating that the deleterious health effects attributed to fluoridation are uncontrolled observations and are not based on clinical trials. The article showed that mortality rates and other health statistics in fluoridated and nonfluoridated communities are similar.[†]

The Public Health Service of the United States Department of Health and Human Services has set objectives for water fluoridation for the year 2000. As of 1996, 46,000 public water systems were not fluoridated and just 65% of fluoridated water systems had optimal levels of fluoride. Plans have begun to implement fluoridation programs in the needed areas.

Fluoride therapy has been tried in the treatment of osteoporosis, but there is no convincing evidence that it is beneficial. The procedure is to alternate six months of calcium and vitamin D therapy with six months of fluoride therapy. The theory was to create new bone with calcium and vitamin D and then harden it with fluoride. If enough calcium is not supplied, fluoride actually causes bones to demineralize. In other studies, spinal bone mass increased while other bones fractured more often. Fluoride-treated women experienced stomach irritation and pain in the lower extremities. Bone diseases are prevalent in areas with very high fluoride levels (7 ppm).

In the healthy body, fluoride is necessary for bone and tooth development. When bones and teeth become mineralized, calcium and phosphorus form a crystal called hydroxyapatite. Then fluoride replaces portions of the crystal, forming fluorapatite and making the bones and teeth stronger.

Chromium

Chromium functions with nicotinic acid and amino acids in the body as a complex named glucose tolerance factor. This factor aids the attachment of insulin to cell membranes, helping the cells take up glucose. Chromium stimulates fatty acid and cholesterol synthesis and may help prevent cardiovascular disease as well as diabetes. When there is adequate chromium in the diet, glucose tolerance factor, cholesterol, triglyceride, and HDL levels improve.

Of all the foods, brewer's yeast provides the most chromium, but it is seldom eaten. Spices have been mentioned as having a high chromium content, but they are eaten in such minute quantities that their contributions are negli-

---

[*]Ibid., p. 231.
[†]Newbrun, E., "The Fluoridation War: A Scientific Dispute or a Religious Argument?" *Journal of Public Health Dentistry*, Volume 56, number 5, special issue, 1996.

gible. Mushrooms are a good source but are not a regular part of most diets. Oysters, liver, and other organ meats, rich sources of many nutrients, are also an excellent source of chromium. Eggs, meat, raisins, nuts, some beer, wines, whole grains, bran, seafood, and chicken are also sources of chromium. Potatoes provide more chromium than most vegetables if the skin is eaten.

A nonfood source of chromium is stainless steel cookware, which leaches chromium into the food if some acid, such as tomato, vinegar, molasses, or citrus juice, is used in the preparation. It is not known whether the body can use this form of chromium. The amount of chromium in foods tends to decrease with commercial processing.

The estimated safe and adequate intake for chromium is 50 to 200 micrograms per day for adolescents and adults and 10 to 120 micrograms for infants and children. Some data show that the typical American diet does not provide adequate chromium, but other evidence supports the theory that individuals with less than the recommended intake do not have a chromium imbalance.[*] Only 1 to 2% of chromium intake is available, however, so urinary chromium levels are not good indicators of chromium status. Most of the chromium is lost in the stool.

The hair contains 990 ppm of chromium at birth and 440 ppm at age 3. Hair analysis for chromium is not accurate for adults because of environmental contaminants. The best way to check for chromium deficiency is to look for diabetic-like symptoms. If the symptoms lessen with the addition of chromium to the diet, there is a chromium deficiency. Among the heavy metals, chromium is the only one whose levels in body tissue continually decrease throughout life.[†]

Chromium toxicity is not found in humans. In animals, toxicity is associated with lung tumors. Studies on human runners show that, after running, chromium losses in the urine are increased. Physical traumas produce this same finding.[§]

Molybdenum

Molybdenum functions as part of the enzymes sulfite oxidase and xantine oxidase, which are involved in oxidative and reductive reactions. The best food source of molybdenum is legumes, followed by grains, leafy vegetables, liver, kidney, and spleen. Fruits, berries, and most root or stem vegetables contain some molybdenum. Brewer's yeast is also a source. The molybdenum content depends on where the food was grown, because soil is an important contributing factor.

The estimated safe and adequate daily dietary intake for adults is 75 to 250 micrograms. For young children the safe intake is 25 to 75 micrograms daily, and for children age 7 to 10, 50 to 150 micrograms. Children over 11 years can use the adult recommendation. Excess molybdenum may decrease the body's copper levels, and molybdenum toxicity is possible. It is never recommended to use over-the-counter single supplements because imbalances and excesses could result.

The importance of molybdenum for humans was demonstrated in a case study of a patient on eight months of intravenous feeding who developed molybdenum deficiency. The deficiency symptoms included severe headaches, night

---

[*]Anderson, R., "Chromium in Human Health and Disease." *Nutrition and the M.D.*, Volume 14, number 3, 1988.
[†]Ibid.
[§]National Research Council, *Diet and Health*. Washington, DC: National Academy Press, 1990, pp. 381–382.

blindness, nausea, vomiting, edema, lethargy, disorientation, and coma; all reversed with 300 micrograms of molybdenum. Lack of the sulfite oxidase enzyme, which contains molybdenum, results in severe nervous system problems, as described in this case history.*

Molybdenum helps degrade nitrates in the soil. The nitrate and nitrite concentration of plants is higher when there is a soil deficiency of molybdenum. After the plants are eaten, nitrates can be converted into nitrosamines, which are known carcinogens. Additionally, more vitamin C is found in foods grown in soil with molybdenum fertilizer.

Other minerals

Boron

Boron may be helpful in preventing osteoporosis because it aids the body in retaining calcium, magnesium, and phosphorus in bone. Boron is involved in brain function and low intakes of boron affect alertness. Boron is found in plant foods (especially beet greens), broccoli, nuts, and all noncitrus fruits.

Vanadium

Not enough is known about how vanadium works or how much is needed; thus it cannot be declared an essential nutrient. Research has been ongoing for the past four decades. So far, research proves that some animal species develop problems when vanadium is removed from their diet. Vanadium appears to affect bone development in goats and repair tooth tissue in guinea pigs and rats. Studies have shown that vanadium regulates glucose metabolism in rats in a way similar to insulin. A form of vanadium called vanadate also reverses diabetes in rats. Human studies show that vanadium lowers endogenous cholesterol production in healthy young men but not in older men or in those with hypercholesterolemia or heart disease.

Vanadium occurs in tiny amounts in natural food. Giving very large doses to human beings has shown scientists some of the effects of vanadium, but the mechanism by which vanadium works is unknown. Therefore, nutrition experts believe that the time is not right to declare vanadium necessary. It is thought, however, that in the near future a recommendation will be made.

The best food sources of vanadium are black pepper, dill seed, parsley, mushrooms, and shellfish. Smaller amounts are found in fruits, vegetables, fats, and oils. Some sources claim that there is a moderate amount of vanadium in whole grains, meat, and dairy. (In the past it was difficult to establish food values accurately because of environmental contamination of food samples. Newer equipment and methods now make it possible to analyze small amounts of nutrients found in food.) Current methods of analyzing vanadium use atomic absorption spectrophotometry with a graphite furnace, nuclear magnetic resonance spectroscopy, and neutron activation analysis.[†]

The total body content of vanadium is about 100 micrograms, found mainly inside the cells. The daily intake of vanadium is low in comparison to other trace minerals and averages about 20 micrograms. Ten to one hundred micrograms probably constitutes a safe intake. Large amounts (22.5 milligrams) from

---

*Johnson, J., "The Molybdenum Cofactor Common to Nitrite Reductions, Xanthine Dehydrogenase and Sulfite Oxidate." In *Molybdenum and Molybdenum Containing Enzymes.* New York: Pergamon Press, 1980.
[†]Harland, Barbara F., and Harden-Williams, Barbara, "Is Vanadium of Human Nutrition Importance Yet?" *Journal of the American Dietetic Association,* Volume 94, number 81, August 1994, pp. 891–894.

supplements can cause cramps and diarrhea. There are some reports that elevated vanadium levels are associated with manic depression. Drugs used to treat this disorder are effective in reducing vanadate (a form of vanadium). High intake of vitamin C is also helpful in this regard.

Excess vanadium in the environment is a serious problem. In some industrial environments exposure to vanadium is chronic and high levels of vanadium are inhaled, causing lung irritation, chest pain, coughing, wheezing, runny nose, and sore throat.

Vanadium is used to make steel for automobile parts and is mixed with iron for aircraft engines. It is used in the rubber, plastic, and ceramics industries. It is found in crude petroleum deposits as well.

Everyone is exposed to vanadium to some degree (there are low levels in air, water, and food). Breathing air near an industry that burns fuel oil exposes one to vanadium oxide. Air and drinking water can also be contaminated from waste sites or landfills containing vanadium. Unfortunately, the Agency for Toxic Substances and the Disease Registry do not know the health effects in people of ingesting vanadium. High vanadium levels in the water of pregnant animals, however, has resulted in minor birth defects.* The carcinogenicity of vanadium is not known. Laboratory tests can be performed to measure vanadium in urine and blood, but such tests cannot determine if harmful health effects will occur. People who have high vanadium exposure may develop a green-colored tongue.

The Occupational Safety and Health Administration (OSHA) has set an exposure limit of 0.05 milligrams per cubic meter for vanadium pentoxide dust and 0.1 milligram per cubic meter for vanadium pentoxide fumes in workplace air for an 8-hour workday in a 40-hour work week.

Aluminum

There is no nutritional requirement for aluminum. It is included in this section because of the concern about its possible role in dementia.

It has been suggested that aluminum may cause Alzheimer's disease, but the bulk of the scientific evidence suggests that this is unlikely. Aluminum toxicity does cause dementia in dialysis patients as a result of a high concentration of aluminum in the water used to prepare the dialysate. The accumulation of aluminum seen in Alzheimer's patients may occur as a result of a defect rather than a cause. There are more Alzheimer's cases in England and Wales in areas where drinking water has high aluminum levels. Some of those municipal waters contain as much as 2 to 4 milligrams of aluminum per liter.

Recommendations to avoid using aluminum cookware, aluminum-containing drugs, aluminum-type antacids, and food additives with aluminum are not upheld by most researchers. Little of the ingested aluminum is actually absorbed. The total body content of aluminum does not increase with age.

Aluminum-containing foods include pickles, artificial creamers, and dry mixes. Aluminum additives keep the moisture out of packaged mixes. In pickles, aluminum imparts a crisp texture. Ingestion of aluminum in foods ranges from 3 to 5 milligrams daily. According to the National Research Council, there is no reliable evidence that aluminum is carcinogenic.

Mercury

Mercury, in the form of methyl mercury, is ingested primarily through fish and seafood. Fish heavily contaminated with mercury can cause severe poisoning, with resulting neurological and kidney problems.

---

*TOXFAQS Vanadium, September 1995: http://atsdrl.atsdr.cdc.gov:8080/tfacts58.html

In nature, mercury is found in very low concentrations. Occupational exposure is mainly through inhalation. Safe levels and regulations have been established.

Arsenic

Tiny amounts of arsenic, a known poison, may be essential for health. This is a matter for future research, however. Arsenic is widespread in nature. Arsenic in food may also come from pesticide residue. Daily intakes of arsenic in the United States are estimated to range from 10 to 130 micrograms. Serious health consequences have not been seen in the United States, but studies of countries with high levels of arsenic in well water yield reports of skin and lung cancer.

Cadmium

Cadmium may have a biological role in humans. Cadmium exists in the body in trace amounts but does not appear to be an essential nutrient. The biological function of cadmium is unknown. It is found in minute amounts in food. Higher amounts are found in beef liver and kidney. Plant uptake depends on the soil content of cadmium in which the plants are grown. Because cadmium at certain levels is toxic, crop fertilization is being evaluated as a possible source of cadmium. Soil pH is also a factor in plant uptake of cadmium.

Cigarette smoke contains cadmium, and increased cadmium levels are found in lung tissue from patients with cancer. In some studies, cadmium levels in food and drinking water correlate with the incidence of prostate and other cancers. The association may be a result rather than a cause of the cancers. Findings are inconsistent to establish a relationship between cadmium and high blood pressure. Cadmium contamination can cause kidney and bone disease, however.*

Lead

Lead-free cans are now in use and have eliminated the main source of lead in foods. In the past, the canning industry used lead-soldered cans, which led to lead contamination. Blood lead levels greater than 20 micrograms per deciliter in children are dangerous and lead to anemia, learning disabilities, and behavior problems. The dust particles from lead paint, chipped paint, and soil are the main causes of lead contamination today.

The effects of dietary trace elements cannot be established without a great deal of further research. Until the National Research Council makes specific recommendations, it is unwise to take any of the publicly available trace supplements of lead, vanadium, cadmium, mercury, arsenic, aluminum, or any of the elements for which there is yet no estimated safe requirement.

Review Questions

1. Name the naturally occurring sugar found in milk and the main sugar found in fruit. Why are these sugars, eaten in their natural form, more desirable than processed sugars?

2. What are the names of the monosaccharides and disaccharides that are listed among the ingredients in many commercially processed foods?

---

*Committee on Diet and Health, Food and Nutrition Board, Commission on Life Sciences, National Research Council, *Diet and Health: Implications for Reducing Chronic Disease Risk*. Washington, DC: National Academy Press, 1989.

3. How can lactose intolerant individuals get a good source of calcium in the diet without drinking milk?

4. Discuss two reasons dieters should not follow an extremely low carbohydrate diet.

5. What percentage of our daily calories should come from carbohydrates?

6. Name some foods that are high in water soluble fiber.

7. Explain how water soluble fiber helps to lower blood cholesterol levels.

8. What are two other health benefits of water soluble fiber, and what are the probable mechanisms involved?

9. How does cellulose fiber work to prevent constipation?

10. How many grams of fiber are recommended in the daily diet?

11. Which three food groups contribute to the daily fiber intake?

12. Why should people be cautious when changing from a low-fiber diet to a high-fiber diet?

13. What are the best protein foods to choose for a low-fat omnivorous diet?

14. Explain how a person could possibly gain weight on a high-protein diet.

15. What is the significance of nitrogen balance?

16. Calculate the ideal protein requirement for yourself. Plan a day's worth of food that meets this requirement.

17. Create new recipes or menu ideas utilizing the concept of complementary protein.

18. Why is it wasteful to eat a high-protein diet?

19. In what positive way is cholesterol important in human health?

20. How many milligrams of dietary cholesterol constitute a moderate intake?

21. Name the two food groups in the Food Guide Pyramid that have no cholesterol.

22. Name the two foods in the meat group that are without cholesterol. Which foods in this group are the largest contributing sources of cholesterol in the American diet?

23. Which foods in the milk group are a high cholesterol source?

24. Explain how coconut oil, which has no dietary cholesterol, could raise blood cholesterol levels.

25. Name the two groups of polyunsaturated fats.

26. What happens when a fat is hydrogenated? What is a trans fat?

27. Why is a no-fat or extremely low-fat diet undesirable?

28. Which lifestyle changes affect HDL (good blood cholesterol) levels? What benefit is gained from raising the HDL levels?

29. How would an austere low-fat regime affect vitamin A nutrition?

30. What environmental factors impact on vitamin D nutrition?

31. Name the antioxidant vitamins. What disease protection may these vitamins provide?

32. Enrichment of bread has helped to eliminate two serious deficiency diseases. Name them.

33. List some fruits and vegetables supplying the day's contribution of vi min C in one serving.

34. Name the minerals that play a major role in bone health.

35. Name two minerals that play a role in insulin production.

36. Name the macrominerals, and those that function as electrolytes.

37. Which minerals have no established safe intake level?

Health and Diet

Research and study are illuminating the relationship between health and diet—not diet as a way of losing weight, but diet as it relates to what we eat and how much we consume. Scientists and doctors are beginning to make direct correlations among the foods we eat, the health of our bodies, and the regularity of our bodily functions. It is a good idea to keep abreast of these findings and consider altering our personal lifestyles and eating habits to ensure a long and healthy life.

After completing this chapter, the student will be able to

■ discuss the correlation between health and diet in many common ailments and degenerative diseases

■ describe ways to decrease the risk factors for many diseases that affect the elderly

■ describe conditions that may lead to osteoporosis in women

■ discuss health issues that affect calcium absorption

■ describe diabetes and the health issues it raises

■ describe ways to decrease the risk for heart disease

■ discuss how diet protects against cancer, adult-onset diabetes, and obesity

■ describe how cancer-causing free radicals in the body can be partially countered with antioxidants found in food

■ discuss health issues that may lead to high blood pressure

There is enough of a correlation between health and diet to suggest the importance of learning some basic guidelines about general nutrition. As the science of nutrition continues to be verified through research and experiments, the interaction of health and nutrition will become increasingly evident. In the meantime, there are some commonly accepted tenets of nutrition that are worth noting, and we discuss these in this chapter.

Diet and skin care

The human skin is a living organ, and its health is a clear indication of the health of its host. Clear, glowing skin reflects good health, whereas dry and brittle skin may be indicative of a poor diet. Along with adequate exercise and sleep, a balanced diet contributes greatly to healthy skin. Vitamin A and zinc are essential for producing new skin cells to replace the ones we all lose daily. Fresh vegetables and fruits, particularly citrus fruits, contribute vitamins A and C to the diet.

Diet and aging

Although the aging process cannot be stopped, some of the ill health effects of aging can be postponed or lessened through proper nutrition. Osteoporosis, diabetes, and heart disease can all be caused in part by the foods we eat.

The diet of elderly people tends to be nutritionally deficient because there is a general loss of appetite as people age. Two physical changes contribute to this age-related loss of appetite: (1) the loss of natural teeth, which interferes with chewing (without teeth, only soft or pureed foods are edible), and (2) the deterioration of the olfactory neurons, resulting in the transmission of less taste information to the olfactory lobes in the brain.

There are many ways chefs can help elderly people overcome these difficulties. Chefs can produce healthy soups and stews that supply tender yet nutritional foods or cook meats that are naturally tender, such as beef tenderloin, slow-roasted meats, and poultry and fish. To compensate for a diminished sense of smell, chefs can add more spice and rely more on fresh herbs for pronounced flavors. They can use more ingredients to stimulate the five basic taste sensations of salt, bitter, sweet, sour, and peppery (although salt intake is usually restricted for older consumers with high blood pressure). Chefs may otherwise entice older consumers to eat more regularly by the way foods are presented. Foods presented with a variety of color, tastes, and textures do more to excite the elderly than large portions or fancy foods.

Osteoporosis

Osteoporosis results when bone cell deterioration occurs faster than bone cell production. This condition causes bones to become porous and weak. Fractures occur more easily and the neck bones can collapse, causing the slightly humped look that is associated with women who have severe cases of osteoporosis.

Children, teenagers, and adults should consume proper amounts of calcium because it is the main building material of bones. Vitamin D, vitamin K, magnesium, zinc, fluoride, and boron are also needed for healthy bones. Building a good bone supply early in life helps minimize bone loss later.

Lower than adequate amounts of the hormone estrogen may cause osteoporosis. A lack of estrogen may affect the absorption rate of calcium, which then affects bone cell replacement. Women who have reached menopause or have had their ovaries removed have difficulty maintaining appropriate levels of estrogen in their bodies. Women can take estrogen supplements during and after menopause.

A balanced diet and exercise, especially in early childhood, can help to prevent osteoporosis and other bone diseases. Building a solid bone structure in early childhood creates efficiency and consistency of bone cell replacement for later life. The stronger the bones are in youth and early adulthood, the more they'll hold up to estrogen depletion and short-term deficiencies of calcium and other nutrients.

Milk and all milk products are naturally rich in calcium. Dried beans and peas, tofu (made from soybeans), fish bones from sardines, anchovies, and dark green leafy vegetables are excellent sources of other necessary nutrients and calcium.

Vitamin D ensures the proper absorption of calcium into the human body, but it is not easily obtained through food. Oily fish and egg yolks contain vitamin D, but vitamin D is generally obtained through exposure of the skin to sunlight or by foods that have been artificially enhanced with the addition of the vitamin. Milk has been fortified with vitamin D because it is also a good source of calcium.

As mentioned previously, some people have a deficiency of the enzyme lactase, which prevents them from properly digesting milk and milk products. This is referred to as lactose intolerance. People who must avoid fortified milk and milk products need to get their calcium and vitamin D from alternative sources. Lactase tablets and milk with lactase added are available so people with this deficiency can enjoy the taste and nutritional benefits of dairy products.

Diabetes

Diabetes is a genetic, chronic disease that can affect both the young and the elderly. Its two forms, insulin-dependent diabetes mellitus (IDDM) and non-insulin-dependent diabetes mellitus (NIDDM) affect people in different ways, but both affect the body's ability to convert blood sugar, in the form of glucose, into energy. Insulin is the hormone responsible for glucose metabolism. People either cannot produce enough insulin (IDDM) or cannot respond to insulin (NIDDM). Individually planned diets, exercise, and sometimes medication help balance insulin production and glucose metabolism and modify weight.

For people with IDDM, regular doses of insulin, prescribed by a physician, are usually required to keep the system balanced. Their bodies may never be able to supply the right amount of insulin. People with NIDDM, which is also referred to as adult-onset diabetes, can usually control their symptoms through exercise and diet.

Occurrences of NIDDM are on the rise in America. As the U.S. population ages, more people are becoming susceptible because of a lack of exercise and an increase in obesity. Excessive fat, in itself, may interfere with the body's ability to use naturally produced insulin.

It may be difficult for the elderly to eat a proper diet and get enough exercise. In such cases they may require a doctor's and registered dietician's care.

Registered dieticians are trained to help design diets based on a person's age and particular health problems. For most older adults this usually includes a low-fat, high-fiber diet to help maintain normal body weight and to ensure good nutrition.

Heart disease

The American Heart Association (AHA) estimates that more than 60 million Americans have some form of cardiovascular disease. Risk factors for heart disease include the following: heredity, age, gender (premenopausal women have a lower risk than men and older women), cigarette smoking, diet, and sedentary lifestyle. Diabetes and high blood pressure also can lead to heart disease.

Poor diets include high amounts of foods containing saturated fats and cholesterol, which promote obesity and the buildup of fatty deposits in the coronary arteries. A heart-healthy diet is the same balanced diet that protects against cancer, adult-onset diabetes, and obesity. It is a diet low in fat, high in fiber, and featuring multiple portions of fruits, whole grains, and vegetables daily.

Prudent dietary practices should be started in childhood. Atherosclerosis, the clogging of arteries by fatty deposits, may begin in early childhood (parents often believe, mistakenly, that plump children are healthy children). Although it is true that children burn off more calories than adults, the calories should come from a balanced diet and not one heavily laden with fatty foods.

A list of particularly healthful foods includes all fruits and vegetables, especially those high in vitamin C, beta carotene, and other antioxidants, including all varieties of the cabbage family. Vitamin E may protect against heart disease and is found in eggs, wheat germ, nuts, seeds, and dark green leafy vegetables.

The omega 3 fatty acids found in some cold-water fish species, like salmon, herring, and trout, reduce the tendency for blood to clot. Free-flowing blood helps prevent many forms of heart disease and strokes caused by blood clots. Hemorrhagic stroke is a type of stroke that could be worsened by extreme blood-thinning programs that include extra vitamin E or fish oil. Care must be taken not to use these supplements excessively. Natural sources of vitamin E and omega 3 fatty acids are better choices.

Oat bran, pectin, many fruits, dried beans, peas, and other foods containing soluble fiber also help to lower cholesterol in the blood and regulate glucose absorption.

Cancer

Although there is no cure for cancer yet and no FDA-approved preventive measures to protect against cancer, there is enough evidence to suggest a correlation between eating certain foods and reducing the risks for developing cancers.

Such anticancer foods contain high amounts of antioxidants. Antioxidants are positively charged molecules released into the blood when certain foods are consumed. These positively charged molecules attract the negatively charged molecules referred to as free radicals. The neutral marriage renders the free radicals harmless, and they are excreted through normal bodily functions.

Cancer is partially the result of too many free radicals in the body. Free radicals are the result of the natural bodily process of burning oxygen, which helps convert food to energy, and the natural enzymes deployed to protect healthy cells usually protect against free radical damage. If there are too many free radicals, or if there are other forms of oxidative damage (such as tobacco smoke, ultraviolet sun rays, pollution, and automobile exhaust), cancer becomes possible. Proper diet helps maintain the proper balance between free radicals and the anti-oxidants that counteract them.

The body's immune system tries to maintain balance by seeking out and destroying decaying body cells, much as it does with invading bacteria and viruses, but with age the body becomes more susceptible to free radical damage, and instances of degenerative damage increase. The result may be slight skin blemishes, liver disease, tumor growth, and cancer.

The major sources of antioxidants in foods come from those containing vitamin C and vitamin E, beta carotene (which is the precursor for vitamin A), and selenium, which is found in poultry, seafood, whole grain products, onions, garlic, and mushrooms. The phytochemicals found in food have recently been identified as sources of these antioxidants.

Arthritis

Arthritis affects one in seven Americans and is represented by more than 100 disorders characterized by inflammation of the joints, stiffness, swelling, and pain.

Omega 3 fatty acids, found in fatty cold-water fish, may help reduce inflammation. Some doctors recommend two or three servings of cold-water fatty fish weekly to help supply the omega 3 fatty acids. Excessive amounts of omega 3 fatty acids, however, are not recommended. They may cause internal bleeding in people who are also taking some forms of arthritis medicine, which are designed to interfere with blood clotting. Fish oil supplements, therefore, should be taken only under the advice of a doctor.

There is evidence that the oil capsaicin, found in capsicum peppers and in concentrated forms in the hot pepper varieties, when rubbed onto inflamed knuckles and joints, reduces inflammation in those areas.

Blood pressure

As blood circulates through the body's arteries, it exerts pressure against the walls of the arteries, which doctors refer to as blood pressure. The ability of the heart to pump blood is affected by the health and size of the arteries. As arteries become narrowed, blood pressure rises and the risk for stroke and heart diseases increases.

Stress, diabetes, obesity, smoking, excessive alcohol consumption, and sedentary lifestyles may contribute to hypertension, the common name for high blood pressure. Salt also has a negative effect on blood pressure in those who already suffer from hypertension.

Dietary means of controlling high blood pressure include a low-fat diet (to help maintain healthy body weight) and a restricted salt intake (2400 milligrams per day, or less). Exercise, stress-relieving activities, smoking cessation, and reduced alcohol intake can also help the body keep blood pressure at normal levels. High-potassium foods such as fruits and vegetables also help control high blood pressure.

Review Questions

1. What degenerative diseases, which affect mostly the elderly, can proper diet and nutrition reduce the risk of or postpone?

2. What can chefs do to encourage proper eating habits in the elderly?

3. How does osteoporosis occur, and why does it affect mostly women?

4. What is the best source of vitamin D, and why has it been introduced into many milk products as an additive?

5. What is insulin, and what use does it have in the human body?

6. What are some of the risk factors that may contribute to heart disease, and which ones are diet or nutrition related?

7. Why is food containing omega 3 fatty acids beneficial in the reduction of risk for heart disease and stroke?

8. Which foods contain large amounts of antioxidants? What are the benefits of antioxidants?

9. Why are the elderly more susceptible to cancer?

10. Why are omega 3 fatty acids and capsicum peppers used to treat arthritis patients?

11. What is the suggested amount of daily sodium intake for good health?

12. When does the consumption of sodium become a health concern?

Smell and Taste

The art of nutritional cooking is more than following dietary guidelines in designing recipes; it is also preparing the foods to look and taste good. Although how foods look is purely a visual response, taste is a combination of many sensory perceptions. The perception of taste is influenced by smell; the five basic tastes of sour, sweet, bitter, salty, and savory; texture; heredity; and even tradition. The dietician's role is to design diets for their nutritional benefits, whereas the cook's role is to please the palate.

After completing this chapter, the student will be able to

■ describe the human perception of taste as a combination of data input from physical and environmental sources

■ discuss how tradition and custom play important roles in a person's willingness to try certain foods

■ list and describe the five basic tastes stimulated by the tongue

■ describe the characteristics and use of human taste buds

■ describe the four general taste zones of the human tongue affected by organic and inorganic compounds

■ describe the causes for the sensation of pepper

■ discuss the placement of olfactory neurons and their contribution to taste

■ list and describe the basic categories of smells

■ describe the effect of a loss of smell on taste, and means of heightening tastes to compensate for such a loss

Taste is a sensation that many of us take for granted. If something tastes good, we ask for more; if it tastes bad, we put it aside. Cooks, however, are mechanics of tastes and must understand the true intricacies of this sense. Taste was once described by the French gastronome Brillat-Savarin as "one of the most pleasurable of all the senses."

What we perceive as taste is actually a combination of physical, genetic, and environmental stimuli. The physical properties of taste are a combination of smell (the olfactory process) and taste, by way of more than a thousand taste buds implanted in the tongue and the roof and back of the mouth. Genetic information tells us instinctively what tastes good and is safe to eat, and what tastes bad and is better left alone. Environmental stimuli come from family traditions and customs.

Traditions and customs do not affect the physical sensation of taste; rather, they affect our willingness to try various foods. In some cases, traditions and customs may even dictate our perceptions of good- and bad-tasting foods. What we learn to eat as children and what our families like to eat contribute to our own food choices.

Traditional food choices are partly based on geography (i.e., food choices indigenous to certain regions), cultural heritage, and religious or philosophical beliefs. Those of us raised on fresh cow's milk, for example, would find pasteurized milk unsatisfactory. Those of us accustomed to drinking only pasteurized milk from a grocery store would probably choke if offered a glass of warm cow's milk right from the udder. In Alabama and Georgia the smell of chitterlings cooking might create a sense of great anticipation for the afternoon meal. The same smell might invoke nausea and disgust in a Northerner.

Some of us might assume that the sense known as taste is fabricated in the mouth, because this is where food generally enters the body. In fact, only five basic taste sensations are disseminated there; the rest occur in the olfactory passages above our nasal cavity.

In the mouth the tongue has a dual purpose: (1) as a muscle that holds food in place for chewing and then carries the food to the back of the mouth for swallowing; and (2) as a harbor for tiny organs known as taste buds. Similar taste buds are also found on the roof of the mouth and in the air passageway at the rear of the mouth known as the pharynx.

Taste buds are classified as organs because they have a very specific function in the human body: taste discrimination. They are one of the few types of human organs that completely regenerate themselves almost weekly.

Each taste bud is a collection of modified epithelial cells, the taste cells, which act as receptors for the stimuli created through the ingestion of food. Taste buds themselves are somewhat spherical, with small openings on the surface known as taste pores. Through these pores and then onto tiny hairs (microvilli), called taste hairs, pass the essence of the flavors of foods after being dissolved in saliva. It is believed that the taste hairs are a part of receptor cells. The receptor cells bridge the taste impulses to connecting links in the brain (see Figure 5–1). The brain identifies the taste by linking the impulse sensation with similar sensations already learned.

Microscopically, taste cells in all taste buds appear quite similar, yet there is evidence that five types of taste cells exist. Each of these is designed to identify primarily one of the basic tastes: sweet, sour, salt, bitter, and umami (a new taste recently identified by scientists). Umami, which translated from Japanese means "wonderful taste," is a possible fifth basic taste. The English word "savory" best describes umami taste. Researchers at the Monell Chemical Senses Center in Philadelphia are trying to understand the biological basis of this "new" taste and to identify natural sources. One primary stimulus comes from the sodium salt of the common amino acid glutamate, which is known as monosodium glutamate, or MSG, and is commonly used as a flavor enhancer.

Although all taste cells can detect a variety of tastes, there are collections of cells on the surface of the tongue that appear to be more sensitive than others to a specific taste sensation.

Near the tip of the tongue are the taste cells that are predominantly sweet sensitive. The sensation of sweetness can be created either through the ingestion of organic or inorganic sources. Organic sources are from the family of sugars: cane sugar, beet sugar, honey, and fructose. Inorganic sources include lead and beryllium salts. Other organic sources are organic chemicals such as saccharine and aspartame.

The sour taste sensation is predominantly detected along the margins of the tongue to the right and to the left. This sensation is generated through the ingestion of any one of the many acids present in foods: citric (e.g., oranges, lemons, limes), malic (e.g., apples), tartaric (e.g., grapes; tartaric acid is a

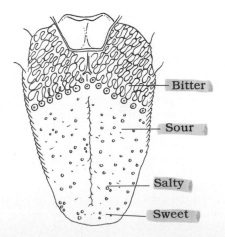

Figure 5–1 Human tongue: flavor zones. (© 1998 Jessica A. Delfino.)

byproduct of the wine industry), and oxalic (e.g., rhubarb, spinach, and other leafy green vegetables). In fact, all plant tissues are acidic to some degree, with pH levels at 7 or below.

Saltiness in food is detected at the tip and upper front portion of the tongue. This sensation is generated by a number of ionic compounds regardless of the positive or negative nature of the present ions. Sodium chloride (table salt) is the most common source, but other chlorides, fluorides, and nitrates also create the salty sensation in taste.

The fourth basic taste sensation, bitter, has the majority of its taste receptors at the back of the tongue. Most bitter sensations are caused by organic materials, although some inorganic salts, like magnesium and calcium, also generate a bitter response from the taste buds. It is believed that bitter taste, a primal reflex, acts as a warning about the presence of poisonous alkaloids in some plant and animal species, and unsuspecting animals are thus spared from ingesting poisonous foods. The common rejection of bitter foods may be related to this protective mechanism, which is at work in even the most primitive of life forms. Examples of poisonous alkaloids are strychnine, nicotine, and morphine; similar alkaloids are present in minute amounts in coffee, tea, and chocolate.

The sensation of peppery taste is not a true taste sensation. The taste buds do not generate a sensation of pepper as a specific taste; this sensation is a physical response to acidlike irritants burning the tissues in the mouth and tongue. Chili peppers, pepper corns, and ginger contain chemicals that stimulate pain receptors in the mouth, which causes the burning sensation we associate with spicy food. (Capsaicin is the alkaloid in chili peppers and jalapeños that causes the peppery sensation, and the piperine is the alkaloid in black and white pepper corns.)

The basic tastes and the taste of pepper only begin to define flavors in food. The sense of smell and the olfaction process give flavors greater dimension and complexity. As Brillat-Savarin described the process so elegantly in his book *The Philospher in the Kitchen,* "Smell and taste form a single sense, of which the mouth is the laboratory and the nose is the chimney."

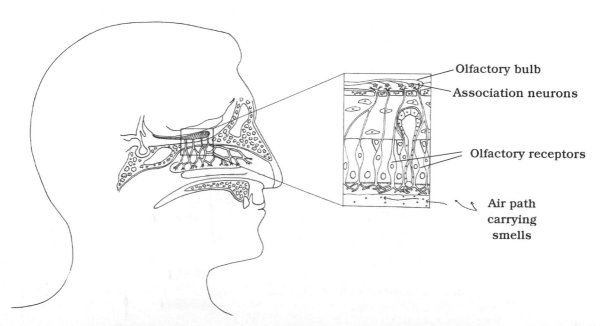

- Olfactory bulb
- Association neurons
- Olfactory receptors
- Air path carrying smells

Figure 5–2 Human olfactory system. (© 1998 Jessica A. Delfino.)

As air is breathed into the nose, thousands of microscopic organic and inorganic particles are carried in with it. These particles are then exposed to olfactory neurons (from the Latin *olfacere*, meaning "to smell"), which act as smell receptors and protrude into the nasal cavity. The olfactory lobes in the brain translate the many different scents into recognizable smell sensations. The olfactory bulbs are found in the front of the brain and are connected to brain centers where, according to Monell scientists, association and other higher mental processes, including pleasure, take place. This theory is partially proved by our many experiences in which smells, and therefore tastes, are triggered by memory. Memory can affect olfaction more than any other human sense.

There are at least seven primary odors detectable by the olfactory neurons in the human nose:

camphoraceous: the scent of camphor, unmistakably present in some insect repellents and lacquers but also in the herb sage, and used as a stimulant, expectorant, and diaphoretic

musky: the scent of sexual attraction between animals and humans

floral: the scent associated with flowering vegetables, herbs, and plants

pepperminty: the scent found in various strengths in all members of the mint family (e.g., peppermint, basil, marjoram, and oregano)

ethereal: the scent of ether, any of a class of organic compounds derived from the distillation of ethyl alcohol and sulfuric acid and used widely as an anesthetic

pungent: the scent of spices

putrid: the scent of decay, of aged meat, and of some cheese molds

Any odor may be described as one or a combination of several primary odors.

Scientists at Monell are studying the effects of time on the perception of smells. When we are first exposed to an odor, it is very distinct; but after continued exposure, the smells often seem to fatigue or disappear altogether. Examples include cigarette smoke (smokers often cannot smell their own smoke) and perfumes and/or colognes, which often smell very strong when first applied and then fade away a few seconds later. The source of the odor may remain, but our ability to detect the odor fatigues with time.

Our perception of taste comes partly through our ability to smell, so it is also affected by this fatigue phenomenon. When the flavor of herbs or spices dominates rather than enhances the flavors of food (because a chef has used a heavy hand with spices or repeats the same spices on multiple menu items), our ability to recognize the odors, and therefore the taste, of the food fatigues with every bite. Use of multiple flavorings in every dish and throughout the meal keeps the olfactory neurons stimulated, the sense of taste heightened, and customer satisfaction intact.

When people suffer from colds or any other nasal infection or obstruction, the olfactory neurons lose the ability to send accurate messages to the brain. (This is why the sense of taste is diminished in such circumstances.) Unfortunately, the direct exposure of the olfactory neurons to external elements makes them susceptible to damage and destruction. Olfactory neurons are not easily regenerated, so damage caused by heavy smoking, chemical abuse, and aging can be permanent.

Complete loss of smell is known as anosmia. Partial anosmia affects people whose olfactory center is damaged or who have some temporary malady that interferes with the reception and transmission of smell impulses. People with partial or total anosmia, including the elderly, need special encouragement to eat balanced meals. They may eat primarily fatty and high-sodium foods in an attempt to experience the sensations of taste (as noted previously, too much of those foods can cause serious health problems). Continued disinterest in eating will cause malnutrition, sickness, and possibly death.

People with partial anosmia should eat foods that stimulate the basic taste sensations assimilated in the mouth rather than in the nose. For example, foods flavored with sour, salty, bitter, sweet, or peppery ingredients. In this way, they can still sense "taste" in their food while bypassing the dependence on the olfactory for smell stimuli.

For those of us without a diminished sense of smell, even before we put food into our mouths, we can usually judge by its smell whether we'll like to eat it. Foods served hot give off a greater effervescence of odors than foods served warm or cold. The smells of hot foods are carried to the nose even as the fork or spoon approaches the mouth. Cold foods must first be placed in the mouth for taste to occur. As they are warmed by our body temperature, their smells are released and carried to the nasal cavity through the pharynx, a passage at the back of the throat.

Tastes are a combination of flavors, smells, and the customs we are used to. Cooks should learn to build tastes by choosing flavors and smells that complement each other and do not overpower the basic food flavors. Food should taste like food, not like spices, fat, or wine.

A good analogy can be drawn between the building of taste and the creation of music. Musical notes, by themselves, do not generally invoke great emotion; nor do single flavors create real satisfaction. When notes are combined in certain ways to form chords, they begin to form music. Flavors combined can create great tastes just as magically.

Paul Prudhomme, the famous Louisiana chef and inventor of the blackened redfish process (well-seasoned redfish fillets are seared in a smoking hot iron skillet to intensify flavor while creating a blackened crust), has great admiration for categories of flavors and adds a simple procedure to many of his recipes to ensure the continuation of certain categories of flavors throughout the cooking process. He may begin a dish with the flavors of certain herbs, flavoring vegetables, wines, or brandies, and then he will add more of these flavors about halfway through the cooking process. At the end, just before plating, he may add the same key flavoring elements a third time to the same dish. The flavors of the dominating ingredients thus evolve along with the dish itself. The original flavors cook, mellow, and blend with the other ingredients; the second addition of flavors does the same thing but at a different pace; the third addition returns the original taste of the ingredients to the pot at the very end, just before plating, and ties together the beginning, middle, and end.

Flavors can be divided into ten categories: sweet, sour, bitter, salty, savory, peppery, floral, peppermint, pungent, and putrid. Using multiple ingredients from within single categories gives definition and depth to particular flavors or tastes; selecting items from various categories can create dimension in those tastes. Items from single categories can be combined to emphasize a certain taste; items from multiple categories can be combined to create interesting contrasts and pleasant discord:

sweet: sugar, carrots, sweet bell peppers, pimentos, liqueurs, many fruits

sour: lemons, limes, vinegars, wine, rhubarb

bitter: endive, turnips, mustard greens, chicory, dandelions, radichio

salty: table salt, sea salt, oysters, MSG

savory: mushrooms, sage, truffles

pepper: black pepper, white pepper, red pepper, jalapeños, habeñeros

floral: vanilla, anise, fennel, celery, parsley, berries, artichoke

peppermint: basil, oregano, marjoram, spearmint, peppermint

pungent: cloves, allspice, cinnamon, nutmeg, thyme, rosemary, sage

putrid: Limburger cheese, blue cheese, aged meat

Review Questions

1. What are the three main sources that collectively determine taste for humans?

2. What factors help determine traditions in food choices that are hard to break?

3. What are the five basic tastes identified in the mouth by human taste buds? What is the sixth sensation of taste, which is not truly a taste but a physical reaction to an ingredient?

4. If the tongue were divided into five parts, front, top, right, left, and rear, where would each of the basic tastes usually be detected?

5. What happens when someone receives a peppery taste?

6. What is the result when information taken from the olfactory neurons in the nasal cavity is transferred to the olfactory lobes in the front of the brain?

7. Name five of the seven primary odors detected by human olfactory neurons that are represented by food and drink.

8. Why do people with colds and the elderly have difficulty tasting foods?

9. What other factors affect a person's ability to smell and therefore taste foods?

10. What can chefs do to help people who experience partial anosmia?

11. Name eight categories of flavors.

God's natural Sweetners -
- Sweetners -
onions

6

Taste with Herbs and Spices

Herbs and spices have long been the champions of taste and flavors in cuisines around the world. Used since ancient times, they have had a long history of intrigue, suspense, and adventure. Once worth their weight in gold, they are now readily available year-round for the average consumer and cook.

By looking back at the development of the spice trade, we can see how it helped shape the world as we know it today. This retrospective will lead us to a better appreciation of spices and may inspire us to use them more frequently in preparing food.

After completing this chapter, the student will be able to
- state the botanical and culinary definitions of herbs and spices
- discuss a short history of the spice trade and how it has developed over the past 2000 years
- discuss, in brief, the history of herbs and their uses in culinary and medicinal arenas
- describe the role herbs and spices play in the creation of flavors and tastes
- describe various market forms of spices and herbs
- discuss methods of obtaining the most flavor from herbs and spices
- list and describe the most commonly used herbs and spices and their uses in cooking and in the promotion of health

Leaves, needles, flowers, blossoms, seeds, berries, fruits, bark, and roots are items you would not generally attribute much importance to, yet their cultivation and trade has influenced the shape of world history and the flavor of world cuisine. These substances represent a whole spectrum of natural flavorings known as herbs and spices.

The American Heritage Dictionary defines *herb* as follows: "1. A plant that has a fleshy stem as distinguished from the woody tissue of shrubs and trees and that generally dies back at the end of each growing season. 2. Any of various often aromatic plants used especially in medicine or as seasoning."* Spices include all "various aromatic and pungent vegetable substances such as cinnamon or nutmeg, used to flavor foods and beverages."† This definition seems to segregate herbs as a subcategory of spices. The culinary definition may be a little different because of a need to characterize similar ingredients with similar applications. Herbs are the leaves of plants and have the greatest flavor value when fresh, used in chopped or whole form, and added to the cooking preparation at either the beginning or final stages of preparation. Spices are all other vegetable aromatics, including the bark, seeds, and roots of some plants. Spices usually require a drying or curing process to enhance their flavor and are used in whole or ground form. Spices are added early in the cooking procedure to maximize their characteristic flavors.

History of spices

Over the centuries, some varieties of spices have wielded great value and importance. Cassia and cinnamon were once bartered for fine silks and jewelry. Sesame seeds were used to pay ransoms and taxes for ancient kingdoms. Anise, cumin, and marjoram were used in the embalming of ancient Egyptians.

The history of the spice trade is associated with the course of development of world cuisine, cultures, and civilizations. For centuries the issue of sovereign power in Europe and the Middle East was settled by the city, country, or nation that controlled the flow of spices from the Orient to the Mediterranean.

It was often the route of the spice traders, from India and the Orient through the Middle East and into Europe, that determined which ancient cities would last through the centuries and which would perish. Constantinople and Alexan-

---

The American Heritage Dictionary, 2nd college ed. (Boston: Houghton Mifflin, 1985), p. 606.
†Ibid., p. 1176.

dria became great market centers for the collection of precious spices and for their further sale and transport into Europe. Venice, the beautiful Italian canal city, owed much of its development as a major European city and political power to the spice trade. Situated at the head of the Adriatic, Venice's maritime position would lead to its control of all shipping in the Mediterranean Sea, including the shipment of spices from the East to the West. Spices became Venice's most valuable commodity.

The Portuguese quest

The search for a direct sea route to India and China, the land of spices, led the Portuguese south along the western coast of Africa. Their plan was to sail south around the great continent of Africa and then back north to China and India, completely circumventing the land route (and thus the Arabs and Venetians) in the quest for valuable spices.

At the beginning of the fifteenth century, Prince Henry of Portugal was a well-learned man who had a keen interest in maritime adventures, astrology, and cartography (the making of maps). He was also a shrewd ruler who knew that finding a sea route to the land of the spices would secure a dominating position in world trade. Because of their exotic appeal and the difficulty in obtaining them, aromatics were beginning to cost as much as precious metals and jewels.

Prince Henry died in 1460, twenty-seven years before Bartholomew Diaz rounded the Cape of Good Hope and thirty-seven years before Vasco da Gama completed the journey to India with three small ships on May 20, 1498. Prince Henry's dream was finally realized, and Portugal became a major player in the trading of priceless aromatics.

Christopher Columbus

The adventures of the famous Italian captain Christopher Columbus were merely an attempt to beat the Portuguese in discovering a sea route to the lands of spices. Whereas the Portuguese were headed south, Columbus was able to convince King Ferdinand and Queen Isabella of Spain that the quickest route was to the west. He believed that the world was round and that Spain and India were on the same parallel at the top of the sphere.

Columbus had no way of knowing that whole continents stood in the way of any direct route to the west. He even named the natives he found "Indians," thinking he had indeed been successful in winning the race to India.

Columbus didn't find the spice islands he was looking for, but his discovery was to have an even greater impact on world cuisine than anyone could have imagined. Discovery of the Caribbean islands opened the door for new food discoveries that would influence world cuisine forever. Allspice, vanilla, hot and sweet peppers, tomatoes, corn, potatoes, beans, sugar cane, cocoa, and turkeys were soon brought back across the waters for the world to enjoy. Although they might have been poor substitutes for the pepper corns and cinnamon Columbus risked his life for, future generations of chefs and bakers would be forever grateful.

History of herbs

Herbs may not have as romantic and adventurous a history as that of spices, yet their use in cooking dates back to humankind's earliest attempts at cooking. Their availability throughout the world made them more convenient and less expensive to use than spices.

The development of agriculture and herding, nearly twelve thousand years ago, meant that the nomadic search for food became obsolete in most of the world. Growing food from seeds and moving grazing livestock over open fields made food a more reliable resource. Hunting became a less risky business, and hunger was better controlled.

Once food supplies became steady and the fear of hunger subsided, variety and flavor began to play a greater role in cooking and eating. Herbs and spices became regular ingredients in a multitude of recipes from cultures around the globe.

Cooking progressed hand in hand with advancements in metallurgy. When iron could be forged and shaped into long spears for hunting and fighting, people also used such implements for roasting meats and vegetables. These spears could pierce large and small pieces of meat and hold them over fire. This method was far better than placing the foods directly onto burning embers. Foods could be turned repeatedly over the fire without danger to the cook, and the foods would be roasted evenly on all sides.

Further advancements in metallurgy made iron pliable enough that it could be shaped into large round cauldrons. These cauldrons were so large that they could be used to cook soups and stews for a dozen families. It took several men, using pulleys and chains, to move the cauldrons on or off the fire. Stews would cook for days at a time, with meats, vegetables, spices, and water replaced regularly as portions were drawn out. Strong-flavored roots and seeds were rubbed into the flesh of meats or tossed directly into the cooking liquid because their flavor lasted through long cooking times. Fresh herbs, grown locally, were also used but usually at or near the end of the cooking time. Often herbs would be chopped and tossed with the finished product before it was consumed.

Most herbs grew wild and were free for the picking. Many reseeded themselves and grew back in the same locations every year; others were evergreens or grew up from root stocks. As towns began to grow, people found it easy to grow most herbs right in their own flower gardens.

Herbs were easily dried for winter storage. Many of their seeds, such as celery, fennel, dill, and mustard, could also be used for flavor. Herbs were versatile, cheap to use, and easily replenished.

Availability and use of spices and herbs today

Today spices are easily obtained from a variety of sources. Large corporate spice companies take the place of the ancient Arab caravans and Venetian spice merchants. Price, quality, and availability are more consistent today than they have ever been.

Spices are adaptable to many cooking and baking procedures. They are available in whole and ground forms.

Herbs that were only available in certain regions of the world are now available throughout the globe. At the local market, fresh, dried, and ground herbs are now available year-round because of the shrinking global marketplace and modern greenhouse techniques, which assure perfect climate control all year. Chefs want to use fresh herbs in their culinary creations, and this demand has also increased the supply. Fresh herbs contribute the greatest amount of flavor and should be used whenever possible.

Like all living plants, fresh herbs need proper handling. They need moisture and cool air to preserve freshness. Herbs purchased from quality vendors should arrive prewashed and stored in individual plastic bags to help retain their freshness. It is a good idea to rinse the herbs once more before putting them in the refrigerator and to allow some excess water to remain in the bag. Plastic containers work just as well for storage and are better suited for larger quantities. Set the herbs so they stand on their stems, as you would cut flowers, and fill the container partway with water. Cover the herbs loosely to help retain moisture without crushing the leaves. Fresh herbs are now available in sealed, plastic containers. The herbs should remain in such containers until ready for use.

Fresh herbs can be chopped prior to storage. Chop only what is required for the day's use, and keep the chopped herbs in tightly closed containers. Fresh herbs contain a lot of water; place stale bread in the containers with the chopped herbs to absorb some of the moisture released by chopping and to keep the herbs from sticking or matting together.

For the most pronounced tastes, use fresh herbs whenever possible, dry leaf forms next, and ground forms last. Ground herbs and spices loose their flavor quickly and should be avoided. There is no way to know how old an herb is when purchased in dry or ground form. The containers chosen for herb storage should be in line with the amounts of herbs used. For example, if you use basil and oregano often, then large containers are economically feasible, but if you use them only in a few preparations, purchase smaller containers.

Whole and ground spices are also available from all parts of the world. Seed and small berry-type spices can be cracked lightly or ground using a standard pepper mill. To crack spices, place them in a plastic bag or wrap them in a piece of cheese cloth and crush them with a meat tenderizer or with the broad side of a knife. The bag or cheese cloth keeps the cracked pieces from being strewn all over the kitchen. The pepper mill can be used to grind many seed types of spices as well as pepper corns. Pepper mills are particularly good for grinding anise, fennel, mustard, caraway, allspice berries, cardamom, and white and black pepper corns.

The use of herbs and spices depends on personal choice and preference. Traditions that prescribe rosemary for lamb, sage for turkey, nutmeg for spinach, and cinnamon for muffins should be set aside for a more open approach to the versatility of spices in cooking and baking. Creativity comes into play when the chef uses other combinations of herbs and spices for traditional and new preparations of meats, poultry, seafood, vegetables, and baked goods.

Early cultures took full advantage of all the flavors that were at hand to create their food. Apicius, the great Roman culinarian of the first century A.D., had recipes calling for cinnamon and ginger as the main flavors in many meat and fish sauces. Greeks have a national dish, called mousaka, that calls for layered noodles, ground lamb, cream sauce, and cinnamon. The people of India, who live in the land of spices, show no hesitation using mace and nutmeg to flavor rice and curries, or cinnamon and cassia to flavor cabbage and turnips. A study of cookbooks from other countries will give you ideas for using herbs and spices in your own cooking. If you consider it an adventure to use different herbs and spices in cooking and baking, you can make great, exciting food with little difficulty.

Try not to confuse the taste buds by using too many opposing flavors in the same recipe. A recipe that uses rosemary, thyme, tarragon, and sage may produce a dish that is simply too confusing for the human palate to appreciate and may give the impression of bad taste. Most recipes can produce great dishes when combining one or two of the strong-flavored spices and herbs with one or more of the gentler ones. Combining rosemary and thyme with cinnamon and mace could produce excellent results. Using tarragon and sage with fennel and allspice could produce exciting flavors in otherwise plain meat, poultry, or fish dishes.

The use of a sachet should always be considered when using spices or dried herbs to flavor stocks, soups, and sauces. A sachet is a bag used as a type of spice or herb infuser. It can be easily pulled from the stock or sauce and discarded after it has released all its flavor. The bag is usually made from cheese cloth, which is wrapped around the spices and herbs and tied with a piece of butcher's twine. The twine should be long enough to allow the spices to settle well below the level of liquid in the pot and long enough to reach the handle of the pot for tying. Tying the twine to the pot handle allows for easy removal at the end of the cooking time. At the beginning of the cooking process, the sachet is tossed into the pot. It should remain in the pot for 45 minutes to an hour, with the stock or sauce simmering. If the entire cooking process is shorter than 45 minutes, the spices should be fully crushed to release their flavors quickly.

The flavors and smells of herbs and spices

Herbs and spices contribute a wide range of flavors to foods and beverages and can be used singularly and in combinations to create hundreds of complex flavors.

Herbs and spices contain oils, which are primary flavoring agents. These oils can be released either by simmering the herbs and spices in a liquid or frying them in fat. In nutritional cooking, simmering in liquid is preferred. Simmered herbs and spices retain their fresh taste and distribute their flavors throughout the cooking liquid.

Some tastes are merely enhanced through the sense of smell, and others depend on this sense. Herbs and spices, which depend on the properties of smell for their flavor, must be handled properly to ensure that their scents are not released until needed.

Dried herbs and spices should be kept in tightly closed containers and stored in a cool part of the kitchen whenever possible. Exposure to the air weakens their flavors, as does light and heat. Ground or powdered herbs and spices dissipate their scents even more quickly; therefore, it is important to grind your own spices whenever possible and use fresh herbs, which contain their full flavors.

Add herbs and spices at intervals during the cooking process. A good practice is to add herbs and spices at the beginning of the cooking process, again during cooking, and add them at the end of the cooking process to complete the flavor package. Dried herbs and spices may require up to 30 minutes to release their flavors completely, whereas fresh herbs and freshly ground spices need only a few minutes.

Detecting flavors through smell

The art of nutritional cooking is in the utilization of herbs and spices to enhance the natural flavors of foods in which fat and salt have been reduced or eliminated. Nutritional cooking is not a hodgepodge or free-for-all use of spices, but a constructive manipulation of flavors based on experience, knowledge, and creativity.

The experienced chef knows hundreds of flavor combinations that work well together. By copying other successful recipes, or by trying combinations of their own, chefs learn which spices and herbs complement each other and which do not.

In addition to experience and knowledge, creativity plays an important role in the development of exciting tastes. This is the art of cooking.

Herbs and spices can be grouped according to the primary odors that they share. Some are primarily pepperminty in origin, others flowery and more pungent. Although not all herbs and spices fit neatly into these designations, the many that do set a good standard for comparison. Here is a list of the most common herbs and spices grouped by their primary odors:

pepperminty	*flowery*	*pungent*
mint	anise	thyme
basil	fennel	rosemary
marjoram	caraway	bay
parsley	celery seed	cloves
oregano	dill	cinnamon
chervil	saffron	nutmeg
tarragon	juniper	cumin

Use selections within the same groups to build complementary flavors and from different groups to build contrasting flavors.

Take advantage of the importance of smell when trying to create new flavors or new combinations of flavors. Test the flavor of foods, through your olfactory, without actually adding or changing spices. Chefs may be interested in a certain taste but may not be sure how a certain herb or spice might react to other flavors. They'll want to test the result before committing the change to the whole recipe. One way to do so is to hold the herb or spice in question over the product that is being prepared. Smell the aroma from the spice and the product at the same time. The smells will combine in your olfactory to give you a prelude to the actual taste. Next, take a small amount of sauce, liquid, or raw product being cooked and mix in or rub on a small amount of the herb or spice that is being considered. Cook raw samples before proceeding, and then taste the new combinations.

This test is especially important as chefs try to follow nutritional cooking practices, reducing salts and saturated fats by cooking with more herbs and spices. Chefs should be experimenting with nontraditional taste combinations to create new and exciting flavors, and they should test those new flavors before serving them to their guests.

An anthology of the most generally used herbs and spices

Allspice was a relatively new spice to the Europeans who settled America, although it is one of the only spices native to the Americas. Found abundantly in the Caribbean islands, it is the fruit of a tropical evergreen of the myrtle family. Often referred to as the Jamaican pepper, the berries are picked green and allowed to sun dry. This transforms them into a form resembling plump pepper corns, without the hot bite. Allspice gets its common name because of its resemblance in flavor to a blend of other spices, such as cloves, cinnamon, and nutmeg. It can be bought in dried berry form, which is preferable to crushed or ground, and is easily crushed under a rolling pin before being added to a variety of dishes. Allspice is excellent in flavoring meat, poultry, and seafood stews and sauces, especially venison, rabbit, duck, turkey, shrimp, and mussels. Although tradition prefers the use of allspice in pies and puddings, it is also excellent in vegetable dishes, including the family of winter squashes, greens, and root vegetables.

Anise is an old spice known throughout the Mediterranean region. It has been used to flavor everything from alcohol (anisette) to curries. Combined with mace, allspice, ginger, coriander, and cumin, anise adds character to many vegetarian dishes, which are the mainstay of southern Indian cuisine. Anise can be bought as an extract, which is distilled with alcohol, and it is excellent for flavoring cream sauces and puddings. Its seeds can be easily ground and used to flavor many stews and fricassees or left whole as desired. It is excellent in salad marinades in combination with dill and sweet peppers, or just by itself with cucumbers and sour cream.

Basil is one of the Mediterranean's most widely used herbs. It grows easily in most climates, and its seeds are successfully stored for replanting the following growing season. Because of the ease of growing basil in hothouses, it is available fresh year round. Basil is part of the mint family and has a slightly mint taste when first eaten. In dried leaf form that minty taste is almost lost, but basil's characteristic sweet flavor remains. Besides its popular use in Italian tomato sauce and salad dressings, basil is also a good seasoning to use for roasting meats, poultry, and fish. It is an excellent blending herb when used in combination with some of the more powerful-tasting herbs like cumin and tarragon. Fresh basil leaves may also be chopped and mixed with salad greens or marinated eggplant for excitement and character. There are at least four related basils for the modern cook to use: lemon basil, cinnamon basil, red basil, and Israeli basil (lemon and cinnamon because of the related flavors they impart; red basil for its color; and Israeli basil for its hardiness).

Bay, or laurel leaves, as they are sometimes called, come from an evergreen whose cultivation dates back to ancient history. In Greece and Imperial Rome bay leaves were used as a symbol of wisdom and glory; they were often tied into a crown worn by emperors and kings (bay leaves are also a symbol for scholarship; the word *baccalaureate* means "laurel berries"). As a gardening shrub, laurels add a robust aroma to gardens throughout Europe. Bay is well known for its contributions to stews and meat pies. It gained this reputation because of its year-round availability: In the cold winters, when herbs were unavailable and imported spices costly, farmers would merely pick a few bay leaves from their gardens to lend spice to their soups and stews. Along with the game they hunted and the dried beans that were stored for the winter, they could easily make great-tasting meals with the addition of a few bay leaves. Bay has a very strong flavor when fresh, and only a few leaves are needed. To impart its flavor in sautéed dishes, bay leaves can be fried in hot oil and then removed from the dish, leaving behind their aroma.

Caraway is known to most Americans only as the seeds found in rye breads. This is unfortunate because the flavor is an excellent enhancer for many other dishes as well. Germans and Austrians know about the benefits of caraway, and this seed finds its way into many of their dishes. Goulash is a stew with caraway and paprika as the main flavors. Sauerbraten and sauerkraut both complement the taste of caraway. Caraway is an excellent spice for strong-flavored dishes like these and others made with lamb or venison. It is also an excellent accompanying spice with flavors like sesame, sage, or sweet potato.

Cardamom is an underestimated spice today. It is found rarely in some bakery items and sausage recipes, but it is generally forgotten. At one time, however, it was so popular that its rich fragrance was used as the essence in some of the more valuable perfumes and oils of ancient Rome. Cardamom is the second most expensive spice (saffron comes first), because the pods containing the seeds are cut from the plant by hand, for a crop yield of only 250 pounds per acre. It is native to India, although modern sources also include Guatemala. Cardamom comes in seed form and is easily crushed or ground as needed. It is excellent when used in dishes that need a subtle yet distinguishing taste (e.g., rice pilaf or creamed onions), but it can also be used in combination flavors (e.g., curries and meat pies). Cardamom was one of the original curry spices and rightfully has a reputation of being one of the great blending spices.

Cassia is similar in taste to cinnamon yet a little more pungent. It also comes from the bark of an evergreen, and it is harvested and dried in the same way as cinnamon.

Cayenne pepper was one of the "spices" discovered by Christopher Columbus when his ships reached the Caribbean islands. One of the varieties of the genus *capsicum*, cayenne is related to sweet bell peppers, jalapeños, and chilies. Cayenne pepper pods grow three to four inches long, are narrow and taper to a point, and are red. The pods are first dried and then crushed (leaving the whole seeds and similar sized pieces) or ground very fine. Like all spices, in ground form cayenne will eventually lose its potency; however, this fact is not generally known because when freshly ground, cayenne pepper's potency is extreme. Cayenne is also used to produce liquid hot sauces used as flavoring spices for soups and stews.

Celery seed, because of its close resemblance in taste to its mother plant, is used frequently as a spice in various food preparations. It is a small seed that does not have to be crushed or ground to release its flavor. Its concentrated celery flavor adds quick identification to almost any dish it is used in, and it is excellent in cold food preparations and hot food recipes. Celery seed offers a unique blending taste that can smooth out otherwise pungent tastes or enhance some of the most delicate flavors.

Chervil has long been considered one of the essential herbs in French and other Mediterranean cuisines. It shares a place with tarragon and parsley as one of the three *fines herbes* used in many French dishes and soups. In dried form it has almost no taste, just as dried parsley has no distinguishing taste, and therefore it has not gained much popularity in American cooking. Now that it is available in fresh form throughout the world, its popularity is sure to rise. Chervil can be used in meat and vegetable dishes and has a clean and refreshing taste. Its flavors are easily extracted when sautéed in oil or steeped in stock or sauces. It should never be added too early in the cooking process; in fact, it should only be added to the dish or soup just before removing it from the heat source because its delicate flavor dissipates quickly.

Cinnamon has had one of the most romantic and adventurous histories of all the spices. The Arabs, who transported cinnamon from the East into Europe, were determined not to share in the trade of this valuable spice and created unbelievable stories about its collection and transport to scare off anyone even thinking of competing. A story recorded by Herodotus tells of a great bird in the Far East who builds its nest high in the rocky peaks of great mountains out of sticks of cinnamon. According to Herodotus, to collect the spice, traders must climb these peaks and risk their lives. Naturally, stories like these also kept the price of cinnamon very high.

Actually, cinnamon comes from the bark of a laurel-like evergreen found in Ceylon. It was not until the Portuguese captain Vasco da Gama reached India by sea in 1498 that the myths about cinnamon were finally put to rest. Modern traditions dictate that cinnamon can be used only in bakery items. In truth, cinnamon has as much flexibility as any other spice. It is excellent for sautéed potatoes and for June peas, carrots, sweet potatoes, and even brussels sprouts. Cinnamon has long been used in cream sauces for famous dishes like Greek moussaka and in meat pies and stuffing for a turkey, quail, pheasant, and duck. It is also good for seafood stuffing for flounder or for making deviled crab. Cinnamon should be bought and used in stick form whenever possible; the stick can be used to flavor a stock or sauce and then removed and used over again. When the stick form cannot be used, fresh ground cinnamon is adequate. Like any preground spice, cinnamon's potency is lost quickly with age.

Cloves are dried, unopened blossoms of a tall evergreen nearly 30 feet high. The tree's crimson buds are picked before they open and dried on palm leaf mats (in the drying process, the buds turn reddish-brown). Cloves can be purchased either whole (which are easily crushed) or ground (ground cloves are potent when fresh). Cloves, and especially their oil, have been used throughout the centuries as a cure for many ailments. The use of clove oil as a pain reliever is well documented. Clove oil is used in medicinal teas to aid in digestion and to reduce fevers. Cloves are traditionally used to flavor hams and spice cakes. Their distinctive taste, however, could be used to flavor a variety of dishes (e.g., vegetable dishes and savory pies and fillings). Cloves are also one of the great blending spices; they blend well not only with cinnamon, nutmeg, and allspice but with sage, fennel, caraway, anise, and bay leaves.

Coriander has a marked place in history. In the Bible (Exodus, chapter 16, verse 31) there is a description of the life-saving bread called manna, which fell from the sky to help feed the Israelites in the desert: "The bread from heaven tasted of coriander seed and honey." Coriander blends well with the taste of whole grains, which have a similarly nutty taste when roasted. Coriander seeds are small round spheres, light brown, with a thin shell easily ground or crushed with a rolling pin. Coriander is excellent in sausage recipes and savory dishes of all descriptions. Coriander is used in some of the world's best chutneys, and it blends well with most varieties of fish and shellfish.

Cumin has long been recognized as one of the world's most widely used spices. It is native to Egypt (which gives it one of the oldest histories of any spice used in cooking) and is predominant in foods of the Near East and Latin America. It comes in seed and ground form and is the characteristic flavor of chorizo, the famous Spanish sausage. Cumin is the main flavor in two very different spice blends, chili powder and curry powder. Cumin has a fairly dominant flavor that blends well with sage, thyme, garlic, or ginger; it gives exciting flavor to rice, beans, potatoes, vegetables, meat dishes, fish, and poultry. Fresh ground cumin seeds can also be used to flavor biscuits or wafers; cumin lends a certain Mediterranean flair to such foods.

Dill can be used either for its leaves or its seeds, although its seeds are more pungent than its leaves. Dill is not a true perennial, but it will grow back every year from seeds that fall on the ground. Dill is the characteristic flavor of the world-famous dill pickle, and dill seems to do extremely well with other marinated preparations as well. Dill has an intense flavor and should be used with other dominant flavors (e.g., with sour cream and in vinegar dressings).

Fennel, or finocchio, as it is called by the Italians, has a flavor similar to anise yet is a little more delicate. Fennel's flavor blends well in many cooking and baking preparations. Fennel may be used for its leaves (like dill), for its seeds, or as a vegetable. Fennel produces a stalklike plant similar in texture to pascal celery with a slightly rounder bulb at the root. Fennel, as a vegetable, can be braised, simmered, or sautéed; it can also be used as a flavoring vegetable for stews and soups and a variety of other dishes. Fennel is the characteristic flavor in Italian sausage and has gained world popularity for its use in tomato sauces, soups, and stews. It is used to flavor many European-style hearth breads and is a popular ingredient in foccacia and sandwich rolls.

Garlic, which originally comes from Asia, enjoys as intriguing a history as any of the other herbs and spices. Its medicinal properties, though only scientifically evidenced in the twentieth century, have long been associated with warding off evil spirits (in medieval times sickness was perceived as the work of an evil spirit) and with promoting lasting youth. Modern research suggests that garlic can help lower cholesterol and strengthen the immune system, but these findings are still speculative. Garlic is a bulbous plant made of several smaller cloves. It is generally used fresh and is preferred in this form. Because of its popularity, garlic can also be found in several dried forms, from chopped and minced to flakes and powder. The juice from garlic can be processed and used in its liquid form to flavor sauces and stews. Garlic's flavor changes dramatically when roasted or fried, producing a milder and sweeter version, respectively.

Ginger is one the oldest spices used in cooking. Centuries ago, Chinese sailors carried potted ginger on long journeys so they could enjoy its fine flavor and benefit from its medicinal properties. Today ginger is used frequently in Asian and Pacific island cuisine. Ginger has a peppery flavor and gives curry powder its spicy hot characteristic. The fresh ginger root can be easily shredded, chopped, or grated and is available year-round. Ground dried ginger loses most of its characteristics and should be avoided. Ginger is excellent with summer and winter squash, celery, rutabaga, and turnips; it is also good with savory poultry and meat dishes and seafood stews.

Horseradish is a root that is native to Eastern Europe. Today it is grown around the world wherever other root crops are grown. The roots are first washed thoroughly and then ground with their skins (the skins give horseradish its characteristic tang). A small amount of water is added during the grinding process to provide a smooth consistency. Horseradish should be refrigerated to help retain its highly volatile properties. Grinding fresh horseradish releases vapors 10 times more potent than the vapors released from opening a jar of horseradish; these vapors may be too powerful for the average person to bear. Buy fresh ground horseradish from a reputable vendor and you will be guaranteed a consistent product ready for use in your recipes.

Horseradish is used mainly in cold sauces like cocktail, barbecue, and mustard. Because of its potency, it is generally used as a condiment spice.

Juniper is a berry that is widely known for its use in the flavoring of some English gins. Its sweet aromatic taste has been used for many years as an essential ingredient in game stews like venison or rabbit, but juniper can also be used to flavor vegetable dishes like cabbage, broccoli, and onion. Juniper has a strong but sweet taste that can blend well with other characteristic tastes without being lost.

Mace is the aril, or thin skin, around the nut of the nutmeg that is removed and then dried and ground. Its taste, therefore, resembles the nutmeg yet is somewhat milder. Mace is much more versatile than nutmeg because its sweet taste is easily blended with other tastes without overpowering them, as is sometimes the case with nutmeg. Mace is more expensive than nutmeg because it is only a small part of the whole nut, yet its delicate fragrance can enhance the most subtle of flavors. Mace can also be used to stimulate vibrant flavors because its sweet taste lingers in the mouth and in the nostrils.

Marjoram, which is sometimes called sweet oregano, is one of the most popular herbs of the southern Mediterranean region. It grows wild almost everywhere dirt and sun are found and is a hardy perennial. Marjoram is similar in taste to thyme but not as pungent and can therefore blend well with thyme and oregano. Whenever a dish calls for a subtle flavor of fresh herbs, marjoram is an excellent choice.

Mint has a sweet and slightly peppery taste. It, too, is a hardy perennial that renews itself every spring for fresh cuttings. Mint has a strong characteristic flavor that should be used in moderation in cooking. A little mint can enhance the flavor of green peas; too much mint can dominate the delicate flavor of some vegetables. As a replacement for salt in vegetable cooking, a touch of mint gives both sweetness and a peppery spice to many foods.

Mustard is related to the cabbage family and is used for its green, broad leaves, which are high in vitamin A, magnesium, potassium, iron, and fiber, and for its dried pungent seeds. Mustard seeds produce the characteristic spicy taste of prepared mustard. Mustard has been used in cooking for thousands of years. Its leaves can be cooked and served like a vegetable, and its seeds can be ground into a spicy condiment. The ground seeds are mixed with water and allowed to rest for 10 to 15 minutes; the water stimulates enzyme growth, resulting in a hot and volatile flavor. Mustard seeds are very small and can be easily crushed, or they can be used whole to develop their taste through longer cooking processes. In creating recipes, however, it is difficult to judge how much mustard to use because the flavor is not released until late in the cooking process. Recipes using mustard should be tested thoroughly and adjustments made until a satisfactory amount of mustard is identified. Generally, too little mustard is used to give any value to the taste, or too much is used and overpowers the taste.

Nutmeg is the nut, or kernel, of a large fruit that resembles a yellow plum. Nutmeg grows on a large evergreen and is allowed to ripen and dry on the tree. When the fruits are dry they split open, revealing a bright red aril, the mace, with the nutmeg in the center. Nutmeg has a strong characteristic taste that can easily overpower other more subtle tastes. A few specks of nutmeg can beautifully enhance the flavor of greens and potatoes, whereas a half teaspoon of nutmeg can overwhelm other flavors. Nutmeg is excellent when used with some of the stronger flavors like venison, lamb, sweet potatoes, and cabbage, but in small amounts nutmeg can be used in almost all preparations. Nutmeg blends extremely well with cinnamon, mace, and allspice (an American spice blend commonly referred to as pumpkin pie spice) and can be used for other fruit, squash, or potato pies.

Oregano, commonly referred to as the "pizza pie spice," is related to marjoram yet has a much more pungent flavor. Oregano is a perennial that grows wild throughout the southern Mediterranean, and it has been used in all types of recipes from meat stews and pies to fish soups and shellfish chowders. Oregano's potency holds up well when dried; however, fresh leaves are preferred.

Paprika is the dried ground flesh of a red capsicum pepper called *capsicum annum.* Until the nineteenth century, paprika was always hot, and then Hungarian spice millers developed a process to remove the seeds and hot membrane inside. Paprika takes its name from a Hungarian word meaning "Turkish pepper." Although Christopher Columbus was the first to bring paprika peppers back to Spain, paprika's full introduction as a dried spice did not come until much later. Today there are both Spanish and Hungarian paprikas. The Spanish variety is less pungent. Paprika is one of the main flavoring ingredients in Hungarian goulash and is often used in spice mixes like chili powder, Old Bay, and Caribbean jerk.

Parsley has been underrated as an herb and overrated as a garnish. Because of its ease in growing, parsley is available fresh year-round. It has a sweet slightly minty taste when eaten fresh, but it loses its flavor quickly when dried. Fresh chopped parsley can be stored for several days by following this simple procedure: Place the chopped parsley in a cheese cloth bag and rinse it thoroughly with cold water. Then, using the bag, squeeze the parsley until no more water comes out. Remove the parsley from the cheese cloth and place it in a closed container with a few pieces of stale bread. The bread will help remove all the excess moisture and keep the parsley in a semidried state. Parsley is one of the better edible garnishes. When eaten fresh, it acts like a breath freshener and leaves the palate clean and fresh.

Pepper has long been one of the most prized of all the world's spices. It adds excitement to almost every dish and is identifiable in any combination. Green, white, and black pepper corns are all the same berry. Green pepper corns are picked green, cured in brine, or freeze dried. Black pepper corns are picked green and dried in the sun, which turns their outer skin black. White pepper corns are ripened on the tree and have a slightly crimson color. Their outer skin is removed, leaving behind the white pepper corn.

Black pepper corns are the most pungent and green the least pungent. Black and white pepper corns are usually cracked with the flat blade of a knife or ground in a pepper mill for the most flavor. Because of the prevalence of pepper in recipes, the practice of cracking or grinding your own pepper may be too cumbersome. In this case it is better to buy cracked or restaurant-grind (course) pepper corns for a rich peppery taste. Fine ground pepper should be avoided unless a recipe specifically calls for its use. Ground white pepper is usually used to season white or blonde sauces because black pepper will leave behind small specks in the sauces. Red pepper should not be confused with the other peppers. Red pepper is of the *capsicum* family called cayenne and is related to chili peppers and bell peppers.

Peppercress has bright, light green leaves with parsleylike foliage. Its peppery flavor gives it its characteristic name. It can be used in whole leaf form as a salad green, or it can be chopped and used as an herb.

Rosemary is most popular in the eastern Mediterranean. Its leaves come from an evergreen that grows on the rocky coasts of Italy, Greece, and Turkey. Rosemary has a distinct flavor that is excellent in any number of savory dishes. Fresh rosemary is available year round because it comes from an evergreen. The fresh leaves can be chopped finely and left in the preparation; if the dried form is used the leaves are tough and should be removed from the dish before serving. A sachet may be needed to remove the leaves easily when the cooking is complete.

Saffron is the dried stigmas from the flower of the saffron crocus, which grows throughout the Mediterranean region. The tiny stigmas must be picked by hand. An estimated 750,000 plants are needed for 1 pound of saffron, so the price of this flavorful spice has always been extremely high. Saffron has a flavor that is worth the price. It is one of the primary spices used in the world-famous French seafood stew called bouillabaisse, and it is used to flavor many Spanish dishes, like paella. The beauty of saffron is that only a small amount is needed to give a recipe a unique signature taste.

Sage is another of those spices for which, in America, tradition has dictated only a few culinary applications (e.g., turkey with sage dressing, country breakfast sausages). In other areas of the world, sage is used most for its medicinal properties rather than for cooking. The people of the Mediterranean believe that a tea made from the leaves of fresh sage can relieve almost every kind of digestive or intestinal problem. Sage has a very distinctive taste, which makes it more versatile than other delicately flavored herbs and spices. Its flavor can enhance stews, pies, stuffings, and sausages. Sage is also good on its own as a flavoring for potato dishes, corn, carrots, celery, turnips, and vegetable greens. Purple sage is also available; its taste is the same as regular sage.

Savory is an herb whose taste most closely resembles that of thyme, yet it is not as pungent. Savory can be used in a variety of savory dishes or as the primary seasoning for beans, peas, rice, leeks, and potatoes.

Sesame is a spice that has lost its allure over the centuries. At one time in history, sesame was so favored that it was believed to possess supernatural powers. The Arabian prince Ali Baba, in searching for a city's hidden treasure, commanded the secret passage door to open by chanting the words, "Open sesame." Sesame seeds contain 60% oil. This extracted oil was once used to light lamps and has been used in Asian cooking for thousands of years. Today, a common use for the toasted seeds is to flavor and garnish hamburger buns and other breads. Sesame deserves a more vibrant place among the world's seasonings: Its flavor is unique, especially when roasted before use. Sesame can be used to highlight the flavors of any stuffing or breading or to flavor salad dressings and marinades. Sesame oil can be used alone or as part of other frying mediums in many sautéed dishes. Sesame oil is great in oriental stir fries, where it is commonly used, and also in sautéed lamb, venison, chicken, and veal dishes.

Tarragon has earned a high place among the world's seasonings for its unique taste and versatility. Tarragon is not as easily grown as some of the other herbs, yet the demand for this herb has created a world market for its fresh leaves as well as for tarragon leaves preserved in brine. Dried tarragon should be avoided because it tends to have a very "grassy" taste. Tarragon gained world recognition for its use in béarnaise sauces and in cream sauces for poached fish and shellfish. A simple dish of a toasted English muffin with Gruyère cheese and crab meat becomes an excellent luncheon item or appetizer when topped with fresh béarnaise sauce. Tarragon oil and vinegar are used commonly in salad making and in vegetable and meat marinades.

Thyme is a popular spice. Not only does it provide good-character tastes by itself, as in Cajun jambalaya, but it is excellent in blending with other spices. Thyme has small leaves that dry well, but the dried herb has a more pronounced flavor than fresh thyme and can overpower delicate tastes. Fresh thyme has a distinctive flavor, yet it enhances other flavors rather than hiding them. Thyme can be used in almost any type of dish, including as a flavoring in biscuits, rolls, and muffins. Lemon thyme has just a hint of lemon flavor. Israeli thyme is a little more pungent with slightly larger leaves.

Turmeric is a spice with little flavor of its own and is generally used as a coloring spice in curries, soups, and rice dishes. Turmeric is sometimes used in place of saffron in paella and other dishes because of its low cost; however, the taste is sacrificed.

Vanilla is not usually thought of as a spice, yet it fits both the botanical and culinary definition of spices. Vanilla is the pod of a climbing orchid grown in tropical America. The pod is dried slowly in the sun, on top of palm leaves, and turned many times during the drying process. Vanilla is most readily available as an extract, which has been distilled with alcohol, yet its dried pods are superior. The pods can be infused for their flavor in stocks or sauces and then rinsed off and stored for later use. One single vanilla bean can last through several applications. Tradition dictates that vanilla is used primarily in dessert applications. Its versatility is much greater than that, however. Vanilla is great with fish and seafood, chowders, and savory meat dishes; its slight sweetness can enhance an otherwise unexciting flavor. Only a small amount of vanilla is needed to turn the taste completely around to one that is unique and pleasant.

Wasabi is an Asian spice that is gaining in popularity in Western cuisine. It is the root of *wasabia japonica* and is ground into either a dry powder or a wet paste. The character flavor of wasabi resembles a combination of mustard and horseradish. Wasabi can be found in most Asian food stores and is available from specialty food vendors.

Review Questions

1. How is the accepted culinary definition of herbs and spices different from the dictionary version?

2. What influence did the spice trade have on the development of nations and capital cities?

3. Which sea route had the Portuguese, in their quest for spices, decided would be the fastest way to India and the Orient?

4. On May 20, 1498, Vasco da Gama made what historical discovery?

5. Why was Christopher Columbus successful in convincing the Spanish royalty to try a sea route to the west?

6. Why were herbs and other aromatic leaves a common ingredient in ancient cooking styles?

7. What development in cooking equipment created a great demand for the use of herbs, spices, and other strong-flavored vegetables?

8. What are the primary market forms of herbs and spices?

9. What is a sachet, and what is it used for?

10. Why might a chef add spices and herbs more than once to a single recipe?

11. How do you balance the flavors of herbs and spices with the natural flavors of foods?

Natural Flavorings

In addition to herbs and spices for flavoring foods, cooks use an array of other highly flavorful foods to heighten tastes. These include flavoring vegetables, oils, and vinegars. Accomplished cooks use these flavoring ingredients as freely as they use spices and herbs. When used correctly, such ingredients add taste, color, and, in some cases, texture to the finished product. The ready availability of these foods means that knowledgeable cooks worldwide can fine-tune tastes and thus increase dining pleasure.

After completing this chapter, the student will be able to

■ identify the most commonly used flavoring vegetables and their flavor contributions

■ describe the effect of national trade associations, innovative chefs, and popular TV cooking shows on the American consumer

■ use flavoring ingredients to enhance the natural flavors of a dish

■ list and describe cooking techniques designed to manipulate the natural flavors of foods

■ list and describe commonly available capsicum peppers

■ list and describe commonly available cultivated and wild mushrooms

■ discuss the use of vegetable stocks in low-fat recipes and vegetarian cooking

■ describe ways of using flavored vinegars, oils, and fats to flavor foods while maintaining nutritional standards

Along with herbs and spices, many natural ingredients are used to enhance the flavor of food: bulb and root vegetables, including garlic and ginger; flavored oils; vinegars; and fruit juices. These natural flavorings contribute distinctive flavors, textures, and nutrients to an assortment of hot and cold foods.

It may seem confusing at first to talk about carrots, celery, and onions in the same reference as basil, oregano, and marjoram. The former are not herbs, but they have distinctive flavors, colors, and textures that can enhance the flavor and appearance of many culinary applications.

It takes time to learn and appreciate the versatility of natural flavoring ingredients and the contributions they can make to many hot and cold dishes. Knowing what, when, and how to use them to create great-tasting foods will come with experience and study. Today's chefs are not limited to regional ingredients and can choose from a world of flavors and textures. Ginger, once only available dried or in powdered form, is now available fresh year round in most common grocery stores. Jalapeños no longer have to be bought in pickled form, and avocados have become a household item.

The general public is becoming increasingly aware of the variety of food ingredients available in American markets. Publicity from chefs' associations like the American Culinary Federation and the World Association of Cooks Societies; the popularity of innovative chefs across the United States; and television cooking shows, which have become one of America's passions, have all contributed to this increase in the general public's knowledge. Americans are willing to experiment with new foods in their own homes. They see TV chefs using innovative ingredients, and they can taste the great results by visiting restaurants and bakeries that keep up with culinary trends.

American consumers soon find out that there is more to mushrooms than the common white mushroom *agaricus* and more to onions than Spanish and Vidalia. Grocery store managers are eager to please, and they set aside entire sections of their produce counters to new and exotic foods. They take previously unheard of portabella, crimini, and enoki mushrooms; celeriac; leeks; and ginger and mix them right in with white button mushrooms, spring onions, lettuce, and tomatoes.

Chefs who learn about these new foods and how to use them in cooking and baking help to raise consumer awareness. They redevelop traditional recipes and create new ones.

Commercial vendors have observed this trend and are trying to do their best to keep restaurants stocked with seasonal local produce, exotic vegetables, fresh herbs, and other natural flavorings. If they don't carry something that a chef wants to use, they can get it with little trouble.

Cooks who take the time to learn their craft well learn that vegetables and other natural flavoring foods are as much tools of the trade as they are food for the table. Learning about these specific tools requires study, experimentation, and, most important, a willingness to put aside the perception that traditional foods restrict creativity. Creativity, in fact, is built up from traditions and culinary foundations.

Experience tells cooks what combination of foods, flavoring vegetables, and seasonings seems to work best in many traditional cooking procedures. Chefs come to understand that low-fat sour cream can transform a basic brown sauce into a sauce fit for stroganoff, and that celery and onion can turn stale bread into turkey stuffing. They imagine what dried plums can do for duck sauce or raisins and almonds for rice pilaf, and they experiment.

Adventure, for the sake of good taste, is what gives cooks the courage to use their knowledge and their appreciation for fine foods to look beyond the recipe and beyond the single ingredient in their quest to satisfy an educated palate and to stimulate creativity in the kitchen. The art of nutritional cooking uses natural flavors and natural ingredients, in low-fat and controlled-salt preparations, to provide healthy foods. It incorporates a thorough knowledge of discriminating and complementary flavors from natural food sources with the use of proper cooking techniques in the creation of great-tasting foods—nutritional foods balanced by nature.

A trained and knowledgeable hand that uses the natural flavors in foods to overcome shortfalls in flavor associated with nutritional, low-fat foods can create as exciting a dish as any traditionally cooked preparation.

Flavoring vegetables

Chefs must keep in mind the role of the natural flavors of foods when creating recipes: to enhance rather than disguise taste. Green beans should taste like green beans, and steak should taste like steak. Following the same tasting principles discussed earlier, chefs should choose flavor combinations using vegetables and other natural flavorings that will contribute flavors at multiple levels of taste.

Dishes can be sweetened without the addition of sugar. Using any one or a combination of the following vegetables will contribute sweetness without sugar, honey, or molasses:

caramelized onions	pears
Vidalia onions	almonds
carrots	hazelnuts
parsnips	macadamia nuts
vine-ripe tomatoes	fennel
celery	sweet bell peppers
yellow turnips (rutabagas)	sweet banana peppers
apples	pimentos
sweet berries like strawberries, blueberries, and raspberries	pineapple

There are many bitter-tasting foods and ingredients to choose from, ranging in flavor from mild to medium to strong. Whether you are using a bitter taste to balance other flavors (as in adding turnips to potatoes for creamed potatoes) or to stand on its own (as in braised Belgian endive), bitter foods play an important part in world cuisine.

Some of the more common bitter-flavored foods follow:

endive	dandelion
Belgium endive	turnip
radichio	turnip greens
mustard greens	kale
collard greens	escarole
watercress	

Sour is the easiest taste sensation to produce in cooking because of the pronounced flavors of its host sources. Some of the common sour foods are the following:

lemon	rhubarb
lime	vinegar
white grapefruit	sour wine
sour cherries	sour cream*
plain yogurt	

A peppery taste is easily accomplished with the use of any one of a number of hot capsicum peppers. Remember that the seeds of any hot pepper can contain as much as four hundred times the amount of spiciness as the pod itself. Therefore, if you want a slight peppery taste, use the pod or part of the pods only; if you want more heat, use part or all of the seeds and seed membranes as well as the pods. Here are some common examples of peppers:

jalapeños	anchos
cayenne	habañero
relleño	serraño

The taste of savory, as defined by umami, has not yet been well defined. Scientists worldwide are trying to isolate flavors attributed particularly to this sense. Mushrooms, truffles, sage, and many wildflowers may make the list one day.

Vegetable mirepoix

Vegetable flavors play a critical role in the production of many restaurant dishes. Their flavors contribute a vast array of tastes, vitamins, and minerals when used to season food. They contribute to sauces, stews, soups, and roasts.

A mirepoix of vegetables is a selection of rough-cut vegetables used primarily as a flavoring tool. A commonly used collection of vegetables would include one member of the onion family, from Spanish onions to leeks, celery, carrots, and turnips. Chefs may also use fennel, parsnips, ginger, or garlic for a variety of recipes, resulting in distinctive flavor combinations unique to each dish.

---

*Low-fat sour creams are available with as little as 2% fat, and no-fat sour creams contain 0% fat.

Chefs use a mirepoix of vegetables when making stocks, soups, or sauces. A vegetable mirepoix is also used to lift large pieces of meat or poultry off the bottom of a roasting pan while cooking; these vegetables will be used later to make a sauce for the finished item.

The flavors of the vegetables, which are layered on the bottom of the pan, are extracted slowly over a long and slow cooking process into the liquid of stocks or into the pan drippings of roasting meats and poultry. The vegetables are usually discarded at the end of the process because most of the flavor, texture, and nutrients have been cooked out. The strained stocks hold the blended taste of the vegetables plus the vitamins and minerals that were extracted from them. The vegetables are sometimes puréed into a fine-consistency sauce or soup, thus contributing all the body and fiber of the vegetables to the final product.

For white stocks or sauces, the mirepoix would not include carrots or yellow turnips because the carotene color pigments would bleach out when cooked. White stocks could include the center stalks of celery (a cream-colored green) or celeriac (a white-fleshed root whose taste resembles pascal celery), onions, and white turnips. The amount of onion would remain the same, whereas the amount of turnips would likely increase to replace the flavors of the missing carrots.

In making brown stocks, the mirepoix is usually browned along with the bones so that the natural sugars in the vegetables caramelize, thus adding more color and sweet flavor to the final product. In making white or neutral stocks, the fresh-cut vegetables are simply added to the bones.

Sweating versus browning

Two variations in the taste of cooked flavoring vegetables can be easily achieved through varying the cooking process. These variations are what chefs refer to as browned versus sweated vegetables. Vegetables that are cooked uncovered in hot oil, allowing the cooked moisture to escape through evaporation, will brown as their natural sugars caramelize as the fat approaches a cooking temperature of 310°F. These vegetables will add color and a slightly sweet taste to the final product. Vegetables that are cooked in a covered pan will not brown as quickly because the evaporated liquids are trapped in the pan during the cooking process. This moisture, which condenses on the lid of the pan and falls back down onto the vegetables and the cooking medium (thus the descriptive term *sweating*), inhibits the coloring process because the moisture makes it difficult for the fat to approach the high temperature needed for browning. Sweated vegetables will have the most natural taste.

Both browned and sweated vegetables have their place in culinary preparations depending on the desired taste of the end product. Some recipes may even use both to deepen the taste sensation. A recipe for French onion soup, for example, may have the chef start out with a portion of the onions browned in hot fat for color and flavor. Another portion of onions is added but not browned just before adding the flavored stock. This combination of browned and sweated onions in the same preparation gives a unique depth of flavor not possible using only one of the vegetable preparations.

The onion family

There are many varieties of onions that chefs can use as seasoning vegetables in their recipes: the round bulb types, including Spanish onions (yellow), white onions, red Bermuda onions, shallots, and pearl onions; and the elongated bulb varieties, including green onions, leeks, and chives. Garlic is also a member of the onion family but is treated more like an herb or spice than a vegetable because of its high concentration of flavor.

Onions have varying amounts of cysteine derivates. Cysteine is a sulfur-laden amino acid responsible for onions' distinctive tastes. Cysteine compounds are stored in the cells of the plant in a relatively stable state until those cells are broken through the cutting or chopping process. The end result is a mixture of ammonia, pyruvic acid, and a third compound that is later broken down into diallyl disulfide, the precursor of the smell of garlic.

The sharp and biting taste of onions and garlic is most prevalent in the raw, chopped state and is lost slowly during the cooking process. A milder taste is achieved if these vegetables are used in whole or large cut form. A sweetened lighter taste can be developed through a dry cooking process (sautéed, pan fried, grilled, or roasted), which helps caramelize the natural sugars of the onion and creates a sweeter and more delicate onion flavor.

These three distinguishable taste variations—sharp and biting, mild, and sweet—help chefs create versatility in their cooking and baking using only onions and garlic. An example is the production of many of the small sauces (derivatives of the five basic or mother sauces). In making stocks, large pieces of onions are used for the blending quality of their characteristic taste, but for flavor excitement finely chopped shallots are often used in the final preparation of sauces. The taste of the cooked onion in the stock, which has blended with the other vegetables, and the sharp, biting taste of the shallots in the final cooking step contribute relative yet distinctive flavors to the final sauce.

Within each variety of onion there exists a wide range of flavors and smells depending on where the onions were grown and how long it has been since they were harvested. Each type of onion has a distinctive flavor and may not be interchangeable in all recipes. The Spanish onion usually has the strongest onion flavor (even this varies throughout the year, depending on storage time and geographic growing location) and the spring onion the slightest. White onions, including the pearl onion, the Vidalia onion (from Vidalia, Georgia), and Bermuda onions, lean toward a sweeter taste even when raw and caramelize extremely well.

Some chefs have been experimenting with a variety of onion types in the same recipe. Three-onion quiche and veal sauté with three-onion soubise (cream sauce highlighted with onion essence) are two examples. Combinations of related yet distinct flavor ingredients add depth to flavors.

The following are the most popular onion varieties:

Bermuda onion: A sweet-flavored variety of a bulbing onion that comes both in white and burgundy colors. Used primarily in salads and sandwich preparations.

Garlic: Related to the onion, garlic is composed of several individual bulbs, called cloves, each protected by a thin dried leaf base with a thick fleshy body, which contains the bud for the next year's growth. This collection of tiny bulbs is itself referred to as a bulb. *Elephant garlic* gets its name from the enormous size of its cloves and subsequently its collective bulb. Each bulb can grow as large as 1 pound and contain five to seven huge cloves. Elephant garlic is much milder than its smaller brother. The flavor of garlic, like onion, changes slightly depending on the geography in which it is grown. Southern and western varieties tend to be spicier than northern or eastern crops.

Green onions: Also called scallions, spring onions, bunching onions, and multipliers, these are easily identified by their slender, straight leaf bases, which never form a true bulb, and green tops. Both the white and the tender portions of the green tops are used in cooking. Green onions are primarily used in salads for their subtle sweet flavor and crisp texture; they are popular in Pacific rim and Asian styles of cooking.

Leek: The largest of the nonbulbing onion, leeks look like oversized green onions and are the sweetest of all members of the onion family. The white parts are very tender. The green tops add flavor to vegetable stocks.

Pearl onion: A very small white-skin and white-fleshed onion with a mild flavor, pearl onions are ideal for stews, for roast meat accompaniments, and for pickling.

Shallot: A small reddish-brown-skinned onion with pinkish-white, sweet flesh. Sweeter than scallions, shallots hold up well in cooking applications and are used to flavor many sauces and sautéed preparations.

Spanish onion: Another type of bulbing onion with a pale, straw-colored outer skin and white flesh. Spanish onions are somewhere in between Bermudas and regular yellow onions with regard to flavor.

Vidalia onion: This onion variety is the namesake of Vidalia, Georgia, where this variety of the yellow onion was originally grown. Vidalias are reputed to be the sweetest bulbing onion in the world.

Yellow onion: This is the most powerful-tasting onion. It has yellowish-brown skin and slightly off-white flesh. The Texas onion is an extra large yellow onion.

Flavoring stalk, root, and tuber vegetables

Stalk, root, and tuber vegetables contribute flavor to many culinary applications, both hot and cold.

Most of these vegetables are served as individual accompaniments to meals, and they make excellent vegetable choices. The art of nutritional cooking examines their flavors and textures more closely and uses them to replace flavors lost by reducing or eliminating fats and sodium.

The following are the most popular stalk, root, and tuber vegetables. These can be used individually or as flavor and texture additives to recipes:

Carrot: Originally red, purple, and even black carrots were common table food; the familiar orange variety, rich in carotene, was developed in Holland in the seventeenth century. Brought to the United States via the colonists, the carrot became one of America's most popular vegetables. Carrots are eaten raw and cooked and are used in multiple recipes, including salads, relishes, soups, and desserts.

Celeriac: A relative of the popular stalk vegetable celery, celeriac shares celery's distinctive flavor yet is more concentrated, with a slight hint of parsley. Although its common name is celery root, celeriac is not a root but rather a mass of swollen stalks that grow below the ground and take the form and texture of a bulbous root. Celeriac is generally shredded and eaten raw in salads and slaws, but it is just as versatile in soups and stuffing and as a vegetable accompaniment.

Celery: A member of the carrot family, celery is grown for its fleshy leaf stalks, which are used in great variety of culinary applications. Used primarily as a flavoring vegetable in soups, stews, and salads, celery is also regularly found raw on salad bars and relish trays. Celery has a cool, sweet, crispy taste and texture. The outer stalks contain stringy fibers that should be removed if the vegetable is intended for the table, either cooked or raw. These strings can be easily removed using a vegetable parer.

Daikon: Also called Oriental radish, this long, cylindrical-shaped, white version of the radish has a spicy, mustardlike flavor. A relative of mustard, the Daikon radish can grow as large as 50 pounds, but it is generally harvested in sizes that range from a half pound to 2 pounds.

Fennel (finocchio): Adored by the Italians for its sweet, subtle flavor, this plant can be utilized to flavor food. Its leaves, like dill, are fragrant; its seeds, like anise, are sweet; and its fleshy stalks, like celery, can be used to flavor other dishes or as a vegetable in their own right.

Horseradish: A member of the mustard family, this rooted plant is more often used as a condiment spice rather than as a vegetable. Horseradish can be purchased in grated form or you can grate your own, but beware of its effervescent aroma, which may sting and even burn your eyes and nose. Horseradish is also shaved into very thin strips or slices and served to accompany varieties of roasted meats and other highly flavored foods.

Jerusalem artichoke: Actually not an artichoke but a member of the sunflower family, the Jerusalem artichoke was *not* originally cultivated or sold in Jerusalem but is a native of North America. Therefore, its name can be misleading. A tuber of a flowering plant with bright yellow blossoms, the Jerusalem artichoke looks much like an oversized, pale-colored ginger root, with smooth skin and lumpy bulbous growths. The flavor is said to resemble artichoke hearts and salsify, and its texture is much like the water chestnut.

Kohlrabi: Like celeriac, kohlrabi is actually a collective mass of swollen stems rather than a root, but it is treated in much the same way as other root vegetables. Kohlrabi has both the wild turnip and wild cabbage as its ancestors and has a flavor reminiscent of both. The swollen stem mass that makes up the bulb and the greens are used in culinary applications.

Parsnip: A member of the carrot family, parsnip has a creamy white color and distinctively sweet flavor, especially when harvested after the first frost. Parsnips can be served baked, braised, simmered, fried, or raw. They are a versatile vegetable usually associated with the cuisines of cold-climate countries (e.g., Germany, Russia, Poland, and Canada).

Radish: A member of the cabbage family, radishes come in many varieties: pink and red, white and black, round and long, small and large (some are as small as marbles and others as large as grapefruits). The flavor of radishes also varies, although the flavor is always on the spicy side; black radishes, a common vegetable for Russians and Poles, may be as spicy as horseradish and are treated in the same way.

Peppers for flavor

The family of capsicum peppers includes sweet bell peppers, pimentos, and the hot varieties like the jalapeño and cayenne. The range of temperature from sweet and mild to extremely hot determines the particular fruit's culinary applications.

The sweet and mild varieties, like bell peppers, pimentos, and sweet banana peppers, can be used in a variety of culinary applications to provide flavor, texture, and color to the final dish. They also add a touch of sweetness that can balance acidic, bitter, or naturally salty foods. Red, yellow, purple, and green sweet peppers are now available year round.

Hot capsicum peppers are used for their spiciness and distinctive flavors. The amount of spiciness can be controlled by removing part or all of the internal seeds and seed membrane. As mentioned previously, the seeds and membrane can be as much as four hundred times as hot as the peppers themselves.

The following are the most common peppers from the capsicum family:

Anaheim: A mild green chili pepper that grows to 8 inches in length; used in chili relleños (a stuffed pepper identified with Mexican cuisine).

Ancho: Called *poblano* when fresh, *ancho* when dried; heart shaped and slightly milder heat than the jalapeño.

Banana: A sweet chili pepper; gets its name from its long tapered shape and bright yellow color; may turn green and then red when fully ripe.

Bell: Named for its shape, this sweet pepper comes in colors ranging from green to yellow, red, and black (actually dark purple); color does not affect flavor or spiciness.

Cayenne: A fiery red slender pepper that grows 5 to 8 inches long; dried cayenne is commonly called red pepper.

Cherry: A mildly hot green pepper that turns red when fully ripe; gets its name from its resemblance to the fruit with the same name.

Habañero: One of the hottest peppers in the world, this shriveled bell-shaped fruit turns fiery orange/yellow when fully ripe.

Hungarian wax: A spicy yellow pepper that grows 6 inches long and turns red when mature.

Jalapeño: A spicy pepper that grows 3 to 4 inches long and is usually harvested green yet turns red when fully ripe.

Pimento: A heart-shaped chili pepper ranging in spiciness from sweet to mildly hot; fruits turn from olive green to scarlet red when ripe.

Relleño: Commonly called green chili and most widely used in Mexican and Southwest American cuisine; a mildly hot chili.

Serraño: Slender 1- to 2-inch-long fruits fiery hot in flavor.

Mushrooms for flavor

Mushrooms are a separate class of vegetables. They represent a class of edible fungi; fungi are one of the most simple life forms found on earth today.

Mushrooms are extremely flavorful and find their way into many cold and hot culinary dishes. Mushrooms are served raw or cooked, but the advantage of cooking mushrooms is that the full flavor of the mushroom can be passed on to the accompanying ingredients of the dish.

The mushroom is the one class of vegetable that does not lend itself to genetic alteration. The same mushrooms available today were gathered and eaten thousands of years ago by our ancestors. There are over a quarter million mushroom varieties, but only about thirty thousand that are edible and only a few dozen that have been successfully cultivated. Poisonous mushrooms range from slightly poisonous, to hallucinogenic, to deadly.

Picking wild mushrooms is a science practiced in most of the ancient world: Europe, Asia, and the Far East. It is extremely dangerous for the novice to pick and eat wild mushrooms. If you are determined to pick wild mushrooms, it is better to learn a few varieties that are easily recognizable and only harvest them wild. Some poisonous mushrooms look like edible varieties when immature, and there are *no* simple rules for distinguishing delicious from deadly.

Here are some of the most common varieties of mushrooms found in many neighborhood grocery stores in raw and dried forms and readily available from any good produce company:

Agaricus: Also known as the common white mushroom, agaricus is the most familiar mushroom in the United States today because it grows very well in controlled environments. Agaricus are gilled mushrooms with a mild flavor and are suitable raw in salads or lightly cooked. Larger agaricus caps are sometimes stuffed and baked. Agaricus mushrooms are harvested with caps 1 to 4 inches in diameter.

Crimini: Similar to the common white mushroom except with a brown cap and stem; stronger flavor than the common white mushroom.

Chanterelle: The most readily available chanterelle is a golden yellow trumpet with a spicy, almost fruity flavor.

Enoki: Long-stemmed mushroom with small caps and a sweet fruity flavor. Used mainly raw in salads and in sandwich making.

Morel: The most familiar cup-shaped mushroom; grows 2 to 5 inches long throughout the United States and France; has a sweet, earthy, and slightly nutty flavor.

Oyster: Found in the wild on living trees, but cultivated on fresh straw or hardwood sawdust and compost; flavor is said to resemble the familiar mollusk from which they get their name.

Porcini: One of the many edible boletes, also called cepes in France; can have a cap as large as 8 inches across, but are usually harvested when they are from 2 to 4 inches in diameter; brown mushrooms with slightly swollen, almost bulbous stems. Boletes have pores instead of the gills common to other mushroom types.

Portabella: A meaty, large-capped gill mushroom related to the crimini mushroom, excellent grilled because of their size and firm texture.

Shitake: Originally grown in China; Japan now grows more shitakes than any other country; grown on teak or oak logs or in hardwood sawdust in a controlled environment; buff brown with a shaggy, rolled-in cap and pronounced flavor.

Straw: Grow naturally on the decaying straw of rice plants in China and Japan; have small grayish-brown caps and short stems.

Truffle: An underground fungus grown in clusters attached to the roots of fir, oak, and beech trees 3 to 12 inches below the ground; two major varieties of true truffles: the French black truffle and the Italian white Piedmont truffle; the white truffle is more pronounced in flavor and odoriferous. The Oregon white truffle is not a true truffle but resembles a small puffball that grows on or just below the ground.

Vegetable stocks

Vegetable stocks are an excellent substitution for the meat-based stocks commonly used in production kitchens. They are less costly to make, contain little or no fat, and can be used in a multitude of culinary applications.

On most professional production cooking lines, there is a token pot full of chicken, veal, or beef stock on hand for a variety of finishing and/or presentation procedures for hot and cold foods. Vegetable stocks can be used instead.

Many varieties of vegetables stocks can be prepared easily and with little cost from ingredients already in the kitchen. Vegetable scraps and pieces as well as fresh-cut vegetables, canned vegetables, herbs, and spices can make the most flavorful cooking medium when combined with deliberate action and professional care. Vegetable stocks require considerably less time to make than meat stocks (only minutes) because their flavors are extracted quickly. Stocks made from animal bones take hours to produce properly.

It is not absolutely necessary to use meat-based stocks in many standard culinary practices. The use of meat-based stocks has been promoted more out of convenience than for effect. If vegetable stocks replaced the chicken or veal stock used as *mise en place* (readied ingredients) on many hot food production lines around the country, cooks would use them just as frequently in soup making, in the reheating of vegetables for service, and in the thinning down of already prepared sauces. Vegetable stocks can also make great accompanying sauces for meats, fish, poultry, or vegetable-based menu items.

Standardized recipes are followed for meat-based stocks; this standardization can carry over to vegetable stocks as well. Following the same basic vegetable stock formulas time after time will help to ensure consistency of the final flavors. The same need for consistency that inspired Escoffier's *Le Guide Culinaire* now inspires a realm of basic stocks and sauces made without bones and other animal products.

Whether used to reheat vegetables, thin down a sauce in the steam table, or become the foundation for a soup, sauce, or braising liquid, the stock's flavor is paramount to the success of the final dish. Vegetable stocks are no different. If they are made with the same directness and confidence as all of the other parts of the meal, the final product will be full of flavor and may satisfy the most discriminating of tastes. If not, then flavor becomes captive to the whims of the cooks and an accidental hodgepodge of ingredients. Only in a planned and well-orchestrated vegetable stock preparation can the end flavor be a creation and not an accident.

Two general axioms of color and flavor dominate in the making of vegetable stocks; everything else is open to interpretation. First, strong-flavored vegetables like cabbage and broccoli should be avoided in standard or basic vegetable stock formulas. These vegetables have characteristic flavors that may overpower the delicate flavors of the other vegetables used in the stock and may interfere with the flavor of the main dish item. If readily available and used with consistency, however, strong-flavored vegetables can be used in vegetable stocks destined for braising liquids and other full-flavored cooking preparations. Second, green and red vegetables are likely to have leached out some of their color and flavor into the stock and should not be used in making white vegetable stocks. White vegetable stocks might be used for poaching or reheating of already cooked vegetables or rice dishes. Color that may transfer to the products being cooked or reheated must be part of the planned result and not a chance happening. Parsley, pimentos, tomatoes, and the dark green outer stalks of celery should be used only when the color of the stock is of the least importance or when making browned or red vegetable stocks.

Vegetable stock pots should not become garbage pots for vegetable trimmings. Use vegetables for their flavor and color contributions; do not use all the bits and pieces off the prep table. Chefs need to present dishes that have consistent flavors. A sauce made from a vegetable stock containing broccoli stems and parsley will have a very different taste from one that uses tomatoes and bell peppers. Decide what flavors you would like to present and keep the recipes for your vegetable stocks consistent.

Chefs can make at least three different vegetable stocks to contribute flavor and color to final preparations. White vegetable stocks can be made using onions, the center stalks of celery, and turnips. Red vegetable stocks may use tomatoes and carrots to enhance their flavors. Browned vegetable stocks can be made by browning the vegetables used in the process before adding the liquid. Browned vegetable stocks can have the greatest depth of vegetable flavors because any vegetable color added through the cooking of the stock will only enhance the darker color desired. In browned vegetable stocks, the chef can use any of the celery stalks, including the darker outer ones, carrots, parsley, turnips, onions of any type or description, tomatoes, peppers, and so on.

Here are three basic vegetable stock formulas. Recipe is the wrong word to describe these formulas because they are not meant to be exact.

⋙ *White Vegetable Stock*

Makes 1 gallon

1 pound of onion, any variety, not browned
1 pound of celery, center stalks only, or 1/2 pound diced celeriac
1/2 pound of white turnips
1/2 pound of parsnips
1½ gallons water
2 teaspoons salt
2 teaspoons cracked white pepper corns

1. Rough cut all vegetables and add to stock pot with water and seasonings.

2. Cook for 1 hour only. Strain vegetables and adjust seasonings.

⋙ *Red Vegetable Stock*

Makes 1 gallon

1 pound onions, any variety, not browned
1 pound celery, any stalks
1 pound chopped tomatoes
1/2 pound carrots
1/2 pound turnips, yellow preferred
1/4 cup chopped parsley
1½ gallons water
2 teaspoons salt
2 teaspoons cracked white or black pepper corns

1. Rough cut all vegetables and add to stock pot with water and seasonings.

2. Cook for 1 hour only. Strain vegetables and adjust seasonings.

⚜ *Browned Vegetable Stock*

Makes 1 gallon

1 pound onions
1 pound celery, any stalks
1 pound chopped tomatoes (optional)
1/2 pound carrots
1/2 pound turnips
1/4 cup chopped parsley
1½ gallons water
2 teaspoons vegetable oil
2 teaspoons salt
2 teaspoons cracked black pepper corns

1. Rough cut all vegetables.
2. Heat oil in sauce pot and add onions; cook until well browned.
3. Add the rest of the vegetables and cook until they are also browned.
4. Add water and seasonings.
5. Cook for 1 hour only. Strain vegetables and adjust seasonings.

Uses of vegetable stocks in cooking

Vegetable stocks may be substituted easily for meat stocks in many typical culinary applications. Vegetable stocks might be used wholly or in part for traditionally meat-based sauces and soups to give a different taste to the finished product. Such stocks would offer consumers a lower-fat item without sacrificing flavor.

For example, use all or part vegetable stocks when braising meats. Chefs instinctively use meat-based stocks as the basis of braising liquids and prefer to use stocks made from the braising item itself—beef stock for beef, chicken stock for chicken, fish stock for fish, and so on. These are easily at hand and match the flavors of the braising meat item. Vegetable stocks that are rich in flavor and freshness could just as easily be used if they too were convenient. Vegetable-based stocks would not match but would complement the flavors of the braising meat item. The meat juices blended into the vegetable stock during the cooking process would create a final product with many complementary flavors. The end product will have more well-rounded tastes, a heightened flavor, and less fat than if meat stocks had been used.

Through evaporation, already prepared sauces become thicker as they continue to cook slowly in steam tables or on the stove. Many chefs use veal or chicken stock to thin them back down to their desired consistency. It is not the flavor that has evaporated away, however, but only the moisture or water content. Although you could use plain water to thin down sauces thickened through evaporation, you could use vegetable stocks instead of traditional chicken or veal stocks. Vegetable stocks have the same effect on thinning as plain water or other stocks and contribute fresh flavors without the added fats and cholesterol of meat-based stocks.

Rice pilafs are excellent when made with vegetable stocks. You don't have the problem of the rice tasting like chicken because you used chicken stock or veal because you used veal stock. Rice dishes should taste like rice and the vegetables added to them for flavor. Vegetables like celery, onion, bell peppers, hot peppers, and even tomatoes can be added in rice preparations. Their flavors combine with the herbs and spices in the rice dish.

Cream soups, like cream of broccoli, potato, or leek, which traditionally use chicken or veal stock as the base, could be made with vegetable stocks instead. Legumes, potatoes, and pastas can be cooked in vegetable stocks for nutritious and delicious dishes. This practice enhances the flavors of the dominant vegetables.

Oils and fats for flavor

If it is confusing to think of using fats and oils for flavorings in nutritionally prepared foods, it is because of old habits and unqualified traditions. Fats and oils can be used in cooking applications for the media that they are and for the flavors they impart when used moderately.

There are many different oils and fats for chefs to choose from, depending on the cooking temperatures used and the flavor results desired. Whole butter burns easily when heated, whereas peanut oil can consistently withstand temperatures over 350°F. The oils that present the strongest flavors are sesame, olive, any of the nut oils (hazelnut, walnut, etc.), butter, and margarine.

A stir-fry dish using a small amount of sesame or walnut oil will accentuate the taste of the other ingredients and allow the chef to reduce the amount of soy sauce (a fermented sauce high in sodium) or other flavor enhancers, such as MSG, without sacrificing flavor.

Sautéed dishes or pan-fried items take on a whole new character when olive oil is the cooking medium. Even omelets cooked in a small amount of this ancient oil take on a different characteristic. Olive oil provides an exciting change with virtually no difference in the cooking process.

Some chefs stay away from these highly flavorful oils in their cooking. They believe that if they use enough of these oils for the proper application of the cooking method, then the flavor of the oil will dominate the dish (sesame oil has an extremely dominating flavor, and virgin olive oil is a close second). They need to think of these oils as seasonings rather than frying media. In a recipe that calls for a fat to stir fry, sauté, or pan fry, use an oil with little or no dominant flavor, like canola, soybean, or sunflower, as the primary oil, with the flavorful oil as only a portion of the frying medium. In this fashion, sesame oil, walnut oil, or olive oil is used more like a spice to accent the flavors of the final product.

Flavored oils

Flavored oils allow chefs to give their recipes a complex taste by utilizing flavor extraction techniques and the cooking medium to disperse flavors evenly throughout the entire dish. Chefs make flavored oils by infusing the essence of their favorite herbs and spices into any of the pure cooking oils they would regularly use in their operations.

A garlic/tarragon oil can be made easily, for example, by taking a safflower or soybean oil and adding crushed cloves of garlic and sprigs of fresh tarragon (approximately four cloves of garlic and two full sprigs of fresh tarragon per quart of oil). The oil can then be used to sauté or pan fry or in a marinade or salad dressing to give the final dish a signature taste.

There is some concern that the procedure of making flavored oils could present an ideal situation for botulism and should be handled carefully. *Clostridium botulinum*, a spore-forming bacteria, is found in the soil and may be present on fresh garlic cloves. The bacteria thrives in oxygen-free environments, such as in canned foods and foods immersed in oil. You can prevent this problem by making only small quantities that can be used quickly and by keeping the oils refrigerated at all times.

Some restaurant chefs keep chopped garlic and chopped shallots as part of the hot line *mise en place* and cover the chopped bulbs with fresh oil. If the recipe calls for a stronger garlic or shallot taste, they have access to the actual chopped product. When the recipe calls for just a hint of these flavors, they merely spoon off a tablespoon or so of the oil and add that during the cooking process, replenishing the oil at the end of the shift for later use.

Fresh herbs and cracked whole spices are best suited for this type of oil infusion, because the freshness of their flavors stands out. Olive oil and other flavorful oils can also be used for these herbal infusions. Their strong natural oil flavors will add even greater dimension to the infused taste.

Chefs may develop their own herbal/oil blend. These blends could be used for many cooking procedures. Just like a chef's own restaurant blend of spices, these oil blends give character and depth to the most simple applications.

Butter and margarine

Two more fats to consider in the application of taste are butter and margarine. Many people are concerned with the amount of cholesterol and saturated fats in their daily diets and want to reduce their intake of these types of fats. Nutritional diets do not dictate the total elimination of these fats (10% of the total daily caloric intake should consist of saturated fats) but simply the reduction of these fats in the diet.

As cooking media, butter and margarine should be avoided because the same results can be achieved easily through the use of liquid oils. When it comes to flavor, nothing tastes the same as fresh whole butter. Margarine is merely vegetable oil that has been hydrogenized, making it solid at room temperature. Some products today have been flavored artificially to resemble the taste of butter without the cholesterol.

If your recipe calls for the taste of butter, think of butter as a seasoning. Add a small amount of it at the final stages of cooking so that the pure taste remains with the final product. If the recipe calls for butter as the cooking medium, replace it with a combination of a nonflavored oil and a smaller amount of butter.

Compound butters

Compound butters are flavored butters that can be used as seasonings for a variety of sautéed, roasted, grilled, poached, or broiled preparations, including vegetables, poultry, beef, fish, and veal.

Compound butters are a combination of fresh sweet butter, herbs, spices, and other highly flavored ingredients. Combined, rolled into cylindrical shapes, and refrigerated, compound butters can be used easily and quickly by slicing off an appropriate amount and adding it to the cooked item just before service.

The advantage to using compound butters is their high flavor concentration. One thin slice, less than a teaspoon (which contains approximately 36 fat calories), can significantly alter the taste of a food item without exceeding nutritional guidelines for fat percentage based on overall calories.

Compound butters get their concentrated flavors from the other ingredients that make up each individual formula. Maître d'Hôtel butter, perhaps the standard by which other compound butters are compared, is a mix of fresh sweet butter, fresh chopped parsley, lemon juice, salt, and pepper. Other compound butters might include other herbs and seasonings, finely chopped shallots or garlic, or even ground shellfish like shrimp or lobster. A shrimp-flavored compound butter might be an excellent accompaniment to poached, grilled, or broiled fish, whereas a garlic, chive, and thyme compound butter might be used for grilled chops or steaks.

Acid products

Sour is one of the five true tastes discussed in Chapter 5. It is distinguishable from other tastes and acts as an influencing flavor over other flavors. Just as salt is used to heighten the taste of many recipes, adding some type of acid product would have the same stimulating effect without the sodium. In some cases the use of an acid product eliminates the need for salt as a flavor enhancer.

There are many forms of acid products, including citrus juices from lemons, limes, and oranges; tomato products; vinegars; and sour cream and yogurt. Each of these gives chefs great flexibility in preparing the finest recipes. In the creation of new recipes, chefs can take advantage of the versatility of these products to bring excitement to the most simple of preparations.

The excitement that makes beef stroganoff more than just beef stew is the addition of sour cream to the final sauce. Flounder meuniére is a fantastic variation of sautéed flounder with the addition of a few drops of lemon juice, which makes all the difference. The use of acid products as seasonings can transform tastes from average to gourmet.

When using fresh citrus zest, be careful not to use any of the white membrane that attaches the zest (peel) to the fruit. The white membrane has a bitter taste.

Flavored vinegars

Flavored vinegars can be made in much the same way as flavored oils, by the simple infusing of herbal and spice essences into a favorite vinegar. Fresh herbs and cracked whole spices give the best results. A rosemary/thyme white vinegar gives extra definition to seafood marinades, whereas dill/garlic vinegar gives character to cucumber, potato, and pasta salads.

Fruit-flavored vinegars are also gaining in popularity for the preparation of salad dressings and marinades. These vinegars use crushed berries or chopped fruit for flavor; once the flavor of the fruits has been fully steeped out (three to four days), the vinegar is strained off the fruit residue and can be stored indefinitely. Fruit vinegars can be made more rapidly for quick service by using fruit that has been finely puréed and adding some of the fruit to the dressing. The presentation will be quite different, however, and the versatility of use not as great.

In making flavored vinegars, you can use white, red, red wine, cider, and balsamic vinegars as the base. The resulting flavors will be dependent on the base vinegar used.

To make a fruit-flavored vinegar, like raspberry vinegar, add 1 cup of broken raspberries to 1 quart of vinegar. Allow this to steep for at least 48 hours to allow the flavors of the berries to permeate the vinegar. To spice it up even more, add 1 tablespoon of cracked black pepper per quart to make raspberry and black pepper vinegar. Peach vinegar can be made by adding 1 cup of cut peaches or 1/2 cup of peach nectar to 1 quart of cider vinegar. The combination of fruit flavors creates an excellent vinegar blend.

Refrigerating flavored vinegars that used fresh fruit as a main ingredient keeps them from becoming rancid. Straining the fruit out of the vinegar after steeping them will also add shelf life to the flavored product.

Review Questions

1. What other food groups, besides herbs and spices, contribute great amounts of flavor to foods?

2. How are consumers becoming aware of the variety of foods that are available in modern American markets?

3. What does experience teach cooks about certain combinations of foods and flavoring ingredients?

4. What does the spirit of adventure allow cooks who have a thorough knowledge of foods and are practiced in modern cooking methods to do?

5. Which of the basic taste sensations are not easily found naturally in foods?

6. How can you use natural flavorings to heighten the presence of sweet, bitter, sour, and peppery in many recipes while maintaining appropriate nutritional guidelines?

7. Why are vegetable mirepoixs important for the traditional and modern cook?

8. What is the difference between sweating and browning of vegetables, and what are their appropriate applications?

9. Which family of onion is usually considered a spice?

10. What are some of the more commonly used flavoring root, stalk, and tuber vegetables?

11. Why are so many varieties of mushrooms available in today's market?

12. What safeguards should be practiced in making vegetable stocks?

13. In what culinary applications can vegetable stocks substitute for meat-based stocks while maintaining great-tasting results?

14. How can fat and oil be used to enhance flavors in foods while maintaining nutritional fat percentage guidelines?

15. How can the chef and home cook develop their own flavored oils and vinegars for kitchen applications?

Flavoring with Wines and Spirits

Wines, beers, and spirits have long been enjoyed as beverages but have taken on a new role as flavoring ingredients in cooking and baking. Although some countries have used them liberally in the past, they are now being used in many traditional and nontraditional cuisines and cooking applications throughout the world.

The cook does not have to be a bartender or wine steward to use these beverages properly in the kitchen. A basic understanding of types of beverages, and the flavors that dominate them, is an important aspect of modern nutritional cooking.

After completing this chapter, the student will be able to

- list and describe the general categories of alcoholic beverages and the flavors associated with them
- list and describe the four classifications of wines
- list and describe popular drinking and cooking wines from each of the world's major wine-producing countries
- discuss the use of sweet versus dry, fortified, or aromatized wines
- describe how consistency of flavor is obtained through the process of producing sherry and port wine
- list and describe other nongrape fruit wines that can be used in cooking and baking
- discuss the uses of beers and ales in cooking and baking
- discuss the use of brandy in the commercial kitchen
- list and describe the large variety of flavored liqueurs chefs can use in the kitchen and pastry shop

Alcoholic beverages provide another way to enhance the flavor of foods. Although most people think of alcoholic beverages only as drinks, they are used by professional chefs to impart unique tastes to cooked foods or pastry items.

Many different kinds of alcoholic beverages may be used to flavor foods and pastries before, during, and after cooking or baking. Wines, beers, ales, brandies, and various liqueurs have been used for centuries to flavor some of the most common and exotic foods and pastries.

Alcoholic beverages represent part of an entire spectrum of flavors that can blend in with or dominate the flavors of any particular dish and can give character to the final presentation. When enhancing flavors in food, chefs cannot afford to overlook the versatility provided by using these liquid flavor enhancers.

The history of wines and beers is as old as recorded history itself. How they were discovered and when they were first used may never be known but have often been the subject of speculation. Humans have enjoyed the spirit (alcohol) of these drinks for thousands of years. As cooking and baking developed, so did the use of these natural flavor enhancers. Brandies and liqueurs can give extraordinary distinction to otherwise simple tastes. These liquids can impart character and excitement to the easiest of preparations without fat or other unhealthy components.

Nutritional components

Not only do wines, beers, brandies, and liqueurs impart flavors to foods, but many may add to the nutritional value of a finished product. Alcohol by itself does not add nutritionally to the human diet (and is usually reduced or eliminated by evaporation during cooking or baking), but the beverages containing alcohol can contribute to nutrition.

Some wines contain potassium, calcium, phosphorus, magnesium, and iron. Most other wines aid in the absorption of these minerals as well as zinc when made a part of a meal. Researchers are investigating any correlation between moderate wine consumption and a healthy level of high-density lipoproteins (HDL, or the "good" cholesterol) in the bloodstream. If true, then moderate wine consumption (one to two glasses per day) may play a role in reduced risk for heart attack and stroke.

Beers contain traces of protein or amino acids, fats, and some B vitamins, which remain in the bottle or can from the yeast used in the fermentation process. Liqueurs are often flavored with the essences of herbs and spices and were originally created as medicinal cures. Their contribution to health can be argued but not totally denied.

Wines

All of the four wine classifications—table, sparkling, fortified, and aromatized—can be used in cooking and baking. Each imparts its own special quality and flavor.

Table wines (or still wines, as they are sometimes called) are wines whose fermentation has completely ceased before the bottling process. They may be named with a particular variety of grape (cabernet sauvignon, merlot, etc.), or they may consist of a blend of various types of grapes and be known simply as red, white, rosé, or blush table wines.

Sparkling wines go through a second fermentation process after they are bottled. This traps the yeast-produced carbon dioxide inside the bottle, which creates bubbles (the sparkle) when the bottle is opened. Only sparkling wines produced in the French region of Champagne are allowed to carry the family nomenclature, although many champagne-type sparkling wines appear throughout the wine-producing world.

Fortified wines have had brandy added before bottling to help raise the alcohol content of the wine. Familiar types of fortified wines are Madeira and Marsala.

Aromatized wines, sometimes fortified and sometimes not, have been flavored by herbs and/or spices. Vermouth is the most familiar of the aromatized wines.

It is important to use wines for cooking or baking that would be considered good for drinking as well. Often, chefs try to use inferior wines in the kitchen as a way to save money, not realizing that they are also sacrificing taste and quality. The opposite, however, is not necessarily true—using only the most expensive wines will not always produce a better end product.

Many young chefs make the mistake of substituting a similar yet inferior wine for the specific wine called for by the recipe. In more than a few restaurants, the kitchen staff is given the two- or three-day-old opened bottles of wine from the bar to use in cooking. This practice naturally dictates the substitution of many types of wines as long as they are similar in color (red versus white) and in the degree of sweetness or dryness. There are so many other discriminating differences between varietal wines (wines produced primarily from a single variety of grape), even between similar varietals produced in different regions or countries, that this practice leads to inconsistency in taste and quality. The right wines should be selected for the right dish.

France, Italy, Germany, Spain, Portugal, Australia, and the United States all produce excellent wines—from the common table wines to the sophisticated varietal and sparkling wines. The only way to learn the proper use of these different wines is to taste them and cook with them.

France

The French wine makers have worked diligently to develop an excellent wine-making tradition. It is wise to investigate the different French wines when choosing the right wine for the kitchen.

All of France's six main wine-producing regions—Bordeaux, Champagne, Burgundy, Alsace, Rhone, and Loire—offer a variety of excellent wines. Each region is further divided into distinct districts that produce their own types and qualities of wine. Bordeaux, for example, is subdivided into nine districts where specific wines are produced; Médoc, Graves, Saint Émilion, Pomeral, Sauternes, Premières Côtes de Bordeaux, Côtes de Bourg, Côtes de Blay, and Entre-Deux-Mers. Wines produced in each of these regions and subdistricts have distinct characteristics, which make the task of choosing the right wine difficult but enjoyable.

Although complex, the task of choosing the right French wine can also be educational and fun. It may be best to start with the Bordeaux region, which is well known for its red wines from Médoc and Saint Émilion. Burgundy is known for its world-famous whites, especially from the Chablis and Maçonnais districts.

A sweeter wine, such as one of the whites from Sauternes, would be appropriate to mellow the bitter taste of turnips and endive. These wines are produced from overly ripe grapes that are almost raisins. In these grapes, the juices have partially evaporated, which leaves behind a high concentration of sugars, increases the glycerin, and thus reduces the acids. The resulting wines will be fruitier and sweeter than most other varieties.

Champagnes, when used in cooking, give a light body to many sauces, especially berry and other fruit sauces served with duck, lamb, or pork. Although the effervescence of champagne is lost during cooking, the character of the excellent wines used in the making of champagne remains on the palate. When Dom Perignon, the seventeenth-century Benedictine monk associated with the invention of champagne, invented the bubbly wine, he insisted on using only the finest white wines for the base. The true champagne producers of today still insist on this tradition.

Italy

An excursion through Italy's wine regions would be equally exciting and educational. Perhaps because of the great influence and financial support of the Catholic Church in the production and distribution of wines, Italy can boast of having one of the finest array of wines in the world. The Catholic monks who raised vineyards to produce their sacrificial wines took great pains to produce the finest wines in the world.

Wines are produced almost everywhere in Italy, from the Piedmont, one of the northernmost regions, to Sicily, the southern island that is the home of the Marsala wines.

Some of the best Italian red wines come from the northern Piedmont. The noble grape of this region is called the nebbiolo. Barbera and grignolino grapes are also important in the Piedmont and Lombardy regions for producing a wide range of reds. These wines are excellent cooking wines whose character withstands longer cooking methods like braising and stewing.

The white grape trebbiano, also grown in the north, is the base grape for soave, one of Italy's most popular white wines. Soave is excellent for use in poultry dishes, seafood sauces, and stews.

From Tuscany come the popular chianti and chianti classico wines. Although it is among the most famous Italian wines in the United States because of its straw-wrapped bottle, chianti governato has few culinary attributes. This particular chianti is intended to be drunk while quite young and is sold in the popular straw fiaschi more for decoration than for any other purpose. Because of its youth, however, chianti governato cannot contribute a full-bodied character to sauces or stews. Many chefs believe, therefore, that chianti does not make a good cooking wine. The other varieties—chianti vecchio and chianti classico riserva—are excellent cooking wines. These wines are aged from two to three years and acquire a more developed character suitable for cooking and for marinades. Chianti classico riserva is the perfect flavoring liquid for braising rabbit and quail and for shellfish ragouts and sauces.

From Sicily come some great wines used in kitchens around the globe. Mount Etna, the volcano on the eastern end of Sicily, has contributed a fertile volcanic ash to much of the island. This ash is a perfect grape vine fertilizer. The best wines are produced from grapes grown directly on the volcano's slopes and bear its name: Etna bianco, Etna rosso, and Etna rossato.

Perhaps the most famous Sicilian wine is Marsala, a fortified wine, which means that brandy has been added after the fermentation ceased to raise alcohol content in the bottle. The volcanic soil in which the wine's grape is grown gives Marsala an acid undertone that withstands the highest cooking temperatures, as in sautéing techniques. Marsala is not only popular for cooking but also for drinking. The sweet Marsala makes an excellent dessert wine; the dry Marsala is generally used for cooking.

Germany

Germany is also divided into several wine-growing regions. The three that are most famous are the Rheingau, Rheinhessen, and Rheinpfalz.

From Rheingau come some of the most famous wines in the world. Johannisberg, Hallgarten, and Rauenthal are a few of the most popular. This region's wines have excellent body, flavor, and character and are among the longest lived of any German wines. They are generally fruity in nature and can add great depth to sauces, marinades, and desserts.

From the region of Rheinhessen come the most popular liebfraumilchs. Liebfraumilch is neither a district nor a vineyard but is rather a blending of wines. Liebfraumilch is an excellent drinking wine that may be used as an aperitif (before-dinner cocktail), as a beverage consumed with the meal, or as an after-dinner wine. Liebfraumilch's consistent flavor makes it a great cooking wine for soups, stews, and sauces.

Rheinpfalz is Germany's largest wine-producing region. Although much of this region's product is consumed by Germans, its excellent white and red table wines make good cooking wines when available in the United States. Table wines are usually blended from multiple varieties of grapes and usually have less distinctive characteristics than varietals; in Rheinpfalz, this is not the case.

Spain

Spain's southernmost wine region, Andalucía, is the home of the country's most prized viniculture possession, sherry wine. The lands that produce the finest of these wines are situated between the Guadaquivir and the Guadalete rivers. Jerez de la Frontera is the primary shipping port for sherry.

The sherry we know today is the product of soil, fruit, and the intricate solera system. Solera is a controlled blending system that takes seven to ten years to complete. Sherries are also fortified with brandy.

The best sherries for cooking are the finos, which range from the very dry manzanilla to the pale dry amontillado, which also has a slightly nutty flavor. The sweet sherry wines, oloroso, cream, and tawny, may be used in dessert sauces and fillings.

Portugal

Of all the wines produced in Portugal, the fortified port wine is the most prized in the culinary arena. Port is fortified before fermentation has completely ceased, which leaves some of the unused sugars behind. Port is, therefore, always a sweet wine. Port's significant character gives distinction to sauces and stews.

Port comes in three types: vintage, ruby, and tawny. Each of these wines is excellent for drinking and as flavoring liquids for cooking.

Vintage port is produced only during exceptional years, when nature has cooperated fully with the wine growers. If rain, sun, and the soil work together through the entire growing season, an exceptional wine full of character, bouquet, and flavor can be achieved. These conditions usually occur about every three to four years. Vintage ports need several years to mature fully in the bottle and may be too costly for regular kitchen use. For the special occasion or feast, however, there can be no substitute.

Ruby and tawny ports are aged in wooden casks, which give character to these otherwise young, fruity wines. They are usually blended wines, which ensures a consistency in style and quality similar to that achieved in the sherry solera system. Tawny ports that are blended and well wooded (aged) are generally more consistent and thus better for culinary use than younger aged ports.

Another Portuguese wine is the popular Madeira, which takes its name from the island on which the grapes are grown. The name *Madeira* means the "wooded isle." The island of Madeira was founded by Portuguese sailors on their way south around Africa in search of the spice islands. Captain Joso Goncalves of the Portuguese navy was given the task of settling the island and establishing it as a resting place for other ships. Finding it to be completely covered by a dense forest, and being short of manpower and time, Goncalves decided to burn the trees as a quick means of clearing the land.

Captain Goncalves was later rewarded for his deed. The volcanic island covered by a thousands of years of decaying organic matter was completely covered by several feet of freshly consumed potash as a result of Goncalves's actions. Captain Goncalves accidentally made Madeira one of the most fertile wine-producing islands in the world. This combination of volcanic soil, organic debris, and potash was perfect for the cultivation of grape vines and, later, sugar cane. One of the oldest domesticated grape varieties, the *malvasia candiae,* was transplanted from Crete to this new, lush home. Before long Portugal had a thriving wine-producing colony.

There are four types of Madeira: sercial, verdelho, bual, and malmsey. Sercial is the driest and is suitable in most culinary applications. Verdelho is less dry. Bual is almost sweet. Malmsey is the sweetest and is almost liqueur-like in consistency and taste.

Other wine-producing countries

Excellent wines are produced today in many other countries. Austria, Greece, Hungary, Switzerland, Australia, Brazil, and the United States are all fine wine producers. Chefs should not halt their wine exploration before tasting a few examples from each of these countries.

Aromatized wines

As their name suggests, aromatized wines are those that have been made more aromatic by the infusion of herbs, spices, and other flavoring ingredients. Primarily used as aperitifs, some aromatized wines also make excellent cooking wines. Aromatized wines are almost always fortified with brandy.

Vermouth is perhaps the most popular aromatized wine used in the kitchen. It is made from white wine grapes. Vermouth is aromatized with twenty to fifty different herbs, plants, roots, seeds, barks, flowers, and citrus fruit peels. Using vermouth in the kitchen in place of white wine adds the flavor of a well-developed spice blend. Vermouth is produced both dry and sweet; each has different culinary advantages.

Other aromatized wines that may have a place in the kitchen pantry include French dubonnet, which is excellent for dessert sauces and currant pies; campari from Italy, which can accent salad dressings or chutneys; and cynar, whose flavor comes from the artichoke and can add softness and elegance to a variety of cream sauces and vegetable dishes.

Other fruit wines

Grapes are not the only fruit whose juices are made into wine. Apples, pears, cherries, plums, and various berries are all capable of producing some fine wines. These specialty wines do not contain the tannins and other acids of grape wines and therefore need to be drunk while still very young. They are usually fortified with brandy made from a similar wine (for example, pear wine is fortified with pear brandy). Usually sweet, these wines are excellent flavoring liquids for fruit sauces, soups, and desserts.

Beers and ales

Beers and ales are fermented beverages that use grains instead of fruit to feed the alcohol-producing yeast.

Beer is produced in varying degrees of lightness and body. Lager is the clearest and lightest of the beers. Lagers are effervescent, which is caused by an artificial carbonation before bottling. Most of the American beers are of the lager type. Stout, on the other hand, is a dark beer that takes its color from the roasted malt and the addition of roasted barley to the brew. Stout is slightly bitter tasting with no effervescence.

Before the mass production of beers, beer and ale were used in cooking and baking throughout Europe, but not as much as wine or brandy. Perhaps this was a result of the bitterness in beer (most beer was home brewed and lacked consistency in taste and color). Beer made in the traditional manner does not age, as do wines, and therefore had to be drunk or used right away.

Beer production has become more scientific today, and its consistency in taste, body, and color can be guaranteed.

Some European chefs are fond of using the darker ales and stouts for cooking and baking. Several of the most flavorful roasts and stews can be made even more tasty with the addition of a good ale to the marinade or sauce. Sauerbraten, the German version of potted roast beef, can be accentuated with a bottle or two of dark, malty ale.

Barley wine is a style of ale with an alcohol content that approaches 9 to 14% by volume. Barley wines are aged up to two years and have a deep well-developed flavor. A popular brand is Young's Old Nick™, made in London. Barley wines are excellent flavor enhancers for food.

Beer is also excellent as part of the poaching liquid for highly seasoned meat sausages and blood puddings and for steaming strong-flavored vegetables such as cabbage, mustard greens, and kale.

In bread baking, beer contributes taste and color and aids in the dough's fermentation. In fact, no one knows for sure which came first, the discovery of raised bread or fermented beer. More than likely, the discoveries were simultaneous.

Brandy

Brandy is a distilled beverage taken from a variety of host wines. Although the science of distillation dates back thousands of years, the art of commercial brandy making was not realized until the sixteenth century.

Brandy can be made from any of the fruit wines: grape, apple, pear, or even berry. Brandy retains some of the characteristic flavor of the base wine and can be a great flavoring liquid in cooking.

Because of its high alcohol content (from 80 to over 100 proof), brandy burns off its alcohol quickly, leaving behind its distinctive flavor in just a few seconds. For example, brandy can be added directly to the sauté pan just before plating. Once the brandy has flamed (burned down), the sauce can be finished quickly. This is why brandy is the perfect liquor to use for tableside cooking presentations. The high alcohol content flames up fairly easily, giving the customer an exciting show, and what remains in the sauce is excellent flavor.

Liqueurs

During the Middle Ages, an invention of alchemists, liqueurs (distillations flavored with all kinds of herbs, seeds, roots, and other spices) were supposed to help prolong life. Often, they were prescribed as medicinal cures and even love potions.

Liqueurs were always sweetened with the addition of one or more types of sugar and then laced with brandy. Liqueurs contain anywhere from 2½ to 35% sugar by weight. Liqueurs, therefore, must be used sparingly in cooking.

The following are some of the more widely used liqueurs and their flavoring agents:

Amaretto: almond flavored; used in desserts and dessert sauces

Anis or *anisette:* aniseed; used in Italian cookies and candies

Benedictine: perhaps the oldest known liqueur, developed in the early sixteenth century; made from twenty-seven different herbs with a cognac brandy base

Coffee liqueur: based on the coffee bean; Kahlua and Tia Maria are two types

Creme de cacao: flavored from cacao and vanilla beans

Creme de cassis: black currant–flavored liqueur

Creme de menthe: white or green (with food color added); flavored primarily from peppermint

Creme de noyaux: also almond flavored; derived from crushed fruit stones (pits)

Curacao—flavored from the fresh peel of green oranges; comes from the island of Curacao

Drambuie—made from old Highland malt Scotch whiskey and heather honey in an area of Scotland known as the Highlands

Galliano: Italian, made from flowers and herbs

Gran Marnier: orange curacao liqueur with a cognac brandy base

Kummel: caraway-flavored liqueur; made in Germany

Pear liqueur: made from fresh pears

Peppermint schnapps: also a mint-flavored liqueur, usually with a higher proof than creme de menthe

Sambucca: a licorice, candy-flavored liqueur from the elderbush

Sloe gin: considered a flavored gin; a sweetened liqueur flavored from the sloe berry

Triple sec: a white, orange-flavored liqueur

Review Questions

1. What beverages have been used for centuries to flavor foods and bakery products?

2. Do alcoholic beverages contribute any nutritional value to foods or pastries?

3. What are the four classifications of wine, and how is each produced?

4. How can you protect the consistency of flavor in dishes that call for wine or other alcoholic beverages in their preparation or service?

5. Why would the Bordeaux region of France be a good place to start in the search for good cooking wines?

6. Why are some chiantis suited only to drinking whereas others are suited to drinking or cooking?

7. What soil factor contributes to the taste of Marsala, and which variety (sweet or dry) is used mainly in cooking?

8. Why is liebfraumilch a good choice in cooking wine for soups, stews, and sauces?

9. What is the Spanish solera system, and how does it maintain consistency for the taste of sherry wine?

10. How often is vintage port produced, and what are the controlling factors?

11. Where does the name *Madeira* come from, and why does the island now make excellent wines?

12. What is the most popular aromatized wine that is used in cooking, and why?

13. What are the main classifications of beers and ales, and what are some of their culinary applications?

14. Why does brandy make the perfect liquor to use in tableside cooking presentations?

15. What are some of the more popular liqueurs, and what flavors do they contribute to cooking and baking?

Cooking for Nutrition

The art of nutritional cooking not only designates certain ingredients and cooking methods for proper nutrition but also includes critical procedures for the buying, storing, and fabrication of foods. Only through proper care, cooking, and serving techniques can the nutrients that are natural to foods remain intact from the farm to the table.

The trained cook can also take standard recipes and transform them into more nutritional offerings (e.g., through careful measurement of fat and salt and low-fat meat or dairy substitutions). With a little planning and with knowledge about foods and the nutrients they contain, the accomplished cook can prepare a multitude of healthy dishes that rival more traditionally prepared foods in taste and presentation.

After completing this chapter, the student will be able to

- discuss the effects of time, shipping, and handling on nutrition
- describe some of the biggest destroyers of vitamins
- ensure receipt of the freshest vegetables possible from vendors
- prepare foods for maximum nutrient retention
- discuss frying methods that can maintain the RDA of 30% calories, or less, from fat
- list and describe the cooking methods usually associated with healthful food preparation
- substitute fats in cooking and baking to reduce saturated fats and cholesterol
- substitute meats in standard recipes to reduce fat in the final dish

The ability of foods to retain their nutritional value is heavily influenced by storage procedures, length of storage, shipping, handling during shipping and storage, and preparation and cooking methods. Improper handling or cooking can destroy the natural nutritional benefits of food, whereas proper preparation and cooking can help preserve them. Establishing standards in receiving, storing, handling, and preparing foods can help assure that the foods served are of the highest nutritional value possible.

The nutrients of foods are at their peak just at the point of harvest. Whether the food source is vegetable or animal, its nutritional value begins to diminish as soon as the life process has ended.

Oxidation is one of the biggest enemies of vitamins in food. Oxidation occurs when air comes in contact with food and oxygen binds with the hydrogen and carbon that make up all animal and vegetable tissue. The oxidation process causes rancidity in fats and a breakdown of many vitamins. Vitamins are also affected by acidity or alkalinity. Vitamins most affected by oxidation are A, B_{12}, B_6, C, D, K, and riboflavin. Vitamins most affected by acid are A, D, and folacin; vitamins most affected by alkalinity are C, D, riboflavin, and thiamin.

To protect foods and their vitamin content, preparation and cooking should begin as soon after harvest as possible. Buying food, especially produce, from a reputable dealer who can guarantee a fast turnover of products can assure the freshest produce available. Buying produce from bargain dealers may guarantee poor nutrient value. The bargain prices usually are due to overstocking, and the produce can be several days old.

Cutting and chopping of foods during cooking preparation will accelerate the oxidation process because more tissue or cells are exposed to air for longer periods of time. If the foods must be cut, do so just before they are cooked; this will help retain their vitamin content.

Light and heat affect the composition of vitamins in food because they also accelerate the oxidation process. Foods should be prepared and cooked as quickly as possible to assure vitamin retention. Already prepared foods should be refrigerated, with the lights off, until ready for the pan.

Keep lids on pans and pots during cooking as much as possible to prevent exposure to air and light and subsequent vitamin loss. Water-soluble vitamins are especially vulnerable to loss during preparation and cooking. Protect water-soluble vitamins by steaming foods instead of poaching or boiling. One of the biggest culprits in vitamin loss is soaking precooked vegetables during the cleaning process and shocking vegetables in cold water after cooking. Both processes are necessary and acceptable cooking techniques, but the vegetables must not soak in the water longer than is needed. Consider using cooking liquids, whenever possible, in sauce preparations that are served with cooked foods. In this way, many vitamins and minerals leached into the cooking liquid will end up on the plate or bowl.

Proper cooking techniques

If low-fat cooking is the goal, then pan frying and deep-fat frying should be avoided. There are many alternative cooking techniques that provide nutritionally balanced foods.

Sautéing can be considered a low-fat cooking process if done properly. Using nonstick coated cooking pans will help reduce the amount of fat needed in cooking. Measure the amount of fat used carefully. In a nonstick pan, you can reduce the amount of fat needed as a cooking medium to one-half teaspoon per serving, or approximately 4 grams of fat. In contrast, as much as 1 tablespoon of fat may be needed if noncoated pans are used.

Stir-frying is the one frying technique that allows foods to cook rapidly with the addition of only a fraction of the amount of fat needed for sautéing the same foods. The large round shape of the wok; the high cooking temperatures required; and the fine chopping, slicing, or dicing of foods all add up to fast cooking with little need for fat. (Just remember to chop the foods immediately prior to cooking.) Particularly if the wok is seasoned properly (i.e., prepared in such a way to help prevent the sticking of foods) or coated with a nonstick material, the amount of fat needed becomes minimal.

One of the criticisms of stir-frying is that the amount of fat used still adds up to more than the 30% of daily caloric intake recommended by the American Dietary Association. Free pouring of fat into the wok is the biggest culprit in the fight against fat control. Because fat contains 9 calories per gram, a tablespoon of fat—about 1/2 ounce or approximately 14 grams of fat—contains 126 calories, all from fat. If the wok is prepared properly or is coated with a nonstick material, only 1 teaspoon of fat is needed to help keep the food moving quickly in the pan.

The use of vegetable oil sprays or a pastry brush to dispense oils and melted fats reduces the amount of fat by controlling the amount used. Whereas 1 tablespoon of butter contains approximately 104 calories and 1 tablespoon of oil contains 122 calories, one spray from a commercially prepared vegetable oil cooking spray may contain as few as 2 calories and work just as well in a properly prepared pan or nonstick pan. A single brush stroke from a pastry brush dipped into liquid fat will distribute slightly more fat but still in a controlled amount. Free pouring oil or other fats into cooking pans adds more fat than is required and can easily turn a nutritious meal into a high-fat one.

If a chef wants to add the traditional flavor of oriental oils into the stir-fry preparation, he or she can add two or three drops of sesame oil (less than 1 gram of fat) for flavor at the end of the cooking process. In this way the chef reaps the benefits of low-fat cooking and the flavor of the oriental oil.

Braising and stewing are great ways to prepare nutritional dishes because these methods incorporate some of the leaner and tougher parts of the animal. Trimmed chuck roasts, first-cut brisket, and flank steak are ideal for braising and stewing. These muscles are naturally low in fat (compared to other pieces of meat) and therefore make excellent nutritional choices. In braising and stewing, meats are served along with the cooking sauces, so any nutritional elements that leach out during the cooking process remain with the dish.

Roasting is a low-fat cooking process, but the extended cooking times required for roasting may affect the vitamin retention of some meats. When roasting meats, cut the meats into smaller pieces. Cutting 20-pound top rounds into 4 equal pieces of 5 pounds each will accelerate the cooking time, as if each piece were cooked separately. The vitamin retention will be greater, and the product will have great versatility. Roast all meats and poultry on a rack, which allows melted fats to settle on the bottom of the pan, away from the meat.

Grilling and broiling are fast becoming the two most popular cooking techniques for nutritional cooking. Direct heat cooks items rapidly and requires no additional fat. Meats and poultry can be trimmed of all exterior fat: the fatty edge can be trimmed from steaks and chops and the skin from poultry before grilling or broiling. The items are cooked so rapidly that vitamin retention is high and excess interior fat melts and falls away from the food. Extremely lean cuts of poultry or fish may be brushed with a seasoned oil mixture to help prevent them from sticking to the grill and to add flavor to the final dish. Most of the oil is cooked off the product, whereas the flavors from the seasonings remain. Use well-trimmed meats and poultry parts and cook quickly, without charring the outsides.

The blackened technique, attributed to chef Paul Prudhomme of Louisiana, is also a no-fat cooking procedure. It requires the use of a cast-iron skillet and a relatively thin cut of chicken, fish, or steak. The pan is put onto a very hot fire with no oil or fat added. Once the pan is smoking hot, the seasoned meat item is added to the pan. The extreme heat from the pan actually lifts the item off the pan (the steam that is generated from the meat's natural juices vaporizes when in contact with the extreme heat). In this way, meats can be cooked rapidly without sticking to the pan and without oil or fat.

The American Cancer Society warns that charred meats from broiling, grilling, and blackening techniques may contain carcinogens (cancer-causing compounds), but the studies are not complete. The amount of charred meats that would have to be consumed to create a health problem is considerable. Broiling, grilling, and blackening gives consumers no-fat and low-fat cooking choices. Diets should not be based on any one of these cooking methods alone, however.

Poaching is an excellent no-fat cooking technique. Vitamins and flavor are leached into the cooking liquid, however, and although some liquid may be used in an accompanying sauce, most is discarded. The design of the cooking liquid can add some flavor back to the dish. A well-flavored cooking liquid will add more flavor than is lost. Return water-soluble vitamins to the dish by using the cooking liquid in making any sauces; add aromatic and vitamin-rich vegetables (e.g., carrots, celery, and onions) in the sauce-making process.

Steam cooking offers the benefits of extremely fast, no-fat cooking with little loss of vitamins or flavor. Although steam is created by boiling water, there is no cooking medium, liquid or fat, to trap the flavors or leach out the vitamins. Most foods can be cooked by steam. The temperature of steam is only slightly higher than boiling water (212°F, 100°C), however, and browning will not occur (browning requires temperatures of 310°F, or 154°C, or higher).

En papillote is a technique that incorporates steaming as the cooking method. Fish, shellfish, poultry, and vegetables are most suitable for this method because browning will not occur. Foods are placed onto cut heart-shaped pieces of baker's parchment paper or aluminum foil; doused with some liquid like wine, juice, or sauce; and sealed by folding the paper over the product and crimping the edges. The tight package is placed into a hot oven, which quickly turns the trapped liquid into steam. The trapped steam then puffs the package, creating a miniature steam oven. When finished, the steam condenses back into a liquid, which contains all the flavors originally wrapped inside.

Substituting fats in cooking

Although it is recommended that Americans reduce all of their fat consumption, the biggest culprits are those fats that contain large amounts of saturated fatty acids (e.g., butter, clarified butter, margarine, bacon grease, lard, and vegetable shortenings). Most recipes that call for these fats can be altered by making simple substitutions that will reduce the amounts of unhealthy saturated fats and still provide a high level of flavor and taste.

First, the purpose of using particular fats in recipes must be determined before changing them. Are they used as cooking media, to keep foods from sticking to hot pans or grills, for flavor only, or for a combination of cooking method and flavor? In some cases, exchanges can be made with few other recipe adjustments. In other cases, exchanges may require significant changes in the recipe to achieve the same or a similar dish.

Problems arise when you try to take an item like pound cake, which is very high in fat and saturated fat, make substitutions based on levels of saturated fats only, and expect something that tastes and looks the same as before. This is an unrealistic expectation. Although there are low-fat pound cakes on the commercial market, these are made by large bakery conglomerates with all the latest scientific knowledge and skills. Such companies are using technology that is not available to restaurant chefs. This technology uses microparticulated proteins and special gums that create the feel of fat in the mouth.

Other bakery items, like sponge cakes, pies, and muffins, can have acceptable tastes and mouth feel using vegetable oils (which are naturally low in saturated fatty acids) as a substitute for butter, margarine, lard, or shortening. To offset the loss of moisture in finished baked products, add apple juice concentrate to the recipe. Apple juice concentrate will not significantly affect the taste of the finished product but will remain sweet during baking and drying. Sweetness, one of the five basic tastes, will stimulate the taste buds and saliva secretions from the mouth. The end result will be a moist product, full of flavor and with an adequate mouth feel.

If the baking structure is lessened because of a reduction in eggs and/or saturated fats, which trap air molecules during mixing and provide rise and solid, internal structure, then the addition of whipped egg whites can help. Whipped egg whites, folded into other mixed ingredients, can help regain structure through trapped air.

Substitution of vegetable oils for butter, margarine, bacon fat, or other highly saturated fats in many dry-heat cooking methods, such as sautéing or pan frying, can be accomplished either partially or entirely without significantly changing the cooking method. To reduce fats even further, use nonstick cooking pans or grills. Measuring the amount of fat that is actually needed, instead of free pouring fat into the pan, is another helpful practice.

A cook will often use a 2-ounce (or larger) ladle to carry oil or clarified butter to the pan for cooking when 1 or 2 teaspoons are all that is required. It can be cumbersome to measure this small amount in a spoon. A smaller ladle can be used instead. Similarly, a cook will often ladle a generous supply of fat across the face of a grill to make sure that enough fat remains on the surface for proper cooking and does not all end up in the grease tray. Simply transferring oil or clarified butter into a spray bottle and giving a pan or grill one spray at a time will distribute the fat in a fine mist (less than 1 teaspoon per spray) evenly over small and large surfaces. For easiest application, keep both oil and clarified butter spray bottles in a hot *baine marie*, either on or near the stove, to keep the fat as free flowing as possible.

In the many recipes that call for butter, whole or clarified, as the fat in sautéing, use a nonflavored vegetable oil instead. Nonflavored vegetable oils include safflower, sunflower, and canola oils. Flavored oils include peanut, corn, and olive oils. These oils produce the same effect in cooking as does butter (an even exchange of heat and a nonstick medium) but without the saturated fat.

In reducing fat, you lose some flavor. This is where most nutritional recipe conversions leave off: Their translators forget the importance of taste in a healthier recipe. Chefs must realize that flavor must be re-created. When fat used in part or entirely for flavor is replaced or removed from the original recipe, then an equivalent level of flavor must be added by other ingredients. This practice will maintain full taste satisfaction in the finished product.

If you want the flavor of butter but the health benefits of oil, then sauté in oil and add butter, as you would any seasoning, at the end of the cooking process. A recipe that might call for 2 or 3 tablespoons of butter as a frying medium may be cut back to only 1 teaspoon of butter when the butter is treated as a seasoning. The delicate flavor of the butter is present in the final dish, but the benefits of cooking with oil are realized.

In sautéing vegetables, the use of stock as the sautéing medium greatly affects the amount of fat in the finished dish. Although the use of stock is not part of the true definition of sautéing, the results are the same: the heating through of already prepared vegetables for table service. A carefully measured amount of butter (about 1/2 teaspoon per serving, for approximately 17 calories) added to the sauté pan after the vegetables have been heated through gives the taste of butter without all the fat of cooking in butter.

If butter is not the desired flavor, then your choices are many. The use of fresh herbs and aromatic vegetables in combination with the main ingredients can add great amounts of flavor to the most simple preparation. Instead of green beans sautéed in butter, try green beans sautéed with red pimento slices and sweet basil; add a little garlic or shallots if you want even more flavor. Instead of chicken breast sautéed in butter, try chicken breast sautéed with fresh thyme, lemon, and cracked pepper corns.

In place of bacon fat (a seasoning fat used by many southern cooks to flavor vegetables), try using a vegetable oil in combination with hickory-smoked turkey wings, backs, or necks. Sauté the turkey parts in plain vegetable oil for 10 minutes; then strain and reserve the oil. Using a teaspoon or two of this oil in flavoring braised cabbage, steamed brussels sprouts, sautéed green beans, or any other bean recipe will impart a great smoky flavor without the saturated fat of bacon.

In grilling or broiling steaks, chops, and chicken, first remove all the exterior fat and skin from the meat. Use a knife to trim the solid fat as close to the meat as you can. Then prepare a marinade of flavored liquids, herbs, and spices that can be brushed onto the item just before cooking. This gives flavor back to the items in which the flavor of the fat has been drastically reduced. The little amount of oil that is needed to keep these items from sticking to the grill can be supplied by brushing or spraying a 1/2 to 1 teaspoon of oil onto the cooking surface. This method reduces the amount of fat in grilled or broiled items by as much as 60%.

To reduce the amount of fats in other cooking and baking preparations, make these substitutions: evaporated skim milk for heavy cream, low-fat yogurt for sour cream, and part skim-milk cheese for whole-milk cheeses. Take a careful look at the remaining flavors and make substitutions or additions that will replace the level of flavor.

Reducing natural saturated fats in cooking

The simplest way to reduce saturated fats in cooking is to trim meats closely. The visible fat on steaks, chops, and roasts can be cut away with a sharp knife. What does this do to the flavor of the food, however? Everyone knows that fat contains a lot of flavor. You can add flavors back by using fresh herbs and spices; flavorful vegetables like onions, celery, and garlic; and wines, beers, and brandies in food preparation. These ingredients can be used in a marinade (with the addition of an acid product like lemon, tomato, or wine) to help the flavors penetrate into the flesh of the trimmed meat or in a sauce to accompany the meats after they are cooked.

Leaner cuts of meat, such as flank steak and first-cut brisket, are less tender than fattier meats. You need to create some tasty marinades that help tenderize tough muscles or use slow-cooking methods like braising or stewing to make the flesh more palatable. Then come up with a creative way of serving these normally unsophisticated entrees, such as braised beef brisket with raspberry wine sauce, marinated beef flank steak with Indian spices and curried rice pilaf, or country beef terrine (stew) with whole wheat biscuit topping.

Substituting less fatty cuts of meat and poultry for the more traditional fatty meats in many everyday recipes can drastically reduce the amount of fat on the plate. Why not try turkey parmesan instead of veal parmesan or turkey chili instead of beef chili? How about chicken chasseur or chicken roulade florentine? Flank steak bourgignone and chuck roast montmorency are other enticing options.

There are ways to create delicious desserts with less fat. Feature low-fat yogurt parfaits with fresh berries instead of traditional ice cream or sponge cake with raspberry melon sauce in place of butter cream or other high-fat icing.

Substituting meats in cooking

Many traditional recipes that call for meat high in saturated fat, like beef and pork, can be made with another meat low in saturated fat. Turkey, chicken, and game meats like venison and rabbit are good choices.

Substitution of meats will greatly affect the flavor of the dish. Add something back: Use fresh herbs, fresh ground spices, and aromatic vegetables to create new and flavorful dishes using traditional recipes. For example, a beef chili becomes turkey chili with cilantro and sun dried tomatoes. Beef stroganoff

---

SUBSTITUTING MEATS

For	*Substitute*
Beef Ribeye	Beef Tenderloin
Beef Top Round	Beef Eye Round
Beef Brisket	Beef Flank Steak
Beef Strip Steak	Beef Sirloin Steak
Ground Beef	Ground Turkey
Any Beef Cut	Any Venison Cut
Pork Ribs	Lean Pork Chops
Pork Shoulder	Fresh Ham
For Any Red or White Meat	Rabbit, Venison, or Turkey
Veal Scallopini	Turkey Scallopini

becomes venison stroganoff with plum tomatoes and fresh yogurt. Braised pork and plum sauce becomes braised rabbit with currants, plums, and fennel. A great number of variations can be achieved by having an open mind and using a little creativity.

Portioning

The proper portioning of foods that are high in fat is a simple way to control the amount of fat consumption. Simple answers are usually not the complete story, however. Although both the ADA and AMA recommend that meat consumption be limited to 3 ounces 3 times per week, most Americans eat much more than that, often in a single meal. The 10-ounce filets, 12-ounce ribeyes, and 16-ounce sirloin steaks on restaurant menus across America make it difficult to follow more stringent guidelines.

Imagine a diet that starts out with a three-egg omelet in the morning, a ham and cheese sandwich for lunch, and roast beef for dinner. The amount of fat, especially saturated fats and cholesterol, soars off any recommended dietary chart. The problem, however, is a humanistic one: Does a two-egg omelet satisfy the consumer's hunger? Will 3 ounces of roast beef leave the consumer wanting more?

In making omelets, some or all of the eggs can be substituted with commercially prepared nonegg products that contain no fat and no cholesterol, but taste may be sacrificed. A two-egg omelet made with real eggs seems small and unsatisfying unless you incorporate air into the egg mixture before cooking it and serve the omelet with many varieties of vegetable fillings. Whipping air into eggs, either by hand or with a blender, will cause the omelet to soufflé during cooking. This will add height and structure to the small amount of product. Filling the cooked omelet with steamed julienne vegetables, like carrots, celery, onions, fresh chopped parsley, chopped basil, or spinach, will present a satisfying array of flavors and a quantity of food that will please even the hungriest of diners. Adding extra egg whites, which contain no fat or cholesterol, also increases the bulk of the final omelet.

Reducing the amount of meat in a serving will reduce the amount of fats in the diet, but if diners walk away hungry, they are likely to eat other foods later to compensate. Likewise, customers who leave restaurants unsatisfied with the size of portions are reluctant to return.

Don't simply reduce the amount of meat in dishes, but add back volume by creating combination dinners like stews, stir-fries, and casseroles. A braised beef ragout full of tournéed turnips, potatoes, carrots, pearl onions, green beans, herbs, spices, and a sauce made from lean beef stock or vegetable stock limits the amount of meat consumed and satisfies the heartiest appetite as well. Try serving beef with pasta, chicken with rice. These combination dinners, when created with flavor as the number one priority, reduce the amount of meats the average diner consumes, but still satisfy even the most discriminating of restaurant guests. Perhaps the chef doesn't call the dish beef stew, but ragout of beef primavera (with fresh tournéed garden vegetables and a rich-flavored sauce). Instead of chicken and rice, a dish is called fricasse of chicken Portugese (with fresh chopped broccoli flowers and diced fresh tomatoes, cumin, and scallion tops).

If reduction of fats is the goal, there are thousands of alternative solutions. Meat and fat substitution replaces foods high in saturated fats with other foods lower in saturated fats. The use of modern cooking pans and grills that are treated with nonstick surfaces reduces the need for fat as a cooking medium.

Measuring the amount of fat either with a spoon or small ladle or with a spray bottle will help guarantee lower-fat results in cooked products. Portioning, with a plan to satisfy both flavor and hunger, becomes a tool the chef can use to design great dining pleasure while maintaining nutritional guidelines.

Review Questions

1. What effect do storage, length of storage, shipping, handling, and preparation and cooking methods have on the ability of foods to retain nutrients?

2. What effect do oxidation, acidity, and alkalinity have on vitamin retention?

3. How can the cook protect against the oxidation of foods?

4. Which forms of frying can produce menu items within the RDA of 30% of calories from fat?

5. What are three ways of controlling the amount of fat used in cooking?

6. Why are braising and stewing preferred nutritional cooking methods for meats?

7. Why are grilling and broiling becoming two of the most popular nutritionally based cooking methods for meats and vegetables?

8. What are four no-fat cooking methods that can be used to cook meats or vegetables?

9. How can the chef substitute foods low in fat for foods higher in fat without drastically changing the taste of the recipe?

10. What techniques can the chef use to reduce fat in recipes, particularly the saturated fatty acids?

11. What must the cook remember when reducing fat in traditional recipes?

Weight Control

One of the biggest health problems facing Americans today is the ability to control their body weight. As modern civilization becomes increasingly mechanized, people are performing less physical activities than their ancestors did. In addition, the availability of foods today and the fast food phenomenon have given Americans ample opportunities to overindulge in food and dining pleasures.

This problem is obviously on the minds of millions of Americans, as evidenced by the multitude of program diets, like Weight Watchers, and fad diets, like the "no carbohydrate diet" or "cabbage soup diet," exercise shows, and home exercise videos on the market today. In reality, the best defense against becoming overweight is to eat sensibly, exercise regularly, and drink plenty of water.

After completing this chapter, the student will be able to

■ discuss the importance of maintaining ideal body weight

■ describe methods of assessing obesity

■ produce formulas for calculating individuals' caloric needs

■ discuss theories explaining weight problems

■ explain why strict diets may not work for everyone

■ produce sample moderate diet plans

It is important to maintain a healthy body weight to maximize good health. Obesity, however, is an unhealthy body state that affects millions of Americans.

The suggested body weights given in height and weight charts produced by insurance companies are based on mortality rates for upper-income white Americans. The insurance companies do not take into account that death from cancer is often preceded by weight loss before diagnosis of the disease. Therefore, excess mortality associated with obesity is underestimated. In general, overweight people—especially those who are overweight during their younger adult years—die sooner than individuals of average weight.

Excess poundage creates a burden on the body that can lead to disease, especially when people are two to three times heavier than their "normal" weight. (Figure 10–1 shows three formulas for calculating "normal" weight for adults.) Obesity enhances risk factors such as elevated blood cholesterol and low HDL (the good cholesterol) and can lead to heart disease. Hypertension, which can damage coronary vessels and cause heart disease, is also aggravated by obesity. High blood pressure can also cause stroke and kidney disease. Modest weight reduction is effective in lowering high blood pressure.

Obesity can also create the onset of diabetes in those who are genetically prone. Diabetes, in turn, can lead to heart disease, blindness, and neuropathies. Osteoarthritis and gout are also seen more often in the obese population. People who are overweight seem to be at particular risk for osteoarthritis of the knees and hands.

Gallbladder trouble is more prevalent in obese people, and obesity appears to be a risk for colon cancer in men. Heart disease and diabetes are associated with obesity characterized by fat over the abdominal area: "Some recent research indicates cardiovascular disease is probably as closely related to general obesity as abdominal obesity."* Fat over the hips and thighs apparently is a normal female attribute that does not correlate with the incidence of heart disease and diabetes.

Nondiet approaches

Weight control programs abound everywhere, and diet books are best sellers. Frequently, the person who succeeds in losing fat does so only temporarily. The success rate for keeping off weight lost while dieting is not encouraging. More than 50% of dieters regain their weight within five years. Failure to stay lean leads to guilt and repeated efforts at dieting.

---

*Seminars in Nutrition and Healthy Weight Maintenance, A Challenge for Dietitians, Volume 16, number 2, Nov./Dec. 1996, p. 1.

1. Height in inches × wrist in inches = _____ divided by 3 = _____
   (*Note:* Wrist and ankle measurements are not influenced by body fat and are accurate sites for measuring frame size.)
2. Men: 106 pounds for the first 60 inches + 6 pounds for each inch over 60 inches.

   Women: 100 pounds for the first 60 inches + 5 pounds each inch over 60 inches.

   For both sexes: Add 10 pounds for large frame.
   Subtract 10 pounds for small frame.
   Subtract 1 pound for each year under 25.
3. Body Mass Index
   a. kilograms = $\dfrac{pounds}{2.2}$

   Determine kilograms by dividing pounds by 2.2
   b. height in inches
   $\underline{\times .0254}$
   = height in meters
   c. Square height in meters
   d. Divide weight in kilograms by your height in meters squared.
   e. Desirable 22.4
   24.8 = 10% overweight
   27.2 = 20% overweight (obese)

   Body mass index formula using pounds:

   $$BMI = \frac{\text{weight (pounds)} \times 703}{\text{height (inches)}^2}$$

Formula 1: Dr. Roger Sherwin, Professor of Epidemiology. University of Maryland School of Medicine. Used with permission.

Formula 2: Hartmann, P., and Bell, E., *Nutrition for the Athlete, Sports Medicine for the Primary Care Physician*, East Norwalk, CT: Appleton-Century-Crofts, 1984, p. 108.

Formula 3: Nutrient Data Laboratory, Agricultural Research Service, Beltsville Human Nutrition Research Center, 4700 River Road, Unit 89, FDA. http://ww.fda.gov/search.html

Figure 10–1   Three Weight Formulas for Adults

Restrictive diets are unreasonable programs that can spell failure in the long run. We live in a society in which food abounds, and it is not easy to resist the vast array of culinary pleasures, whether of the gourmet or the fast food variety. Even if the temptations presented at holidays, birthdays, and office parties are overcome, the diet effort is often a disappointment.

This failure is not the fault of the dieter. The dieter's body, fearing starvation and death, lowers its metabolism, burns fewer calories, which causes the dieter to gain weight. As long as four years after going off a drastically calorie reduced diet, the basal metabolic rate can remain reduced by 28%.

Two possible ways to keep the metabolic rate up while dieting are to exercise and to change the time and frequency of eating. Exercising the body so the metabolism increases is based on the premise that a toned body burns more calories than a flabby one. (Figure 10–2 lists the approximate calorie expenditures associated with various activities.)

Recommendations to change the time and frequency of eating stem from the science known as chronobiology. One of the theories of this science is that medicines work best if taken at certain hours of the day. Research in chronobiology is not definitive with regard to eating, but some studies show that changing the day's food intake so that heavier meals are eaten earlier in the day and lighter meals later results in weight loss. Circadian rhythms (biological rhythms in a 24-hour period), such as those of insulin, glucagen, and growth hormone, respond to a change from breakfast only to dinner only. Subjects who eat all of their calories in the morning lose weight, whereas those who eat the same number of calories at the evening meal gain weight. For example, an individual who ate 1500 calories at breakfast and skipped lunch and dinner would lose weight. Someone who ate no breakfast or lunch but consumed 1500 calories at dinner would gain weight.

Another idea is that food intake spread out into frequent, small meals helps promote weight loss. There are studies to support and refute this. One group of

Activity	Calories Expended per Hour
Lying quietly	80–100
Sitting quietly	85–105
Standing quietly	100–120
Walking slowly (2½ mph)	210–230
Walking quickly (4 mph)	315–345
Light work, such as ballroom dancing, cleaning house, office work, shopping	125–310
Moderate work, such as cycling (9 mph), jogging (6 mph), tennis, scrubbing floors, weeding garden	315–480
Hard work, such as aerobic dancing, basketball, chopping wood, cross-country skiing, running (7 mph), shoveling snow, spading the garden, swimming (the "crawl")	480–625

Figure 10–2 Approximate Energy Expenditure by a Healthy Adult (about 150 pounds) *(Source: Nutrition and Your Health: Dietary Guidelines for Americans, Home and Garden Bulletin No. 232, 2nd ed., U.S. Department of Agriculture/U.S. Department of Health and Human Services, Rockville, MD, 1985.)*

scientists reported that it did not matter whether the calories were divided across the day into four meals or eaten in two large meals. The total daily energy expended (the thermic effect of food) for digestion was the same in both cases. Another study found that a person's metabolic rate rose after each meal, and much of what was eaten was burned off. This effect was reduced after three meals were eaten in one day, however. According to the study, eating fewer than three meals will burn fewer calories, but eating more than three meals does not increase metabolism.*

Most of the studies were done on small numbers of subjects for short periods of time. Because the rearranging of meal times and sizes is easier to do than placing people on restrictive diets, this author believes that the method merits a try; it has worked for some of the author's patients. Exercise is always recommended for emotional and physical health, when it has the approval of the patient's physician and when it is done in a supervised setting with a knowledgeable trainer. A self-prescribed exercise program could lead to injury, especially in those who are obese. One who is extremely obese has to consider that shortness of breath may not be from obesity itself but from respiratory and heart problems that have already developed. Therefore, it is essential to have a physician's clearance before initiating any exercise program. Some hospitals are sponsoring supervised exercise programs for such people.

Behavior modification is another nondiet approach to weight loss and involves careful analysis of the activities that lead to eating and a plan of action to change those patterns that trigger overindulgence. The help of a professional, such as a dietitian or psychologist, may be necessary. Some patients may begin to regain weight when they are on their own and without continued support from the health team. After keeping careful records of what is eaten and when, the obese person will disrupt the activity that leads to eating or will substitute another activity. Eating will be done more slowly, with the patient chewing longer or counting bites of food so the total intake will be less. Celebrations and social situations involving food will be thought out before the person attends them so that binging will not occur. Behavior modification works with those who were not aware of their self-abusive eating habits. For obsessive-compulsive eaters, however, this method may trigger even greater degrees of overeating. These people may have deep psychological problems, and simple techniques do not work.

Nutrition and weight control

The quality of a diet, along with an exercise program and timing of meals, is important if the diet is to work and the person's health is to be protected. Attention to the diet's quality is especially important when behavior modification is selected as the weight loss program, because food intake must be well balanced and nutritious.

It is not advisable to follow any program that emphasizes or de-emphasizes a particular food or group of foods. According to the Committee of Diet and Health of the National Research Council's Food and Nutrition Board, the daily diet should contain 55% carbohydrates, 15% protein, and 30% fat. Saturated fat should comprise 10% of the total calories, polyunsaturated fat 7%, and monounsaturated fat 14%. Cholesterol intake should be no more than 300 milligrams daily. Sodium levels should be around 2400 milligrams per day.

Nutrition and the M.D., Volume 15, number 12, December 1989, p. 6.

The number of calories in a diet should be individualized. Each of us eats an amount of food to which our body has become accustomed. By keeping an accurate record of our daily food intake for one week, we can find the calorie level that supports our present weight and then decide how many calories to eliminate in a controlled diet (Figure 10–3).

It is easy to slice off some of these calories, but calories must not be reduced drastically. A very-low-calorie diet (500 kilocalories) over a period of two months has been shown to cause gallstones. On the other hand, obesity, especially in women, is also a positive risk for gallstones.

It seems that reducing weight with a sensible diet is the safest program. Fasting is worse than low-calorie diets because it results in muscle loss. If a person normally eats 4000 calories daily and goes on a 1200-calorie diet, he or she will be miserable and will soon go off the diet. If, on the other hand, this

▨

By keeping an accurate record of daily calorie intake for a week, one can find the calorie level that supports one's present weight.

Time	Food Eaten	Portion Size	Calories
6 A.M.	Orange juice	4 ounces	60
8 A.M.	Coffee	8 ounces	0
	Cream (half & half)	1 teaspoon	15
	Sugar	1 teaspoon	20
	Bagel	One-half	80
	Jelly	1 teaspoon	20
12 noon	Sandwich:		
	bread	2 slices	160
	mayonnaise	1 tablespoon	135
	meat (roast)	3 ounces	225
	Milk (2% fat)	8 ounces	120
	Apple	1 (medium size)	60
	Ice cream	1 cup	300
5 P.M.	Fried fish:		
	fish	2 ounces	110
	flour	2 tablespoons	70
	oil	2 teaspoons	90
	Vegetable	1/2 cup	25
	Margarine	1 teaspoon	45
	Salad	1 cup	25
	Dressing	2 tablespoons	270
			Total 1830

Figure 10–3 Sample Diet Record

person cuts back to 3500 calories, the pain of dieting is minimized and weight loss progresses slowly but successfully. There are calorie reduction formulas that can be used (Figure 10–4), but none is as accurate as keeping an individual record.

Keeping a diet record is easy if one learns a few basic calorie counts (Figure 10–5). Records should be kept for at least three days, with each record done on a separate page. Eating a variety of foods will balance out the calorie differences among foods within the group. For example, if one eats a banana and an orange and some strawberries, the calories will "average" out to the group number. Although the banana has the most calories, strawberries the least, and oranges

---

Formula 1:

For men, 18 calories/pound
For women, 16 calories/pound

Formula 2:

The Harris Benedict equation:
For men, 66.47 + 13.75 (weight in kilograms) + 5.0 (height in centimeters) – 6.76 (age)
For women, 65.10 + 9.56 (weight in kilograms) + 1.85 (height in centimeters) – 4.68 (age)
(This formula is for basal calories. Add 5 to 20% for activity, or multiply by 1.3.)

Formula 3:

For sedentary individuals, 25 to 30 calories/kg
For moderately active individuals, 30 to 35 calories/kg
For very active individuals, 35 to 40 calories/kg

Formula 4:

Body weight × 10 = basal calories
 + body weight × activity calories = total calories
where activity calories = 3 for sedentary activity
 = 5 for moderate activity
 = 10 for strenuous activity
To this total, one may add additional calories for sports or exercise—for women, 6 calories/minute and for men, 10 calories/minute.

ADJUSTMENTS FOR AGE ARE NEEDED FOR METHODS 1, 3, AND 4:

For individuals aged 35 to 45, 94% of calories
For individuals aged 45 to 55, 92% of calories
For individuals over age 55, 89% of calories

Figure 10–4 Calorie Requirement Formulas for Adults

Starchy foods	80 calories	1/2 cup
Fruit and juices	60 calories	1/2 cup
Vegetables	25 calories	1/2 cup cooked
		1 cup raw
Meats (lean)	55 calories	Per ounce
(medium fat)	75 calories	Per ounce
(fatty)	100 calories	Per ounce
Milk (whole)	150 calories	1 cup
Plain yogurt (whole milk)	150 calories	1 cup
2% low-fat milk	120 calories	1 cup
Skim milk	90 calories	1 cup
Cheese	100 calories	1 ounce
Pudding	150 calories	1/2 cup
Custard	150 calories	1/2 cup
Ice cream	150 calories	1/2 cup
Flour	400 calories	1 cup
Cake	350 calories	1 slice
Pie	400 calories	1 slice
Cookies	77 calories	Each
Alcoholic beverages	0.8 × ounces × proof = calories (double alcohol to get proof)	
Sweet beverages	10 calories	Per ounce
Chocolate	180 calories	1 ounce
Fats and oils	2000 calories	1 cup
	1000 calories	1/2 cup
	500 calories	1/4 cup
	135 calories	1 tablespoon
	45 calories	1 teaspoon
Sugars, syrups, honey, and jelly	1000 calories	1 cup
	20 calories	1 teaspoon

Note: Based in part on Exchange Lists for Weight Management, American Diabetes Association, Inc., and the American Dietitic Association.

Figure 10–5 Calories in Food

are in the middle, it is not wise to always eat strawberries and miss out on the nutrients from the other higher-calorie fruits. This same concept applies for each of the food groups. The diet should always be nutritious.

Eating according to the Food Guide Pyramid is one way to a nutritious diet. A minimum of two servings daily of low-fat milk or cheese; two servings of lean meats, poultry, fish, eggs, nuts, or legumes; two servings of fruit; three servings of vegetables; and six servings of grain foods meets the Food Guide Pyramid recommendations. Care must be taken to choose the leaner and less salty foods within each group, most of the time.

Rich desserts and sweet beverages have many calories because of the large amounts of fat and sugar they contain. Some dieters feel guilty after eating sweets or salty snacks. They feel that they have failed to stay on the diet because they gave in to their craving for a sweet or salty treat. They think, "I've blown it anyway, so I might as well eat this whole box of cookies." This self-destructive thinking often begins in childhood, when reward and punishment are metered out as food (e.g., a child is told that he or she can have an extra piece of cake for dessert if a particular task like homework is completed). There is nothing wrong with eating desserts, however, if they are eaten in moderation; they will not cause any disease or obesity by themselves. Unless desserts replace all nutritious foods, they are not bad. Desserts, in fact, can be made nutritious if fruits, nuts, whole grains, molasses, milk, and other valuable foods are used (Figure 10–6 shows examples of two desserts made with ingredients from the Food Guide Pyramid groups). A small portion of dessert every so often will give the dieter the satisfaction of eating something delicious while staying on a weight loss program. The use of skim milk lowers the calories in custard and pudding recipes.

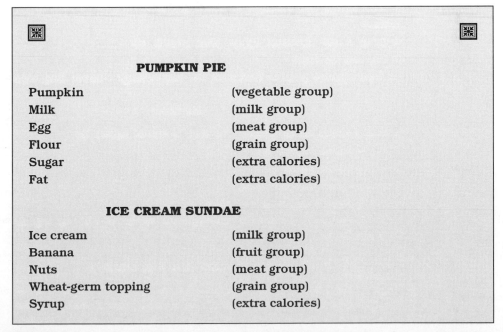

PUMPKIN PIE

Pumpkin	(vegetable group)
Milk	(milk group)
Egg	(meat group)
Flour	(grain group)
Sugar	(extra calories)
Fat	(extra calories)

ICE CREAM SUNDAE

Ice cream	(milk group)
Banana	(fruit group)
Nuts	(meat group)
Wheat-germ topping	(grain group)
Syrup	(extra calories)

Figure 10–6 Examples of Two Desserts Made with Ingredients from the Food Guide Pyramid

A diet should feature enough variety and flexibility that one can follow it for the rest of one's life. Obesity is mostly due to bad habits: eating too much food and eating too many foods with fat and sugar. A sample 2000-calorie weight reduction plan is shown in Figure 10–7.

Some people prefer to use formulas to determine ideal body weight and calorie requirements, and for them the formulas shown in Figure 10–4 can be used. It is important to realize, however, that achieving an ideal body weight is an unrealistic goal for some people, especially those who are extremely overweight. In these cases, a reasonable, reachable goal should be set. A weight loss program should always be gradual, no matter what the final goal is (5 to 10% of body weight is reasonable, according to the 1995 Dietary Guidelines).

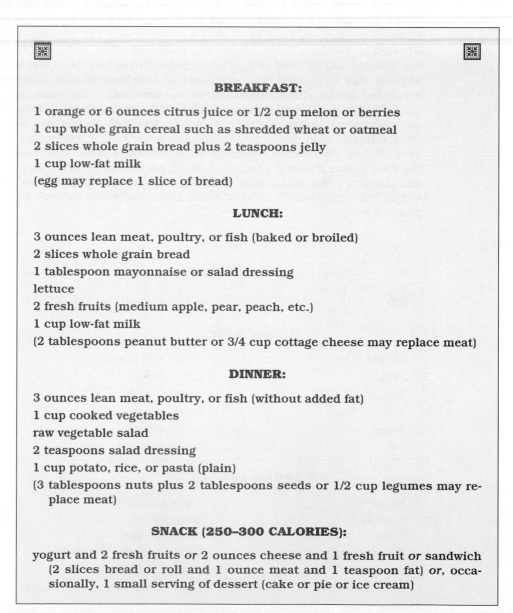

BREAKFAST:

1 orange or 6 ounces citrus juice or 1/2 cup melon or berries

1 cup whole grain cereal such as shredded wheat or oatmeal

2 slices whole grain bread plus 2 teaspoons jelly

1 cup low-fat milk

(egg may replace 1 slice of bread)

LUNCH:

3 ounces lean meat, poultry, or fish (baked or broiled)

2 slices whole grain bread

1 tablespoon mayonnaise or salad dressing

lettuce

2 fresh fruits (medium apple, pear, peach, etc.)

1 cup low-fat milk

(2 tablespoons peanut butter or 3/4 cup cottage cheese may replace meat)

DINNER:

3 ounces lean meat, poultry, or fish (without added fat)

1 cup cooked vegetables

raw vegetable salad

2 teaspoons salad dressing

1 cup potato, rice, or pasta (plain)

(3 tablespoons nuts plus 2 tablespoons seeds or 1/2 cup legumes may replace meat)

SNACK (250–300 CALORIES):

yogurt and 2 fresh fruits *or* 2 ounces cheese and 1 fresh fruit *or* sandwich (2 slices bread or roll and 1 ounce meat and 1 teaspoon fat) *or,* occasionally, 1 small serving of dessert (cake or pie or ice cream)

Figure 10–7 2000-Calorie Weight Reduction Plan

An inexpensive and widely available "high-tech" method uses bioelectric impedance measurements.* Some health spas use this machine, which is somewhat like an electrocardiograph. Electrodes are applied to the ankles and arms. A computer printout tells the individual his or her body proportions of lean body tissue, fat, and water. These machines are reliable indicators of body composition for healthy people. For those who suffer from conditions that are accompanied by abnormal water fluctuations, other equipment, such as skinfold calipers, may be more appropriate. A skinfold caliper is a sort of pincher that measures fat in millimeters. A subscapular skinfold thickness, 12 millimeters in men and 15 millimeters in women, corresponds to a healthy body weight.

The simplest method for determining healthy weight is to use the body mass index (BMI). The Dietary Guidelines for Americans recommend a BMI of 19 to 25 for adults under 35 years and a BMI of 21 to 27 for adults over the age of 35. A BMI over the stated recommendation but less than 30 is considered as overweight, whereas a BMI over 30 is considered obese. Figure 10–1 shows how to determine BMI. The Futrex 5000 Near Infrared Body Composition and Fitness Analyzers provide direct measurement of body fat. During operation, a light wand sends a safe infrared light beam into the biceps of the dominant arm at a wavelength that allows fat to absorb the light and lean mass to reflect it back. The light absorption is measured by the Futrex 5000 to determine the percent of body fat. This is the latest equipment used today.

Common sense is another method for determining healthy weight. Mathematical calculations aren't always a suitable assessment. They can overestimate or underestimate weight for a given individual. A look in the mirror and a feeling of physical and psychological well-being are two methods that should not be overlooked.

The causes of chronic obesity

A few extra pounds caused by overeating does not pose the concern that obesity (20% or more over desirable body weight) causes. Inability to succeed in achieving and keeping weight off is explained by many theories including the following:

1. *Set point theory:* The set point theory maintains that the hypothalamus in the lower portion of the brain programs a set point for body weight. This hypothesis explains the plateau phase in dieting (when weight loss stops despite continued efforts at dieting). It also explains why dieters often return to their former weight after the initial weight loss.

2. *Enzyme theory:* According to this theory, the obese person has 15 to 25% less ATPase enzymes. These enzymes exist in all cells and help burn off calories not used during physical activity.

3. *Thermogenesis theory:* This theory is related to body temperature. The hypothalamic area regulates body temperature, and heat production influences food intake. Cold induces even more eating. Anorexia nervosa patients are found to have abnormal responses to heat and cold.

4. *Brown fat theory:* Brown fat, a special type of fat that contains extensive blood vessels and lobes, is found in babies and hibernating animals. Adults have only insignificant amounts of brown fat, in particular around the neck and chest. Brown fat burns calories rather than storing them, as regular fat tissue does. There are theories that obese persons have less brown fat than those who are thin.

Nutrition and the M.D., Volume 13, number 3, March 1987.

5. *Insulin theory:* Insulin in the brain's cerebrospinal fluid suppresses appetite, whereas insulin in the blood stimulates it. According to this theory, the obese person may have alterations in insulin function. Large fat cells have diminished insulin receptors.

6. *Hormone theory:* This theory is based on the fact that hormones are known to affect fat cell growth, as seen during pregnancy. Appetite is enhanced in many women in the days before each menstruation (at this time, there are heightened cravings for carbohydrates). Around the time of ovulation, when estrogen levels surge, women eat less. Estrogen causes fat to accumulate on the hip. Glucocortical hormone causes fat to accumulate over the back and trunk.

7. *Genetic theory:* The results of various studies conducted on twins reared apart lean toward the probable role of genes in obesity. An overfeeding experiment on identical twins showed that weight gained in response to overfeeding is influenced by the genotype of the individual.

More recently, there have been scientific breakthroughs in understanding the body's weight regulatory system. New insights into the causes of human obesity are likely to follow. The genetics involved revolve around the hormone leptin, secreted by fat cells, which signals the central nervous system.[*]

8. *Medications:* Many medications cause weight or appetite changes. Some antidepressants cause a craving for carbohydrates. Literature on food/drug relationships is usually supplied by pharmacists upon request.

9. *Compulsions and obsessions:* Some people are obsessed with being lean, whereas others feel compulsions to eat. The resulting eating disorders, anorexia nervosa and bulimia, are currently treated as psychological problems. Scientists are investigating the appetite-regulating neurotransmitters that may play a role in these disorders. Experimental studies in animals have shown that damage to the hypothalamic area results in overeating.

Psychiatrists and psychologists do not treat eating disorders as stemming from concern over food, weight, or appearance. Instead, they believe that thinking about food and dieting blocks thinking about other problems. Depression, fear, guilt for not being in control, and low self-esteem are characteristics of patients with eating disorders. Antidepressant and psychotherapeutic drugs are being tried in cases of eating disorders. Interestingly, eating disorders do not exist in countries that do not have the constant food supply available to most of us.

Appetite suppressants

In the 1960s amphetamines were the popular diet pills. They sped up metabolism, were addictive, and caused mood swings.

The amphetamines were replaced by newer appetite suppressants, phentermine and FenPhen (Pondimin). Fenfluramine is the fen in FenPhen.[†]

Phentermine caused sleeplessness, constipation, and jitteriness. FenPhen caused drowsiness and diarrhea.[§]

---

[*]Bouchard, Claude, "Human Variation in Body Mass: Evidence for a Role of the Genes." *Nutrition Reviews*, Volume 55, number 1, Jan. 1997, pp. 521–530; Schwartz, Michael W., and Seeley, Randy J., "The New Biology of Body Weight Regulation." *Journal of the American Dietetic Association*, Volume 97, number 1, January 1997, pp. 54–58.
[†]Gallo, Nick, *Better Homes and Gardens*, Volume 75, number 4, April 1997, p. 64.
[§]*FDA Consumer*, Volume 31, number 7, Nov./Dec. 1997, p. 2.

A combination of these two drugs did not produce unpleasant side effects. The new drug, Redux (dexfenfluramine) works like FenPhen, increasing serotonin levels in the brain. High serotonin levels decrease appetite in some people.

Redux was approved by the Food and Drug Administration in April 1996.[*] The FDA issued guidelines, reserving Redux for people who were at least 30% overweight or at least 20% overweight with weight-related health problems (high blood pressure, high cholesterol, or diabetes).[†]

The FDA announced in September 1997 that about 30% of patients who were taking Redux and who were evaluated for heart valve function had abnormal echocardiograph readings, even without symptoms.[§] Redux can also cause a rare but deadly condition called primary hypertension (the blood vessels that supply the lungs thicken so that the heart has to work harder).

The manufacturers withdrew Redux and Pondimin from the market at the FDA's request.[**] The FDA did not request withdrawal of phentermine, however.

The manufacturers' findings contradict earlier reports of heart valve troubles in Redux users, some of whom took the pill for longer than the time recommended.

The "miracle" pill, according to a report in the British medical journal, *Lancet,* failed to produce more than a few pounds of weight loss in over a third of 822 people in a year-long study on Redux.

New drugs are being tested in the search for a solution to the obesity problem.[††]

Exercise and weight control

Aerobic exercise, the kind that involves steady rhythmic movement, will help a person burn off body fat. (A doctor's approval should be obtained before beginning an exercise program.) If one gradually increases a program of walking, cycling, skiing, rowing, running, jogging, or the like, the enzymes that metabolize fat will perform better. When one is not in good physical condition and gets out of breath easily, fat will not be burned and weight will not be lost. The enzymes that do the job of burning fat require the high-quality protein, vitamins, and minerals of a well-balanced, low-fat diet free of excess processed sugar. Beginning slowly and progressing to a level of fitness is the surest way to succeed in reducing excess body fat and maintaining healthy body weight. The endorphins released in the body as a result of exercise produce a feeling of euphoria, which provides motivation to stick with the exercise program. Forming a lifestyle habit such as taking a daily walk decreases not only excess body fat, but the stresses that lead people to overeat.[§§]

---

[*]Ibid.
[†]Gallo, *Better Homes and Gardens.*
[§]*FDA Consumer.*
[**]Ibid.
[††]Welch, C. B., "The Miracle That Wasn't: Fen/Phen and Redux," *Diabetes Forecast,* April 1998, pp. 40–45.
[§§]"Healthy Weight Maintenance, A Challenge for Dietitians." *Seminars in Nutrition,* Volume 16, number 2, Nov./Dec. 1996, p. 1.

Review Questions

1. Calculate your ideal body weight using each of the formulas shown in Figure 10–1. Which formula gives an answer that is best for you?

2. Keep a 24-hour dietary record. Count your calories for the day.

3. Use one of the formulas shown in Figure 10–4 to determine your calorie needs.

4. Compare your answer for question 3 with your answer for question 2. Discuss the reasons for basing a diet on individual needs.

5. Plan a well-balanced diet using the Food Guide Pyramid. How many calories are in the diet you planned? Use the average numbers in the calorie chart shown in Figure 10–5.

The Food Label, Daily Values, and Goals 2000

Sometimes it is hard for the average consumer to tell the difference between food product marketing and nutrition hype. Catch phrases like low fat, no cholesterol, reduced calorie, and high fiber abound on food packages and in TV and radio advertisements. Are consumers supposed to believe everything they read or hear? Can they rely on the accuracy of such labels?

With the mandated Nutrition Labeling and Education Act of 1990, the Food and Drug Administration and the U.S. Department of Agriculture have championed the consumer's cause in the fight against false nutrition advertisement. This act provides that all manufactured food products must display on their exterior packaging accu-

*rate information that follows the USDA's accepted nutri-
tional guidelines. Consumers are encouraged to study
these labels to ensure that the products they
are buying do, in fact, meet the standards the marketing
and advertisements claim and to determine which products are low in fat, cholesterol, and sodium and high in
fiber, Vitamin C, and Vitamin A.*

After completing this chapter, the student will be able to

- explain why most health professionals consider the FDA food label to be a triumph
- discuss the relevance of the information that is included on food labels
- discuss what nutritional information is excluded from food labels
- discuss any shortcomings of the current food label information
- describe how information is listed on food labels
- interpret the information from various food labels
- explain why daily values are not the same as recommended dietary allowances

Most health professionals consider the FDA food label to be a triumph. Not only is it informative, but the average American consumer can understand it easily. The information that the label contains addresses the major health problems of our society (i.e., cardiovascular disease, high blood pressure, cancer, osteoporosis, tooth decay, and iron deficiency). Consumers can examine the total fat, saturated fat, cholesterol, sodium, and fiber contents of a product and can compare brands to select the one best suited to their particular diet. Portion sizes are uniform and allow easy comparison of similar foods. The important vitamins A and C are given as a percentage of the recommended daily values, as are the minerals calcium and iron.

Unfortunately, there is only so much information that can fit on a label. The former B vitamin information, for thiamin, riboflavin, and niacin, is no longer deemed necessary on food labels. Illnesses associated with deficiencies of these vitamins have been eliminated for the most part because of the enrichment of certain foods, such as flour, breads, and cereals, with B vitamins. The decision has recently (1997) been made to include folic acid on food labels (folic acid, as you will recall, is the B vitamin that may prevent heart disease and birth defects). There is a new folic acid fortification program, which began in January, 1998.

The revised food labeling requirements do fall short on some issues, however. For example, labels do not include trans fatty acid information, although some product labels boast of an absence of these fatty acids. The data on trans fatty acids are not available for many products, and the issue of the role of trans fat as a risk factor for cardiovascular disease is controversial. As the label stands today, trans fats are included with the monounsaturated fat values. This can be misleading because the general belief is that monounsaturated fat is beneficial and helps to lower the bad cholesterol levels in the blood. With trans fats making up part of this monounsaturated total, people could be led to believe that they're doing something good for their body when in fact they may not be.

Another labeling problem is that polyunsaturated fat is not divided into its two families. Polyunsaturated fat is thought to be preferable to saturated fat. Excesses of one type of polyunsaturated fat, however, can contribute to blood clot formation, artery constriction, and inflammatory responses in certain medical conditions, for example, arthritis. A particular type of oil is not always used consistently in a product, and several options may be stated on the ingredient label. It such cases, it would be impossible for the label to provide specific information on the quality of the polyunsaturated fat. When a specific oil is routinely used, this information can be stated clearly on the label.

Daily values are used on labels to indicate how much of a nutrient is found in a particular food product. The daily values are listed as percentages of the RDIs to avoid the complexity of all the different units that are used to measure nutrients (e.g., retinol equivalents, grams, milligrams, and micrograms).

The daily values are not the same as the recommended dietary allowances and are based on the 1968 edition of the RDA. An amount higher than the RDA is listed on food labels to include consumers with the highest nutrient needs. For example, if a man needing 800 milligrams of calcium as his recommended dietary allowance consulted a food label that stated that the product contained 50% of the daily value for calcium, he would be getting over 50% of his daily need (the daily value is set at 1000 milligrams for calcium).

The daily values for calories come in two ranges. The 2000-calorie level is thought to cover most moderately active women and sedentary men. The 2500-calorie level is for more active people. Many women and the elderly may need fewer calories.

"Healthy People 2000" is a report developed by the U.S. Department of Health and Human Services. In it, the "Year 2000 Goals" will set into progress the educational programs needed to enable future generations to calculate and personalize the data on food labels. Great strides have been made, but nutritional programs for the public must follow. Nutrition, which dramatically affects every human being, should be part of basic schooling, national health objectives, and disease prevention.

The Vegetarian Diet

Vegetarianism, in one form or another, is on the increase in the late twentieth century. People choose to become vegetarians because of concern over health and diet and because of ethical or religious reasons.

Although totally vegetarian restaurants are few in number, vegetarian entrees are now appearing on a wide array of restaurant menus. Management and cooks alike must ensure that vegetarian menu items taste good and meet established nutritional standards. Some vital nutrition issues confront vegetarians; cooks must make sure that meals prepared for vegetarian customers are as healthy and balanced as meals prepared for nonvegetarians.

After completing this chapter, the student will be able to

■ discuss why many people are choosing to eat vegetarian for perceived health benefits

■ list and describe the three main categories of vegetarians

■ explain why many ethnic cuisines, like Asian, South Indian, and Mexican, have long histories of vegetarian-based recipes

■ describe ways of using fresh and seasonal ingredients to ensure the quality of flavors and nutrients for vegetarian diners

■ explain the concept of complementary proteins

■ list and describe food choices that aid in proper nutrition for vegetarians

In the fall of 1991 the National Restaurant Association (NRA) did something it has rarely done before: It issued a statement to all of its members advising them to add vegetarian menu items to their daily offerings. Based on overwhelming results from a Gallup Poll designed to register the dining public's interest in vegetarian restaurants and vegetarian choices on standard restaurant menus, then-President John R. Farquharson of the NRA advised restaurant owners and chefs to feature a few vegetarian main dish items on their menus. He added that restaurants may wish to put a vegetarian section on their menu and list vegetarian entrees in that section.

According to that same Gallup Poll, "twenty percent of American adults are likely or very likely to look for a restaurant that serves vegetarian items when they decide to eat out." Further, the poll suggested that "interest is higher among women and respondents 35 and older." These are fast-growing dining-out markets because many women are now career oriented and therefore choose to dine away from home frequently, and the baby boomers are finally settling into middle age.

The NRA-sponsored Gallup Poll also showed an increasing desire among respondents to choose vegetarian entrees because of the assumed healthy implications rather than for ethical or religious purposes. A concern about cholesterol and fiber in the daily diet has steered many customers toward vegetarian-type menu items.

Professional chefs must learn how to satisfy the demands of vegetarian customers through the preparation and service of truly vegetarian appetizers, salads, soups, and entrees.

Vegetarian classifications

Vegetarians are divided into three main categories: *vegans,* who consume no meat or animal products; *lacto vegetarians,* who eat or drink some dairy products, like milk and cheese; and *lacto-ovo vegetarians,* who include eggs and dairy in their diets. The latter two groups are not as difficult to satisfy as the first. For example, vegetarian lasagna and vegetarian quiche, with their cheese, milk, and/or egg ingredients, are acceptable for the latter two groups. But for the vegan these menu choices would not suffice. Pasta primavera without the parmesan cheese is acceptable for the vegan; eggplant lasagna with tomato sauce and no cheese is also an excellent choice. The trick is to design vegan menu items and lacto-vegetarian menu items that would also be suitable for a meat-eating diner who simply chooses vegetarian meals once in a while (a fourth category of vegetarian, but not a true vegetarian).

Curly Parsley

Basil

Oregano

Fennel

Sage

Marjoram

Tarragon

Bay
Leaves

Chives

Thyme

Cilantro

Dill Weed

Rosemary

Fresh Herbs

Green Bell
Pepper

Parsnips

Shallots

Jumbo Yellow Onion

Carrots

Spring Onions

Jumbo White
Onion

Red Bermuda
Onions

Leeks

White Pearl
Onions

Jerusalem
Artichoke

Ginger

Pascal
Celery

Fennel
Bulb

Garlic

Elephant
Garlic

Flavoring Vegetables

Grilled Chicken
Breast with Spanish
Sauce and Ham and
Cheese Grits

Eggplant
Pate

Curried Rice Salad

Broccoli and Cauliflower Coleslaw

Caraway Beef
with Pearl Onions/
Glazed Yellow Turnips
and Figs

Smothered Chicken
and Onions

Flounder en Papillote with
Cauliflower Creole

Herbed Black-Eyed Peas with
Almonds and Raisins

Many diners have decided to reduce drastically their meat protein consumption but are not willing to give up meat entirely. Some of these diners may further restrict their diets by choosing only seafood or poultry instead of red meat. Such diners may include people who are counting calories and/or are concerned about fat and cholesterol intake. Many people age 35 to 49, America's fastest-growing population group, are as much interested in the uniqueness of vegetarianism as in its propounded health benefits. Vegetarian entrees are perceived to be new and exciting choices on menus. Offering these choices increases the depth of menu appeal.

For all of these groups flavor is the most important factor determining the repeat selection of vegan, lacto-vegetarian, or lacto-ovo-vegetarian choices. It becomes the chef's job to understand the demands of each of these groups of people and to offer menu items that satisfy their dietary restrictions. This must be accomplished with the same dedication to texture, color, flavor, and cooking style that is given to meat-based menu items.

There is nothing more irritating to a vegetarian customer, or one who chooses vegetarian items, than to dine at a restaurant where a plate of boiled vegetables is the only vegetarian choice. Such restaurants demonstrate a lack of concern and/or a lack of understanding of vegetarianism and a failure to read the trends in the market and make changes to keep pace with the competition.

Restaurants that cannot or will not offer complete menu items based on vegetarian ingredients (complete in the sense of dietary needs) will not attract vegetarian diners. You may say, "I don't serve vegetarians, and they had better go elsewhere." Remember that all vegetarians have nonvegetarian friends, and many nonvegetarians have vegetarian friends. Do you want to alienate anyone? Being business smart means offering a versatile product in a demanding market. Vegetarian menu items are not complicated to prepare and are generally less expensive to prepare yet demand the same price as meat-based items. Doesn't it make good business sense to add a few vegetarian items to your menu?

Cooking for vegetarians

Learn what a true vegetarian meal is, and train your front staff and kitchen staff to offer vegetarian suggestions. Offer complete vegetarian accompaniments for your regular meat-based menu items. Specialized vegetable and starch accompaniments for all main entrees offer variety for nonvegetarians and complete dishes, when combined, for vegetarian customers. Instead of buttered broccoli, you might offer steamed broccoli and cauliflower topped with toasted pine nuts tossed in a warmed balsamic vinaigrette. In place of glazed carrots, try spaghetti squash with fresh diced tomatoes, chopped spinach, and toasted almonds. Curried mashed potatoes, broccoli in garlic oil, and grilled portabella mushrooms make excellent accompaniments to meat dishes. When they're combined on a single plate, such choices make a good vegetarian meal. These complete accompaniments will please many of your vegetarian guests, demonstrate that you are an educated professional, and add greater variety to the accompaniments you already serve.

Asian, South Indian, and Mexican cuisines have always included vegetarian-style entrees. People from these parts of the world added meat, fish, or poultry to their meals only when it was readily available, which was rare. Recipe books from these cultures could give chefs many ideas about vegetarian menu items, which they could use as menu specials or add to their daily menus to broaden their customer pool.

Staffs must be trained to prepare vegetarian dishes at the same level of culinary innovation and presentation as is representative of all items on the menu. In creating vegetarian dishes, chefs must consider the flavors of the vegetables or seasonings and build dishes that have complex flavors and textures. Satisfying the palate of vegetarians is no different from satisfying the palate of nonvegetarians. A dish that is full of flavor keeps customers from missing the meat.

To guarantee the purity of vegetarian entrees, the kitchen staff should keep vegetable stock on hand at all times. The vegetable stock can be used freely in many culinary applications where chicken or veal stock are called for. Many chefs reheat vegetables for service in chicken stock, whereas others use chicken or veal stock to make rice pilafs. The use of vegetable stocks will supply flavor without the meat. Vegetable stocks do not really cost anything to make because all the vegetable trimmings are put to use. Onions, celery, tomatoes, and rosemary provide a savory and long-lasting vegetable stock.

Some nonvegetarians would be interested in choosing vegetarian menu items when proper thought, planning, and execution are combined in the creation of these items. For example, a dish like eggplant lasagna is tasty and would appeal to most diners. Layers of caramelized onions, roasted eggplant slices, crimini mushrooms, fresh tomato marinara, herbs, spices, and imported cheeses make up this particular dish, which can be served as a main entree portion or to accompany any other dish.

When cooking vegetarian dishes, start with good ingredients that are both fresh and flavorful so you can use the natural flavors of produce the way they were intended. Design multiple applications for all your produce just as you do for your meat and seafood menu ingredients. Using each type of vegetable in many applications makes inventory control easier and ensures freshness.

The use of flavored oils, vinegars, cooking wines, onions, shallots, fresh citrus juices, zest, fresh herbs, freshly ground spices, and cultivated and wild mushrooms can make vegetarian entrees exciting and satisfying for the most discriminating diners. Nature has provided an endless array of vegetable flavors that, when combined skillfully, can make for memorable meals.

Special equipment can also add depth to the flavors of vegetarian entrees. For example, a mesquite barbecue grill can be used to grill vegetable kabobs, marinated tofu, and polenta. The mesquite gives vegetables more depth of flavor in the same way that it gives depth to grilled chicken or steak kabobs. The open flames and smoldering wood chips combine to preserve the natural flavor uniqueness of vegetables. (Grilled tofu must first be marinated in a flavored oil, which adds flavor and protects the tender curds from sticking to the hot grill during cooking.)

Seasonal menus

If you have decided to offer vegetarian menu choices and to commit the same degree of planning to vegetarian dishes that you do to meat-based dishes, then take advantage of the versatility of vegetables and their seasons: for example, asparagus in the spring and early summer, berries in May and June, yellow squash and zucchini in the summer, acorn squash and butternut in the fall and winter. Take advantage of seasonal ingredients at their peak because they are never more fresh, tender, and full of nutrients. Seasonal vegetables often cost less than out-of-season vegetables, especially when locally grown produce is used.

Balanced vegetarian items

The term *complementary proteins* refers to the combination of foods in the diet that add one or more of the essential amino acids. In combination, all essential amino acids can be made present in a single meal without any meat source. Although it is not necessary that every dish contains all the essential amino acids, it is helpful if vegetarian diners get as much balance as they can in every meal.

A vegetarian diet is balanced through the combination of various vegetable, grain, seed, legume, and nut sources to supply the essential amino acids. This is not as complicated as it may sound, but it does take a little planning.

Create entrees that combine vegetables, grains, and nuts in the same dish. Try brown rice pilaf with early peas, carrots, and toasted almonds, or mixed summer vegetables with lentils and roasted sunflower seeds. Succotash (corn and lima beans) is another good choice. (Did the American Indians know something about complete proteins when they invented this dish?)

Soybean is the one vegetable source that contains almost all the essential amino acids, as meat sources do. Tofu, or soybean curd, makes an excellent nutritional choice for strict vegetarians. You can create satisfying entrees using tofu, such as tofu stir fry with snow peas and wild mushrooms, or breaded deep-fried tofu with honey mustard sauce and warm bitter greens.

Vegetarian plates are built with at least three distinct segments: for example, a single vegetable, or a combination of vegetables prepared in a specific way; a starch or grain product prepared and seasoned as a proper accompaniment; and some form of condiment, such as chutneys, chick pea spreads, or bean salsas. These segments help pull together all the flavors and textures on the plate. They can supply great taste, texture, and eye appeal along with the needed amino acids without meat, meat-based items, or animal products.

Review Questions

1. Why did then-president of the National Restaurant Association, John R. Farquharson, advise restaurant owners to add vegetarian sections to their menus?

2. For what reasons do people choose vegetarian menu items?

3. What are the differences between vegans, lacto vegetarians, and ovo-lacto vegetarians?

4. What frequently happens to vegetarians that is irritating and may cause them never to return to certain dining establishments?

5. If vegetarianism is not your restaurant's specialty, then why offer a few vegetarian selections on your menu?

6. How can you design the rest of your menu to make supplying vegetarian choices easier to handle with accuracy and efficiency?

7. When would nonvegetarians decide to order vegetarian-style menu items?

8. What things can you do to help ensure the success of your vegetarian offerings?

9. How can you use the seasonality of certain types of produce to keep customers, cooks, and wait staff excited about the vegetarian menu items that you offer?

10. What is meant by complementary proteins?

11. What vegetable-food combinations give the most complete set of complementary proteins?

12. What plate configuration would ensure proper nutrition for vegetarian diners?

Menu Planning

Preparing food to meet nutritional standards is only one concern of restaurant chefs and cooks; designing a menu that allows this flexibility without increased work or expense is of equal importance. Most restaurants will offer a mix of standard menu items and nutritionally sound ones. Taking extra care in menu planning before committing to special needs is critical for the efficiency and profitability of the dining establishment.

After completing this chapter, the student will be able to

- discuss the importance of offering a variety of menu items to please a diverse marketplace and a discriminating customer
- describe the difference between a food fad and a food trend
- describe the chef's role in guaranteeing customers' rights to make nutritional food choices
- discuss how variety in menu items can be achieved
- use world cuisine for examples of naturally prepared nutritional foods
- build nutritional and vegetarian choices from existing menu items
- create satisfying menu items with the 3 to 4 ounces of meat recommended by nutritional guidelines
- substitute fats to reduce the saturated fats and cholesterol in classical preparations
- substitute meats and protein alternatives in traditional recipes to create new recipes full of flavor and lower in fat, saturated fat, and cholesterol

Nutrition is not something that is likely to disappear from the consumer conscience. As knowledge of the relationship between health and nutrition continues to strengthen, so will consumer demand for nutritionally prepared foods. Despite this focus on healthy foods, it is probably not a good idea to alter all restaurant menus to conform to low-fat, high-fiber, and low-sodium guidelines.

Not all customers want these restrictions. Those who do also have friends and family members who do not. Successful restaurant operators understand the dynamics of their particular marketplace and can offer products and services to attract a wide range of customers. The greater the diversity of customers, the more consistent the traffic flow for the restaurant and ultimately the more flexibility in menu planning for the chef.

Restaurants that only wave the nutritional flag may not be as successful as restaurants that offer nutritional choices. Unless they are located in exact markets, such as near health and fitness clubs and close to a substantial customer pool that wants or needs a restricted diet, restaurants that use strict nutritional guidelines for all menu items lose their overall appeal. The marketplace is diverse, and multiple segments must be satisfied through various menu choices.

Professional chefs play a crucial role in supplying nutritionally sound menu choices for otherwise standard menus. They are the technicians who must bring nutrition to the dining table either by introducing new menu items or by transforming standard menu items into more nutritionally oriented versions.

Nutrition: fad or trend?

Food fads and food trends are two distinct manifestations of consumer choices for restaurant and home cooking. Although they are closely related, food fads and food trends have different life spans and require different forms of commitment from professional food servers. Fads are usually short term and often are the result of media attempts to promote certain regions of the country, particular restaurants, or celebrity chefs. Food trends, on the other hand, are usually reflections of a change of attitude in eating or dining habits. Trends last for longer periods of time than fads and may in time become acceptable, common practice. Trends may have been influenced by several different fads but are sure to continue after those fads have subsided.

Nutrition is neither a fad nor a new trend: It is simply one way of legitimately pursuing the oldest trend of all: the human quest for a long and healthy life. For thousands of years humans have searched for the fountain of youth; it can finally be found in the basics of good eating.

There will always be a place on American menus for traditional foods with high percentages of cream and/or fat, like cheese cake, alfredo, and prime rib. Increasing numbers of customers, however, are choosing healthier foods as whole or part of their daily menus. Professional chefs who understand this may create for themselves a special niche among their competitors.

The chef's role

Chefs have a specific role in guaranteeing the rights of their customers to make nutritional choices. Although not every restaurant patron is counting calories or fighting high blood pressure, those who are should have the option of choosing a menu item or items to meet their specific needs.

Chefs have a dual role in the development and presentation of nutritional choices on their menus: first, in constructing the menu and listing a variety of menu items both traditionally and nutritionally prepared; and second, in designing the recipes and in training the staff who will ultimately produce and serve the recipes. Both roles are supported by an understanding of basic nutritional guidelines and aided by simple culinary substitutions that can transform traditional recipes into formulas for good nutrition.

Menu construction

Except in specialty restaurants (e.g., Italian restaurants serving only Italian food), a well-constructed menu is one that offers a variety of menu items for the adventurous, for the traditionalist, and for the nutritionally aware customer. This variety can be achieved through cooking methods and styles and the use of herbs and spices to create particular taste and flavor combinations.

By carefully selecting menu items from a variety of cooking styles, chefs can offer nutritionally prepared foods that are low in salt and saturated fat without having to label the items as consumer healthy. Clear menu descriptions can lead consumers to make their own decisions about what foods to eat.

Many of the ancient cuisines embody some of the same nutritional guidelines that are proposed in this text. South Indian cuisine, Mexican cuisine, Spanish cuisine, American Indian cuisine, and Asian cuisine are based on the simple and natural preparation of foods, but with an emphasis on taste and substance. Selected items can be offered as part of a restaurant menu: Oriental-style stir fries, South Indian curries and vegetarian entrees, Mediterranean pasta dishes with olive oil and herb sauces, and native North American cuisine with legumes and wild rice are just a few examples. Not all foods from these cuisines are low in fat, but most have low amounts of animal and saturated fats and therefore contain little or no cholesterol.* Those that are not low in fat can be altered by following the guidelines presented in this book.

---

*The ancient cuisines may explain, in part, the survival of entire civilizations through the development of smart eating habits. Perhaps this development was mere coincidence resulting from the use of fresh foods available in each region, as opposed to the twentieth-century compulsion for processed foods.

Modern chefs can select menu items representing as many of the ancient cuisine food styles as they want. These choices offer customers variety, excitement, and good nutrition in their dining experiences.

The use of a variety of cooking methods is essential to the task of supplying good nutrition to customers without taking away the pleasure of eating. Ideal nutritional cooking would use steaming or poaching as the primary cooking methods and would offer simple fruits for dessert, but who would want to base his or her whole diet on these foods? Chefs must offer their customers a choice of menu items prepared in many different ways. This will allow customers to create their own balanced meals while in the restaurant and to balance their restaurant meals with their other daily meals.

It is not necessary that *all* menu items embody nutritional guidelines. Customers who follow strict diets during the day may want to splurge a little at dinner, especially with dessert. Customers who eat freely during the day may want to cut back on calories and fat at dinner. Menu selections should accommodate both cases and a range of choices in between.

As many cooking methods as possible should be employed in each menu category: appetizers, soups, salads, entrees, and desserts. Perhaps not all of the methods will be used in each category, but variety is the key. Menus that feature only fried appetizers or broiled and sautéed entrees are too restrictive for the average customer. For example, not everyone likes thin, healthy consommés, broths, or vegetable soups. Hearty, thick soups also have their place in a nutritional menu.

Traditional menu items can be altered to conform to nutritional cooking guidelines. For example, grilled chicken or shrimp Caesar salad is a popular menu item and transforms a classic dish, the Caesar salad, by adding a few ounces of grilled marinated chicken or shrimp. If a customer wants a Caesar salad but not the high fat content of Caesar dressing, he or she should have a choice in the type of dressing that is used. For a completely vegetarian main-dish salad, the chef might include grilled wild mushrooms, like portabella or shitake, and tofu or beans instead of chicken or other meat.

Commercially prepared low-fat dressings come in all flavors, including the popular ranch, blue cheese, and Caesar. Menus should state that these low-fat substitutes are available. No-fat dressing alternatives should also be available, like honey and lemon or plain lemon. Oil and vinegar served on the side allow customers to construct their own dressing with as little oil as they want.

Entrees should include grilled or broiled meats as well as roasted meats. Lean cuts of meats should be available as well. Ribeye steak, for example, contains less fat than prime rib even though it comes from the same cut of meat. Broiling steaks releases more of the fat in the muscle than roasting. In broiling, fat falls off the steak during the cooking process and is not served. Roasting (especially low-temperature roasting, which is the preferred method for prime rib) does not release as much fat as broiling does, and the fat does not have a chance to fall away from the cooking meat. In roasting, much of the melted fat is absorbed back into the muscles along with the other meat juices.

Entrees should also include combination dinners like fettucini and grilled chicken with wild mushroom sauce, or tenderloin tips over wild and brown rice pilaf. In combination dinners, the amount of meat served is less than the traditional 10- and 12-ounce portions found in steak houses or prime rib restaurants, yet the customer walks away satisfied.

Vegetarian entrees should also be considered, especially if quality vegetable and starch accompaniments to entrees are on the menu. The toasted almonds, polenta, beans, and lentils that are used in vegetarian accompaniments can be used in vegetarian entrees. Creating great-tasting vegetarian entrees does not have to be difficult, but it does take planning and organization.

For desserts, the key is balance, not elimination. Not all desserts need to be on the heavy side. A good selection of sherbet, yogurt, sponge cakes, and fresh fruit cups should be offered along with heavier, more traditional choices.

To create an exciting menu for customers—especially for repeat customers, who are always looking for different experiences—chefs should always consider taste as the number one priority. Taste may be dictated by the herbs and spices used in a dish. Chefs should avoid using dominant flavors more than once in the same meal plan. For example, marinated basil chicken kabobs for an appetizer, basil vinaigrette for a salad, pesto for fettucini, and wild mushroom sauce with basil for broiled flounder will be redundant. The main ingredients—chicken, lettuce, fettucini, and flounder—are only part of the taste sensations. The taste of the basil will dominate after the first two choices. Taste is the collection of different flavors and must have balance as well as complexity. Taste is also dictated by the other flavoring ingredients used. Chefs need to be careful, for example, that everything does not end up tasting like olive oil, garlic, or bell peppers.

Another way to orchestrate variety is through the accompanying vegetables and starches. Many chefs tend to oversimplify the preparation of these accompaniments, as though they were unimportant fillers. Common accompaniments include buttered carrots, cauliflower mornay, broccoli hollandaise, and rice pilaf, but these are so unimaginative that they take away from the full effect of the dining experience. With some creative planning, these accompaniments can become an integral part of the overall impressions of a well-executed meal. A few good examples include sesame seed carrots, cinnamon noodles, turnips with dried figs, and brown rice with dates and toasted almonds.

The recipe

Just as important as menu selection is the development of individual recipes. Procedural and ingredient substitutions can be made, thus ensuring the product's quality and offering more nutritional choices.

Herbs, spices, and other natural ingredients should be used as taste enhancers, as discussed in Chapter 6. When the amount of salt and saturated fats is reduced, a dish's flavors can be increased through the addition of other flavorful ingredients. In recipes that call for herbs, spices, and natural flavor enhancers, these ingredients can be added during the final cooking or marinating stages as well to ensure flavor. Freshly chopped herbs or freshly ground spices stirred into a dish just before service give character to the overall flavors. A small amount of wine, liqueur, or brandy laced into a soup or sauce before plating can enliven flavors without overpowering the main ingredients.

Substituting for fats

Although butter and lard have traditionally been used in cooking and baking, new information regarding the use of vegetable oils makes substitution a simple and healthy process in most cases. Margarine is often substituted for butter and vegetable shortening for lard, but these hydrogenated fats have the same ill effects as saturated fats. It is better to use one of the many liquid vegetable oils whenever possible because they contain no cholesterol and low amounts of saturated fats.

Olive and sesame seed oils are ancient in origin, but some chefs won't use them today because of their pronounced flavors. Using them in moderation and in combination with nonstick pans, which require little or no oil, can produce tasty results.

New techniques in oil extraction have given chefs a greater variety of vegetable oils to choose from. Sunflower, safflower, rape seed, corn, peanut, walnut, and sesame oils are readily available. Even the traditional oils, like olive oil, are now available in lighter-tasting forms. Olive oil can be purchased in extra virgin, virgin, pure, and light versions, each with a different level of the olive flavor.

One problem with using liquid instead of hydrogenated oils is lower smoking points. Smoking point is the temperature at which the oil will burn and give off an unpleasant taste. For frying, a simple solution to the lower smoking points of liquid oils is to trim the size of foods and remove bones whenever possible. By doing so, the foods cook quickly at lower temperatures. When it is impossible to do so, the items can be completed in a very hot oven, which will finish the cooking process and retain the desired crisp texture.

A lower smoking point also means that fat in oil breaks down more quickly and must be replaced sooner. A sign that the oil is breaking down is that it will smoke while heating up in the fryer. Filtering the oil after each day's use will help remove food particles and keep the oil fresher longer.

For baking, vegetable oils are not easily substituted in all cases. In rolled-in doughs and pastries, such as puff pastry, Danish, and flaky pie crusts, the substitutions do not work. In cakes, muffins, and breads, oils work just as well as butter or shortening, with only a slightly lower volume. The difference in volume can be overcome by the addition of whipped egg whites before baking. Whipped egg whites give volume to bakery products because of the air that is trapped in their protein strands.

Replacing butter with oil is a sound nutritional choice, but taste is compromised. The lost buttery flavor should be replaced with other flavorful ingredients, such as pureed fruits, vegetables, vanilla, extracts, or liqueurs.

Another way to replace saturated animal fats with vegetable oils and to increase taste at the same time is to marinate meats and poultry. The exterior fats can be trimmed and fatty skins removed before cooking. These leaner meats, however, tend to become dry and lose their flavor during cooking. Marinades that consist of vegetable oils, flavoring liquids, herbs, and spices allow the products to be cooked quickly under higher-temperature broilers while preserving more of the natural juices and flavor of the meats. Marinades also allow flavors to penetrate throughout the flesh because of the tenderizing effect of marinating acids.

Substituting meats

In some cases, it is possible to substitute one meat for another in a particular recipe and still have a quality product. Much like milk, which can be purchased in whole form and in less fatty forms, and coffee, which can be purchased in regular and decaffeinated forms, some meat recipes allow for the whole or partial substitution of meats with lower fat concentrations. Customers can thus eat their favorite meals with many of the traditional flavors they enjoy but with less fat.

Casseroles, stews, sausages, stuffings, and many meat sauce recipes can use meat substitutions with little effect on overall taste. If complete substitution makes too great a change, then partial substitution is possible. For example, 2% milk is better than whole milk and has more flavor than skim milk. The end result will be reduced fat and cholesterol but great flavor and appearance.

Turkey is one of the best meats for substitutions. It is naturally low in fat and is suited to most cooking procedures and taste combinations. For example, half the amount of ground beef or pork can be replaced with ground turkey without a noticeable taste difference. Venison and other game meats, which are naturally more lean than most domesticated animals, also make excellent substitutes. Game meats may be more expensive, but portion sizes can be smaller because of their pronounced flavors.

Substituting protein alternatives

There are many forms of protein substitutes available on the market. These substitutes are usually derivatives of soybeans and soybean curd. Tofu is the most common protein substitute, but other textured vegetarian proteins are available.

There is no mistaking the taste of protein substitutes for the taste of meats, but their use adds the needed proteins and amino acids and adds substance to otherwise light vegetarian entrees.

Tofu and other textured vegetable proteins can be grilled, sautéed, stir fried, or mixed with other ingredients to make substitute meatloafs, hamburger, or other traditional meat items.

Staff development

The chef or dining room manager may be concerned with offering low-fat, low-sodium choices for customers, but their plans are easily foiled if their wait staff and kitchen staff are not properly trained to deliver such alternatives.

The wait staff are the salespersons and ambassadors for the restaurant. They must be trained to answer the questions customers will ask. Servers must know the preparation methods and ingredients for all menu items. They must also have a basic understanding of nutritional cooking so they will know what substitutions will help transform a traditional recipe to a more nutritionally balanced recipe. Can the chef use oil instead of butter or no fat at all in any particular recipe? Can the flounder be broiled or baked instead of fried? Can the customer substitute a small salad for the baked potato, or a vegetable for the fries? Nutritional awareness will enable the wait staff to help customers make sensible choices. Customers will view an informed wait staff as a valuable part of the dining experience.

Make sure all wait persons taste all new menu items, all specials, and all nontraditional menu items. They can then give their honest opinions to inquiring customers. If a wait person does not like the taste of a dish, the chef must find out why. Customers may agree with the wait person.

The kitchen staff must also be trained in nutritional cooking concepts so they can make alterations and substitutions within company policy and sound nutritional guidelines. It doesn't help to send out a baked flounder, requested by the customer for its lower fat content, if the cook brushes butter on top just before serving. If the chef has vegetable stocks available for vegetarian diners, then the staff must be trained in when and how to use such stocks. Kitchen staff must be further trained to use their own judgment in adding flavors back to certain dishes when the fat or salt is reduced or removed. Cooks must have plenty of fresh ingredients on hand, including fresh herbs and an abundance of flavoring vegetables, to add flavor and substance to dishes.

Review Questions

1. Why does the trend toward nutritional cooking not suggest changing entire menus to meet nutritional guidelines?

2. What are the difficulties in maintaining too many nutritional items on any particular menu?

3. Is nutrition a food fad, with a limited life span, or a food trend that is part of the evolution of humankind?

4. What is the chef's role in developing and presenting nutritional choices on menus?

5. What styles of cooking offer easy adaptations for nutritionally prepared foods?

6. How does offering a variety of cooking methods help consumers make nutritional choices?

7. What combination dinners satisfy the hungry diner while meeting nutritional guidelines?

8. How can you design dessert items that are low in fat but high in customer appeal?

9. Why should chefs not use the same powerful seasonings on multiple menu items?

10. Why are vegetable oils healthier substitutions for butter in cooking and baking than vegetable shortening and/or margarine?

11. What problem is inherent in using vegetable oils for traditional fried menu items, and what techniques can chefs adopt to overcome this difficulty?

12. When steaks, poultry, and chops have their natural fats trimmed before cooking, how can the chef protect them from drying out during the high cooking temperatures of broiling and grilling?

13. When is partial substitution of meats more appropriate than full substitution?

Marketing Nutritional Menus

The business of offering nutritional choices on restaurant menus can go unnoticed if not presented and marketed well. People need to know what is available to them without having to go to long lengths to find out. Proper marketing of nutritional menu items can go far toward satisfying existing clientele and attracting new clientele.

Restaurant management, wait staff, and cooks are all responsible for marketing nutrition. All share in the success or failure of nutritional programs. Nutritional claims must be supported by written documents similar to the labels found on manufactured food products, so care must be taken in promoting and supplying nutritionally labeled menu items.

After completing this chapter, the student will be able to

◼ discuss the costs associated with adding nutritional menu items

◼ explain the guidelines established by the Nutrition Labeling and Education Act and the act's effect on food service

◼ discuss how chefs can promote good-tasting, nutritionally prepared foods

◼ explain why the wait staff should be prepared to answer typical questions relating to nutritional menu items

◼ explain the liability inherent in giving customers false information about menu items and their nutritional components

◼ list and describe some of the more common food allergies and foods that contain these components

Marketing a nutritional program involves everyone in the restaurant. Owners, managers, chefs, kitchen staff, and wait staff must all be willing to buy into a nutritional program if the program is going to succeed. Restaurant owners must be willing to spend the money to train staff, print menus, and give away samples of food as promotion and advertisement. Managers must be thorough trainers. They must insist on a high level of service and hospitality for customers who want nutritional choices or have concerns about food allergies. Chefs and kitchen staff must be willing and able to offer nutritional alternatives that follow dietary guidelines. The wait staff must sell the program to customers. They must accurately inform customers of the cooking procedures and ingredients used in each dish, and they must clearly communicate any requested changes to the chef.

The trend toward nutritional menu choices is still evolving. No one knows where it will end up. Will all menus gravitate toward nutritional offerings? Probably not. Will nutrition fade away like many other food trends and fads? Very unlikely.

Food Service Director, a leading food service management publication, cites an NRA study announcing that more than "half of customers 35 and older and two out of five consumers 18 to 34 look for lower fat menu items when eating out."* The trend continues to grow, and food service operators must meet the challenge.

Another recent survey conducted for *Food Service Director* supports the hospitality industry's strong commitment to meeting nutritional demands.[†] According to a survey conducted by Find/SVP, 84% of all food service operations, including hospitals, colleges, and businesses and industries, include nutritionally prepared items on their daily menus. A total of 77% of breakfast menus across the United States offer healthy choices, whereas 96% of all nutritional choices are requested at lunch and dinner. A majority, 64%, of operators who serve nutritionally prepared menu items find these items to be profitable and good sellers overall.

Federal guidelines

Federal regulations require restaurant owners and operators to take a more accurate and educated approach to nutrition marketing. They can no longer take a cavalier approach to the use of nutritional slogans or catchy phrases but must

---

*"Nutritional Menus Gain Steam," *Food Service Director,* June 15, 1997, Vol. 10 No. 6, p. 26.
[†]"Nutrition in Schools," *Food Service Director,* June 15, 1997, Vol. 10 No. 6, p. 31.

be able to support nutritional claims. Their information must be accurate, well documented, and available to the customer upon request.

When the Nutrition Labeling and Education Act (NLEA) was enacted by Congress in 1990, its purpose was to safeguard consumers from a few food manufacturers who made fraudulent nutritional claims about the products they sold. Nutritional claims appeared on many products, from frozen dinners to pizzas to doughnuts. Many of these claims were exaggerated and misleading.

The NLEA guarantees that products labeled as low in fat, low in salt, or containing no cholesterol follow national dietary standards. Every commercially processed and packaged food must bear a nutrient label that supports health and diet claims (see Chapter 11).

Restaurants were exempted from NLEA guidelines when they were first published in 1993. What appeared to be a victory by the NRA, however, was overturned by a U.S. district court in August 1996.* Consumer groups levied a lawsuit against the Food and Drug Administration claiming gross misrepresentation on restaurant menus regarding "low-fat" and "heart healthy" recipe claims. There didn't appear to be any standard guideline used in making these recipe designations. Waitpersons could not adequately answer questions on fat or sodium content of nutritionally labeled menu items. (These were some of the same complaints made against the food manufacturers six years earlier.)

The district court believed that restaurant owners and chefs were subject to the same liability as food manufacturers. The court ruled that whenever nutritional labeling was used on a restaurant menu, customers had the right to request supporting nutrient documentation. For example, menu items claiming to be low in fat would require standardized recipe cards that accurately depicted the amount and type of fats used and their composition: saturated versus mono- and polyunsaturated. Menu items labeled as low in sodium would require recipe cards calling for specific measurements of salt and processed foods containing sodium. The total amount of sodium had to meet nutritional standards. Documented information would only have to support the specific nutritional claim: sodium counts for low-sodium foods, fat counts for low-fat foods, and cholesterol counts for low- or no-cholesterol foods.

Common menu phrases that can evoke the NLEA ruling are "free," "low," "reduced," "lean," "extra lean," "good source of," "provides," "high," "rich in," and any "fiber" claim. Therefore, if these descriptive words are used, there must be documentation to back up the claims. Even when the wait staff verbally makes nutritional claims, the restaurant can be held liable to document those claims.

Food and Drug Administration officials claim that the new regulations will not stop restaurants from labeling nutritional items on their menus. Because of continuing demand for nutritional, low-fat, and heart-healthy choices, it will remain prudent for restaurants to promote healthy menu items.[†] According to Dr. Joannie Dobbs, a certified nutrition specialist and restaurant consultant, nutritional acknowledgments can be made on the menus themselves or on flyers, brochures, or posters; or they can be stated orally.

Restaurant operators face two problems in trying to market nutritionally prepared alternatives to their customers while maintaining a commitment to quality food service: first, to overcome the perception that nutritionally prepared foods have little flavor, and second, to ensure that the staff is competent to suggest, prepare, and serve nutritionally designed menu items.

---

*Joannie Dobbs, Ph.D., C.N.S., "Menu Labeling: Problem or Opportunity," *The National Culinary Review*, June 1997, Vol. 21 No. 6, pp. 23–24.
[†]Ibid.

Many customers are apprehensive about ordering foods labeled as nutritional, heart healthy, or light fare. In the past, such foods were presented as small-portion, simple vegetable preparations, with accompaniments like low-fat yogurt and no-fat salad dressings. Because these preparations contained little or no fat or cholesterol, they were considered healthy choices. The consumer, however, was left wanting for flavor and substance. Consumers may also be confused by the preponderance of seemingly different opinions about cholesterol, fats, and salt. Chefs try to incorporate nutritional guidelines in their menu items, but often with blind direction and ambiguous information.

Chefs can prepare high-quality foods that meet standardized nutritional guidelines if they are armed with a solid understanding of the importance of taste and substance in nutritionally prepared foods. The task is to present those menu items to customers in a way that will satisfy the customers and thus enhance the restaurant's reputation.

Building a reputation

Chefs can build a reputation for preparing fresh, good-tasting foods by offering fresh vegetables, especially seasonal vegetables, fresh-cut meats, fresh seafood, and fresh poultry for their regular menu items as well as for those labeled as nutritional. If traditional menu items are prepared and presented with fresh ingredients and great flavor, then customers are more likely to try alternative menu choices.

If a restaurant has a reputation for quality accompaniments and a variety of cooking methods, flavors, and presentations, then the addition of nutritionally prepared items to the menu will be equally accepted. Nutritional items thus become simple dimensional developments in an already diverse menu and philosophy of quality food service. Customers who have come to appreciate the technical skill of the chef, kitchen staff, and management are willing to try new menu items more for the fun of it than for health benefits.

Giving samples

Whenever chefs add new items to their menus, it is a common practice to offer small portions, or tasting, free of charge. This practice encourages customers to try foods they might not normally order, and it gives them the impression that their opinion is valued. This can help build loyalty toward the restaurant and a great amount of good will. If customers are pleased with the free samples, they may be encouraged to buy a whole portion. If they are not happy with the presentation, the taste, or the portions, their comments, if freely accepted by the chef, will help customize menu items that will please and sustain customers.

Staff development

As mentioned in Chapter 13, both the front staff and the kitchen staff must be trained with the techniques and philosophies of nutritional cooking. The wait staff must want to promote the nutritional offerings, and the kitchen staff must understand the mechanics of making foods nutritionally balanced.

The wait staff should be trained to answer nutritional questions and provide standard answers to customers. Here are a few of the more common questions likely to be asked and some possible responses:

- "Can this fish be grilled or baked?"
  The tuna or salmon grill very nicely; the flounder is better baked or broiled.

- "Can I have an extra vegetable instead of the baked potato?"
  Absolutely, we have fresh _____ and _____ to choose from.

- "Can I get a lean steak?"
  The filet mignon or sirloin are the leaner cuts of steaks. We have petite, regular, or jumbo cuts available.

- "Can the lasagna be made without meat?"
  I'm sorry, but the lasagna is made with meat sauce as one of its ingredients. I'll tell the chef that you were asking for a vegetarian choice. May I suggest instead the fettucini primavera with fresh steamed vegetables, toasted almonds, and a side of grilled mushrooms?

Giving false nutritional information to customers can cause legal problems. Inaccurate information can also lead to health problems, especially when customers are on restricted diets. Questions customers may ask about fat and sodium content or food ingredients can have a major impact on their quality of life.

In training sessions servers could role-play to demonstrate the types of questions they are being asked and seek advice for answers. It is a good idea to have kitchen staff at these same meetings. They, too, need to hear the types of questions customers are asking and understand the level of authority management allows them to make changes or substitutions. Team effort makes marketing of new ideas and concepts truly successful. If one side says, "Yes we can," the other side must be willing to say, "No problem." If there is a problem, the customer suffers.

The kitchen staff needs the most training. They are the technicians who will execute orders from the dining room. It's not enough that the chef is properly trained in nutritional cooking; the chef may not be available when important questions need to be answered. The prep cooks, line cooks, sous chefs, garde mangers, bakers, pastry chefs, and other kitchen staff should all be trained in nutritional cooking practices.

Keeping staff well trained alleviates a lot of pressure and stress when workers are called on to answer nutritional questions. The ability of staff to address each situation properly will be a major factor in whether these guests have a great, an average, or a poor dining experience.

Food allergies and intolerances

Food allergies and intolerances cause suffering for many individuals. Requests for information about food ingredients should not be taken lightly by the wait staff. Incorrect information given to a customer with a severe food allergy can result in great pain and suffering for the guest and a lawsuit for the restaurant.

It is a major challenge for cooks and wait staff to know exactly the ingredients of the foods they prepare and serve. For example, many people are intolerant to the food additives monosodium glutamate and sulfites, yet these go by various names and are sometimes not listed on food labels. Lemon juice may be listed on a food label as an ingredient, yet the juice itself may have been made with sulfites as a preservative. The word *sulfite* would appear only on the original lemon juice container.

Food allergies have been known to cause respiratory problems, particularly in people who have asthma, and have even been known to cause death. Other symptoms of food allergies include headaches, itching, rashes, and hives.

The most common food allergies are milk, eggs, corn, wheat, fish, shellfish, citrus fruits, nuts, soy, processed foods, and chocolate. Such food allergies can be complex, as the following examples indicate:

- Peanuts, which are actually legumes, can be consumed safely by many people who are allergic to nuts.
- Milk allergy calls for avoidance of all forms of milk and milk constituents. Casein, whey, lactose, cream, and butter must also be avoided.
- Celiac disease, also called nontropical sprue, is caused by a sensitivity to gluten. For people with this sensitivity, wheat, oats, barley, and rye must be eliminated from the diet.
- Corn allergies include cornstarch and corn oil, which may be harder to avoid in cooking than corn itself.
- Gelatin must be avoided by people who are allergic to pork and beef because gelatin is a byproduct of beef and pork.

WHEAT ALLERGY

White bread
Whole wheat bread
Rolls
Muffins
Biscuits
Pancakes
Waffles
Rye bread (usually contains wheat)
Cornbread (usually contains wheat)
Soy bread (usually contains wheat)
Cookies
Cakes
Pies
Cereals made with wheat
Breaded foods
Malt
Beer
Ale
Postum
Puddings thickened with flour
Commercial ice cream, sherbet, etc.

Meats dredged in flour
Chili con carne thickened with flour
Meatloaf made with bread or bread crumbs
Any sauce or salad dressing thickened with flour
Gravies
White sauce
Cream soups thickened with flour
Any commercial foods made with wheat
Graham flour
Farina
Semolina
Wheat germ
Wheat bran
Cracked wheat
Sprouted wheat
Cracker meal
Matza meal
Matzos
Noodle and spaghetti products

Figure 14–1 Foods Not Allowed (Partial List)

In food allergies, antibodies form that may react with increasing strength every time the person affected is exposed to the offending food. This is especially true for peanut allergy, which can be life threatening. Food intolerances, unlike allergies, do not involve the immune system, but the symptoms are similar.

Food allergies usually cause itching and bloated stomachs; food intolerances cause increase in stomach gasses, bloating, constipation, dizziness, or difficulty sleeping. People with food allergies usually cannot eat any of the offending foods, while people suffering from food intolerances may be able to consume small amounts of the offending food without any ill health effect. For example, a person may be intolerant to milk and milk products but may be able to consume some cheeses and some dairy products with small amounts of dairy included, but someone else who is allergic to peanuts cannot eat anything fried in peanut oil or cooked in the same pan as something cooked with peanuts or peanut butter.

While most food allergies are easy to protect against, others are more complicated. Wheat allergies, for example, may be triggered by a number of foods

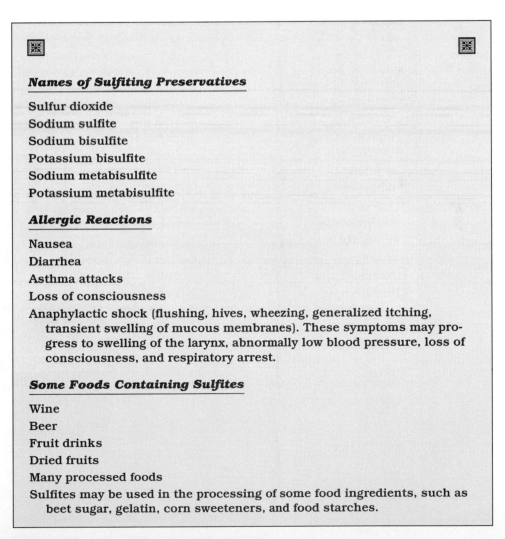

Names of Sulfiting Preservatives

Sulfur dioxide
Sodium sulfite
Sodium bisulfite
Potassium bisulfite
Sodium metabisulfite
Potassium metabisulfite

Allergic Reactions

Nausea
Diarrhea
Asthma attacks
Loss of consciousness
Anaphylactic shock (flushing, hives, wheezing, generalized itching, transient swelling of mucous membranes). These symptoms may progress to swelling of the larynx, abnormally low blood pressure, loss of consciousness, and respiratory arrest.

Some Foods Containing Sulfites

Wine
Beer
Fruit drinks
Dried fruits
Many processed foods
Sulfites may be used in the processing of some food ingredients, such as beet sugar, gelatin, corn sweeteners, and food starches.

Figure 14–2 Specifics of Sulfite Allergies

and food products in which wheat may not be known as an ingredient, such as in noodles and spaghetti products (Figure 14–1). People intolerant to sulfites may have an equally difficult time identifying foods that contain the offending ingredient. Many food preservatives, for example, contain sulfites but may not say so (Figure 14–2). MSG is a chemical flavor enhancer that may cause allergic reactions in many people. It was once referred to as "Chinese Restaurant Syndrome" because of the heavy use of MSG in American Chinese cooking. Since adverse reactions are similar to other common ailments (Figure 14–3), such as diarrhea and headaches, many people who have symptoms may not know the source of the reaction. MSG is found in many common foods (Figure 14–4). Read the labels carefully to see if MSG, or its longer name, monosodium glutamate, is listed as an ingredient. The chemical aspartame can also cause reactions in some people. Aspartame is found in many popular diet drinks and foods as an artificial sweetener. Symptoms may resemble those for MSG sensitivity (Figure 14–5).

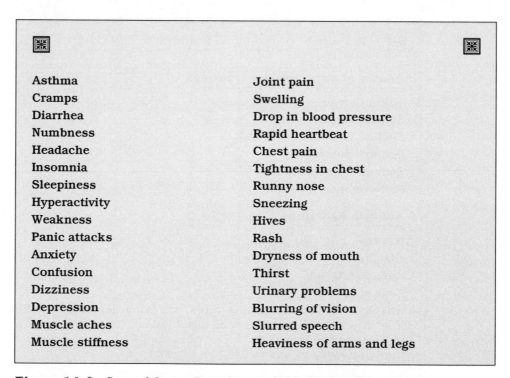

Asthma	Joint pain
Cramps	Swelling
Diarrhea	Drop in blood pressure
Numbness	Rapid heartbeat
Headache	Chest pain
Insomnia	Tightness in chest
Sleepiness	Runny nose
Hyperactivity	Sneezing
Weakness	Hives
Panic attacks	Rash
Anxiety	Dryness of mouth
Confusion	Thirst
Dizziness	Urinary problems
Depression	Blurring of vision
Muscle aches	Slurred speech
Muscle stiffness	Heaviness of arms and legs

Figure 14–3   Some Adverse Reactions to MSG (Monosodium Glutamate)

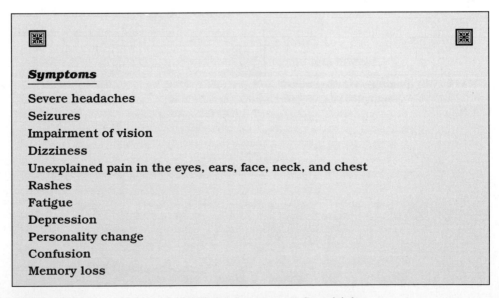

Accent™
Chinese seasoning
Gourmet powder
Zest
Natural flavorings
Flavoring
Hydrolyzed plant protein
Hydrolyzed vegetable protein
Texturized vegetable protein
Soy sauce and some other soy products
Glutamate
Glutamic acid
Commercial broth, soup mix, boullion
Seasonings (mixtures)
Canned soups, meats, tuna, gefilte fish, sauces
Hot dogs, sausages, lunch meats
Salad dressing
Frozen prepared entrees, side dishes, and dinners
Diet foods
Snack foods such as chips, cookies, and crackers

The substances listed are either aliases for monosodium glutamate or contain significant amounts of it. Not all brands of prepared food will contain MSG.

Figure 14–4 MSG-Containing Foods

Symptoms

Severe headaches
Seizures
Impairment of vision
Dizziness
Unexplained pain in the eyes, ears, face, neck, and chest
Rashes
Fatigue
Depression
Personality change
Confusion
Memory loss

Figure 14–5 Aspartame (Artificial Sweetener) Sensitivity

Review Questions

1. With whom does marketing a nutritional program begin?

2. What costs are associated with the decision to offer nutritionally prepared menu items?

3. During what meal periods are the majority of nutritionally prepared menu items offered?

4. Why are consumers reluctant to try nutritionally prepared menu items?

5. How can chefs build a reputation for good-tasting foods?

6. How can a restaurant's reputation foster the success of nutritional menu programs?

7. What can restaurants do to promote nutritional menu items?

8. What is the NLEA, and how does it affect the food service industry?

9. What are some of the typical questions wait staffs are asked regarding nutritional choices?

10. Why must the front staff and the kitchen staff agree on a nutritional menu program and menu alternatives?

11. What are the most common food allergies, and in what various forms are some of the offending foods found?

Preface for the Recipe Chapters

As described in Chapter 1, nutritional cooking is a philosophy of cooking that considers dietary guidelines for low fat, moderate cholesterol, controlled sodium intake, increased fiber, and increased complex carbohydrates. The art of nutritional cooking is making such foods look and taste good at the same time.

The next 11 chapters demonstrate how to achieve both of those premises. The chapters contain easy-to-prepare recipes intended for a large audience of practicing culinarians. The recipes embody information from the previous chapters and offer alternatives to traditional recipes or traditional styles of cooking.

The measurements for these recipes are given in volume and weight measures to accommodate a variety of culinary operations. Standardized equivalent weight and volume measures do not exist for most foods. For example, a cup of small diced onions may weigh between 7 and 10 ounces, depending on the size of the dice and how tightly the measure was packed. To compensate for these differences, 1 cup of vegetable has been equated to 8 ounces of dry weight whenever feasible.

To remedy any confusion, the cook should use only weight *or* only volume measures when trying to reproduce these recipes. The recipes have been tested using both sets of measures and work well in normal situations.

For convenience, here are the main equivalencies that were used:

1 cup honey/molasses	=	8 ounces	1 cup raisins/dates	=	6 ounces
1 cup chopped nuts	=	8 ounces	1 cup mushrooms	=	6 ounces
1 cup flour	=	4.5 ounces	1 cup diced onion	=	8 ounces
1 cup granulated sugar	=	6 ounces	1 cup diced celery	=	8 ounces
1 cup brown sugar	=	7 ounces	1 cup barley	=	5 ounces
1 cup cornmeal	=	7 ounces	1 cup dry lentils	=	8 ounces
1 cup oats	=	3.5 ounces	1 cup dry macaroni	=	2.5 ounces
1 cup bran cereal	=	2 ounces	1 cup sliced fruit	=	8 ounces

Breakfast Foods

American breakfast habits alternate between eating no breakfast at all and eating high-fat, cholesterol-packed meals such as bacon and eggs and sausage and biscuits. People are in too much of a hurry to eat breakfast or too groggy to cook for themselves, or they rely too heavily on fast food breakfasts. With a little planning and foresight, however, healthy breakfast preparations can be made easily and with as much creativity as any other meal of the day.

Some people skip breakfast as a form of dieting. This is a self-defeating practice, however, because people who don't eat breakfast are usually ravenous by lunchtime and tend to overeat at that meal.

The human body needs a regular supply of energy foods and nutrients throughout the day. The first meal of the day is the most important meal because it helps the body recover from its night of repose and fasting. Other meals taken at intervals of four to five hours help the body balance its energy needs with its energy consumption. (Some researchers attest to the benefits of snacking between meals to stave off the urge to overeat at the next meal. Healthy snacks include raw vegetables, fruits, and other nonfattening foods.)

People who choose to eat breakfast away from home need nutritional choices for breakfast, just as they do for any other meal. Without such choices, people will either eat high-fat foods or choose to eat elsewhere. It's not that difficult to offer nutritional choices; it's another way of practicing the art of nutritional cooking.

Here are some simple strategies that will help transform traditional breakfast meals into healthy choices:

- In place of regular bacon, which is full of fat, use Canadian bacon, which is mostly meat.
- In place of ham or Canadian bacon, use smoked turkey breast or grilled chicken as breakfast meats.
- In place of pork sausage, use turkey- or soybean-based sausage.

- Poach eggs, instead of frying, and serve one egg with steamed, seasoned vegetables in place of home fries or hashbrowns.
- In making omelets or scrambled eggs, add one extra egg white for every whole egg used.
- Add fruit to pancake and waffle mix; the added moisture and flavor will reduce the need for a large amount of calorie-laden syrups.
- Add whole wheat flour or a combination of wheat flours and oats to traditional pancake and waffle mixes to increase fiber, vitamins, and minerals.
- Make your own fruit syrups with reduced calories and great natural flavor.

The following recipes are examples of reduced-fat and reduced-cholesterol breakfast items. They do not all fit into the definition of low fat, but the amount of fat and cholesterol is significantly reduced from more traditional breakfast items, whereas fiber, vitamins, and minerals are increased.

Sunflower Seed Pancakes with Honey Roasted Figs

This is a variation on a popular breakfast food, the American pancake. Rolled oats add fiber and iron; sunflower seeds supply fiber and extra protein. The egg whites take the place of oil in traditional recipes, giving moisture and structure to the finished product. The stewed figs and the honey make their own syrup when roasted together; this syrup can substitute for more calorie-laden maple and other pancake syrups.

Makes 20 4-inch pancakes

2 cups, or 12 ounces, dried whole figs
1 cup, or 8 ounces, water
1 teaspoon cardamom, ground
1/4 cup, or 2 ounces, honey
6, or 6 ounces, egg whites
2 cups, or 9 ounces, pastry flour
2 cups, or 7 ounces, rolled oats
2 tablespoons baking powder
1/2 teaspoon salt
1 tablespoon cinnamon, ground
1/4 cup, or 3 ounces, dry roasted, shelled, sunflower seeds
2 cups, or 16 ounces, 1% milk
2 teaspoons vanilla extract
1/2 cup, or 3 ounces, white raisins, plumped
1/4 cup, or 2 ounces, vegetable oil for griddle

1. Mix figs, 1 cup (8 ounces) of water, and cardamom in a saucepan and simmer until the figs are plump and tender. Add honey and place in moderate oven (350°F) for 20 minutes.

2. Whip egg whites to soft peaks and set aside.

3. Mix pastry flour, rolled oats, baking powder, salt, and cinnamon together.

4. Add sunflower seeds, and stir in the milk.

5. Add vanilla and plumped raisins.

6. Fold in whipped egg whites, but do not overmix.

7. Brush or spray just enough oil onto the griddle to cook each batch of pancakes.

8. When pancakes are done, pour roasted figs on top and serve immediately.

Approximate values per serving: **Calories** 366, **Carbohydrates (grams)** 60.4, **Protein (grams)** 9.8, **Fat (grams)** 11.4, **Cholesterol (milligrams)** 1.8. Carbohydrates = 63% calories, Protein = 10% calories, Fat = 27% calories.

⬛Vanilla Bran Pancakes with Strawberry Yogurt

The bran adds fiber and flavor to an otherwise simple preparation. With the vanilla, strawberries, and yogurt, there is plenty of flavor to satisfy your guests. Any fruit can be substituted for the strawberries, giving many variations to this nutritious breakfast.

Makes 20 4-inch pancakes

2½ cups, or 13.5 ounces, all-purpose flour
2 tablespoons baking powder
1/4 teaspoon salt
3 cups, or 6 ounces, bran cereal
1 tablespoon cinnamon, ground
2 cups, or 16 ounces, 1% milk
2 teaspoons vanilla extract
4, or 4 ounces, egg whites
1/4 cup, or 1.5 ounces, granulated sugar
1/2 cup, or 4 ounces, water
1 pint, or 4 ounces, frozen strawberries
1/2 pint, or 6 ounces, fresh strawberries, sliced
1 pint, or 16 ounces, plain, low-fat yogurt
1/4 cup, or 2 ounces, vegetable oil for griddle

1. Sift together flour, baking powder, and salt.

2. Add bran cereal and cinnamon; stir well.

3. Mix milk and vanilla with the flour mixture; stir well.

4. Whip egg whites to soft peaks.

5. Fold in whipped egg whites, but do not overmix.

6. Add sugar and water to frozen strawberries.

7. Heat the frozen strawberries on top of the stove and let them simmer for about 10 minutes.

8. Add sliced strawberries and remove from heat.

9. Fold in yogurt.

10. Cook pancakes on lightly oiled griddle and top with strawberry yogurt; serve immediately.

Approximate values per serving: **Calories** 300, **Carbohydrates (grams)** 52.2, **Protein (grams)** 10.2, **Fat (grams)** 8, **Cholesterol (milligrams)** 4. Carbohydrates = 65% calories, Protein = 13% calories, Fat = 22% calories.

Gingerbread Pancakes with Applesauce and Yogurt

Adding familiar flavors, like ginger and apple, to pancakes adds a level of satisfaction to this simple breakfast for people who are watching their fat and calorie intake.

Makes 20 4-inch pancakes

1/2 cup, or 4 ounces, dark molasses
1/2 cup, or 4 ounces, boiling water
1/4 teaspoon salt
2 teaspoons ginger, ground
1 tablespoon baking powder
2 teaspoons baking soda
2 cups, or 9 ounces, pastry flour
1/2 cup, or 4 ounces, plain, low-fat yogurt
1/2 cup, or 4 ounces, applesauce, unsweetened
1/2 teaspoon cinnamon, ground, for garnish
1/4 cup, or 2 ounces, vegetable oil for griddle

1. Place molasses in mixing bowl and add the boiling water; stir until well mixed.

2. Add salt, ginger, baking powder, and baking soda; stir well.

3. Add flour, a little at a time, while stirring lightly; add only enough flour for a pouring-batter consistency.

4. Cook gingerbread pancakes on lightly oiled griddle until lightly browned on both sides.

5. Mix together applesauce and yogurt.

6. Top each serving with the applesauce and yogurt mix, and sprinkle cinnamon on top for color and flavor.

Approximate values per serving: **Calories** 190, **Carbohydrates (grams)** 30.5, **Protein (grams)** 3.4, **Fat (grams)** 6.1, **Cholesterol (milligrams)** 0.55. Carbohydrates = 64% calories, Protein = 7% calories, Fat = 29% calories.

Spanish Pancakes

People who enjoy Spanish omelets will find this an interesting substitute. Reproducing the flavorful Spanish sauce used in Mexican and Spanish preparations and using it to flavor a fiber-rich cornbread pancake makes this a full-flavored and full-bodied breakfast.

Makes 20 4-inch pancakes

1/4 cup, or 2 ounces, onions, small diced
1/2 cup, or 4 ounces, green bell peppers, small diced
1/2 cup, or 4 ounces, celery, peeled, small diced
1 tablespoon olive oil
2 cups, or 16 ounces, fresh tomatoes, peeled, seeded, small diced
1/4 cup, or 2 ounces, tomato puree
1 teaspoon cumin, ground
1 teaspoon black pepper, ground
1/8 teaspoon red pepper, crushed
1 tablespoon fresh parsley, chopped
3 cups, or 13.5 ounces, pastry flour
2 tablespoons baking powder
1/4 teaspoon salt
1 cup, or 7 ounces, yellow cornmeal
1 tablespoon sugar, granulated
4 ounces egg whites, slightly beaten
2 cups, or 16 ounces, 1% milk
1/4 cup, or 2 ounces, vegetable oil
1/4 cup, or 2 ounces, cheddar cheese, shredded

1. Sauté onions, bell peppers, and celery in olive oil until onions are tender.

2. Add tomatoes, tomato puree, and spices and bring to a quick boil.

3. Reduce sauce to a simmer and cook slowly for one hour.

4. Sift flour, baking powder, and salt together.

5. Add cornmeal and sugar; mix well.

6. Mix together egg whites, milk, and corn oil, and add to cornmeal mixture.

7. Cook cornbread pancakes on lightly oiled griddle until golden brown on both sides.

8. Ladle 2 ounces of Spanish sauce on top of each stack of cooked pancakes; top with shredded cheddar cheese before serving.

Approximate values per serving: **Calories** 338, **Carbohydrates (grams)** 50.8, **Protein (grams)** 10.4, **Fat (grams)** 10.5, **Cholesterol (milligrams)** 7.8. Carbohydrates = 60% calories, Protein = 12% calories, Fat = 27% calories.

Country Waffles with Hazelnut Yogurt

Waffle recipes can be altered to provide more fiber, vitamins, and minerals than standard waffle recipes. Whole wheat flour is partially substituted for the all-purpose flour traditionally used. Rolled oats and cornmeal provide fiber and minerals; their combined flavors make this a satisfying breakfast.

Makes 10 large waffles

1/2 cup, or 2.25 ounces, all-purpose flour
1/2 cup, or 2.25 ounces, whole wheat flour
2 tablespoons baking powder
2 cups, or 7 ounces, rolled oats
1 cup, or 7 ounces, white cornmeal
1 teaspoon cardamom, ground
1 teaspoon coriander, ground
1/2 cup, or 3 ounces, raisins
1/2 cup, or 3 ounces, dates, chopped, pitted
2 cups, or 16 ounces, 1% milk
2 teaspoons vanilla
1/4 cup, or 2 ounces, molasses
1/4 cup, or 2 ounces, vegetable oil
2 tablespoons, or 1 ounce, Frangelica liqueur
1/4 cup, or 2 ounces, hazelnuts, chopped
1 pint, or 16 ounces, plain, low-fat yogurt

1. Sift together all-purpose flour, whole wheat flour, and baking powder.
2. Stir in oats, cornmeal, spices, raisins, and dates.
3. Add milk, vanilla, molasses, and vegetable oil and stir well.
4. Make sure waffle iron is hot and lightly oiled before adding batter.
5. Add Frangelica to sliced hazelnuts in small saucepan and cook until liqueur is almost gone.
6. Allow hazelnuts to cool and fold in yogurt.
7. When waffles are done, top with hazelnut yogurt and serve immediately.

Approximate values per serving: **Calories** 397, **Carbohydrates (grams)** 68, **Protein (grams)** 9.8, **Fat (grams)** 10.6, **Cholesterol (milligrams)** 4. Carbohydrates = 67% calories, Protein = 10% calories, Fat = 23% calories.

✎ *Whole Wheat and Almond Waffles*

Although nuts contain a large amount of fat, the slight amount of almonds used in this recipe does not substantially increase the overall fat content of this meal. The almonds add texture and flavor to a traditionally nontextured product.

Makes 10 large waffles

1½ cups, or 6.75 ounces, all-purpose flour
1½ cups, or 6.75 ounces, whole wheat flour
2 tablespoons baking powder
2 tablespoons, or 1 ounce, almond slivers
4, or 4 ounces, egg whites
1/4 cup, or 2 ounces, vegetable oil
2 cups, or 16 ounces, 1% milk
1 teaspoon almond extract

1. Sift all dry ingredients together except almonds.

2. Stir almonds into dry mix.

3. Whip egg whites to soft peaks.

4. Mix together oil, milk, and almond extract.

5. Add liquid ingredients to dry and stir well.

6. Fold whipped egg whites in batter, but do not overmix.

7. Make sure waffle pan is very hot and lightly oiled before adding batter.

8. Serve fruit syrup (see following recipes) with waffles; serve immediately.

Approximate values per serving: **Calories** 231, **Carbohydrates (grams)** 33.4, **Protein (grams)** 6.5, **Fat (grams)** 8.1, **Cholesterol (milligrams)** 1.8. Carbohydrates = 58% calories, Protein = 11% calories, Fat = 31% calories.

Apple Syrup

Traditional breakfast syrups are made using various natural liquid sweeteners, including corn syrup, maple syrup, and other sugar-based syrups. Using fruits to flavor syrups adds flavor and sweetness without as many calories. The following recipes use natural sugar, natural fruits, and cornstarch to produce flavorful breakfast syrups with more vitamins and minerals and less calories per serving than traditional maple or breakfast syrups.

Makes 16 2-ounce portions

1 cup, or 4.5 ounces, cornstarch
1½ cups, or 12 ounces, water
2 cups, or 16 ounces, sliced apples, Macintosh or Wine Sap
1/2 cup, or 4 ounces, apple juice concentrate
2 teaspoons cinnamon, ground
1/2 teaspoon nutmeg, ground

1. Dissolve cornstarch in water and add to the rest of the ingredients in a small saucepan.

2. Bring to a boil and simmer for 10 minutes.

3. Serve hot or cold on any pancakes, waffles, biscuits, or toast.

Approximate values per serving: **Calories** 47, **Carbohydrates (grams)** 10.8, **Protein (grams)** 0.4, **Fat (grams)** 0.4, **Cholesterol (milligrams)** 0. Carbohydrates = 89% calories, Protein = 3% calories, Fat = 8% calories.

Peach Syrup

This syrup recipe and the preceding one can be adapted to any fruit desired. Blueberries, raspberries, strawberries, and even melons make a wonderful syrup for breakfast meals. In some cases, you may need to add a little sugar or corn syrup to sweeten the syrup to your specific taste, but try to rely on the natural sweetness found in the ripe fruit.

Makes 16 2-ounce portions

1 cup, or 4.5 ounces, cornstarch
1 cup, or 8 ounces, water
2 cups, or 16 ounces, peaches, sliced
1 cup, or 8 ounces, peach nectar
2 teaspoons allspice, ground

1. Dissolve cornstarch in water and add to the other ingredients in a small saucepan.

2. Bring to a boil and simmer for 10 minutes.

Approximate values per serving: **Calories** 54.1, **Carbohydrates (grams)** 13.7, **Protein (grams)** 0.4, **Fat (grams)** 0.1, **Cholesterol (milligrams)** 0. Carbohydrates = 95% calories, Protein = 3% calories, Fat = 2% calories.

Blueberry Oatmeal Crunch

Granola and granola-type cereals add fiber, vitamins, and minerals in tasty combinations of natural foods for breakfast and snacks. This is a baked version of a granola cereal that adds variety to standard menu choices. Any seasonal berries or cut fruit can be substituted for the blueberries to create even greater variety.

Makes 10 4-ounce portions

3 cups, or 10.5 ounces, rolled oats
1 cup, or 4.5 ounces, light buckwheat flour
1 cup, or 7 ounces, light brown sugar
1/2 cup, or 3 ounces, raisins
1/4 cup, or 2 ounces, honey
1/4 cup, or 2 ounces, butter, lightly salted
1 tablespoon cinnamon, ground
1 quart, or 32 ounces, fresh blueberries

1. Mix all ingredients together except the blueberries.

2. Place blueberries in the bottom of a shallow baking pan, or in individual dishes, and spread oatmeal topping on top, making sure to cover the berries as evenly as possible.

3. Bake in oven for 20 minutes at 350°F.

4. Can be served hot or cold, with or without yogurt or light ice cream.

Approximate values per serving: **Calories** 292, **Carbohydrates (grams)** 61.2, **Protein (grams)** 3.3, **Fat (grams)** 5.7, **Cholesterol (milligrams)** 12.4. Carbohydrates = 79% calories, Protein = 4% calories, Fat = 17% calories.

Peach Granola

This simple recipe creates a healthy topping for pies, coffee cakes, light ice cream, and yogurt. With the addition of skim milk and orange juice, fruit granola makes a complete morning meal by itself. Again, the simple substitution of fruits and nuts offers variety.

Makes 10 4-ounce portions

3/4 cups, or 6 ounces, honey
1 teaspoon vanilla extract
4 cups, or 14 ounces, rolled oats
1/2 cup, or 3 ounces, dry roasted pecans, chopped
1½ cups, or 12 ounces, fresh peaches, sliced
1 cup, or 6 ounces, raisins
1 tablespoon cinnamon, ground

1. Mix honey and vanilla together.

2. Stir together all other ingredients in a separate bowl; be careful not to break up the peach slices.

3. Pour honey and vanilla mixture over granola and stir gently.

Approximate values per serving: **Calories** 223, **Carbohydrates (grams)** 43.6, **Protein (grams)** 3.1, **Fat (grams)** 6.2, **Cholesterol (milligrams)** 0. Carbohydrates = 72% calories, Protein = 5% calories, Fat = 23% calories.

Strawberry Granola Parfait

Makes 10 6-ounce parfaits

2 cups, or 7 ounces, rolled oats
1/2 cup, or 2 ounces, walnuts, chopped
1/2 cup, or 3 ounces, raisins
1/3 cup, or 3 ounces, honey
1½ teaspoons cinnamon, ground
1/2 teaspoon vanilla extract
1 pint, or 16 ounces, fresh strawberries, sliced; reserve 5 large berries for garnish
2 pints, or 32 ounces, plain, low-fat yogurt

1. Mix together oats, walnuts, raisins, honey, cinnamon, and vanilla.

2. In parfait glasses, layer first some sliced strawberries, then yogurt, and finally granola.

3. Continue with two more layers, finishing with granola on the top and a half of a fanned strawberry for garnish.

Approximate values per serving: **Calories** 205, **Carbohydrates (grams)** 35.3, **Protein (grams)** 6.9, **Fat (grams)** 5.3, **Cholesterol (milligrams)** 4.4. Carbohydrates = 72% calories, Protein = 5% calories, Fat = 23% calories.

Maple-Flavored Vegetable Blintzes

Many studies have been done on the health benefits of eggs. It has been shown that eggs contain less cholesterol than saturated fats such as palm oil and coconut oil. Eggs contain all the essential amino acids, iron, and vitamins A, D, and B_2.

The butter used in this recipe to brown the blintzes imparts a superior flavor to that of other fats. Butter is a better choice than margarine because the trans fatty acids in margarine have been shown to raise cholesterol more than naturally occurring saturated fats in natural butter.*

Blintzes can be made nutritious by using low-calorie and full-flavored foods for fillings. The amount of butter used to cook the blintzes does not significantly increase the overall fat content. Using nonstick frying pans will enable you to decrease the butter even more, yet the flavor of the butter is still a desired result.

Makes 20 blintzes, or 10 portions

1 cup, or 8 ounces, water
2, or 4 ounces, whole eggs
1 cup, or 4.5 ounces, all-purpose flour
1 teaspoon coarse salt

Filling:
2½ cups, or 20 ounces, carrots, julienne
2½ cups, or 20 ounces, celery, julienne
2 cups, or 12 ounces, shitake mushrooms, julienne
2 teaspoons olive oil
1 teaspoon white pepper, ground
2 tablespoons, or 0.25 ounces, fresh parsley, chopped
1/4 cup, or 2 ounces, pure maple syrup
2 cups, or 16 ounces, plain, low-fat yogurt
1/2 cup, or 4 ounces, butter for frying

1. To make blintzes, mix water and eggs with flour and salt and beat together well.

2. Pour 1/2 ounce batter on lightly oiled crepe pans and cook until lightly browned; turn blintze over and cook on second side until lightly browned.

3. To make the filling, steam carrots and celery until tender.

4. Lightly sauté mushrooms in olive oil and mix in with cooked carrots and celery.

5. Add white pepper, parsley, and maple syrup; stir gently.

6. Place some filling on each blintze sheet and roll in envelope form.

7. Heat whole butter in a sauté pan and cook each blintze in butter until lightly browned on both sides.

8. Top with yogurt.

Approximate values per serving: **Calories** 209, **Carbohydrates (grams)** 31.8, **Protein (grams)** 6.9, **Fat (grams)** 7, **Cholesterol (milligrams)** 76.6. Carbohydrates = 58% calories, Protein = 13% calories, Fat = 29% calories.

---

*Nutrition Close-Up 1990, "Hydrogenated Vegetable Fats Shown to Increase Serum Cholesterol," Washington, DC: Egg Nutrition Center, 7, no. 3, pp. 1, 2.

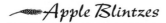 *Apple Blintzes*

Use previous blintz recipe for blintze shells

Makes 20 blintzes, or 10 portions

Filling:
1/4 cup, or 2 ounces, unsalted butter
8, or 16 ounces, cooking apples, peeled, cored, and small diced, Macintosh or Wine Sap
1/4 cup, or 2 ounces, apple juice concentrate
1/4 cup, or 2 ounces, water
1 teaspoon vanilla
1/2 cup, or 3 ounces, raisins
1/4 cup, or 2 ounces, roasted chestnuts, chopped
1 pint, or 16 ounces, plain, low-fat yogurt
2 tablespoons cinnamon, ground

1. Place all ingredients except walnuts in small saucepan and bring to a boil; remove from heat immediately.

2. Place apples in refrigerator overnight.

3. Add walnuts to apple mixture and fill blintze sheets.

4. Roll blintze sheets in envelope shape and heat in melted, whole butter until browned on both sides.

5. Serve with plain, low-fat yogurt and ground cinnamon.

Approximate values per serving: **Calories** 219, **Carbohydrates (grams)** 35.5, **Protein (grams)** 5.7, **Fat (grams)** 7, **Cholesterol (milligrams)** 76.6. Carbohydrates = 62% calories, Protein = 10% calories, Fat = 27% calories.

Ham and Cheese Grits

Instead of an entire portion of ham or bacon, this recipe gives you the taste of ham and cheese without supplying large amounts of fat. This dish represents a complete meal when accompanied with a good breakfast juice such as tomato or orange juice.

Makes 10 3-ounce portions

1/4 cup, or 2 ounces, green bell peppers, small diced
1/2 cup, or 3 ounces, lean baked ham, small diced
1/4 teaspoon cloves, ground
1 tablespoon vegetable oil
1½ cups, or 10.5 ounces, corn grits
3/4 cup, or 6 ounces, 1% milk
3/4 cup, or 6 ounces, water
1 teaspoon white pepper, finely ground
1/2 cup, or 4 ounces, part skim ricotta cheese, shredded

1. Sauté bell peppers and ham together with ground cloves in vegetable oil for 1 minute.

2. Add grits, milk, and water, and bring to a boil.

3. Reduce to a simmer and allow to cook until most of the water is absorbed.

4. Add pepper and cheese and stir well.

Approximate values per serving: **Calories** 156, **Carbohydrates (grams)** 24.4, **Protein (grams)** 6.4, **Fat (grams)** 3.4, **Cholesterol (milligrams)** 9.3. Carbohydrates = 63% calories, Protein = 17% calories, Fat = 20% calories.

Turkey Breakfast Sausage

Even with 38% of its calories coming from fat (compared to pork sausage, at 77% of calories from fat), turkey sausage makes a healthier substitute for traditional breakfast sausages. In a complete meal with one of the modified breakfast pancakes or waffles, the combined fat intake will be below the recommended guideline of 30% of calories from fat.

Makes 20 3-ounce links

4 pounds ground turkey, skin removed
6 cloves garlic
1 tablespoon celery seed
2 tablespoons sage
2 teaspoons white pepper, finely ground
1/4 teaspoon red pepper, crushed
1 teaspoon salt
12, or 12 ounces, egg whites

1. Mix ground turkey, spices, and egg whites together.

2. Make a small patty of the mixture and sauté in a small amount of oil to test the seasoning.

3. Add more spice, if desired, make links or patties, and refrigerate overnight.

4. Sauté links or patties in a small amount of vegetable oil, browning completely on both sides, or broil for no-fat cooking.

Approximate values per serving: **Calories** 141, **Carbohydrates (grams)** 2.4, **Protein (grams)** 19, **Fat (grams)** 5.8, **Cholesterol (milligrams)** 49.8. Carbohydrates = 7% calories, Protein = 55% calories, Fat = 38% calories.

Cornbread Biscuits and Tomato Gravy

Serve with a portion of turkey breakfast sausage, grilled chicken breast, or grilled portabella mushrooms for a satisfying breakfast. The traditional sausage gravy and biscuits contain 728 calories, with 54% of the calories coming from fat. This recipe is a healthier choice.

Makes 10 2-inch biscuits

Cornbread Biscuits:

2 cups, or 14 ounces, cornmeal
1 cup, or 4.5 ounces, all-purpose flour
1/2 teaspoon salt
1 tablespoon sugar, granulated
2 tablespoons baking powder
1/4 cup, or 2 ounces, butter, lightly salted
3/4 cup, or 6 ounces, 1% milk

Tomato Gravy:

1 quart, or 32 ounces, fresh tomatoes, diced
2 tablespoons fresh basil, chopped
1 teaspoon salt
1/2 teaspoon white pepper, ground
2 tablespoons, or 1 ounce, butter, lightly salted

1. Sift all dry ingredients together for the biscuits.

2. Cut butter into dry mix, leaving butter in pea-size balls.

3. Mix in milk and knead lightly into a round ball.

4. Roll dough out to 1/2-inch thickness, and cut into 2-inch round biscuits.

5. Bake on sheet pan lined with parchment paper until lightly browned on top.

6. Mix tomatoes, basil, salt, and pepper in a sauté pan and cook on medium heat for 15 minutes.

7. Stir in butter.

8. Serve 1 biscuit cut in half with tomato gravy spooned on top.

Approximate values per serving: **Calories** 340, **Carbohydrates (grams)** 59.3, **Protein (grams)** 7.6, **Fat (grams)** 8.1, **Cholesterol (milligrams)** 19.3. Carbohydrates = 70% calories, Protein = 9% calories, Fat = 21% calories.

Shirred Eggs and Turkey Primavera

Instead of frying eggs, try shirred or poached eggs to reduce the overall fat content. This recipe calls for turkey and vegetables to add body, texture, flavor, and nutrients. The amount of ingredients allows you to use only one egg per serving and still provide a satisfying breakfast.

Makes 10 4-ounce portions

1 cup, or 8 ounces, zucchini, small diced
1 cup, or 8 ounces, yellow squash, small diced
1 cup, or 8 ounces, cucumber, small diced
1½ cups, or 12 ounces, tomatoes, peeled, seeded, and small diced
1 cup, or 6 ounces, white mushrooms, sliced
1 tablespoon virgin olive oil
2 teaspoons marjoram
1 teaspoon sage
1/2 teaspoon salt
1 teaspoon white pepper, ground
10 slices, or 20 ounces, turkey breast, cooked, sliced
10 whole eggs
5 teaspoons, or 0.75 ounce, parmesan cheese

1. Place all vegetables and seasonings in a saucepan and cook for 10 minutes.

2. Brush olive oil on the inside of 10 8-ounce ramekins or similar containers.

3. Line each ramekin with one 1½-ounce slice of cooked turkey breast.

4. Spoon 3 ounces of vegetable mix on top of turkey.

5. Place one raw egg on top of each dish and sprinkle 1/2 teaspoon of parmesan cheese on each.

6. Bake in 400°F oven for 15 minutes, or until egg reaches desired degree of doneness.

Approximate values per serving: **Calories** 104, **Carbohydrates (grams)** 4.3, **Protein (grams)** 14.8, **Fat (grams)** 3.2, **Cholesterol (milligrams)** 24.8. Carbohydrates = 17% calories, Protein = 56% calories, Fat = 27% calories.

Grilled Chicken Breast with Spanish Sauce

Replace fatty breakfast meats like bacon and sausage with less fatty meats like chicken, veal, and beef. Marinating boneless, skinless chicken or lean pieces of veal or beef can help add flavors not usually present in these less fatty meats. This recipe can accompany many of the previous breakfast recipes to make a complete meal.

Makes 10 4-ounce portions

Spanish Sauce:

1/2 cup, or 4 ounces, celery, small diced
1/2 cup, or 4 ounces, bell pepper, small diced
1/4 cup, or 2 ounces, onion, small diced
1 tablespoon olive oil
2 teaspoons garlic, freshly chopped
1 tablespoon parsley, freshly chopped
1/2 tablespoon cilantro, freshly chopped
1 teaspoon cumin, ground
1 teaspoon black pepper, ground
1/2 teaspoon salt
1 quart, or 32 ounces, tomatoes, diced

Chicken Breast:

10 4-ounce skinless, boneless breasts
1/4 cup, or 2 ounces, balsamic vinegar
1/4 cup, or 2 ounces, onion, finely diced
2 teaspoons paprika, ground
1 teaspoon black pepper, ground
1/2 teaspoon salt

1. Heat olive oil in saucepan and cook celery, bell peppers, and onion until tender. Do not brown.

2. Add garlic and spices and cook for an additional minute.

3. Add tomatoes and simmer for 1 hour.

4. Combine vinegar, onion, and spices for chicken marinade.

5. Soak chicken breasts in marinade for at least 15 minutes.

6. Grill or broil chicken breasts until done.

7. Serve one breast with 2 ounces of Spanish sauce.

Approximate values per serving: **Calories** 216, **Carbohydrates (grams)** 7.4, **Protein (grams)** 34.3, **Fat (grams)** 5.1, **Cholesterol (milligrams)** 87.2. Carbohydrates = 14% calories, Protein = 64% calories, Fat = 22% calories.

Appetizers

Well-planned appetizers play an integral part in the overall enjoyment of the dining experience. If they are properly designed, appetizers can act as a bridge between hunger and the main course and set the tone for the entire meal.

Appetizers need to be distinctive in flavors and textures but not overpowering in style or presentation. They should encompass a wide variety of flavors, cooking techniques, and portion sizes to satisfy a wide range of customers. Customers who regularly order appetizers are usually looking for value, variety, and often nutritional choices.

Value-minded customers may select appetizers that are neither complicated nor expensive. They are looking to round out their meal with tasty, bite-size portions of foods, and they don't want to become overly full with the first course. Appetizers should be large enough to satisfy customers' initial hunger but not too large to ruin their appetite.

Customers want a variety of foods, flavors, and cooking techniques to choose from. Offer appetizers in all categories of foods: vegetables, proteins, grains, fruits, and dairy, prepared in as many cooking methods as is practical. Fried appetizers may be acceptable, but also offer grilled, poached, baked, and cold preparations to allow customers to choose the appetizer that best complements the rest of the meal.

Plan appetizers with flavors and ingredients that complement the entrees, but do not duplicate them. Small portions of entrees do not always make satisfying appetizers; large appetizers must not take the place of the main course.

Using the techniques outlined in this text, it is easy to plan and construct appetizers that meet the aforementioned requirements yet maintain a high level of nutrition. Exciting flavors can be achieved using herbs, spices, and other flavoring ingredients. Flavors do not have to be dominated by fat or sodium.

Some traditionally prepared appetizers that are relatively high in fat can be augmented with no-fat or low-fat accompaniments to lower the total plate value to recommended standards. For example, the batter-fried popcorn shrimp recipe, which contains 32% fat, can be served with a small portion of the brunoise salad on a piece of leaf lettuce (21% fat) as an accompaniment to lower the total plate fat percentage to 30%. Adding sliced fresh vegetables like tomatoes, celery, and carrots; small portions of other low-fat salad recipes; or sliced fruits and berries will have the same effect on the overall plate fat content.

⬤ *Wild Rice Corn Fritters with Sour Cream Cinnamon Sauce*

Wild rice is not a rice but the seed of a marsh grass. It is found in fresh and brackish waters in Minnesota and Wisconsin. At one time it was abundant, but overharvesting has nearly brought it to extinction in the United States.

It takes longer to cook wild rice than regular white or brown rice. The kernels will still have a slight bite when fully cooked, giving a nice texture to the final dish.

One cup of raw wild rice has 22.6 grams of protein, 120.5 grams of carbohydrate, and a slight amount of fat. It has more than double the iron of brown rice.

The buckwheat flour in this recipe is a special food. Buckwheat is grown extensively in Siberia and parts of Europe. It is also known by the names *beechnut* (because the seeds resemble beechnuts) and *saracen* (because of its dark color). Until the end of the nineteenth century, buckwheat was a staple food in northeastern Europe. Botanically, buckwheat is not a cereal, but its seeds yield a flour, so buckwheat is correctly called a grain. Many people consider buckwheat a weed and use it as a cover crop to fertilize their farms.

Buckwheat is fed more to animals than to humans. This is unfortunate because this gray flour with black flecks is rich in minerals and B vitamins and has a lower caloric value than any of the cereal grains.

The corn oil in this recipe helps balance out the small amount of saturated fat in the low-fat sour cream. The recipe contains less than 25 milligrams of cholesterol.

Makes 20 2-ounce fritters

1/2 cup, or 4 ounces, wild rice
1½ cups, or 12 ounces, water
1 cup, or 8 ounces, whole kernel corn
1/4 cup, or 2 ounces, celery, peeled and finely diced
1 cup, or 4.5 ounces, buckwheat flour
1 tablespoon baking powder
1/2 teaspoon white pepper, ground
1 teaspoon allspice, ground
2, or 2 ounces, egg whites
1 tablespoon corn oil
1 tablespoon vanilla extract
1/2 cup, or 4 ounces, 1% milk

1½ cups, or 12 ounces, low-fat sour cream
1 tablespoon cinnamon, ground

1. Cook wild rice in water until tender.

2. Sift together buckwheat flour, baking powder, white pepper, and allspice.

3. Whip together egg whites, oil, and vanilla until well mixed, and add to dry ingredients.

4. Add milk and stir well.

5. Add corn, celery, and rice to the mixture and stir to incorporate all ingredients.

6. Measure 2 ounces of batter for fritter, and cook on lightly oiled griddle.

7. Cook fritters on one side until batter begins to show bubbles; flip over gently and cook the other side until firm.

8. Mix the sour cream and cinnamon, and spoon over each serving of fritters.

Approximate values per serving: **Calories** 164, **Carbohydrates (grams)** 25.7, **Protein (grams)** 4.6, **Fat (grams)** 5.5, **Cholesterol (milligrams)** 8. Carbohydrates = 60% calories, Protein = 11% calories, Fat = 29% calories.

Eggplant Pâté

Eggplant's nutritional value is its scarcity of calories—only 24 in a 3½-ounce portion. This beautiful vegetable has been used in Mediterranean and east Mediterranean cuisines for centuries. An eggplant can weigh from 1 to 5 pounds.

A 3½-ounce portion of eggplant contains 92.7 grams of moisture, 1.2 grams of protein, 0.2 grams of fat, and 5.5 grams of carbohydrate. Almost a fifth of the carbohydrates come from fiber. Although eggplant is not a great source of any one vitamin or mineral, it is a storehouse of small amounts of vitamins A, C, B_1, B_2, and B_3 and calcium, chlorine, copper, iron, magnesium, manganese, phosphorus, potassium, and fluorine.*

Makes 10 4-ounce portions

1/2 gallon, or 2 pounds, eggplant, peeled and diced
2 tablespoons, or 1 ounce, virgin olive oil
1 cup, or 8 ounces, onion, small diced
1/2 cup, or 4 ounces, bell pepper, small diced
2 tablespoons garlic, finely chopped
2 cups, or 16 ounces, tomato concassé (peeled, seeded, and small diced)
1/4 cup basil, fresh chopped
1/4 cup, or 2 ounces, ripe olives (Sevillan), chopped
2 teaspoons black pepper, coarsely ground
1 lemon, for its juice
1 head of lettuce leaf for base of plate
1 French baguette, sliced, for croutons
2 tablespoons, or 1 ounce, butter, lightly salted

1. Sauté diced eggplant in olive oil until lightly browned; remove from pan.

2. In the same pan, sauté onions, bell peppers, and garlic for 2 minutes (vegetables should still have some texture, and garlic should not brown).

3. Mix everything else together in a large bowl with the cooked vegetables; squeeze the lemon for its juice.

4. Refrigerate overnight.

5. Serve a large scoop of pâté over a bed of leaf lettuce with French bread croutons (toasted with a small amount of butter).

Approximate values per serving: **Calories** 203, **Carbohydrates (grams)** 31.2, **Protein (grams)** 5.6, **Fat (grams)** 7.2, **Cholesterol (milligrams)** 7. Carbohydrates = 59% calories, Protein = 11% calories, Fat = 30% calories.

---

*Douglas M. Considine and Glen D. Considine, *Foods and Food Production Encyclopedia*. New York: Van Nostrand Reinhold, 1987, pp. 593–596.

Brunoise Salad

Diced fresh vegetables contribute large amounts of flavor to a simple dish. This dish can be served with toasted French bread or simply on a bed of salad greens. Because of the tremendous amounts of flavor from the vegetables, the balsamic vinegar, and the lemon juice, little oil is needed to enhance flavors or mouth feel.

Makes 10 4-ounce portions

1 cup, or 8 ounces, celery, finely diced
1 cup, or 8 ounces, carrots, finely diced
1 cup, or 8 ounces, cucumbers, peeled and seeded, finely diced
1 cup, or 8 ounces, zucchini, finely diced
1/2 cup, or 4 ounces, onion, finely diced
1/2 cup, or 4 ounces, red bell peppers or pimentos, finely diced
1 tablespoon virgin olive oil
1/4 cup, or 2 ounces, lemon juice
1/4 cup, or 2 ounces, balsamic vinegar
2 tablespoons fresh basil, chopped
1/2 teaspoon white pepper, ground
1/2 teaspoon salt
10 leaves green leaf lettuce
20 slices French bread, sliced, dry toasted, or Melba toast

1. Combine all ingredients except lettuce leaves and French bread toast.

2. Stir well, and refrigerate overnight.

3. Serve a 4-ounce (1/2-cup) portion on top a piece of green leaf lettuce with two pieces of dry toasted French bread, Melba toast, or other dry crackers.

Approximate values per serving: **Calories** 85, **Carbohydrates (grams)** 15.1, **Protein (grams)** 2.6, **Fat (grams)** 2.1, **Cholesterol (milligrams)** 0.4. Carbohydrates = 67% calories, Protein = 11% calories, Fat = 21% calories.

Vegetable Pancakes with Sour Cream Horseradish Sauce

Vegetable pancakes, or fritters, are not unusual foods. The simple combination of fresh ingredients makes this a healthy and delicious dish. A small amount of flour and baking powder is needed to bind the ingredients together and to give a little leavening to the pancakes.

Makes 20 2-ounce pancakes

1 cup, or 8 ounces, carrots, shredded
1 cup, or 8 ounces, zucchini, shredded
1 cup, or 8 ounces, yellow squash, shredded
1 quart, or 2 pounds, white potatoes, shredded
1 cup, or 8 ounces, whole kernel corn
3/4 cup, or 6 ounces, onion, finely diced
2 tablespoons parsley, chopped
1 tablespoon fresh marjoram, chopped leaves
2 teaspoons fresh savory, chopped leaves
1 teaspoon white pepper, finely ground
1/2 teaspoon salt
1 cup, or 4.5 ounces, all-purpose flour
1 tablespoon baking powder
2, or 2 ounces, egg whites
2 tablespoons peanut oil
1½ pints, or 24 ounces, low-fat sour cream
1/4 cup, or 2 ounces, horseradish, ground

1. Stir together all shredded vegetables and corn with onion and spices.

2. Mix together flour and baking powder and add lightly beaten egg whites; mix well.

3. Add batter to vegetables and fold ingredients together.

4. Grill 2-ounce portions of batter on a hot grill brushed with peanut oil or in a sauté pan; the starch from the potatoes and the egg whites will hold the vegetables together.

5. Brown on both sides.

6. Mix horseradish and sour cream together and serve with pancakes.

Approximate values per serving: **Calories** 187, **Carbohydrates (grams)** 33.1, **Protein (grams)** 6.7, **Fat (grams)** 4.2, **Cholesterol (milligrams)** 2.7. Carbohydrates = 67% calories, Protein = 13% calories, Fat = 19% calories.

Popcorn Shrimp with Chili Sauce

Always make sure the oil in the fryer is at the desired temperature for frying before placing ingredients in the basket. Also make sure the peanut oil is clean and fresh. These two precautions will ensure the least amount of oil absorption in the product. For recipe analysis, assume that 1/2 cup of oil has been absorbed by the amount of batter-fried shrimp this recipe yields.

Makes 10 4-ounce portions

2½ pounds medium shrimp (36 to 41 count), peeled and deveined

Sauce:
1/2 cup, or 4 ounces, bell peppers, small diced
3/4 cup, or 6 ounces, onion, small diced
1 tablespoon garlic, finely chopped
2 tablespoons, or 1 ounce, olive oil
1 tablespoon chili powder
1 teaspoon coriander, ground
1 teaspoon cumin, ground
2 bay leaves
1 tablespoon fresh basil, chopped
1 teaspoon black pepper, coarsely ground
1/8 teaspoon red pepper, crushed
1 quart, or 32 ounces, tomatoes, seeded, and diced
2 teaspoons lemon juice, freshly squeezed

Batter:
2 cups, or 9 ounces, corn flour
2 cups, or 9 ounces, all-purpose flour
2 tablespoons paprika
2 teaspoons white pepper, finely ground
2 bottles, or 24 ounces, regular beer
1/2 cup, or 4 ounces, peanut oil for frying

1. To make sauce, sauté bell peppers and onions in oil until tender.

2. Add garlic and spices and cook for two more minutes.

3. Add tomatoes and lemon juice and cook at a simmer for one hour.

4. To make batter, mix all dry ingredients together and slowly stir in beer; add only enough beer for a pouring consistency.

5. Dip shrimp in batter and deep fry in peanut oil until brown and crispy.

6. Serve with chili sauce on the side for dipping.

Approximate values per serving: **Calories** 481, **Carbohydrates (grams)** 51.4, **Protein (grams)** 27, **Fat (grams)** 16.6, **Cholesterol (milligrams)** 169. Carbohydrates = 44% calories, Protein = 23% calories, Fat = 32% calories.

Skewered Sesame Shrimp

A simple preparation that might normally be high in overall fat can have its fat content reduced by grilling and by adding fresh vegetables to the body of the dish. Although sesame seeds are high in fat, their strong flavor can be imparted with small amounts. Sesame seeds can also be dry roasted in a hot oven without fat. They will not easily adhere to the grilled shrimp, so simply sprinkle a few on top of the finished dish.

Makes 10 4-ounce portions of combined shrimp and vegetables

20 ounces small shrimp, 41 to 50 count, peeled and deveined
1 cup, or 8 ounces, stout beer
1 cup, or 8 ounces, small cocktail onions
1 cup, or 8 ounces, bell peppers cut into 1/2-inch squares
bamboo skewers
1/4 cup, or 2 ounces, sesame seeds, dry toasted
1/2 cup, or 4 ounces, carrots, julienne
1/2 cup, or 4 ounces, zucchini, julienne
1/2 cup, or 4 ounces, yellow squash, julienne
1 bunch spring onions, sliced
1 teaspoon fresh ginger, grated
1 teaspoon lemon juice, freshly squeezed
1 teaspoon white pepper, ground
1/2 teaspoon salt

1. Marinade shimp in beer for at least one hour.

2. Alternate shrimp, cocktail onion, and green pepper squares on bamboo skewer three times.

3. Grill shrimp skewers quickly; be careful not to overcook shrimp.

4. Roll cooked skewers in toasted sesame seeds so that some of the seeds stick to the shrimp and vegetables.

5. Add julienne vegetables, spring onions, ginger, and lemon juice into a sauté pan and heat until vegetables are tender.

6. Season vegetables with salt and pepper, and serve two skewers on top of a bed of julienne vegetables.

Approximate values per serving: **Calories** 123, **Carbohydrates (grams)** 8.5, **Protein (grams)** 12.9, **Fat (grams)** 3.8, **Cholesterol (milligrams)** 85. Carbohydrates = 28% calories, Protein = 43% calories, Fat = 29% calories.

Oyster Fritters with Apple and Raisin Chutney

The fat content of a normally fatty recipe, such as fritters, can be decreased by adding other nonfatty ingredients. Apple and raisin chutney served with oyster fritters helps make this dish a nutritious appetizer. Substituting part of the flour requirement with cornmeal adds flavor, texture, and fiber to a delicious preparation. For the recipe analysis, assume that 1/2 cup of oil has been absorbed by the amount of fritter batter used. Accompany each serving with a small portion of any no-fat or low-fat salad, vegetable sticks, or sliced fruit to reduce the total plate fat percentage.

Makes 20 2-ounce fritters

Chutney:
4 each, or 12 ounces, baking apples, peeled, seeded, and small diced
1/2 cup, or 4 ounces, apple juice, unsweetened concentrate
1/2 cup, or 4 ounces, water
1 cup, or 6 ounces, golden raisins
2 teaspoons lemon zest
1 teaspoon fresh ginger, grated
1/2 cup, or 4 ounces, bell pepper, small diced
2 tablespoons corn starch

Fritters:
1 cup, or 7 ounces, yellow cornmeal
2 cups, or 9 ounces, all-purpose flour
2 tablespoons baking powder
1/2 teaspoon white pepper, finely ground
1 tablespoon fresh oregano, chopped
4, or 4 ounces, egg whites, slightly beaten
2 pints, or 32 ounces, select oysters, chopped (reserve oyster juice for batter)
1/2 cup, or 4 ounces, peanut oil for frying

1. To make chutney, place apples, apple juice, water, raisins, lemon zest, ginger, and bell peppers in a sauce pot and bring to a boil.

2. Add cornstarch dissolved in a small amount of water and simmer until thickened.

3. Refrigerate chutney overnight.

4. To make fritters, mix cornmeal, flour, and baking powder thoroughly.

5. Add white pepper, oregano, and egg whites; mix until smooth.

6. Add chopped oysters and just enough liquid to make a thick batter.

7. Use a number 16 disher to measure each fritter.

8. Drop oyster batter in hot peanut oil until the fritters are golden brown.

9. Drain fritters on paper towels to remove excess oil, and serve with chutney.

Approximate values per serving: **Calories** 401, **Carbohydrates (grams)** 56.2, **Protein (grams)** 13.6, **Fat (grams)** 13.7, **Cholesterol (milligrams)** 45.3. Carbohydrates = 51% calories, Protein = 13% calories, Fat = 31% calories.

Peppered Cornsticks with Mexican Lime Salsa

Makes 10 3-ounce portions

Salsa:

1/2 cup, or 4 ounces, onion, small diced
1/2 cup, or 4 ounces, bell pepper, small diced
1/2 cup, or 4 ounces, celery, peeled and small diced
1 quart, or 32 ounces, tomatoes, peeled, seeded, and small diced
1/4 cup, or 2 ounces, jalapeño peppers, seeded and chopped
2 teaspoons cumin, ground
2 teaspoons coriander, ground
2 tablespoons fresh parsley, chopped
1/4 cup, or 2 ounces, fresh lime juice
1 tablespoon lime zest

Corn sticks:

2 cups, or 14 ounces, yellow cornmeal
1 cup, or 4.5 ounces, corn flour
2 teaspoons baking powder
1/4 cup, or 2 ounces, corn oil
1/2 teaspoon salt
6, or 6 ounces, egg whites, slightly beaten
1 teaspoon black pepper, coarsely ground
1/2 teaspoon white pepper, coarsely ground
1/8 teaspoon red pepper, ground

1. To make salsa, mix onion, bell pepper, celery, tomatoes, jalapeños, cumin, coriander, parsley, lime juice, and lime zest; refrigerate overnight.

2. To make corn sticks, mix cornmeal, corn flour, baking powder, salt, and spices.

3. Add oil and egg whites and knead the dough until everything is well incorporated.

4. Roll cornmeal dough on lightly floured table top to 1/4-inch thickness.

5. Cut dough into long strips and twist dough to make ribbons.

6. Bake cornbread ribbons in 450°F oven until golden brown.

7. Serve peppered cornsticks with lime salsa.

Approximate values per serving: **Calories** 290, **Carbohydrates (grams)** 50, **Protein (grams)** 7.4, **Fat (grams)** 6.9, **Cholesterol (milligrams)** 0. Carbohydrates = 68% calories, Protein = 10% calories, Fat = 21% calories.

Cornbread Pizza

Using cornmeal for part of the flour in traditional pizza dough recipes gives added texture and fiber to a simple dish. The use of Monterey Jack and feta cheese in place of more traditionally used mozzarella cheese significantly reduces the over-all fat content of the finished dish. Topping pizzas with fresh vegetables instead of pepperoni, sausage, or ground beef also significantly reduces the fat content.

Makes 2 12-inch pizzas

1 tablespoon dry yeast
2 cups, or 16 ounces, warm water
2 cups, or 14 ounces, cornmeal
2 cups, or 9 ounces, all-purpose flour
1/4 teaspoon salt
1/4 cup, or 2 ounces, corn oil
1 cup, or 4.5 ounces, corn flour

Sauce:

1/2 cup, or 4 ounces, onion, small diced
1/2 cup, or 4 ounces, bell pepper, small diced
1 tablespoon fresh garlic, chopped
2 tablespoons, or 1 ounce, corn oil
2 cups, or 16 ounces, tomato sauce
2 teaspoons cumin, ground

Topping:

1 quart, or 32 ounces, fresh tomatoes, small diced
1/2 cup, or 4 ounces, bell peppers, julienne
1 tablespoon jalapeño peppers, seeded and chopped
2 tablespoons fresh chives, chopped
1 cup, or 8 ounces, Monterey jack cheese, shredded
1/2 cup, or 4 ounces, feta cheese, shredded

1. Dissolve yeast in warm water and set aside until foam begins to rise.
2. Mix cornmeal, all-purpose flour, salt, and oil with water and yeast.
3. Add corn flour to dough until the dough is well formed and dry to the touch.
4. Roll dough into a round ball and refrigerate overnight.
5. To make sauce, sauté onion, bell pepper, and garlic in 2 tablespoons of corn oil for two minutes.
6. Add tomato sauce and cumin and bring to a boil.
7. Simmer sauce for one hour.
8. Divide dough in half, and roll each piece to 1/4-inch thickness and place on lightly oiled pizza pan or other flat pan; crimp up the edges to help hold sauce on the dough.
9. Pour sauce on top of dough and spread as evenly as possible.
10. Cover sauce with Monterey jack and feta cheeses and toppings.
11. Bake in hot (500°F) oven until crust is lightly browned and cheese is melted.
12. Serve with low-fat sour cream and/or guacamole, if desired.

Approximate values per serving: **Calories** 500, **Carbohydrates (grams)** 72.2, **Protein (grams)** 16.4, **Fat (grams)** 16.5, **Cholesterol (milligrams)** 30. Carbohydrates = 57% calories, Protein = 13% calories, Fat = 29% calories.

◆ Chicken Fingers with Sauce Anisette

Traditionally, chicken tenderloins are breaded and deep fried. This recipe replaces deep frying with pan frying and uses a glaze made from Anisette liqueur for flavor instead of breading. Serving this dish on a bed of lettuce with tomato wedges increases its nutritional value and reduces its overall fat content.

Makes 5 4-ounce portions

20 chicken tenderloins
1/2 cup, or 4 ounces, onion, finely diced
1/4 cup, or 2 ounces, corn oil
1/2 teaspoon white pepper, coarsely ground
1 tablespoon lime juice
2 tablespoons Anisette liqueur
8 leaves romaine lettuce, shredded
3 tomatoes, cut in wedges

1. Sauté onion in hot corn oil until tender.

2. Add chicken tenderloins and sauté until lightly browned on both sides.

3. Pour off any extra oil.

4. Add pepper, lime juice, and Anisette and simmer for three to four minutes, or until sauce is slightly thickened and chicken begins to caramelize.

5. Serve four tenders on fresh lettuce leaves with tomato wedge garnish.

Approximate values per serving: **Calories** 225, **Carbohydrates (grams)** 9, **Protein (grams)** 32, **Fat (grams)** 4.5, **Cholesterol (milligrams)** 82.4. Carbohydrates = 18% calories, Protein = 62% calories, Fat = 20% calories.

Cajun Chicken Tenders

One chicken tenderloin is found beneath each single breast. It is not the same muscle as beef tenderloin, which comes from inside the beef sirloin, but it resembles its beef counterpart in shape, albeit much smaller. Boneless chicken breast meat cut into thin strips can be used in place of or in addition to the chicken tenderloins.

Chicken "Tenders" are commonly a deep fried breaded chicken appetizer. This recipe replaces deep fat frying with sautéing, a less fatty cooking method, and does not call for breading. The seasonings are enough to add the appropriate flavors to this dish. Serve sautéed appetizers with a vegetable garnish, like the lettuce and tomato used here, to present a more nutritious appetizer and lower the percentage of total calories coming from fat.

Makes 5 4-ounce portions

2 tablespoons fresh thyme, chopped
1 teaspoon cumin, ground
1/2 teaspoon coriander, ground
1 teaspoon black pepper, coarsely ground
1/4 teaspoon white pepper, coarsely ground
1/8 teaspoon red pepper, ground
1/4 teaspoon salt
20 chicken tenderloins
1/4 cup, or 2 ounces, peanut oil
1 tablespoon lemon juice, freshly squeezed
8 leaves romaine lettuce, shredded
3 tomatoes, cut in wedges

1. Mix all spices together and sprinkle liberally on chicken tenderloins.

2. Sauté chicken in peanut oil until well browned on both sides.

3. Squeeze lemon juice in pan with chicken and simmer for a few more seconds.

4. Serve with fresh lettuce leaves, sliced tomato wedges, and any cold sauce you desire (low-fat sour cream and chives is an excellent accompanying sauce).

Approximate values per serving: **Calories** 199, **Carbohydrates (grams)** 6.7, **Protein (grams)** 31.8, **Fat (grams)** 4.9, **Cholesterol (milligrams)** 82.4. Carbohydrates = 14% calories, Protein = 64% calories, Fat = 22% calories.

Crab Coins Maryland

Although this is a very simple dish to prepare, it is full of flavor and tradition. The traditional recipe calls for mayonnaise as a binder, but egg whites and bread crumbs do the job just as nicely. Serve with vegetable crudité, lettuce, tomato slices, and corn relish or other low-fat relishes and/or vegetable pickles to reduce the total plate percentage of fat.

Makes 20 1-ounce cakes

2½ pounds lump crab meat, cleaned of all shells
4, or 4 ounces, egg whites, slightly beaten
1/2 cup, or 4 ounces, onion, finely chopped
1/4 cup, or 2 ounces, celery, peeled and finely chopped
2 tablespoons prepared mustard
2 tablespoons lemon juice, freshly squeezed
1 tablespoon Old Bay seasoning
1/2 cup, or 3 ounces, fresh bread crumbs
1/4 cup, or 2 ounces, corn oil for frying

1. Mix all ingredients together and shape into 1-ounce flat cakes; add extra bread crumbs if cakes do not hold their shape.

2. Pan fry in corn oil until well browned on both sides.

3. Serve with spicy mustard or fresh horseradish.

Approximate values per serving: **Calories** 210, **Carbohydrates (grams)** 9.1, **Protein (grams)** 22, **Fat (grams)** 9.2, **Cholesterol (milligrams)** 115. Carbohydrates = 18% calories, Protein = 43% calories, Fat = 39% calories.

Fennel and Artichoke Hearts: À la Grecque

Fennel is a versatile vegetable as well as a spice (its seeds) or an herb (its leaves). In this recipe, with artichoke hearts, spices, and flavoring ingredients, only a small amount of olive oil is used to give a Greek-style flavor. Adding the carrot sticks and radishes reduces the overall percentage of calories coming from fat.

Makes 10 4-ounce portions

1 pint, or 16 ounces, water
1 teaspoon fennel seeds
1 teaspoon coriander seeds
1 teaspoon cracked peppercorns
1 sprig fresh thyme
1 bay leaf
1 quart, or 32 ounces, fennel bulb, peeled and French fry cut
2 tablespoons virgin olive oil
10 artichoke hearts, cooked and sliced
2 tablespoons lemon juice, freshly squeezed
1 tablespoon fresh parsley, chopped
10 red-tipped lettuce leaves
1 cup, or 8 ounces, carrot sticks, 1/2 × 1/2 × 3 inches
10 radish flowers

1. Bring water to a boil and add spices and fennel.

2. Simmer fennel until tender; drain and discard bay leaf and thyme sprig.

3. Heat olive oil in sauté pan and add cooked fennel and artichoke hearts.

4. Heat vegetables together for two to three minutes and add lemon juice and parsley.

5. Drain vegetables of most of the oil and refrigerate; serve cold on a bed of lettuce with carrot stick and radish flower garnish.

Approximate values per serving: **Calories** 76, **Carbohydrates (grams)** 11.3, **Protein (grams)** 2.3, **Fat (grams)** 3.3, **Cholesterol (milligrams)** 0. Carbohydrates = 54% calories, Protein = 11% calories, Fat = 36% calories.

Roasted Sweet Peppers Vinaigrette

Bell peppers are naturally sweet; the roasting technique enhances the sweetness. Spring onions are also sweet and tender and give this appetizer a balanced taste. In the traditional Italian recipe for roasted peppers, 49% of the caloric content is generated from fat. With the addition of the eggplant and zucchini, the fat content is reduced to 36% of calories.

Makes 10 3-ounce portions

5 large red bell peppers
3 large green bell peppers
2 large yellow bell peppers
1/4 cup, or 2 ounces, olive oil
1 bunch spring onions, white and tender greens sliced
1 tablespoon fresh basil, chopped
1 tablespoon fresh oregano, chopped
1 teaspoon garlic, finely chopped
1 tablespoon red wine vinegar
1 tablespoon lemon juice, freshly squeezed
1/2 teaspoon white pepper, coarsely ground
1/4 teaspoon salt
16 ounces eggplant, peeled and sliced
16 ounces zucchini, sliced lengthwise
1 iceberg lettuce head, cut into 10 wedges
1/2 Italian bread loaf, thinly sliced

1. Rub peppers with a little of the oil and roast in 450°F oven until skin blisters (about 15 minutes).

2. Remove peppers from oven and peel off the skins (they should come off easily).

3. Remove seeds from peppers and cut the peppers into julienne strips.

4. Mix together all other ingredients, except eggplant and zucchini, to make a marinade, and pour over pepper strips.

5. Grill eggplant and zucchini slices separately.

6. Add grilled vegetables to the roasted peppers and marinade; refrigerate overnight.

7. Serve with hearts of lettuce and thinly sliced fresh Italian bread.

Approximate values per serving: **Calories** 156, **Carbohydrates (grams)** 22, **Protein (grams)** 4.6, **Fat (grams)** 6.6, **Cholesterol (milligrams)** 0.1. Carbohydrates = 53% calories, Protein = 11% calories, Fat = 36% calories.

═══Chick Pea Dip and Vegetables

This is a tasty and nutritious dish that makes an excellent dip or a spread for a variety of canapés or open-faced vegetable sandwiches. Chick pea spreads are a popular Middle Eastern food used on all occasions in a variety of applications.

Makes 20 2-ounce portions of dip

1 pint, or 16 ounces, cooked chick peas
2 tablespoons fresh garlic, chopped
2 teaspoons black pepper, coarsely ground
1/2 teaspoon salt
1/2 cup, or 4 ounces, olive oil
1/4 cup, or 2 ounces, lemon juice, freshly squeezed
2 tablespoons fresh parsley, chopped
1 cup, or 8 ounces, celery sticks
1 cup, or 8 ounces, carrot sticks
1/2 cup, or 4 ounces, bell pepper strips

1. Place chick peas (also called garbanzo beans), garlic, pepper, salt, oil, and lemon juice in a blender and puree until smooth.

2. Add parsley to the blender and blend for two seconds.

3. Serve with any fresh vegetable sticks and/or dry toasted crackers.

Approximate values per serving: **Calories** 311, **Carbohydrates (grams)** 55, **Protein (grams)** 16.8, **Fat (grams)** 4, **Cholesterol (milligrams)** 0. Carbohydrates = 68% calories, Protein = 21% calories, Fat = 11% calories.

ᜒ*Pear and Pineapple Relish*

Fruit relishes can be stored in sterilized jars for future use. They were developed as a way of preserving ripe fruit in the fall of the year for use throughout the winter months. The addition of the bell peppers gives this relish a taste that will complement a variety of main meals and snacks.

Makes 15 3-ounce portions

1 quart, or 2 pounds, Kieffer pears
1 ripe pineapple
1/2 cup, or 4 ounces, green bell pepper, finely diced
1/4 cup, or 2 ounces, lemon juice, freshly squeezed
1/2 teaspoon white pepper, coarsely ground

1. Peel and core pears and pineapple.

2. Chop fruit in food chopper until fine diced consistency.

3. Add lemon juice, bell peppers, and white pepper.

4. Refrigerate overnight.

Approximate values per serving: **Calories** 85, **Carbohydrates (grams)** 21.8, **Protein (grams)** 0.7, **Fat (grams)** 0.6, **Cholesterol (milligrams)** 0. Carbohydrates = 91% calories, Protein = 3% calories, Fat = 6% calories.

ᜒ*Apple Pickles*

Other interesting variations can be made by adding different fruits to this recipe: apple and pear pickles, apple and cranberry pickles, apple and orange pickles. The terms *pickles* and *relish* are interchangeable in these preparations; either can be used as an appetizing snack with crackers and cheese or as an accompaniment to poultry and meats.

Makes 10 2-ounce portions

12 baking apples, Rome beauties or Macintosh
1½ cups, or 12 ounces, apple juice concentrate, unsweetened
1½ cups, or 12 ounces, water
2 tablespoons lemon juice, freshly squeezed
1/2 teaspoon whole cloves
2 cinnamon sticks

1. Peel, core, and slice apples.

2. Place all ingredients in saucepan and bring to a boil.

3. Immediately remove from the heat and place in refrigerator overnight.

Approximate values per serving: **Calories** 98, **Carbohydrates (grams)** 25, **Protein (grams)** 0.4, **Fat (grams)** 0.7, **Cholesterol (milligrams)** 0. Carbohydrates = 93% calories, Protein = 1% calories, Fat = 6% calories.

Barbecue Fruit with Honey and Poppyseed Dressing

This interesting appetizer can be made utilizing any fruit that has a firm flesh. The amount of honey used for each kabob is very slight, and therefore the caloric value is relatively low. Be sure to serve these kabobs hot off the grill; they lose their appeal when cooled.

Makes 10 3-ounce portions

1 ripe pineapple
5 kiwi fruits
40 large strawberries
5 large peaches
1/2 cup, or 4 ounces, honey
2 tablespoons lemon juice, freshly squeezed
2 tablespoons poppy seeds

1. Cut the fruit in bite-size pieces (leave the strawberries whole).

2. Skewer fruit in alternating colors.

3. Lay fruit on hot broiler or grill for one minute; turn on other side for one additional minute.

4. Mix together honey, lemon juice, and poppy seeds and brush lightly on broiled fruit.

Approximate values per serving: **Calories** 131, **Carbohydrates (grams)** 30.5, **Protein (grams)** 1.7, **Fat (grams)** 1.9, **Cholesterol (milligrams)** 0. Carbohydrates = 84% calories, Protein = 5% calories, Fat = 12% calories.

Soups

Throughout the development of cultures and cuisines around the world, soups have supplied healthy and satisfying meals. Soup making was a versatile cooking method that allowed cooks to rehydrate dried meat and beans; dilute the salty taste from preserved meats; and combine vegetables, herbs, spices, and meats to form a complete meal in a single dish.

Soups continue to play an important part in world cuisine. For some, soups supply complete meals; for others, soup is only one of many courses in a single meal. Soups can be pedestrian in design or sophisticated works of culinary art, depending on the culture in which it is prepared, the ingredients used, and the soup's place in the meal.

In the art of nutritional cooking, soups can be made to supply all essential parts of a healthy meal in a single, satisfying dish. Proteins, carbohydrates, fats (easily kept within the recommended 30% of daily caloric intake), vitamins, and minerals come together in one pot or kettle, satisfying the most ravenous appetites, and the most restrictive diets.

Thin soups and puree soups supply the most nutrition without the fat. Cream soups can be made less fatty by using low-fat dairy products; cornstarch or pureed vegetables for thickening; herbs, tofu, or legumes for protein; and spices and other natural flavorings to heighten the flavors of the finished product.

If a soup is to be a complete meal, it should contain vegetable, starch, and protein. One cup of vegetable; 1/2 cup of grains like rice, barley, or corn; and 2 to 3 ounces of protein could represent a complete meal, depending on individual calorie requirements. A Louisiana-style gumbo, seafood chowder, or Vietnamese noodle soup could all fit into this category. Chicken noodle, cream of broccoli, or vichyssoise contain only one or two of the vegetable, starch, and protein categories and would not provide a complete, balanced meal.

To transform soups into ones that provide fiber and contain 30% or less total fat, follow these eight guidelines:

- Sweat vegetables in stock in place of fat.
- Caramelize vegetables for color and flavor in a nonstick pan or a well-seasoned griddle or grill, without the fat.
- If using fat, substitute a vegetable oil like olive, canola, peanut, or corn for butter, margarine, or other animal fats.
- Thicken soups with cornstarch, arrowroot, or pureed vegetables in place of a roux.
- Utilize a variety of fiber-rich vegetables, especially green leafy vegetables and legumes.
- Use herbs and spices to increase flavors, replacing flavors lost through no-fat and low-sodium cooking.
- Replace cream with low-fat plain yogurt or low-fat sour cream; the added tartness from yogurt or sour cream helps add flavor to the finished soup.
- Decrease fat calories by adding grains, potatoes, noodles, or vegetables.

Vegetable Barley Soup

This soup features two exceptionally nutritious foods: carrots and barley. The carrots are a known source of beta carotene, a precursor for vitamin A. Carotene is converted through the intestinal walls into vitamin A. Some fat is needed for this process, so carrots would not have as high a nutritional benefit if consumed raw.

Vitamin A is needed for growth, night vision, and healthy skin. It also helps us resist infections of the respiratory tract (by keeping the respiratory tract tissues moist). Research shows that beta carotene prevents the growth of certain types of tumors. Further research suggests that cholesterol levels can be significantly lowered when carrots are a regular food source. Similar results have been reported with broccoli, cabbage, and onions.*

Barley is a good source of dietary fiber. Fiber probably lowers cholesterol by binding the bile acids that contain cholesterol. Usually, cholesterol from bile acids is recycled and reused when the liver makes more bile. Soluble fibers are not digested and carry bile acids and cholesterol with them when they are excreted from the body.

Makes 10 10-ounce portions

2 cups, or 16 ounces, carrots, julienne
1 cup or 8 ounces, onion, julienne
1 cup, or 8 ounces, bell pepper, julienne
3 quarts, or 96 ounces, vegetable stock
1 quart, or 32 ounces, tomatoes, peeled, seeded, and diced
1 cup, or 5 ounces, dried barley
1 tablespoon rosemary leaves
1 tablespoon thyme leaves, chopped
1 tablespoon celery seed
2 teaspoons black pepper, coarsely ground
1/2 teaspoon white pepper, ground
1/8 teaspoon red pepper, ground
1 teaspoon salt
2 cups, or 12 ounces, shitake mushrooms, chopped

1. Place carrots, onions, bell peppers, vegetable stock, and tomatoes in a stock pot and bring to a quick boil.

2. Add barley and reduce soup to a simmer.

3. When barley is cooked, about 15 minutes, add spices and mushrooms.

4. Allow soup to simmer for an additional 15 to 20 minutes.

Approximate values per serving: **Calories** 154, **Carbohydrates (grams)** 31, **Protein (grams)** 6.7, **Fat (grams)** 1.5, **Cholesterol (milligrams)** 0. Carbohydrates = 76% calories, Protein = 16% calories, Fat = 8% calories.

---

*Halliwell, Barry, "Antioxidants and Human Disease: A General Introduction," *Nutrition Reviews*, 1997, Vol. 55, No. 1, pp. 44–52.

⟳ *Mexican Lentil*

Lentils, which are also legumes, are an excellent source of calcium. In many parts of the world they are the main source of calcium in the diet. Although milk is the best source of calcium, it is not always available, and some people are lactose intolerant and cannot drink milk. In diets that contain less phosphorus than calcium, either by reduction or elimination of milk and meat, legumes become an adequate source of calcium (the amount of calcium needed in the diet is directly related to the amount of phosphorus). All legumes are an excellent source of copper, a mineral not readily found in other foods but necessary for human life.

Makes 10 10-ounce portions

1 tablespoon garlic, chopped
1 cup, or 8 ounces, onion, small diced
1½ cups, or 8 ounces, celery, peeled and small diced
1½ cups, or 8 ounces, red bell peppers, medium diced
2 tablespoons corn oil
4 cups, or 32 ounces, tomatoes, diced
1 cup, or 8 ounces, yellow turnips, small diced
1 cup, or 8 ounces, whole kernel corn
2 cups, or 16 ounces, dried lentils
1 tablespoon cumin, ground
1 tablespoon coriander, ground
4 bay leaves
1 tablespoon celery seed
2 teaspoons black pepper, coarsely ground
1/2 teaspoon white pepper, ground
1/8 teaspoon red pepper, ground
1 teaspoon salt
2 quarts, or 64 ounces, lean chicken stock or vegetable stock
1 cup, or 8 ounces, fresh blanched or frozen lima beans
1/2 cup, fresh cilantro, chopped
2 limes, for their juice

1. Sauté garlic, onion, celery, and bell peppers in hot oil until tender but not brown.

2. Add all other ingredients except the lima beans, cilantro, and lime juice.

3. Bring the soup to a full boil and reduce to a simmer for one hour, or until lentils are tender.

4. Add lima beans and cilantro; cook for an additional 20 minutes.

5. Adjust seasonings.

6. Finish with lime juice just before service.

Approximate values per serving: **Calories** 178, **Carbohydrates (grams)** 35.4, **Protein (grams)** 10.8, **Fat (grams)** 1.9, **Cholesterol (milligrams)** 0. Carbohydrates = 70% calories, Protein = 21% calories, Fat = 8% calories.

Three-Bean Soup with Kale

This soup is an excellent full-flavored food full of proteins, vitamins, and minerals. Kale, as stated before, is an excellent source of calcium and B vitamins; it also contains vitamin K, iron, and dietary fiber. The strong taste of kale gives body to the flavor of this soup.

The combination of the three beans used in this recipe is a good example of variety in good nutrition. All three beans contain water soluble fibers and protein, along with iron. The lima beans are especially valuable for their folicin. Folicin is an important B vitamin that comes in 213 forms; in the form present in lima beans, the folicin is easily absorbed by the body.

Makes 10 10-ounce portions

1 cup, or 8 ounces, onion, medium diced
1 cup, or 8 ounces, celery, peeled and small diced
1 tablespoon garlic, chopped
3 quarts, or 96 ounces, vegetable stock
1 teaspoon salt
2 bay leaves
2 cups, or 10 ounces, kale, finely shredded
2 cups, or 16 ounces, tomatoes, peeled, seeded, and diced
1/4 cup, or 2 ounces, tomato paste
1 cup, or 8 ounces, red kidney beans, cooked
1 cup, or 8 ounces, baby lima beans, cooked
1½ cups, or 10 ounces, cut green beans
2 tablespoons cumin, ground
2 tablespoons coriander, ground
2 teaspoons black pepper, coarsely ground
1 tablespoon jalapeño peppers, finely chopped, seeds removed

1. Sweat onions, celery, and garlic with a small amount of stock until tender.

2. Add the remainder of the vegetable stock, bay leaves, and shredded kale; cook until kale is tender (about 30 minutes) at a quick simmer.

3. Add all other remaining ingredients and cook for 20 more minutes.

4. Adjust seasonings.

Approximate values per serving: **Calories** 93, **Carbohydrates (grams)** 18.5, **Protein (grams)** 5.1, **Fat (grams)** 1, **Cholesterol (milligrams)** 0. Carbohydrates = 71% calories, Protein = 20% calories, Fat = 9% calories.

Coriander Turkey Chili

Turkey meat can replace all or part of the beef in traditional meat-based recipes to create healthier meals. The change in flavor can be compensated for by adding coriander seeds. Wild and cultivated mushrooms could further increase flavor without adding any fat.

The red beans in this recipe are in the family of legumes. Legumes are a good source of protein. They are also the best source of the mineral nutrient molybdenum. Molybdenum is an important part of the enzymes that are involved in chemical reactions in the body called oxidative and reductive reactions. When molybdenum was inadvertently left out of intravenous diets, patients developed severe neuropathology, with symptoms of headaches, night blindness, nausea, vomiting, lethargy, disorientation, and coma. Immediate reversal occurred when molybdenum was introduced into the diets.

Makes 10 10-ounce portions

1 cup, or 8 ounces, onion, small diced
1 cup, or 8 ounces, bell pepper, small diced
1 tablespoon coriander seed, ground
1 tablespoon vegetable oil
1 tablespoon garlic, chopped
2 pounds turkey breast meat, ground
1/2 cup, or 4 ounces, tomato paste
4 cups, or 32 ounces, tomatoes, peeled, seeded, and diced
2 tablespoons fresh basil, chopped
1/4 cup, or 2 ounces, chili powder
1 tablespoon jalapeño peppers, chopped, seeds removed
2 teaspoons black pepper, coarsely ground
1/2 teaspoon white pepper, ground
2 cups, or 16 ounces, red kidney beans, cooked

1. In a large pot, cook the onion, bell peppers, and coriander seed in the vegetable oil until the onions are translucent.

2. Add garlic and ground turkey and cook until turkey is lightly browned.

3. Add all other ingredients and bring to a quick boil.

4. Reduce to a simmer and cook for an additional 45 minutes.

5. Coriander turkey chili will have a better flavor if allowed to rest overnight and served the second day; adjust the seasonings before serving.

Approximate values per serving: **Calories** 225, **Carbohydrates (grams)** 16.6, **Protein (grams)** 22.5, **Fat (grams)** 9.3 **Cholesterol (milligrams)** 54. Carbohydrates = 28% calories, Protein = 37% calories, Fat = 35% calories.

Cabbage and Broccoli Soup with Chick Peas

This nutritious soup contains cabbage and chick peas. Chick peas are high in iron, which is the one mineral responsible for the prevention of anemia. Especially for vegetarians, whose iron supply cannot come from meat consumption, legumes like the chick pea become essential in the daily diet. Chick peas are also high in protein and fiber and contain no cholesterol.

Cabbage is a good source of vitamin K as well as fiber. Vitamin K is needed for four protein substances that play a role in blood coagulation (i.e., prothrombin, which converts to thrombin, then to fibrinogen, and finally to fibrin, the key substance in coagulation). Vitamin K also plays an important role in our immune systems. Fifty percent of our daily requirement of vitamin K is made through our intestinal tracts, whereas the remaining 50% must come from food sources.

Makes 10 10-ounce portions

1 quart, or 10 ounces, fresh broccoli, chopped
1 cup, or 8 ounces, bell peppers, small diced
1 cup, or 8 ounces, leeks, small diced
2 teaspoons garlic, chopped
2 teaspoons ginger, chopped
1 gallon, or 16 ounces, cabbage, medium diced
2 quarts, or 64 ounces, vegetable stock
1 cup, or 8 ounces, tomato paste
2 cinnamon sticks
1 teaspoon cloves, ground
1 cup, or 8 ounces, chick peas, cooked
2 teaspoons black pepper, coarsely ground
1/2 teaspoon white pepper, ground
1/8 teaspoon red pepper, crushed

1. Cut florets from the broccoli and reserve for the finished soup. Peel the remaining broccoli stems and finely dice the tender centers.

2. Sweat the bell peppers, leeks, garlic, and ginger in some vegetable stock until tender.

3. Stir in the cabbage and cut broccoli stems and sweat for an additional two to three minutes.

4. Add the vegetable stock, tomato paste, cinnamon, cloves, and cooked chick peas and allow the soup to simmer for about 30 minutes.

5. Add broccoli florets and peppers and cook until broccoli is tender.

6. Adjust seasonings.

Approximate values per serving: **Calories** 174, **Carbohydrates (grams)** 32.4, **Protein (grams)** 9.7, **Fat (grams)** 2.1, **Cholesterol (milligrams)** 0. Carbohydrates = 69% calories, Protein = 21% calories, Fat = 10% calories.

Forester Chicken Soup

Adding even a small amount of grains to dishes can significantly change the percentage of calories coming from fat. For example, in this dish, the percent of calories represented by fat was 35% before the addition of rice.

The mushrooms in this recipe are a good source of chromium. Other good sources of chromium include whole wheat breads, meats, and vegetables. Chromium is essential for the body's absorption of sugars and fats and may help prevent diabetes in some cases. Long-term chromium deficiency is associated with cardiovascular disease as well. Studies show that an inadequate chromium intake is anything less than 50 micrograms daily. Physical stress such as running causes a loss of chromium through the urine.

Makes 10 10-ounce portions

1½ pounds chicken breast meat, diced
1 tablespoon olive oil
1 cup, or 8 ounces, onion, small diced
1 cup, or 8 ounces, celery, peeled and diced
1 tablespoon garlic, chopped
1/2 cup, or 2.25 ounces, whole wheat flour
3 quarts, or 96 ounces, lean chicken stock
4 cups, or 32 ounces, tomatoes, peeled, seeded, and diced
1 cup, or 8 ounces, parsnips, small diced
1 tablespoon fresh marjoram leaves, chopped
3 bay leaves
1 tablespoon fresh thyme leaves, chopped
1 tablespoon black pepper, coarsely ground
1/2 teaspoon white pepper, ground
2 cups, or 12 ounces, shitake mushrooms, sliced
1/2 cup, or 4 ounces, dry red wine
1/2 cup, or 4 ounces, arborio rice

1. Sear chicken meat in hot oil until lightly browned; remove chicken from pan and reserve.

2. Add onions and celery to pan and cook until tender.

3. Add garlic and cook for two more minutes.

4. Add whole wheat flour and mix well; cook for five minutes over low flame.

5. Add chicken stock, tomatoes, parsnips, marjoram, bay leaves, thyme, and white and black pepper.

6. Add chicken meat and rice back to the soup; stir well.

7. Bring the soup to a full boil and reduce to a simmer for an additional 20 minutes.

8. Add mushrooms and red wine and finish cooking for 20 additional minutes.

9. Adjust seasonings.

Approximate values per serving: **Calories** 310, **Carbohydrates (grams)** 28.8, **Protein (grams)** 23.9, **Fat (grams)** 11, **Cholesterol (milligrams)** 66. Carbohydrates = 37% calories, Protein = 31% calories, Fat = 32% calories.

Clams are one of the best sources of selenium. Dietary selenium originates as selenium in soil and water taken into food. Selenium has the ability to affect both the initiation and promotion stages of chemically induced cancers as well as tumors. Selenium delays cancer initiation by decreasing cell proliferation. It is part of an enzyme, glutathione peroxidase, which breaks down peroxides before they can attack cell membranes.

Populations living in high-selenium areas have less cancers of the lung, colon, rectum, bladder, esophagus, pancreas, breast, ovary, and uterus.

In animal studies demonstrating selenium's effect against cancer, 20 to 60 times the nutritional requirements for selenium were used. In large doses, selenium is toxic and causes decreased weight gain, liver damage, and death in rats. Recommended safe levels for humans are 50 to 200 micrograms daily, although some fish-eating populations in Japan ingest 750 micrograms daily.

Makes 10 10-ounce portions

4 dozen little-neck clams
1/2 cup, or 4 ounces, dry white wine
1 cup, or 8 ounces, celery, peeled and small diced
1 cup, or 8 ounces, leeks, white part only, small diced
2 cups, or 16 ounces, dried white beans, Navies or Northern
2 quarts, or 64 ounces, water
1 teaspoon salt
3 cups, or 1½ pounds, boiling potatoes, medium diced
3 quarts, or 96 ounces, neutral fish stock, or clam stock preferably
1 cup, or 8 ounces, whole kernel corn
1 cup, or 8 ounces, baby lima beans, fresh or frozen
2 bay leaves
1 teaspoon white pepper, ground
1/8 teaspoon red pepper, ground
1/2 teaspoon nutmeg, ground

1. Wash clams thoroughly.

2. Place clams in a 6-quart sauce pot with white wine, celery, and leeks.

3. Cover the pot and cook on medium high heat until clams open their shells.

4. Remove clams and discard the shells; chop the clams and reserve for later.

5. In another pot, cook the beans in water, with the salt, until almost done, about two hours.

6. Add the diced potatoes to the bean pot and continue to cook.

7. When the potatoes are fork tender (can be broken easily with a fork), the beans should be completely cooked. Divide the beans, potatoes, and remaining liquid into two portions.

8. Add the fish stock and half the beans and potatoes to the pot with the celery and leeks. Puree this all together in a high-speed blender.

9. Add the chopped clams, corn, lima beans, the second half of the white beans and potato mix, and spices to the soup and simmer for approximately 30 minutes.

10. Adjust the seasonings.

Approximate values per serving: **Calories** 246, **Carbohydrates (grams)** 44, **Protein (grams)** 15.5, **Fat (grams)** 2.2, **Cholesterol (milligrams)** 23. Carbohydrates = 68% calories, Protein = 24% calories, Fat = 8% calories.

⟜*Pottage of Winter Squash*

For centuries winter squash have supported the diets of humans through the hard and cold winters of the Western continents. Grown with relative ease, especially in the cooler climates, the fruit can be stored in cold and dry areas for as long as nine months. Before the advent of refrigeration, winter squash were a popular winter vegetable. Winter squash are a good source of vitamin A and fiber.

Makes 10 10-ounce portions

1 large butternut squash
1 large acorn squash
2 cups, or 16 ounces, leeks, white part only, medium diced
4 cinnamon sticks
2 teaspoons nutmeg, ground
1 teaspoon salt
3 quarts, or 96 ounces, white vegetable stock
1 large spaghetti squash
1 teaspoon white pepper, ground
1/4 cup, or 2 ounces, Amaretto liqueur
2 cups, or 16 ounces, plain low-fat yogurt
fresh mint leaves for garnish

1. Peel and seed butternut and acorn squash and dice into 1-inch cubes.

2. Add diced leeks, cinnamon, nutmeg, salt, and vegetable stock and cook for 30 minutes, or until squash is tender.

3. Remove cinnamon sticks and discard; puree soup in a high-speed blender.

4. In the meantime, cut the spaghetti squash in half, remove seeds, and bake, cut side down, in a shallow pan with a little water. When the squash is tender, the pulp can be removed with a spoon and the strands (resembling spaghetti noodles, thus the name) should be added to the pureed soup.

5. Rough cut cooked spaghetti squash, creating small strands; add to pureed soup.

6. Add the pepper and Amaretto and cook for an additional 15 minutes.

7. Adjust seasonings.

8. Serve hot or cold.

9. Garnish with a spoon of yogurt and mint leaves on top.

Approximate values per serving: **Calories** 198, **Carbohydrates (grams)** 41.5, **Protein (grams)** 7.8, **Fat (grams)** 1.8, **Cholesterol (milligrams)** 2.2. Carbohydrates = 78% calories, Protein = 15% calories, Fat = 8% calories.

⇒Pumpkin Soup

Pumpkin is a delicious way to get vitamin A. One cup of pumpkin provides 15,680 IUs of vitamin A. (The recommended allowance for a healthy male is 50,000 units daily.) Vitamin A deficiency results in unhealthy hair, poor night vision, poor growth in children, dry skin, and decreased resistance to colds. A bowl of pumpkin soup is a fresh alternative to the greens that children (and some adults) fuss about.

Makes 10 10-ounce portions

1 cup, or 8 ounces, onion, small diced
1 cup, or 8 ounces, celery, peeled and small diced
3 quarts, or 96 ounces, white vegetable stock
1/2 gallon, or 2½ pounds, pumpkin, fresh, peeled, seeded, and large diced
1 tablespoon garlic, chopped
4 cinnamon sticks
1 teaspoon nutmeg
1/2 teaspoon mace, ground
1 teaspoon salt
1 teaspoon white pepper, ground
1½ cups, or 12 ounces, low-fat sour cream
1 tablespoon cinnamon, ground

1. Cook onion and celery in a small amount of vegetable stock until tender.

2. Add pumpkin, garlic, and spices and cook together for another two minutes.

3. Add the remainder of the stock and simmer for about 30 minutes, or until the squash is tender.

4. Remove cinnamon sticks and discard.

5. Puree soup in a high-speed blender or through a food mill until very smooth.

6. Float 1 teaspoon of low-fat sour cream on top of each portion and sprinkle with ground cinnamon before serving.

Approximate values per serving: **Calories** 117, **Carbohydrates (grams)** 18.6, **Protein (grams)** 10, **Fat (grams)** 1.3, **Cholesterol (milligrams)** 1.9. Carbohydrates = 59% calories, Protein = 32% calories, Fat = 9% calories.

⚊Chicken and the Sea

Peanut oil is a great choice in this recipe because of its high percentage of monounsaturated fat (47%). Lima beans add protein and cholesterol-reducing water soluble fibers. Adding shell macaroni to this recipe reduces the percentage of calories from fat to 31%.

Makes 10 10-ounce portions

3 pounds whole chicken
16 ounces shrimp (medium count)
1 tablespoon garlic, chopped
2 tablespoons peanut oil
3 quarts, or 96 ounces, vegetable stock
1 teaspoon white pepper, ground
1 bunch parsley stems
3 bay leaves
1 cup, or 8 ounces, onion, small diced
1 cup, or 8 ounces, celery, peeled and small diced
1/2 cup, or 2 ounces, all-purpose flour
2 cups, or 16 ounces, yellow turnips, medium diced
1 cup, or 8 ounces, red bell pepper, small diced
2 cups, or 16 ounces, baby lima beans, fresh or frozen
2 cups, or 16 ounces, spinach, cooked, chopped
3 cups, or 18 ounces, white mushrooms, sliced
1/4 cup fresh basil, chopped, or 1 tablespoon dried leaf
1/4 cup fresh oregano, chopped, or 1 tablespoon dried leaf
2 cups, or 5 ounces, shell macaroni

1. Debone the chicken and dice the meat into 1-inch cubes; reserve for later.

2. Peel and devein the shrimp; reserve the shells.

3. Sauté garlic and shrimp shells together in 1 tablespoon of peanut oil for two minutes.

4. Add cracked white pepper, parsley stems, and bay leaves.

5. Add chicken bones and vegetable stock and simmer for two hours, skimming as needed.

6. Strain the stock through a fine strainer (chinois) or cheese cloth.

7. In the second 1 tablespoon of oil, sauté onion and celery until tender.

8. Add chicken meat and cook until chicken begins to turn brown; remove from pan.

9. Add flour to the remaining vegetables and oil to make a roux.

10. Add stock and stir well.

11. Return chicken and add turnips and shell macaroni to the soup and bring to a simmer; cook for 30 minutes.

12. Add all other ingredients and heat thoroughly for another 15 minutes.

13. Adjust seasoning.

Approximate values per serving: **Calories** 384, **Carbohydrates (grams)** 32, **Protein (grams)** 35, **Fat (grams)** 13, **Cholesterol (milligrams)** 140. Carbohydrates = 33% calories, Protein = 36% calories, Fat = 31% calories.

Italian Beef and Tomato

Many studies advocate reduced consumption of red meat to lower cholesterol levels. These same studies, however, do not point out the beneficial properties of red meat.

Red meats are one of the best sources of vitamin B_{12}, also known as cobalamin. A deficiency of vitamin B_{12} may lead to paresthesias (burning or tingling sensations) in the extremities and may even progress to ataxia (loss of ability to coordinate muscular movement) and paralysis. Vitamin B_{12} deficiency may also lead to memory difficulties, which are easily reversed when the deficiency is corrected. Red meats are also one of the best sources or iron, which is necessary for preventing anemia. Iron deficiency is one of the major deficiency states in the world.

Makes 10 10-ounce portions

2 pounds lean beef, 1/2-inch diced
1 teaspoon vegetable oil
1 cup, or 8 ounces, onion, small diced
1 cup, or 8 ounces, bell pepper, small diced
1 tablespoon garlic, chopped
1 teaspoon black pepper, coarsely ground
1/8 teaspoon red pepper, crushed
3 bay leaves
2 quarts, or 64 ounces, tomatoes, peeled, diced, and seeded
1/2 cup, or 4 ounces, tomato paste
1½ cup, or 9 ounces, crimini mushrooms, sliced
1 tablespoon fresh basil, chopped
1 tablespoon fresh oregano, chopped
1 tablespoon fresh marjoram, chopped
1 cup, or 8 ounces, chianti
3 cups, or 24 ounces, cooked ziti noodles

1. Sear beef in a nonstick fry pan or on a well-seasoned griddle until it begins to turn brown (one spray from a vegetable oil spray can releases 1/2 teaspoon of oil, enough to start the cooking).

2. Add onions and bell peppers and continue to cook without fat until vegetables are tender.

3. Add garlic, black and red peppers, and bay leaves and cook for an additional two minutes.

4. Add tomatoes and tomato paste; mix well and cook for one hour.

5. Add mushrooms and herbs and simmer for 15 additional minutes.

6. Add wine and cooked noodles for the last five minutes of cooking.

7. Adjust seasonings.

Approximate values per serving: **Calories** 281, **Carbohydrates (grams)** 25, **Protein (grams)** 25, **Fat (grams)** 7.8, **Cholesterol (milligrams)** 61.8. Carbohydrates = 38% calories, Protein = 36% calories, Fat = 28% calories.

Puree of Cauliflower and Yellow Split Peas

Puree soups are more nutritious than many other soups because there is no need for a thickening agent, such as a roux or cornstarch dilution. Rouxs and cornstarch may help thicken soups, but they add little nutrition. In this recipe, the yellow split peas make an excellent thickening agent, and the pureed cauliflower gives a pleasant taste without overpowering the other flavors.

Makes 10 10-ounce portions

2 pounds cauliflower; reserve some florets for garnish
1 tablespoon garlic, finely chopped
2 cups, or 16 ounces, leeks, white only; reserve some green rings for garnish
2 cups, or 16 ounces, dried yellow split peas
1 tablespoon fresh tarragon, chopped
1 tablespoon fresh cilantro, chopped
3 quarts, or 96 ounces, white vegetable stock
2 teaspoons white pepper, ground
1/2 teaspoon red pepper sauce (Tobasco is one type)
1 cup, or 8 ounces, low-fat sour cream
1 cup, or 8 ounces, Chablis

1. Sweat leeks and garlic together in a small amount of vegetable stock.

2. Add cut cauliflower, split peas, tarragon, cilantro, and the rest of the stock.

3. Bring to a boil and simmer for one hour.

4. Add spices and Chablis and cook for another 15 minutes.

5. Puree in high-speed blender and strain.

6. Steam cauliflower florets that were reserved for the garnish until tender.

7. Stir in sour cream and garnish to serve.

Approximate values per serving: **Calories** 291, **Carbohydrates (grams)** 46.5, **Protein (grams)** 18.6, **Fat (grams)** 3.3, **Cholesterol (milligrams)** 1.2. Carbohydrates = 64% calories, Protein = 26% calories, Fat = 10% calories.

18

Salads
and Entremets

Salads have served many varied functions in the dining experience over the centuries. Depending on culture, dining practices, and health concerns, salads have been an important and an unimportant part of meals.

A salad can be loosely defined as any combination of vegetables, fruits, cheeses, and/or protein foods bound together by a single dressing. They can be designed to accompany a meal or be a meal in themselves with the proper amounts of vegetable, grain, and protein foods in a single serving. Health-conscious diners choose salads as a way of eating a balance of foods, usually low in fat and cholesterol, that have great amounts of flavor and substance.

An entremet is a small course served between large or main courses on a classical menu. Entremets were designed to be light and tasty and easy to prepare so guests would not be kept waiting between courses. Originally, vegetables, fruits, and pastas made up the majority of entremets served. Some culinary history connoisseurs suggest that the modern salad was a type of entremet; it was easily prepared and could be served quickly between courses that took longer to cook and serve. In this way guests would have some food in front of them at all times during the meal.

No matter what their place in the menu, both salads and entremets can be designed to meet dietary guidelines and give guests a variety of food choices and presentations.

Lettuces today are available in many different shapes, sizes, and tastes. The old standby iceberg lettuce has given way to romaine, mâche, red oak leaf, arugula, and about a dozen other specialty lettuces and flavorful green leafy vegetables. Some of these lettuce blends are commercially sold as mesclun. The varied types of lettuces can offer the food service professional great variety in salad taste and appeal without added work.

Commercial no-fat salad dressings are also available in the modern market. A few examples of these should be on hand for customers who request them. Oil and vinegar should be available for those who want oil-based dressings but want to control the amount of oil that is used. A high-quality olive oil and red wine vinegar should be offered.

Low-fat or no-fat salad dressings can also be made in the kitchen. They can be as simple as cold, fruit juice–based sauces thickened with corn starch or arrowroot. Orange, lemon, and apple juices are typically used because of their natural tang, which balances the taste of bitter greens. Other low-fat dressings can be made by substituting low-fat sour cream or plain low-fat yogurt for mayonnaise in many standard dressing recipes.

Salad entrees have become a popular menu choice in the latter half of the twentieth century. They combine a larger quantity of lettuce greens, vegetables, and protein ingredients than the typical salad course. The traditional chef salad, with julienne turkey, ham, and Swiss cheese on a bed of lettuce greens, was one of the forerunners of the grilled chicken Caesar and the Cobb salads of today.

Salad as a main course should contain at least two servings of vegetables (2 cups of raw leafy vegetables or a combination of raw, cooked, and chopped vegetables); 2 to 3 ounces of protein food such as meat, chicken, fish, legumes, or tofu; and either a serving of grains (rice, corn, or pasta), fruit, or dairy.

Lettuces, in general, do not have high calorie counts. Therefore, salads made primarily with lettuce or endive greens and dressed with a simple vinaigrette will contain a high percentage of fat calories overall. To offset these high fat percentages, add low-fat protein items, such as grilled chicken, fish, shrimp, or tofu, or other vegetables to increase calories and substance. In this way a plain salad, high in fat calories, can become a more substantial menu item with appropriate fat content.

Fresh spinach contains adequate calories to offset fat percentages in salads. It should be used whenever possible to reduce overall fat percentages and add extra vitamins and minerals to the final preparation.

⟶ *Marinated Pinto Bean Salad*

This salad is a good example of the total concept of nutritional cooking. The olive oil contains 75% monounsaturated fat, which is known to help reduce LDL (bad cholesterol) without affecting HDL (good cholesterol). When eaten raw, bell peppers are one of the best sources of vitamin C, a water soluble vitamin that must be replenished daily. Dried dates are rich in iron, which is needed to form hemoglobin, and natural sugars, which add a sweetness to the finished salad. Almonds contain a better-quality protein than that found in almost any other plant. Beans contain protein and a high amount of calcium. Peppers, beans, dates, and nuts are also good nutritional choices because of their fiber. When this salad is served on a bed of green lettuce, it becomes a complete meal. The combination of beans and nuts contains complete protein and could substitute for meat.

Makes 10 5-ounce portions

5 cups, or 2½ pounds, pinto beans, cooked
1/2 cup, or 4 ounces, red wine vinegar
1/4 cup, or 2 ounces, lemon juice, fresh
1/4 cup, or 2 ounces, virgin olive oil
2 cups, or 16 ounces, green bell peppers, small diced
1 cup, or 6 ounces, dried dates, chopped
1/4 cup, or 2 ounces, almonds, sliced and dry roasted
1/2 tablespoon cumin, ground
1 tablespoon basil, dried leaf or 3 tablespoons fresh herbs, chopped
1 teaspoon black pepper, coarsely ground
1/8 teaspoon red pepper, crushed
10 leaves red tip leaf lettuce
2 cups, or 16 ounces, carrots, julienne

1. Mix all ingredients together except the almonds, lettuce, and julienne carrots; allow this to rest for at least 1 hour.

2. Mix in the toasted almonds just before service.

3. Plate on a leaf of red tip lettuce and garnish with carrots.

4. Serve with other mixes of lettuce, celery, radishes, tomatoes, etc.

Approximate values per serving: **Calories** 304, **Carbohydrates (grams)** 42.6, **Protein (grams)** 9.9, **Fat (grams)** 10.1, **Cholesterol (milligrams)** 0. Carbohydrates = 59% calories, Protein = 18% calories, Fat = 29% calories.

Cajun Bean Salad

The combination of beans and the highly flavored ingredients in this salad mean that oil need not be used in the dressing to ensure good taste. By eliminating the oil, the natural flavors of the beans, shallots, garlic, herbs, and spices take on the dominant flavor roles. The cooked mustard greens supply a mere 20 calories per cup but a generous amount of vitamins A, E, K, B_6, ascorbic acid, and folate and the minerals calcium, phosphorus, iron, and potassium.

Makes 10 5-ounce portions

1 cup, or 6 ounces, dry pinto beans
1 cup, or 6 ounces, dry black-eyed peas
1 cup, or 6 ounces, dry lima beans
2 quarts, or 64 ounces, white vegetable stock
2 teaspoons garlic, finely chopped
1 tablespoon shallot, finely chopped
1 tablespoon fresh thyme, chopped
1 teaspoon black pepper, coarsely ground

1/2 teaspoon white pepper, coarsely ground
1/4 teaspoon red pepper, crushed
1/2 cup, or 4 ounces, white wine vinegar
1/4 cup, or 2 ounces, lemon juice, freshly squeezed
1/4 cup, or 1.25 ounces, cornstarch
1 cup, or 8 ounces, vegetable stock
1 pound mustard greens, slowly cooked, chopped
1/2 cup, or 4 ounces, pecan halves

1. Soak all three types of beans together in cold water overnight.

2. Cook beans in vegetable stock until tender, about 2 hours.

3. Drain beans, reserving 1 pint of the liquid for the dressing, and cool.

4. Add garlic, shallots, spices, vinegar, and lemon juice to the strained liquid and thicken with a cornstarch slurry (mix 1/4 cup of cornstarch with 1 cup of vegetable stock).

5. Add beans to dressing and marinate for at least 1 hour.

6. Drain beans again and serve on a bed of cooked mustard greens.

7. Drizzle some of the dressing on the greens and garnish with pecan halves.

Approximate values per serving: **Calories** 258, **Carbohydrates (grams)** 37, **Protein (grams)** 12, **Fat (grams)** 8.4, **Cholesterol (milligrams)** 0. Carbohydrates = 55% calories, Protein = 18% calories, Fat = 28% calories.

✒ Curried Rice Salad

This type of marinated rice salad is always better if prepared one day, allowed to rest (letting the flavors blend), and finished and served the second, or even the third, day. The addition of diced apples, orange sections, or any other fruit could further enhance the overall appearance and taste.

Makes 15 5-ounce portions

1 cup, or 8 ounces, celery, peeled, small diced
1 tablespoon peanut oil
3 cups, or 18 ounces, brown rice
1 teaspoon fresh ginger, grated
1 teaspoon cumin, ground
1/2 teaspoon white pepper, coarsely ground
1 tablespoon curry powder
1½ cups, or 9 ounces, raisins, plumped in hot water and strained
1/2 cup, or 3 ounces, pitted dates, chopped
3 pints, or 48 ounces, white vegetable stock
1/4 cup, or 2 ounces, lemon juice, freshly squeezed
1/4 cup, or 2 ounces, almonds, toasted, sliced

1. Sauté celery in hot oil until tender.

2. Add rice and spices and stir well.

3. Add raisins, dates, and vegetable stock and bring to a full boil.

4. Cover pan and bake in 350-degree oven for 20 minutes.

5. Refrigerate cooked rice overnight.

6. Add lemon juice to cold rice and stir with a fork to break up the grains.

7. Serve on bed of lettuce greens with appropriate salad vegetables; garnish with almonds.

Approximate values per serving: **Calories** 367, **Carbohydrates (grams)** 73, **Protein (grams)** 6.7, **Fat (grams)** 7.1, **Cholesterol (milligrams)** 0. Carbohydrates = 76% calories, Protein = 7% calories, Fat = 17% calories.

Barley Salad with Sweet Yellow and Red Peppers

Barley is a grain that has a full flavor and is rich in protein and carbohydrate. Barley also contains generous amounts of calcium, phosphorus, iron, and potassium. Bell peppers add color, texture, and vitamin C to the final salad. The small amount of virgin olive oil gives a distinctive taste without the volume of fat needed from other less flavorful oils.

Makes 15 5-ounce portions

2 cups, or 12 ounces, dry pearl barley
6 cups, or 48 ounces, white vegetable stock
1 cup, or 8 ounces, spring onions, small diced
1 cup, or 8 ounces, celery, peeled, finely diced
2 teaspoons garlic, finely chopped
1 tablespoon virgin olive oil
1/2 cup, or 4 ounces, red wine vinegar
1/4 cup, or 2 ounces, lemon juice, freshly squeezed
1 teaspoon black pepper, coarsely ground
1/2 cup, or 4 ounces, yellow bell peppers, finely diced
1/2 cup, or 4 ounces, red bell peppers, finely diced
1 quart, or 10 ounces, lettuce mix
1 cucumber, cut in circles for garnish

1. Cook barley in vegetable stock until tender.

2. Mix all other ingredients together except the bell peppers.

3. While the barley is still hot, stir in the dressing; refrigerate overnight.

4. Stir in bell peppers and serve on a bed of lettuce greens garnished with cucumber circles.

Approximate values per serving: **Calories** 185, **Carbohydrates (grams)** 35.8, **Protein (grams)** 4.7, **Fat (grams)** 3.5, **Cholesterol (milligrams)** 0. Carbohydrates = 74% calories, Protein = 10% calories, Fat = 16% calories.

Asparagus with Port Wine Vinaigrette

Tawny port gives an interesting accent to this simple vinaigrette and shows how a simple ingredient substitution can transform a basic dressing into a classic sauce. Asparagus salad should be garnished appropriately with tomato wedges, cucumber slices, or carrot shavings to add color, taste, and texture.

Makes 10 4-ounce portions

2½ pounds fresh asparagus, peeled and blanched
2 tablespoons, or 1 ounce, virgin olive oil
1 cup, or 8 ounces, spring onions, whites and tender greens, sliced
1/4 cup, or 2 ounces, tawny port
1/2 cup, or 4 ounces, red wine vinegar
1/2 teaspoon black pepper, finely ground
10 green leaf lettuce leaves
1 cucumber, sliced
3 tomatoes, cut into wedges
1/2 cup, or 4 ounces, carrots, shredded (optional)

1. Cook the asparagus, placing it in boiling, unsalted water for 1 to 2 minutes. Remove the asparagus from the water quickly and place in an ice bath to stop the cooking process. (The asparagus should be bright green and still a little crunchy.)

2. Whisk all other ingredients together except lettuce, cucumbers, tomatoes, and carrots, and pour over asparagus.

3. Allow asparagus to marinate for at least 1 hour.

4. Pull asparagus from marinade, strain out spring onions, and save some for garnish.

5. Serve on top of a single leaf of green lettuce with cucumber, tomato, spring onion, and shredded carrots for garnish.

Approximate values per serving: **Calories** 98, **Carbohydrates (grams)** 9.2, **Protein (grams)** 4.6, **Fat (grams)** 3.3, **Cholesterol (milligrams)** 0. Carbohydrates = 4% calories, Protein = 23% calories, Fat = 30% calories.

Broccoli-Pasta Salad with Fresh Tuna

Tuna is not a newcomer to American salads, but fresh tuna gives this salad an interesting twist. The taste of the salad increases when allowed to marinate for 24 hours or more. Add the tuna at the last minute to retain its distinctive taste and delicate texture.

Makes 15 5-ounce portions

1 quart, or 32 ounces, white vegetable stock
2 pounds fresh tuna steaks, boneless and skinless, cut into 1-inch steaks
1 pound dry pasta, any shape
1 large bunch of broccoli, cut in 2-inch spears
1/4 cup, or 2 ounces, virgin olive oil
1/4 cup, or 2 ounces, lemon juice, freshly squeezed
1/2 cup, or 4 ounces, red wine vinegar
1 cup, or 8 ounces, spring onions, thinly sliced
1/2 cup, or 4 ounces, red bell peppers, small diced
2 tablespoons fresh basil, chopped
2 tablespoons fresh parsley, chopped
1 teaspoon white pepper, coarsely ground
1/8 teaspoon red pepper, crushed

1. In a shallow pan, bring vegetable stock to a simmer.

2. Poach tuna steaks until the flesh can be easily flaked apart with a fork.

3. Remove tuna and cool quickly.

4. Cook pasta separately in plain, unsalted water.

5. Cool pasta quickly to prevent overcooking.

6. Blanch broccoli in boiling, plain water until just tender; cool it quickly to prevent overcooking.

7. Mix all other ingredients together and stir well.

8. Cut cooked tuna into small pieces.

9. Gently mix all ingredients together.

10. Allow salad to marinate for at least 1 hour.

Approximate values per serving: **Calories** 262, **Carbohydrates (grams)** 44, **Protein (grams)** 7.9, **Fat (grams)** 6.5, **Cholesterol (milligrams)** 0. Carbohydrates = 66% calories, Protein = 12% calories, Fat = 22% calories.

Smoked Turkey with Feta and Ziti

Smoked products are usually avoided in the preparation of nutritious meals because of their generally high percentage of salt or natural fats. Smoked turkey breast, however, does not contain a lot of salt or fat. There is some concern that smoked products contain carcinogenic elements, but this is still being investigated. The quantity of smoked products that the average person would have to consume to stimulate cancer growth is likely to be large. Like everything else, moderation is the best course.

Makes 15 5-ounce portions

1 pound dry ziti
1 pound fresh asparagus, peeled, cut in 4-inch spears
1 cup, or 8 ounces, red kidney beans, cooked
1/2 cup, or 4 ounces, celery, peeled, small diced
1 cup, or 8 ounces, spring onions, whites and tender greens, sliced
2 teaspoons garlic, finely chopped
2 tablespoons corn oil
1 tablespoon fresh thyme, chopped
2 tablespoons fresh parsley, chopped
1 teaspoon white pepper, coarsely ground
1/2 cup, or 4 ounces, red wine vinegar
1/4 cup, or 2 ounces, lemon juice, freshly squeezed
2 pounds smoked turkey breast, cooked, julienne
1 cup, or 8 ounces, feta cheese, crumbled

1. Cook ziti in plain, unsalted water.

2. Blanch asparagus in boiling water for 2 minutes.

3. Remove asparagus from water and place in an ice bath to stop the cooking process.

4. Mix together all other ingredients, except turkey, and stir well.

5. Pour dressing over the pasta and stir.

6. Allow the salad to marinate for at least 1 hour.

7. Garnish with asparagus, julienne turkey, and feta cheese.

Approximate values per serving: **Calories** 450, **Carbohydrates (grams)** 43.7, **Protein (grams)** 39, **Fat (grams)** 13, **Cholesterol (milligrams)** 89. Carbohydrates = 39% calories, Protein = 35% calories, Fat = 26% calories.

⟨Tropical Chicken Salad with Raspberry Vinaigrette

The combination of tropical fruits in this recipe gives a variety of flavors, colors, and textures. Papayas, grapefruits, oranges, and raspberries are low in fat yet full of vitamins. Avocados, which are fairly high in fat calories, can be used successfully when paired with other low-fat fruit or protein choices. Avocados are full of vitamins and minerals, are very low in saturated fats, and could be included in a healthy diet. Avocado fat content is mostly oleic fatty acid, with a trace amount of linoleic fatty acid. Grilled chicken breast gives enough protein to make this salad a filling choice. In smaller portions this salad can act as an entremet; the fruit flavors help cleanse the palate.

Makes 10 4-ounce portions

1/2 cup, or 4 ounces, raspberry vinegar
2 tablespoons peanut oil
2 teaspoons fresh orange zest, chopped
1 teaspoon allspice, ground
5, or 20 ounces, 4-ounce skinless, boneless chicken breasts
1/2 teaspoon white pepper, ground
1/2 teaspoon Spanish paprika
1/4 cup, or 2 ounces, dry white wine
3 ripe avocados, peeled, seeded, and thinly sliced

1 papaya, peeled, seeded, and thinly sliced
5 small heads bibb lettuce, cleaned, cut in halves
1 pint, or 16 ounces, fresh raspberries
2 grapefruits, sectioned
2 navel oranges, sectioned
1 tablespoon fresh mint, chopped

1. Mix together raspberry vinegar with oil, orange zest, and allspice.

2. Mix together white pepper, paprika, and wine.

3. Add chicken to wine marinade and allow to rest for 1 hour.

4. Remove chicken from marinade and grill or broil until fully cooked.

5. Slice cooked chicken breast into long strips.

6. Place 1/2 head of bibb lettuce on each of 10 salad plates.

7. Alternate layers of avocado, papaya, and grilled chicken.

8. Pour dressing on salads, and garnish with raspberries, citrus sections, and chopped mint.

Approximate values per serving: **Calories** 256, **Carbohydrates (grams)** 28, **Protein (grams)** 17, **Fat (grams)** 10, **Cholesterol (milligrams)** 36. Carbohydrates = 41% calories, Protein = 25% calories, Fat = 34% calories.

Eggplant Salsa

If you use a nonstick pan for this procedure, reduce the amount of olive oil to 1 tablespoon; you still want the oil for its rich olive flavor. For the lettuce mix, use commercially prepared mesclun, or mix your own using at least three different lettuces and/or endives.

Makes 10 5-ounce portions

2 medium eggplants, peeled, small diced
2 tablespoons virgin olive oil
1/2 cup, or 4 ounces, onions, small diced
1 tablespoon garlic, finely chopped
1 teaspoon black pepper, coarsely ground
1/2 teaspoon white pepper, coarsely ground
1/8 teaspoon red pepper, crushed
2 teaspoons cumin, ground
1 tablespoon fresh marjoram, chopped

1/2 cup, or 4 ounces, green bell peppers, small diced
5, or 25 ounces, cucumbers, peeled, seeded, and small diced
1 quart, or 32 ounces, tomatoes, peeled, seeded, and small diced
1/4 cup, or 2 ounces, lemon juice, freshly squeezed
1 quart, or 12 ounces, lettuce mix
2 cups, or 16 ounces, celery, peeled and cut into 4-inch sticks

1. Sauté eggplant in hot oil until lightly browned.

2. Add onions, garlic, and spices and cook for an additional 3 minutes.

3. Add all other ingredients, stir well, and remove from heat.

4. Refrigerate salad overnight before serving.

5. Serve on a bed of mixed salad greens garnished with celery sticks.

Approximate values per serving: **Calories** 94.4, **Carbohydrates (grams)** 16, **Protein (grams)** 3.1, **Fat (grams)** 3.4, **Cholesterol (milligrams)** 0. Carbohydrates = 59% calories, Protein = 12% calories, Fat = 29% calories.

Broccoli and Cauliflower Coleslaw

This recipe illustrates how a traditional coleslaw can be made more exciting by substituting other cruciferous vegetables for the commonly used cabbage. Broccoli and cauliflower add both taste and dimension to a simple dish. Because of the abundance of flavors from the ingredients, only about half of the normally required oil is used in this recipe. The use of the cider vinegar also makes this slaw a little different by adding a natural sweetness to the dressing. Together with the carrots and the raisins, the cider vinegar gives this recipe full-bodied flavor.

Makes 10 4-ounce portions

2 cups, or 16 ounces, broccoli florets, finely chopped
2 cups, or 16 ounces, cauliflower florets, finely chopped
1/2 cup, or 4 ounces, carrots, shredded
1/2 cup, or 3 ounces, raisins, plumped
1/2 cup, or 4 ounces, onions, finely chopped
1 teaspoon white pepper, ground
1/4 teaspoon liquid red pepper
1 teaspoon celery seed
3/4 cup, or 6 ounces, cider vinegar
2 tablespoons, or 1 ounce, corn oil

1. Mix all ingredients together and allow to marinate overnight for best results.

2. Drain salad and serve on crisp salad greens.

Approximate values per serving: **Calories** 91, **Carbohydrates (grams)** 13.7, **Protein (grams)** 2.8, **Fat (grams)** 3.5, **Cholesterol (milligrams)** 0. Carbohydrates = 58% calories, Protein = 10% calories, Fat = 32% calories.

Country Slaw

Adding finely shredded kale to a fairly traditional coleslaw recipe adds color, vitamins, and minerals to an otherwise plain salad.

Makes 10 5-ounce portions

1 quart, or 2 pounds, green cabbage, finely shredded
2 cups, or 10 ounces, kale, finely shredded
1/2 cup, or 4 ounces, green bell peppers, finely julienned
1/2 cup, or 4 ounces, red radishes, thinly sliced
1/2 cup, or 4 ounces, onions, thinly sliced
2 tablespoons granulated sugar
1/2 cup, or 4 ounces, mustard, coarsely prepared
1 teaspoon celery seed
2 teaspoons black pepper, coarsely ground
1/2 cup, or 4 ounces, cider vinegar
1/4 cup, or 2 ounces, lemon juice, freshly squeezed
2 tablespoons, or 1 ounce, corn oil

1. Mix together cabbage, kale, bell peppers, radishes, and onions.

2. Mix together sugar, mustard, celery seed, pepper, vinegar, lemon juice, and oil.

3. Pour dressing over vegetables, stir well, and refrigerate overnight.

Approximate values per serving: **Calories** 83, **Carbohydrates (grams)** 13, **Protein (grams)** 2.4, **Fat (grams)** 3.4, **Cholesterol (milligrams)** 0. Carbohydrates = 56% calories, Protein = 10% calories, Fat = 33% calories.

Italian Vegetables with Tomato Basil Vinaigrette

Reduced-fat salad dressings can be made more interesting by adding other full-flavored ingredients to the dressing and using full-flavored ingredients in the salad itself. Here the dressing recipe reverses the normal 3:1 oil to vinegar ratio and asks for 2:1 vinegar to oil ratio. Normally this would be too sour to use; however, the tomato paste and fresh basil smooth out the sour taste into a nice balance of flavors. The fennel, artichoke hearts, spinach, and endive give body to the salad but also supply various tastes, textures, vitamins, and minerals to this healthy side dish.

Makes 10 5-ounce portions

2 tablespoons, or 1 ounce, virgin olive oil

1/4 cup, or 2 ounces, tomato paste

1/4 cup, or 2 ounces, red wine vinegar

1 teaspoon black pepper, coarsely ground

1 teaspoon garlic, finely chopped

2 tablespoons fresh basil, chopped

1 cup, or 8 ounces, fresh fennel, julienne

1 cup, or 8 ounces, zucchini, thinly sliced

1 cup, or 8 ounces, artichoke hearts, sliced

5 cucumbers, peeled, seeded, and sliced

1/2 cup, or 4 ounces, onions, thinly sliced

1/2 cup, or 4 ounces, green bell peppers, thinly sliced

1 quart, or 16 ounces, plum tomatoes, 1/2-inch slices

2 cups, or 8 ounces, curly spinach, cleaned and cut into bite-size pieces

1 curly endive, cleaned and cut into bite-size pieces

1. Mix together oil, tomato paste, vinegar, pepper, garlic, and basil for the dressing.

2. Mix fennel with other vegetables except spinach and endive.

3. Pour dressing over vegetables and allow to marinate for at least 1 hour.

4. Mix spinach and endive together and use as bed for marinated vegetables and dressing.

Approximate values per serving: **Calories** 101, **Carbohydrates (grams)** 15.2, **Protein (grams)** 3.1, **Fat (grams)** 2.8, **Cholesterol (milligrams)** 0. Carbohydrates = 63% calories, Protein = 12% calories, Fat = 25% calories.

Sweet Potato Salad with Pecan Honey Dressing

This Southern recipe transforms a simple dish, potato salad, into an exciting taste sensation. Because of the vegetable choices, only a small amount of honey is needed to give the dish a signature taste. In return, the taste of the honey reduces the dependency on oil for flavor and mouth feel.

Makes 15 5-ounce portions

3 pounds sweet potatoes
1 cup, or 8 ounces, celery, peeled, small diced
1 cup, or 8 ounces, carrots, peeled, small diced
1/2 cup, or 4 ounces, bell peppers, small diced
1 tablespoon peanut oil
1/4 cup, or 2 ounces, lemon juice, freshly squeezed
1/2 cup, or 4 ounces, honey
1/2 cup, or 4 ounces, pecans, chopped

1. Cook sweet potatoes in their jackets in hot, not boiling, water.

2. When potatoes can easily be pierced with a fork, they are done.

3. Cool potatoes and peel; cut into medium diced-size pieces.

4. Mix all other ingredients together and stir well.

5. Stir sweet potatoes into mix gently so they don't break up too much.

Approximate values per serving: **Calories** 383, **Carbohydrates (grams)** 47, **Protein (grams)** 4.5, **Fat (grams)** 18, **Cholesterol (milligrams)** 0. Carbohydrates = 59% calories, Protein = 11% calories, Fat = 30% calories.

Green Beans and Potato Salad with International Greens and Walnut Vinaigrette

To make a salad exciting, it is important to choose ingredients that provide great flavors, colors, and textures. The tendency is to use only mild-flavored salad greens and vegetables and spice them up with an overpowering dressing. Instead, salad ingredients should be selected to give as much character to the dish as a wine does to a meal; the dressing should complement the ingredients, not overpower them. In this simple salad, the curly and Belgian endives add character through their mild bitterness. Tossed with the sweet romaine lettuce and the vibrantly colored radicchio, they give color and added textures to an otherwise average salad. Boiled potatoes and green beans add dimensions of taste and substance without added fat.

The walnut oil is only a portion of the total oil used because it is so strongly flavored. It is used more as a seasoning for the dressing than as a main ingredient. Canola oil is used as an accompanying oil because of its bland flavor. It produces the desired effects for a salad dressing (shine, appeal, even distribution of seasonings and vinegars on the main salad ingredients) yet does not conflict with the walnut oil's taste. Using another flavored oil with the walnut oil (olive oil, for example) would confuse the palate.

Makes 15 5-ounce portions

1½ pints, or 24 ounces, red bliss potatoes
1½ pints, or 24 ounces, fresh green beans
1 quart, or 32 ounces, white vegetable stock
1/2 head romaine lettuce, cleaned and cut into bite-size pieces
1/2 head curly endive, cleaned and cut into bite-size pieces
1 head radicchio, cleaned and cut into bite-size pieces
2 heads Belgian endive, cleaned, separated into single leaves
5, or 30 ounces, ripe tomatoes, cut in wedges
1½ cups, or 12 ounces, spring onions, white part only, cut in strips

Dressing:

2 teaspoons walnut oil
2 tablespoons canola oil
1/2 cup, or 4 ounces, red wine vinegar
2 tablespoons lemon juice, freshly squeezed
1 teaspoon black pepper, coarsely ground
1 teaspoon cardamon, ground
1/4 cup, or 2 ounces, walnuts, broken

1. Cook potatoes in vegetable stock until tender; remove and thinly sliced.

2. Cook green beans in same vegetable stock until tender; do not overcook; strain and shock (rinse in ice cold water to stop cooking).

3. Toss together cut romaine, curly endive, and radicchio.

4. Mix together all dressing ingredients except the walnuts. (They will be used as a garnish.)

5. Place salad greens on cold plates and put a few Belgian endive leaves on each; decorate with tomatoes, sliced potatoes, green beans, and spring onions.

6. Spoon dressing over salad just before service; garnish with walnuts.

Approximate values per serving: **Calories** 171, **Carbohydrates (grams)** 23, **Protein (grams)** 5.7, **Fat (grams)** 8, **Cholesterol (milligrams)** 0. Carbohydrates = 50% calories, Protein = 12% calories, Fat = 38% calories.

Grilled Chicken Salad

Grilled chicken salads are typical in American restaurants today. This, however, may not be a typical recipe, for it uses an array of flavoring ingredients to give color, texture, and taste to an otherwise low-fat and light-flavored salad entree. The 4:1 lime juice to oil ratio is far off the traditional 3:1 oil to vinegar ratio of many salad dressings. The fresh lime taste is sour, without being overpowering, and a sweet enough fresh fruit taste to blend well with the fresh chopped mint. The mix of lettuces, iceberg, romaine, and curly endive, gives variety of color, textures, and sweet versus bitter (iceberg versus endive, with the flavor of romaine near the middle of the spectrum) flavor combinations.

Makes 10 5-ounce portions

1/4 cup, or 2 ounces, onions, finely chopped
1 teaspoon garlic, finely chopped
1/4 cup, or 2 ounces, lime juice, fresh
2 tablespoons olive oil
8, or 32 ounces, 4-ounce chicken breasts, boneless, skinless
1/2 head iceberg lettuce
1/2 head romaine lettuce
1/2 head curly endive
1/2 cup, or 4 ounces, radishes, thinly sliced
2, or 10 ounces, cucumbers, peeled and thinly sliced
5, or 30 ounces, tomatoes, cut in 6 wedges each
1/4 cup, or 2 ounces, pine nuts, dry roasted

Dressing:

2 tablespoons olive oil
1/2 cup, or 4 ounces, lime juice, fresh
1 tablespoon fresh mint, chopped
2 teaspoons black pepper, coarsely ground

1. Mix onions, garlic, 1/4 cup of lime juice, and olive oil and stir well.

2. Pour mixture over chicken breasts and marinate overnight.

3. Remove chicken from marinade and broil slowly until done.

4. In the meantime, clean the salad greens.

5. Cut the lettuces in bite-size pieces and mix with radishes and cucumbers.

6. When chicken is cooked, cut into long strips and place on a bed of the salad mixture.

7. Mix together dressing ingredients.

8. Garnish with 3 wedges of tomatoes on each salad, and drizzle some dressing over entire dish.

9. Garnish entire salad with pine nuts.

Approximate values per serving: **Calories** 221, **Carbohydrates (grams)** 8.8, **Protein (grams)** 27.8, **Fat (grams)** 8.9, **Cholesterol (milligrams)** 67. Carbohydrates = 16% calories, Protein = 49% calories, Fat = 36% calories.

Fruit Salad with Honey-Orange Dressing

The interesting twist to this otherwise simple salad is the no-fat orange juice and honey dressing. The same dressing can be used on lettuce-based salads and vegetable salads.

Makes 15 5-ounce portions

5, or 20 ounces, red delicious apples, cored and diced
5, or 20 ounces, Bartlett pears, cored and diced
2 cups, or 10 ounces, red seedless grapes, cut in halves
2 cups, or 10 ounces, fresh peaches, sliced
1/2 cup, or 4 ounces, honey
1/4 cup, or 2 ounces, orange juice, freshly squeezed
1/4 cup, or 2 ounces, walnuts, chopped
1/2 cup, or 3 ounces, raisins

1. Place diced apples in small amount of lemon water to prevent them from discoloring.

2. Place all fruit, except raisins, in a bowl.

3. Mix honey and orange juice and pour over fruit.

4. Garnish with walnuts and raisins.

5. Serve in a fruit cup or on a plate lined with a leaf of lettuce.

Approximate values per serving: **Calories** 176, **Carbohydrates (grams)** 37.4, **Protein (grams)** 2.1, **Fat (grams)** 4.1, **Cholesterol (milligrams)** 0. Carbohydrates = 77% calories, Protein = 4% calories, Fat = 19% calories.

Vegetables, Legumes, Potatoes, and Grains

Vegetables, legumes, potatoes, and grains can be excellent sources of vitamins, minerals, and fiber. The Food Guide Pyramid recommends at least four servings daily of vegetables and six to eleven servings daily of grain products and starch-based foods, so vegetables, legumes, potatoes, and grains could significantly contribute to a well-balanced, nutritionally sound diet.

There are hundreds of varieties of these foods to choose from and thousands of ways of preparing them using nutritional cooking guidelines. Either singularly or combined in myriad flavors and textures, vegetables, legumes, potatoes, and grains play an integral role in the human diet.

The difficulty is to get your guests or customers to eat the appropriate amounts of these foods and still feel satisfied with the meal. Fortunately, vegetable cookery has kept pace with innovations in meat and seafood cookery, so the minimal role vegetables have played in the traditional dining experience can evolve into a major and gratifying part of the dining experience.

Follow these guidelines to ensure the proper retention of nutrients and expand your skills in preparing exciting vegetable, legume, potato, and grain dishes:

- Purchase only the freshest products that are available.
- Purchase vegetables grown in your own locality whenever possible to decrease shipping and storage time.
- Store all products properly, whether fresh, frozen, or dried.
- Prepare products as close to cooking time as possible.
- Never store cut vegetables or potatoes in water for long periods of time.

- If blanching is part of the cooking process, shock vegetables quickly and remove from water/ice bath as soon as cooled off.
- If combining ingredients, learn the different cooking times of leaf, root, stem, flowering, and fruit vegetables.
- Cook vegetables that take the longest amount of time first, and cook the ones that take the least amount of time last.
- Use seasoning vegetables like celery, celery root, onions, garlic, fennel, bell peppers, parsnips, and turnips in addition to herbs and spices to season vegetable, grain, and starch dishes.
- Combine ingredients to present a complexity of textures and flavors.
- Cook vegetables for immediate use only.
- Use a variety of ingredients and a variety of healthy cooking methods.

Creating vegetable and starch accompaniments that stimulate sight, taste, smell, and touch (texture) while maintaining nutritional cooking practices can be challenging and fun. Put aside traditional or common vegetable preparations for exciting and satisfying healthy creations.

Braised Cabbages and Bell Peppers

Cruciferous vegetables are thought to reduce cancer risk in almost all cases. Members of the cruciferous family include cabbage, broccoli, cauliflower, turnips, and brussels sprouts. The National Cancer Institute recommends a low-fat diet containing 20 to 30 grams of fiber daily. An increased consumption of fruits, vegetables, and whole grains would go a long way toward increasing the fiber and micronutrients in our diets and reducing the amount of fat. The use of bell peppers in this recipe is an excellent way of adding flavor, color, and more of the needed fiber and nutrients for a healthy diet.

Makes 20 4-ounce portions

3 pounds green cabbage, finely shredded
2 pounds Chinese cabbage, finely shredded
2 cups, or 16 ounces, onions, thinly sliced
1/2 cup, or 4 ounces, water
2 cups, or 16 ounces, red bell peppers, julienne
2 teaspoons leaf basil, or 2 tablespoons fresh chopped basil
1/2 teaspoon cloves, ground
2 teaspoons black pepper, coarsely ground
1/2 cup, or 4 ounces, white vinegar

1. Place cabbages, onions, and water together in a large pot.

2. Cover the pot and bring contents to a quick boil.

3. Reduce contents to a simmer, and cook until cabbages are tender.

4. Add bell peppers, basil, cloves, and black pepper and stir well.

5. Cook for an additional 15 minutes.

6. Stir in vinegar, and serve immediately.

Approximate values per serving: **Calories** 37, **Carbohydrates (grams)** 8, **Protein (grams)** 2, **Fat (grams)** 0.4, **Cholesterol (milligrams)** 0. Carbohydrates = 73% calories, Protein = 18% calories, Fat = 9% calories.

Summer Squash with Ginger and Spring Onions

This recipe demonstrates the enhancement of mild-flavored vegetables (in this case summer squash) with highly flavorful natural ingredients like ginger and spring onions. The flavors so complement each other that the customer does not miss the taste of salt.

Using stock as a cooking medium, in place of oil, allows you to cook soft vegetables like summer squash, tomatoes, cucumbers, green beans, and snap peas with no fat. Adding 2 tablespoons of whole butter to the finished vegetable would increase the fat content to 23%, still within dietary guidelines.

Makes 20 4-ounce portions

5 pounds yellow squash, zucchini, or any combination of summer squashes
2 cups, or 16 ounces, spring onions, washed and chopped; separate the white from the tender greens; reserve the greens for garnish
2 tablespoons, or 1 ounce, fresh ginger, finely chopped
1 teaspoon white pepper, ground
1/4 cup, or 2 ounces, white vegetable stock
1/4 cup, or 2 ounces, freshly squeezed lime juice

1. Wash the squash thoroughly to remove all sand and dirt. Cut to desired shape.

2. In a sauté pan heat the vegetable stock with the ginger and white spring onions.

3. Add squash and pepper and toss until squash becomes tender.

4. Finish with lime juice and garnish with green onion tops.

Approximate values per serving: **Calories** 42, **Carbohydrates (grams)** 9.2, **Protein (grams)** 2.7, **Fat (grams)** 0.3, **Cholesterol (milligrams)** 0. Carbohydrates = 75% calories, Protein = 18% calories, Fat = 6% calories.

Glazed Yellow Turnips with Figs

Dietary changes can affect high blood pressure. An increase in potassium, a decrease in sodium, and a loss of extra body weight can lower blood pressure. Fruit is the food highest in potassium and lowest in sodium. Increasing fruit in the diet therefore helps reduce blood pressure. In this recipe, the dried figs (a fruit) help lower blood pressure and give body to the sauce and flavor to the dish.

Makes 10 4-ounce portions

1 tablespoon anise seed, crushed
2 teaspoons rosemary leaves
2½ pounds yellow turnips (rutabagas), cut in any uniform shape
2 cups, or 16 ounces, dried figs, chopped
1 quart, or 32 ounces, vegetable stock
1/4 teaspoon white pepper, ground
1 teaspoon pink pepper corns

1. Place anise seed and rosemary in a sachet made from cheese cloth.

2. Place sachet, cut turnips, figs, and vegetable stock in saucepan and bring to a quick boil.

3. Reduce to a slow simmer and continue to cook until the turnips are almost tender (about 45 minutes).

4. Remove sachet.

5. Add white pepper and pink pepper corns, and cook for an additional 10 minutes, fully cooking turnips, and thicken the sauce.

Approximate values per serving: **Calories** 37, **Carbohydrates (grams)** 7.9, **Protein (grams)** 1.4, **Fat (grams)** 0.5, **Cholesterol (milligrams)** 0. Carbohydrates = 77% calories, Protein = 13% calories, Fat = 10% calories.

Southern Greens with Honey Mustard Dressing

Kale, collards, and mustard greens are all relatives of the cabbage family. They are naturally rich in calcium and B vitamins. Their strong tastes can be juxtaposed with the other strong flavors of mustard and honey to present a satisfying flavor combination. The currants and apples add a different texture and a subtle twist to the overall taste.

Makes 10 4-ounce portions

1 pound curly leaf kale
1 pound fresh collards
1 pound mustard, or turnip, greens
1 quart, or 32 ounces, white vegetable stock
2 cups, or 16 ounces, sliced leeks, white part only
1/2 cup, or 4 ounces, dried red currants
2 cups, or 16 ounces, sliced tart apples
1 teaspoon white pepper, ground
1/8 teaspoon red pepper, ground
1/4 cup, or 2 ounces, honey
1/4 cup, or 2 ounces, coarsely prepared mustard
2 tablespoons, or 1 ounce, fresh lemon juice

1. Peel the stems off the greens, and wash thoroughly.

2. Shred and mix all greens together.

3. Place in saucepan with vegetable stock and leeks, and simmer until greens are tender.

4. Add currants, sliced apples, and white and red pepper; cook for an additional 5 minutes.

5. Mix together mustard, honey, and lemon juice, and add to cooked vegetables and remaining stock.

6. Simmer together for 5 minutes.

7. Serve immediately.

Approximate values per serving: **Calories** 155, **Carbohydrates (grams)** 36, **Protein (grams)** 5.3, **Fat (grams)** 0.9, **Cholesterol (milligrams)** 0. Carbohydrates = 83% calories, Protein = 13% calories, Fat = 5% calories.

Oven Roasted Sweet Potato Homefries

Although sweet potatoes are relatively high in calories (200), they are packed full of vitamin A, fiber, and iron. They are also an excellent source of carotene. Carotene is a yellow/orange color pigment that is a precursor for vitamin A.

This recipe transforms a basic breakfast accompaniment, home fried potatoes, into a nutritious alternative with great sensory appeal. Cooking the potatoes in their skins will help add nutrients to the final dish.

Roasting partially cooked potatoes in seasoned stocks allows the cook to reproduce a traditionally fat-laden dish with a low-fat substitute. The high heat of the oven will help caramelize the tops of the potatoes, while the stock continues to cook them through. The resulting potatoes will have a texture that simulates the texture and color of fried potatoes.

The thyme leaves add character to the dish. Other leafy herbs could be added to, or substituted for, the thyme to give multiple variations.

Makes 15 4-ounce portions

2 cups, or 16 ounces, onions, medium diced
2 teaspoons garlic, chopped
1/4 teaspoon white pepper, ground
1 teaspoon black pepper, coarsely ground
1 tablespoon fresh thyme leaves, chopped, 2 teaspoons if dried
5 pounds sweet potatoes
1 cup, or 8 ounces, vegetable stock

1. Simmer the sweet potatoes in plain water, with their skins, until a fork can easily penetrate the flesh; do not overcook them. Cool the potatoes; peel and cut them into large dice.

2. Place stock in a shallow pan, and bring to a boil.

3. Add onions, garlic, and spices and cook until onions are tender.

4. Add sweet potatoes and stir well.

5. Place pan in 450°F oven for 20 minutes, or until potatoes are fully cooked.

Approximate values per serving: **Calories** 227, **Carbohydrates (grams)** 52, **Protein (grams)** 4, **Fat (grams)** 0.8, **Cholesterol (milligrams)** 0. Carbohydrates = 90% calories, Protein = 7% calories, Fat = 3% calories.

Dill and Shallot Hashbrowns

Shallots will give a peppery onion taste with a hint of garlic, and together with the fresh dill will create a complex flavor combination. This added flavor will replace the flavors lost from cooking with very low fats. The paprika will add color and a slightly sweeter taste, blending well with the sharp taste of the peppers and the shallots.

Potatoes are a good food supply. They have no fat and they are not high in calories. The calories associated with potatoes are from the fats traditionally used to prepare them. In this recipe, where added fat is kept to a minimum, potatoes make a tasty and healthy food.

Potatoes are also a plentiful source of potassium and are an excellent source of dietary fiber, vitamins, and minerals.

Makes 15 4-ounce portions

5 pounds russet potatoes, peeled and shredded
2 cups, or 16 ounces, shallots, shredded
1 tablespoon dill, freshly chopped
2 tablespoons paprika
1/2 teaspoon white pepper, ground
1 teaspoon black pepper, coarsely ground
4 tablespoons vegetable oil spray

1. Mix all ingredients together and allow to rest for 5 to 10 minutes.

2. Thoroughly heat a large, seasoned or nonstick fry pan.

3. Spray pan with vegetable spray (approx. 1/2 tsp. each spray), and heat.

4. Spoon 1/4 cup of potato mix, per portion, on the pan.

5. Cook until bottom begins to brown; turn potato mix carefully.

6. Place whole pan in a 450°F oven to finish cooking, about 4 minutes.

7. Serve immediately.

Approximate values per serving: **Calories** 148, **Carbohydrates (grams)** 21, **Protein (grams)** 3.5, **Fat (grams)** 6, **Cholesterol (milligrams)** 0. Carbohydrates = 56% calories, Protein = 9% calories, Fat = 35% calories.

Cranberry Rice Pilaf with Peanuts

Cranberries are a fruit native to North America and were one of the first fruits used to make preserves and relishes in the new country. Their subtle tartness is easily controlled by the addition of sweet flavors to the recipe; in this case those ingredients are the mace and the allspice, but orange juice or apples also blend very well with the distinctive cranberry flavor.

Peanuts are one of the best sources of niacin. Niacin is required for the function of respiratory enzymes. Allowances are based on overall calorie intake. For every thousand calories, 6.5 to 6.6 milligrams of niacin are needed.

Makes 10 4-ounce portions

2 tablespoons peanut oil
1 cup, or 8 ounces, fresh whole cranberries
1 cup, or 8 ounces, onions, small diced
1 teaspoon allspice, ground
1/2 teaspoon mace, ground
1 teaspoon fresh ginger, grated
1/2 teaspoon white pepper, ground
1/2 cup, or 4 ounces, wild rice
1½ cups, or 12 ounces, long grain rice
1/4 cup, or 2 ounces, dry sherry
2 tablespoons granulated sugar
4 cups, or 32 ounces, white vegetable stock
1/2 cup, or 4 ounces, unsalted roasted peanuts

1. Sweat the onions and cranberries together in the peanut oil until the onions are tender and the skins of the berries bust open.

2. Add the spices and rice; stir well.

3. Add the sherry, sugar, and stock; bring to a quick boil.

4. Cover the pan and finish cooking in a 350°F oven. Cooking time should be 20 to 22 minutes.

5. When the rice is finished, there should still be a small amount of liquid in the pan; the hot rice will absorb this very quickly; do not stir at this point.

6. Add chopped or sliced peanuts just before service as garnish.

Approximate values per serving: **Calories** 314, **Carbohydrates (grams)** 51, **Protein (grams)** 7.8, **Fat (grams)** 9.1, **Cholesterol (milligrams)** 0. Carbohydrates = 64% calories, Protein = 10% calories, Fat = 26% calories.

Brown Rice Pilaf with Chickpeas and Pecans

Anemia is caused by insufficient amounts of iron in the blood system and can make us listless, irritable, and mentally sluggish. Chickpeas are an excellent source of iron and are also high in protein and fiber. They have no cholesterol.

Brown rice is the whole kernel of rice with the bran still attached. Therefore, it naturally has more vitamins and minerals. Also, the bran has a high percentage of fiber, which aids in digestion.

Makes 15 4-ounce portions

1 cup, or 8 ounces, onions, small diced
1 cup, or 8 ounces, celery, peeled and small diced
1 cup, or 8 ounces, carrots, small diced
1 tablespoon peanut oil
2 cups, or 16 ounces, brown long grain rice
2 cups, or 16 ounces, cooked chickpeas
1/2 teaspoon celery seed
1 tablespoon sage
1 teaspoon black pepper, coarsely ground
1 quart, or 32 ounces, white vegetable stock
1/4 cup, or 2 ounces, chopped roasted pecans

1. Cook onions, celery, and carrots with hot oil until lightly browned.

2. Add rice, chickpeas, and spices and stir well.

3. Add vegetable stock and bring entire mixture to a full boil.

4. Cover the pan and cook in a hot oven (350°F) for approximately 20 to 25 minutes.

5. Garnish with chopped pecans just before service.

Approximate values per serving: **Calories** 286, **Carbohydrates (grams)** 52, **Protein (grams)** 7.8, **Fat (grams)** 5.7, **Cholesterol (milligrams)** 0. Carbohydrates = 72% calories, Protein = 11% calories, Fat = 18% calories.

Cauliflower Creole

In place of commonly used hollandaise or cheese sauces, try a low-fat vegetable sauce to add flavor and presentation to steamed, boiled, or roasted vegetables. This Creole sauce can be used for a number of different vegetables, including broccoli, squash, cabbage, brussels sprouts, and roasted onions.

Makes 15 4-ounce portions

1/2 cup, or 4 ounces, onions, finely diced
1 tablespoon garlic, chopped
1/2 cup, or 4 ounces, green bell peppers, small diced
1 tablespoon virgin olive oil
2 cups, or 16 ounces, tomato concasse
1 teaspoon black pepper, coarsely ground
1/8 teaspoon crushed red pepper
1 teaspoon fresh lemon juice
1 teaspoon thyme leaves
1 teaspoon dry basil leaf
2 cauliflower heads

1. Sauté onions, bell peppers, and garlic in oil until tender.

2. Add tomatoes, spices, herbs, and lemon juice.

3. Cook for 15 minutes.

4. Cut cauliflower in bite-size pieces, and cook in lightly salted water until done.

5. Place cauliflower in serving bowls and top with Creole sauce.

Approximate values per serving: **Calories** 46, **Carbohydrates (grams)** 7.1, **Protein (grams)** 2.7, **Fat (grams)** 1.7, **Cholesterol (milligrams)** 0. Carbohydrates = 54% calories, Protein = 16% calories, Fat = 30% calories.

Vegetarian Pilaf

A pilaf usually calls for a chicken, beef, or veal stock. Using vegetable stock eliminates fat and cholesterol. It also allows the cook to use this recipe interchangeably with poultry, beef, veal, sea food, or vegetarian entrees.

Makes 15 4-ounce portions

1 cup, or 8 ounces, celery, finely diced
1 cup, or 8 ounces, carrot, finely diced
2 teaspoons shallots, finely chopped
2 cups, or 16 ounces, long grain rice
4 cups, or 32 ounces, vegetable stock (red or white)
1 teaspoon cardamom seeds, crushed
6 cloves
1/2 teaspoon white pepper corns, crushed
1 bay leaf
1 teaspoon salt

1. Using a small piece of cheese cloth, make a bag to hold the cardamom, cloves, white pepper corns, and bay leaf. Tie a piece of twine to the end.

2. Add all other ingredients to a stock pot, and tie the end of the twine to the handle of the pot.

3. Bring to a boil.

4. Cover with foil and bake in hot oven (350°F) for 20 minutes.

5. Remove bag of spices, and serve.

Approximate values per serving: **Calories** 199, **Carbohydrates (grams)** 44, **Protein (grams)** 3.9, **Fat (grams)** 0.3, **Cholesterol (milligrams)** 0. Carbohydrates = 90% calories, Protein = 8% calories, Fat = 2% calories.

Sesame Carrots and Raisins

Sesame seeds and sesame oil contain polyunsaturated fat and can be used successfully when measured properly in a healthy diet. Sesame seeds are also a good source of vitamin E and magnesium.

Peanut butter can also be used in healthy recipes when measured properly. In this recipe, the 1 tablespoon of peanut butter is just enough to provide flavor without adding too many fat calories. Peanut butter contains no cholesterol, is loaded with protein, and is a good source of folic acid. According to the Georgia Peanut Commission, other vitamins and minerals contained in peanut butter include vitamin E, niacin, thiamin, copper, phosphorus, magnesium, and iron.

Makes 12 4-ounce portions

3 pounds carrots, julienne
1 tablespoon sesame oil
1 cup, or 6 ounces, raisins, plumped
1 tablespoon peanut butter
2 tablespoons fresh lime juice
1/4 teaspoon red pepper sauce
2 tablespoons sesame seeds, dry roasted

1. Blanch the carrots by cooking them in simmering water for 10 minutes or in a steamer for 2 to 3 minutes; drain, shock in water bath, and drain again.

2. At service time, heat the sesame oil in a well-seasoned or nonstick fry pan.

3. Add carrots and raisins and heat through.

4. Add peanut butter, lime juice, and pepper sauce and mix well.

5. Add the sesame seeds just before service.

Approximate values per serving: **Calories** 147, **Carbohydrates (grams)** 28, **Protein (grams)** 3.1, **Fat (grams)** 4.1, **Cholesterol (milligrams)** 0. Carbohydrates = 70% calories, Protein = 8% calories, Fat = 23% calories.

⟞ *Walnut French Beans*

This recipe transforms a common vegetable, green beans, into a healthy and tasty accompaniment. The vegetables are cut very thin (French style) and cooked rapidly in the vegetable stock. Strain the excess vegetable stock from the beans before adding the honey and walnut oil.

The walnut oil is used here as a seasoning. Only a small amount is needed to supply the desired flavor. The lemon juice, zest, and honey give this recipe a sweet-and-sour taste.

Makes 10 4-ounce portions

2½ pounds French cut green beans
1 pint, or 16 ounces, white vegetable stock
2 teaspoons walnut oil
1 tablespoon honey
1/2 teaspoon black pepper, ground
1 tablespoon fresh lemon juice
1 teaspoon lemon zest
1/4 cup, or 2 ounces, chopped walnuts

1. In a sauté pan, heat vegetable stock and green beans together.

2. Strain off excess vegetable stock and add the remaining ingredients, except the chopped walnuts; heat through.

3. Add chopped walnuts just before service.

Approximate values per serving: **Calories** 113, **Carbohydrates (grams)** 16.7, **Protein (grams)** 3.6, **Fat (grams)** 5, **Cholesterol (milligrams)** 0. Carbohydrates = 53% calories, Protein = 12% calories, Fat = 35% calories.

Teriyaki Peanut Pasta

A simple pasta side dish can take on an international flavor and appearance with the careful use of highly seasoned ingredients. In this recipe the flavors of the reduced-sodium soy sauce, peanut butter, white wine vinegar, rice wine, fresh ginger, sesame oil, and dry mustard complement each other without being overpowering. The normally bland cooked pasta, dressed with this favorful sauce, turns into an exciting side dish. The addition of broccoli flowers and shitake mushrooms adds great depth to the flavors and more welcomed nutrients to a completely vegan side dish.

Makes 10 4-ounce portions

1/2 cup, or 4 ounces, spring onions, chopped whites and tender greens
1/4 cup, or 2 ounces, creamy peanut butter
1/4 cup, or 2 ounces, reduced-sodium soy sauce
1/4 cup, or 2 ounces, white wine vinegar
2 tablespoons white wine or rice wine
2 tablespoons fresh ginger, chopped
2 teaspoons sesame oil
2 teaspoons dry mustard
1/2 teaspoon white pepper, ground
1/2 teaspoon red pepper sauce
16 ounces dry pasta, any shape
2 cups, or 16 ounces, white vegetable stock
2 cups, or 16 ounces, cut broccoli flowers
2 cups, or 10 ounces, shitake mushrooms, sliced

1. Mix together onions, peanut butter, soy sauce, vinegar, wine, sesame oil, and spices.

2. Cook pasta in large pot of boiling, plain water; drain; rinse with cold water to stop the cooking process.

3. Add vegetable stock to sauté pan and bring to a fast boil.

4. Add broccoli flowers and cook until almost done.

5. Add mushrooms and continue to cook for 2 additional minutes.

6. Add cooked pasta and peanut butter sauce and mix well.

7. Heat through, and serve.

Approximate values per serving: **Calories** 268, **Carbohydrates (grams)** 47, **Protein (grams)** 10.7, **Fat (grams)** 5, **Cholesterol (milligrams)** 0. Carbohydrates = 68% calories, Protein = 16% calories, Fat = 16% calories.

Curried Corn and Lima Beans

Corn and lima beans when combined together form a vegetable dish called succotash, a Native American recipe. Adding the curry flavor to this traditional dish adds a dimension of flavor not possible given only the raw ingredients of corn and lima beans.

Curry powder is a spice blend made to resemble the spices used in East Indian curries. It can be used successfully in many vegetable preparations and adds an international flavor to basic menus.

Makes 15 4-ounce portions

1 cup, or 8 ounces, onions, small diced
1/2 cup, or 4 ounces, green bell peppers, small diced
1/4 cup, or 2 ounces, pimentos, small diced
1 tablespoon curry powder
1/2 teaspoon white pepper, ground
1 cup, or 8 ounces, white vegetable stock
1½ pounds whole kernel corn
1 pound cooked baby lima beans
1/2 cup, or 3 ounces, golden raisins
1/2 cup, or 4 ounces, low-fat sour cream

1. Cook onions, bell peppers, pimentos, curry powder, and white pepper together in the white vegetable stock until the onions are tender.

2. Add corn, lima beans, and raisins; continue to cook until vegetables are heated through.

3. Add low-fat sour cream and stir well.

Approximate values per serving: **Calories** 156, **Carbohydrates (grams)** 31, **Protein (grams)** 4.7, **Fat (grams)** 2.9, **Cholesterol (milligrams)** 0. Carbohydrates = 73% calories, Protein = 11% calories, Fat = 15% calories.

Braised Mixed Greens with Roasted Garlic

It is the mixture of greens that makes the difference in this recipe. A mix gives flavor dimensions that are not possible with single-green recipes. In this recipe, some of the greens are sweeter and some are more bitter than others; together they make a nice blend.

Roasted garlic has a milder flavor than raw or sautéed garlic. Therefore, the use of one whole bulb in this recipe is not overwhelming. The adjusted braising method allows for no-fat cooking and the retention of all the water soluble vitamins in the braising liquid, which will accompany the vegetables on the plate.

Makes 15 4 ounce portions

1 bulb garlic
1½ pints, or 24 ounces, white vegetable stock
1 cup, or 8 ounces, sauterne wine
1½ pounds fresh spinach, washed, with stems removed
1½ pounds escarole, washed and shredded
1½ pounds romaine lettuce, washed and shredded
2 teaspoons black pepper, coarsely ground
2 tablespoons fresh lemon juice

1. Cut garlic bulb in half, and roast at a high heat (450°F) for 30 minutes.

2. Place stock and wine in large, straight-sided pan (rondo) and bring to a boil.

3. Add all lettuces, pepper, and roasted garlic bulb.

4. Cover, and cook in a hot oven (350°F) for 30 minutes.

5. Remove garlic from pan and add lemon juice.

6. Stir well, and serve hot.

Approximate values per serving: **Calories** 97, **Carbohydrates (grams)** 14.6, **Protein (grams)** 4.8, **Fat (grams)** 0.6, **Cholesterol (milligrams)** 0. Carbohydrates = 70% calories, Protein = 23% calories, Fat = 7% calories.

Sweet-and-Sour Brussels Sprouts

Although brussels sprouts are a member of the cruciferous family of vegetables, they are underutilized as a table vegetable. Adding a sweet-and-sour flavor will overcome any strong cabbagelike flavor, which people may find objectionable. Brussels sprouts are commonly served with other strong flavors, like butter or bacon, both of which are high in fat and cholesterol. This recipe is just as flavorful as the traditional dishes but healthier.

Makes 15 4-ounce portions

1 cup, or 8 ounces, onions, small diced
1 quart, or 32 ounces, white vegetable stock
2½ pounds brussels sprouts
2 cups, or 12 ounces, raisins
1/4 cup, or 2 ounces, fresh lemon juice
1/2 cup, or 4 ounces, honey
1 teaspoon black pepper, coarsely ground

1. Add onions to vegetable stock in large sauté pan; simmer until onions are soft.

2. Cut brussels sprouts at the stem end with an X mark to allow for faster and more even cooking. Simmer in vegetable stock for 20 minutes.

3. Strain off two-thirds of the remaining stock, leaving behind approximately 2 cups.

4. Add raisins, lemon juice, honey, and black pepper; heat through.

Approximate values per serving: **Calories** 224, **Carbohydrates (grams)** 55, **Protein (grams)** 6, **Fat (grams)** 0.7, **Cholesterol (milligrams)** 0. Carbohydrates = 88% calories, Protein = 10% calories, Fat = 3% calories.

Winter Squash with Apples and Pears

The flavors of a variety of winter (hard skin) squash blend extremely well with other fall fruit crops, such as the apples and pears used in this recipe. Cooking these together with the wine and amaretto liqueur is a good example of using liquids and fruits to add flavor to common vegetable preparations.

Makes 10 4-ounce portions

2 pounds butternut or acorn squash, cut into 1/2-inch cubes
4 Granny Smith apples
4 Bartlett pears
1/2 cup, or 4 ounces, spring onions, white part thinly sliced
1 quart, or 32 ounces, white vegetable stock
1 cup, or 8 ounces, white Zinfandel wine
1/4 cup, or 2 ounces, amaretto
1/2 teaspoon cinnamon, ground
1/4 teaspoon nutmeg, ground
1/4 cup, or 2 ounces, almonds, dry toasted

1. Place squash in large sauté pan with vegetable stock. Bring to a boil, reduce to a simmer, and cook for 20 minutes or until squash is tender.

2. Add apples, pears, onions, wine, amaretto, and spices; simmer for an additional 15 minutes.

3. Strain to serve; top with toasted almonds as garnish.

Approximate values per serving: **Calories** 139, **Carbohydrates (grams)** 21.8, **Protein (grams)** 2.8, **Fat (grams)** 3.2, **Cholesterol (milligrams)** 0. Carbohydrates = 69% calories, Protein = 9% calories, Fat = 23% calories.

◄──*Braised Red Cabbage with Apple Cider and Sauterne*

Using vegetable stock as the cooking medium eliminates the need to use fat to begin the braising method. The flavors will be developed as a result of the cider and the sauterne wine. Adding the apples at the end will help retain the apples' shape and texture, which will enhance the overall mouth feel of the finished dish.

Makes 10 4-ounce portions

1 tablespoon fresh ginger, grated
2 cups, or 16 ounces, white vegetable stock
2 cups, or 16 ounces, apple cider
1/2 cup, or 4 ounces, sauterne white
3 pounds red cabbage, shredded
2 teaspoons cinnamon, ground
1/2 teaspoon white pepper, ground
1 pound Macintosh or Rome Beauty apples, cored and medium diced

1. Place ginger, stock, cider, and wine in large, straight-sided pan (rondo); bring to a boil.

2. Add cabbage and spices.

3. Cover pan and place it in a hot oven (350°F) to braise for 30 minutes.

4. Add apples just before service.

Approximate values per serving: **Calories** 111, **Carbohydrates (grams)** 23, **Protein (grams)** 3.1, **Fat (grams)** 0.8, **Cholesterol (milligrams)** 0. Carbohydrates = 83% calories, Protein = 11% calories, Fat = 6% calories.

Meat

There are several things to know about meat when deciding on a cut or cooking method: The composition of the muscle(s), the amount of exterior fat, the amount of marbling (interior fat), and tenderness are all critical issues in the nutritional cooking of meat products.

Composition of muscles refers to their shape and size and the direction of the grain (protein strands). Subprimal cuts of meat may contain two or more different muscle types (bottom round roast, for example) and could be broken down into single-muscle cuts to obtain the most flexibility in cooking styles. The following points are also important in evaluating muscle composition:

- The shape of the muscle (e.g., flank steak versus top round) plays a part in determining the cooking method and serving suggestions.
- Size of the muscle determines the type of cooking method that works best: Larger pieces are roasted or braised, and smaller pieces are grilled or broiled.
- Direction of the grain becomes a factor when two or more muscles are connected (such as in the bottom round of beef and veal) or in a thin muscle, like the flank; cooking and cutting of these muscles requires specific care.

All exterior fat on meat should be removed and not consumed. The exterior fat contains the largest concentration of saturated fats and the most fat calories. These fats can be trimmed before or after cooking. (Fat contains concentrated animal flavors because of the natural juices locked inside the fat. During cooking, these juices are released and can add flavor to slow-roasted meats.)

Nutritionists are studying the relationship between cholesterol content and removal of exterior fat before cooking. Results are not yet conclusive. The main health issue is not to consume these fats; the main culinary issue is to make foods taste good without the fats.

All meat contains a certain amount of interior fat, called marbling. This fat is not always visible to the eye and can be removed only by the cooking process. Broiling, grilling, rotisserie cooking, or roasting on a rack are good ways of making sure these fats, when they melt during cooking, fall away from the meat and are not consumed.

Although studies on stearic acid,* one of the saturated fats in meat, showed it to reduce total plasma cholesterol 14% when fed as the sole fat in a liquid formula, we must face the fact that fatty acids do not occur alone in food. Stearic and palmitic fatty acids occur together in many foods. The saturated fatty acids that raise serum cholesterol are palmitic, myristic, and lauric.

We do not need to eliminate meat from our menus, but we do need to eat it in moderate portions, and well trimmed of visible fat whenever possible. Cave dwellers ate a diet in which 35% of their calories came from meat, but the meat was lean and not grain fattened. The fatty acid composition of the meat was completely different from what it is today.

In response to public concern, meat, including pork, is being raised more lean today than ever before. This means that the amounts of exterior and interior fats are naturally being decreased. Because fat is controlled by diet, livestock are now fed special diets to assure more muscle growth and less fat growth. The results are less fatty animal products.

The USDA grading of meat, veal, and lamb evaluates fat content as one of the primary factors in the grade given. Prime meat contains the most fat; Choice meat contains the second most; Select meat (for beef) and Good meat (for veal and lamb) contain the least. Therefore, in selecting meats for nutritional cooking, choose Select or Good grades when possible and Choice grades next; avoid Prime meats.

Meat cuts that are naturally more lean than others include the following:

Beef: flank, top round, eye round, top sirloin, strip loins, tenderloins, first cut brisket

Veal: practically all cuts

Pork: boneless loin roast, boneless rib roast, center loin chops, sirloin roast, tenderloin

Lamb: sirloin roast, loin chops, blade chops, foreshank

Venison: practically all cuts

In spite of all the health concerns regarding meat (especially red meats), beef, lamb, pork, and veal are substantially healthy foods. All meats contain the eight essential amino acids and adequate amounts of vitamins and minerals (particularly the amino acids, vitamins, and minerals not easily found in vegetables). Vegetarians and people who greatly reduce their meat consumption must make sure they get these vitamins and amino acids through other sources. People who eat a moderate amount of lean meat will have a less difficult time meeting their daily nutritional needs.

One of the more difficult health concerns in relation to meat consumption is portion sizes. In America, where large steaks and large roasts are standard dinner fare, the 3- or 4-ounce portions recommended by dietitians may be met with resistance. Hearty appetites must be satisfied while reducing portion sizes. There are two ways to accomplish this: One, prepare meat dishes that are full of

*Hulley, S., Cohen, R., and Widdowson, G., 1977, "Plasma High Density Lipoprotein Cholesterol Level," *Journal of the American Medical Association*, Volume 238, number 2, pp. 2269–2271.

flavor. A simple grilled steak doesn't have enough flavor contrasts or complexities to give the diner a sense of satisfaction when served in smaller portions. Instead, serve beef that has strong and distinct flavors, like tenderloin braised in citrus juice with cloves and cinnamon or sirloin steak marinated in teriyaki sauce. Second, serve smaller meat portions in combination with potato, rice, pasta, or vegetable dishes; an Oriental stir fry is a good example of how this can be accomplished. The bulk of the dinner is made up of several subcourses and is not dependent on the size of any one item.

A variety of meats (beef, pork, lamb, and venison) are used in the following recipes. Each recipe concentrates on a different theme: the type of meat, the marination process, the slow-cooking methods, and the use of natural flavors to create flavorful, nutritious entrees.

✒ Braised Beef Tips au Poivre with Rice Pilaf and Roasted Plum Tomatoes

A traditional beef tenderloin dish, steak au poivre, can be turned into a healthier-choice menu item by changing the cooking procedures slightly. Instead of sautéing the steak in butter or fat, grill the cubes without fat to give them color and firm texture; then braise them in the oven to finish the cooking. Beef tenderloin is naturally tender, so the braising is more to impart the flavors throughout the meat than to tenderize the meat.

Beef tenderloin is the leanest beef muscle. The tenderloin may have a thin fat covering, but this can easily be peeled away from the lean red meat before cutting it into steaks or tips. Serve the recommended 3- or 4-ounce portion on a bed of rice pilaf, cooked noodles, or pasta.

Makes 10 6-ounce portions*

3½ pounds beef tenderloin, trimmed, cut into 1/2-inch cubes
1/4 cup, or 2 ounces, finely chopped shallots
1½ cups, or 12 ounces, dry red wine
1 tablespoon cracked black pepper corns
2 teaspoons thyme leaf
1/2 cup, or 4 ounces, onions, finely diced
1 teaspoon garlic, chopped
1 teaspoon thyme leaf
2 bay leaves
1 teaspoon salt
1/2 teaspoon white pepper, ground

4 cups, or 32 ounces, red vegetable stock
2 cups, or 16 ounces, long grain brown rice
20 fresh plum tomatoes, cut in half
1/2 teaspoon salt
1 teaspoon black pepper, coarsely ground
1½ cups, or 6 ounces, seasoned bread crumbs
1 quart, or 32 ounces, lean beef stock
1 cup, or 4.5 ounces, cornstarch

1. Place 4 ounces of cut tenderloin, about 6 pieces, on a bamboo skewer.

2. Whisk together the shallots, wine, cracked black pepper corns, and first amount (2 teaspoons) of thyme.

3. Place the tenderloin skewers into marinade for 1 hour.

4. Make rice following the vegetarian rice recipe method (p. 294).

5. Place cut plum tomatoes on metal tray.

6. Sprinkle with salt, pepper, and seasoned bread crumbs.

7. Roast tomatoes in very hot oven (450°F) or under a broiler until warmed through.

8. Remove tenderloin from marinade and grill quickly, just enough to color the outsides.

9. Remove tenderloin from the skewer and place in a sauté pan.

10. Heat marinade and pour over tenderloin pieces.

11. Cook tenderloin to desired doneness in a hot oven (450°F).

12. Remove from oven and add beef stock slightly thickened with cornstarch or arrowroot.

13. Place a mound of rice in the center of the plate, and layer tenderloin and sauce over rice.

14. Garnish plate with roasted tomatoes.

*This recipe can easily be adapted to make one order at a time.

Approximate values per serving: **Calories** 451, **Carbohydrates (grams)** 61, **Protein (grams)** 33.6, **Fat (grams)** 7.3, **Cholesterol (milligrams)** 85. Carbohydrates = 55% calories, Protein = 30% calories, Fat = 15% calories.

⟵ Caraway Beef with Pearl Onions

This recipe is a translation of the traditional Hungarian Goulash, which is a beef or veal stew served in a heavy brown sauce flavored with caraway and paprika. This procedure produces only a light-bodied sauce, not thickened with fat and flour (roux), but with a small amount of tomato paste to give flavor, color, and a rich taste that is accentuated with the red wine reduction.

Makes 10 4-ounce portions

3½ pounds lean beef, cubed
2 tablespoons, or 1 ounce, olive oil
2 tablespoons garlic, chopped
3 bay leaves
2 tablespoons shallots, chopped
1 teaspoon black pepper, coarsely ground
1 teaspoon caraway seeds
1 cup, or 8 ounces, tomato paste
1 quart, or 32 ounces, lean beef stock
2 cups, or 16 ounces, dry red wine

1. Cook beef cubes in well-seasoned or nonstick fry pan with olive oil.

2. Add the chopped garlic, bay leaves, shallots, pepper, and caraway; cook quickly for 2 minutes.

3. Remove the meat from the pan and reserve.

4. Add red wine to pan and cook to half its volume.

5. Stir in the tomato paste and stock.

6. Return beef to the pan.

7. Reduce to a simmer and continue to cook for about 45 minutes (or may be finished in a 350°F oven with a cover on the pot).

Approximate values per serving: **Calories** 393, **Carbohydrates (grams)** 6.4, **Protein (grams)** 49.6, **Fat (grams)** 14.6, **Cholesterol (milligrams)** 149. Carbohydrates = 7% calories, Protein = 56% calories, Fat = 37% calories.

⟿ Braised Beef Eye Round Sicilian

Beef eye round is a beef muscle with little internal fat. Much like the tenderloin, the outer layer of fat can be easily removed from eye round. What remains is a relatively lean piece of meat. A major difference between the two cuts of meat is their tenderness. Beef tenderloin is very tender, and beef eye round is much tougher.

The eye round is one of the three muscles that make up the bottom round of the hind quarter. Eye rounds can be cut from veal, venison, and lamb legs for a variety of menu choices.

Because eye rounds come from the inner thigh muscle of the animal, they are not as tender as less used muscles. Braising is one of the preferred methods to tenderize the meat. All the vitamins and minerals from the vegetables, herbs, and spices remain in the braising liquid, which becomes a part of the final dish.

The use of the Chianti wine as a flavor enhancer reduces the need for salt to stimulate taste. The braised fennel will also impart its flavor to the overall dish. The asparagus is a flavorful garnish and side dish, simply prepared to allow the flavor of the asparagus to remain dominant. With the flavors of the eye round, the fennel, and the other seasonings, this dish has many levels of taste.

Makes 10 6-ounce portions

3 to 4 pounds beef eye round, trimmed and cut into 1/2-inch steaks
1 cup, or 8 ounces, onions
1 cup, or 8 ounces, celery, diced
2 teaspoons garlic, chopped
1 tablespoon fresh basil, chopped, or 2 teaspoons dried
1 teaspoon black pepper, coarsely ground
2 cups, or 16 ounces, Chianti wine
3 cups, or 24 ounces, tomatoes, peeled, seeded, and diced
2 fennel bulbs, trimmed and cut into wedges
2 quarts, or 64 ounces, lean beef stock
1½ pounds fresh asparagus
1 quart, or 32 ounces, white vegetable stock

1. Mix together everything except steaks, asparagus, beef stock, and fennel bulb; bring to a quick boil.

2. Immediately remove from the heat and allow to cool.

3. Add steaks to cooled marinade and marinate for a minimum of 3 hours.

4. Remove steaks from marinade and pat dry.

5. Grill steaks just long enough to color the outsides.

6. Add marinade and beef stock to a straight-sided pan (rondo).

7. Bring to a quick boil.

8. Add grilled steaks and cut fennel; cover the pan and cook in a 400°F oven for 1½ hours or until tender.

9. Trim asparagus stems.

10. Poach asparagus in simmering vegetable stock.

11. Time asparagus cooking so that it is done when the meat is ready to be served.

12. Remove the steaks and fennel when cooked, and strain the sauce.

13. Thicken the sauce with 1 cup of cornstarch per quart of strained liquid.

14. Serve each steak with braised fennel, poached asparagus spears, and sauce.

Approximate values per serving: **Calories** 416, **Carbohydrates (grams)** 14, **Protein (grams)** 54, **Fat (grams)** 12.3, **Cholesterol (milligrams)** 149. Carbohydrates = 15% calories, Protein = 56% calories, Fat = 29% calories.

Braised Beef Sirloin with Ginger-Orange Sauce and Broccoli

Beef sirloin is a fairly lean cut of beef. All exterior fat can be easily removed before cooking or plating. It is, however, a relatively tender piece of meat and doesn't require the long cooking times associated with the braising method.

The orange sections and blanched broccoli flowers add color, flavor, and varying textures to the final dish.

Makes 10 6-ounce portions

2 teaspoons fresh garlic, chopped
1 tablespoon fresh ginger, grated
2 cups, or 16 ounces, leeks, whites only, sliced
2 cinnamon sticks
2 teaspoons cloves, ground
1 teaspoon black pepper, coarsely ground
1/8 teaspoon red pepper, crushed
1/2 teaspoon salt
3½ pounds sirloin steak
1 quart, or 32 ounces, lean beef stock
1/2 cup, or 4 ounces, curaçao
1 tablespoon orange zest
1 cup, or 4.5 ounces, cornstarch
2 cups, or 16 ounces, orange sections
2 cups, or 16 ounces, broccoli flowers

1. Add the first eight ingredients to a large pan and bring them to a boil.

2. Grill the steaks just long enough to color all sides.

3. Add steaks to pan; cover and place in 400°F oven for 40 minutes.

4. Remove steaks and strain sauce.

5. Add orange zest to the sauce and mix in 1 cup of cornstarch dissolved in vegetable stock or water; bring to a boil.

6. Add orange sections to thickened sauce.

7. Blanch broccoli flowers and add to sauce.

8. Slice steak, and serve with sauce garnished with orange sections and broccoli flowers.

Approximate values per serving: **Calories** 403, **Carbohydrates (grams)** 16.8, **Protein (grams)** 51.4, **Fat (grams)** 12.1, **Cholesterol (milligrams)** 149. Carbohydrates = 18% calories, Protein = 54% calories, Fat = 29% calories.

Beef Tenderloin Tips in Wild Mushroom and Cherry Sauce

This recipe transforms a classical preparation into a healthy menu choice. The classical dish *Montmorency* refers to the preparation of various dishes flavored with dark cherries, demiglace, and brandy. This related recipe replaces the fat-laden demiglace with a sauce thickened by arrowroot, uses cherry brandy and grenadine to enhance the flavor of the cherries, and uses an assortment of mushrooms for a counterbalance of earthy flavors.

Makes 10 6-ounce portions

3½ pounds beef tenderloin, trimmed, cut into 1-inch cubes
2 tablespoons shallots, finely chopped
2 teaspoons garlic, finely chopped
1/2 cup, or 4 ounces, celery root, finely chopped
1 tablespoon fresh parsley, chopped
1 teaspoon allspice, ground
1 teaspoon black pepper, coarsely ground
1/4 teaspoon red pepper, crushed
1/2 teaspoon salt

2 cups, or 10 ounces, crimini mushrooms, sliced
2 cups, or 10 ounces, shitake mushrooms, sliced
2 cups, or 10 ounces, portabella mushrooms, cut and sliced
2 quarts, or 64 ounces, lean beef stock
1 quart, or 32 ounces, dark, pitted sour cherries
1/2 cup, or 4 ounces, cherry brandy
1/4 cup, or 2 ounces, grenadine
1 cup, or 4.5 ounces, arrowroot

1. Place tenderloin pieces on bamboo skewers, and grill just long enough to color the outsides.

2. In a large shallow pan, place all other ingredients except cherries, brandy, grenadine, and arrowroot.

3. Bring to a boil, and simmer for 10 minutes.

4. Remove tenderloin from the skewers and add it to the pan.

5. Add cherries.

6. Cover the pan and cook inside 400°F oven for 20 minutes or until desired degree of doneness has been reached.

7. Remove the pan from the oven and place it on top of the stove.

8. Dissolve the arrowroot into the grenadine, and add to pan. When the sauce thickens, add the brandy. The brandy will burn if it gets too close to an open flame. Simmer for an additional 2 to 3 minutes.

9. Serve tenderloin with a few cherries and mushrooms.

Approximate values per serving: **Calories** 399, **Carbohydrates (grams)** 16.7, **Protein (grams)** 50.5 **Fat (grams)** 11.9, **Cholesterol (milligrams)** 149. Carbohydrates = 18% calories, Protein = 54% calories, Fat = 29% calories.

⬛ Grilled Flank Steak with Braised Lentils and Chestnuts

Flank steak is one of the lean cuts of beef, but its unusual muscle structure, in which the muscle strands are bundled together in a tight elongated shape, makes it a naturally tough piece of meat. Flank steak is always, therefore, cut on a bias across the grain to expose more of the cut muscle strands in every slice. This will make the cut flank steak very tender. To assure more tenderness, do not overcook it. Flank steak should be served rare to a medium degree of doneness. Medium to well-done flank could also be served, but the slices of cut steak would need to be very thin.

Ale, bay leaves, Worcestershire sauce, garlic, and shallots make up a very potent marinade for the flank steak that will later be incorporated into a flavorful sauce, balanced with the addition of celery, pearl onions, fresh rosemary, juniper berries, and coriander.

Makes 10 6-ounce portions

3½ pounds flank steak, fully trimmed
1 bottle, or 12 ounces, dark ale
2 bay leaves
1 tablespoon Worcestershire sauce
2 teaspoons garlic, chopped
2 tablespoons shallots, chopped
1/4 cup, or 2 ounces, celery, finely diced
20 pearl onions, small
21 chestnuts, boiled and sliced
2 teaspoons fresh rosemary

1 tablespoon juniper berries
2 teaspoons coriander seeds, crushed
1 teaspoon black pepper corns, crushed
1/2 teaspoon salt
1 quart, or 32 ounces, lean beef stock
2 cups, or 16 ounces, lentils
2 cups, or 10 ounces, crimini mushrooms, sliced
1/2 cup, or 2.25 ounces, arrowroot

1. Mix ale with bay leaves, Worcestershire sauce, garlic, and shallots.
2. Add trimmed flank steaks and marinate overnight.
3. Remove steaks from marinade, reserving the marinade.
4. Place juniper berries, coriander seeds, and cracked pepper in cheese cloth sachet. Add to marinade.
5. Add all other ingredients to marinade except chestnuts, mushrooms, beef stock, and arrowroot, and bring to a boil.
6. Reduce to a simmer, and cook until lentils are done (approximately 40 minutes).
7. Remove sachet, and discard.
8. Add mushrooms and sliced boiled chestnuts, and continue to cook for 15 more minutes.
9. Dissolve arrowroot in beef broth and add to sauce; heat to thicken.
10. Grill flank steaks until desired doneness.
11. Slice flank steak and serve with lentils, chestnuts, pearl onions, mushrooms, and sauce.

Approximate values per serving: **Calories** 500, **Carbohydrates (grams)** 38, **Protein (grams)** 56, **Fat (grams)** 12.6, **Cholesterol (milligrams)** 149. Carbohydrates = 31% calories, Protein = 46% calories, Fat = 23% calories.

Roast Leg of Lamb with Honey Berry Sauce

Lamb is ready for slaughter at a very young age, usually between six and nine months old. Therefore, lamb meat is very lean and tender. The fat found on lamb is mostly exterior fat, which can be easily removed before or after cooking.

Lamb is a flavorful meat. With all the excess fat removed, there is still plenty of flavor to enjoy.

The simple preparation of the sauce used in this recipe preserves the full-bodied flavor of the fresh berries. The small amount of honey used is just enough to add a touch of sweetness and not overpower the natural flavors of the sauce. The lemon juice is added for contrast. The end result is a sweet-and-sour berry sauce that marries well with the full flavor of the roasted lamb.

Makes 10 6-ounce portions

1 4- to 5-pound boneless leg of lamb
2 cups, or 16 ounces, dry sherry
1 tablespoon black pepper, coarsely ground
1/4 teaspoon red pepper, crushed
4 tablespoons fresh mint, chopped
2 carrots, rough cut for mirepoix
2 celery stalks, rough cut for mirepoix
1 medium onion, rough cut for mirepoix

1½ pints, or 24 ounces, lean stock (beef, veal, lamb, or vegetable)
2 pints, or 32 ounces, fresh strawberries
1 pint, or 16 ounces, fresh raspberries
1 pint, or 16 ounces, fresh blueberries
1 cup, or 8 ounces, honey
2 tablespoons fresh lemon juice
2 teaspoons lemon zest

1. Mix 1 cup of sherry, chopped mint, and peppers together and rub inside and out of boned lamb before tying for roasting. Tie the boneless leg together to help keep its shape during cooking.

2. Place lamb roast on a bed of mirepoix, and roast in a 300°F oven until desired doneness is achieved.

3. When roast is done, remove from oven and set aside while making sauce.

4. Remove as much fat from the bottom of the roasting pan as is possible.

5. Add 1 additional cup sherry, and cook until almost dry.

6. Add 16 ounces, or 2 cups, of lean beef, veal, lamb, or vegetable stock and cook for 15 minutes.

7. Strain and again remove excess fat.

8. Puree 1½ pints strawberries and ½ pint raspberries; add to strained sauce and heat slowly. Add honey, lemon juice, and lemon zest, and continue to simmer for at least 15 minutes.

9. Dissolve cornstarch in 8 ounces, or 1 cup, of stock and add to sauce to thicken.

10. When sauce is properly thickened, add the remaining whole berries.

11. Slice lamb, and serve over berry sauce and garnished with whole mint leaves.

Approximate values per serving: **Calories** 293, **Carbohydrates (grams)** 17.7, **Protein (grams)** 35.3, **Fat (grams)** 8.6, **Cholesterol (milligrams)** 106. Carbohydrates = 25% calories, Protein = 49% calories, Fat = 27% calories.

~*Roasted Rolled Pork Loin with Turkey Sausage*

Niacin is abundant in pork products, peanuts, fruits, and some vegetables. Although niacin deficiency is rare in the industrial world, its legacy can be destructive where these foods are not found in the average diet. Signs of niacin deficiency include disorientation, confusion, and forgetfulness.

The use of turkey sausage as a filling in this recipe reduces the amount of fat consumed in an average portion. Where as a typical portion might be 4 to 6 ounces of roast pork, this recipe reduces that serving to between 3 and 4 ounces of pork. Served with the vegetable couscous and accompanying vegetables, a 3- to 4-ounce portion of pork is ample for one serving.

Makes 20 6-ounce portions

1 6-pound pork loin, boneless and well trimmed	1/2 teaspoon salt
	2 teaspoons fennel seeds
1/2 cup, or 4 ounces, sesame seeds, dry roasted	1 tablespoon sage
	1/4 cup, or 2 ounces, brandy
2 pounds turkey, ground	1 quart, or 32 ounces, stock (pork, veal, beef, or vegetable)
1/4 cup, or 1.25 ounces, dry milk powder	4 cups, or 10 ounces, dry couscous
1/4 cup, or 2 ounces, sun dried tomatoes, finely chopped	5 cups, or 35 ounces, vegetable stock
1 cup, or 8 ounces, onions, finely chopped	2 cups, or 16 ounces, broccoli flowers
1 tablespoon garlic, finely chopped	2 cups, or 16 ounces, carrots, finely diced
1 teaspoon black pepper, coarsely ground	2 teaspoons cinnamon, ground
1/8 teaspoon red pepper, crushed	2 tablespoons brown sugar

1. Trim the pork loin by cutting into the flesh 1 inch from the bottom side of the loin and rolling the loin as you continue to cut until you have cut the entire loin flat.

2. Mix together all other ingredients except sesame seeds and stock.

3. Spread sesame seeds onto the cut loin, followed by the ground turkey mixture.

4. Roll the loin over the sausage; the two ends should just overlap slightly.

5. Tie the rolled loin, using butcher's twine, to keep the edges sealed together during cooking.

6. Place rolled loin on top of vegetable mirepoix and roast in 350°F oven for 1½ hours, or until done (should reach an internal temperature of 170°F).

7. Remove loin and keep warm while making sauce.

8. Remove as much excess fat as possible from the pan.

9. Deglaze pan with brandy, and burn off excess alcohol.

10. Add stock and simmer for 20 minutes.

11. Strain sauce.

12. Boil vegetable stock in sauce pot.

13. Add cut broccoli flowers, diced carrots, and cinnamon; cook until almost tender.

14. Stir in dry couscous and brown sugar; cover and remove from heat.

15. Let couscous stand for 5 minutes before serving.

16. Serve sliced pork loin over a bed of couscous with sauce.

Approximate values per serving: **Calories** 528, **Carbohydrates (grams)** 25.3, **Protein (grams)** 50.1, **Fat (grams)** 23.3, **Cholesterol (milligrams)** 146. Carbohydrates = 19% calories, Protein = 40% calories, Fat = 40% calories.

Lamb Stew with Cranberries and Madeira

Lamb shoulder is a tough piece of meat with moderate fat content. When butchered properly, most of the exterior fat can be trimmed away before cutting into cubes. It is a tough cut of meat, which requires long slow-cooking techniques, such as the stewing used here. Rather than browning the meat in fat, however, the cubes are placed on a skewer and grilled to add the distinctive brown crust, taste, and aroma achieved through frying in oil. Lamb is a strong-flavored meat that is complemented well with the Madeira wine, a fortified wine, and cranberries. Cranberries are rich in fiber and are a source of calcium, phosphorus, and vitamins A and C.

Makes 10 6-ounce portions

3½ pounds lamb shoulder, trimmed and cut into 2-inch cubes
20 pearl onions
1 tablespoon garlic, finely chopped
2 cups, or 16 ounces, fresh cranberries
2 cups, or 16 ounces, Madeira wine
2 tablespoons fresh parsley, chopped
1 teaspoon black pepper, coarsely ground
1/8 teaspoon red pepper, crushed
1/2 teaspoon salt
2 bay leaves
2 quarts, or 64 ounces, lamb stock
3 cups, or 24 ounces, whole button mushrooms
2 cups, or 16 ounces, early peas
2 cups, or 16 ounces, new potatoes, cut with parisianne scoop into small round balls

1. Place lamb cubes on bamboo skewer with pearl onions.

2. Grill just long enough to color lamb and onions.

3. Combine next 8 ingredients, and cook until pan is almost dry.

4. Dissolve cornstarch in stock and add to pan.

5. Add lamb cubes and pearl onions to pan, and simmer for 1½ hours or until lamb is tender.

6. Blanch potato balls in separate plain simmering water for 10 minutes.

7. Add mushrooms, peas, and blanched potatoes to stew; cook for an additional 15 minutes.

8. Adjust seasonings.

Approximate values per serving: **Calories** 434, **Carbohydrates (grams)** 27.4, **Protein (grams)** 48.5, **Fat (grams)** 11, **Cholesterol (milligrams)** 133. Carbohydrates = 27% calories, Protein = 48% calories, Fat = 25% calories.

⟪Grilled Lamb with Braised Eggplant and Port Wine

Lamb top round, which comes from the upper part of the leg, is a solid meat muscle that can be treated in many different ways to form the foundation of excellent meat entrees. The top round is a relatively tender cut of meat in beef, veal (this is where veal scallopini comes from), and lamb. Because of lamb's pronounced taste, the use of eggplant and port wine helps to create a blend of flavors that is more pleasing in the mouth than any single strong flavor, like the lamb served alone. The artichoke hearts contribute a lighter, almost sweet taste to the eggplant accompaniment, to make the full flavors of this meal a chorus of different tastes.

Makes 10 6-ounce portions

2 teaspoons garlic
1 tablespoon shallots
2 tablespoons coarsely prepared mustard
1 tablespoon fresh oregano, chopped, or 2 teaspoons dried leaf oregano
1 teaspoon black pepper, coarsely ground
1/2 teaspoon salt
2 cups, or 16 ounces, port wine
3½ pounds lamb top round, cut into 1-inch cubes
2 cups, or 16 ounces, leeks, white only, medium diced
2 tablespoons tomato paste
1 quart, or 32 ounces, red vegetable stock
2, or 24 ounces, medium eggplants, large diced
2 cups, or 16 ounces, artichoke hearts, cooked and sliced
1 cup, or 4.5 ounces, cornstarch

1. Mix together garlic, shallots, mustard, oregano, pepper, salt, and port wine.

2. Marinate lamb cubes in sauce for 1 hour.

3. Remove lamb from marinade, and reserve for later cooking.

4. Add the rest of the ingredients, except eggplant, artichoke hearts, and cornstarch, to marinade.

5. Bring this mixture to a boil, and reduce to a simmer.

6. Add eggplant, and allow to simmer uncovered for 40 minutes.

7. Add sliced, cooked artichoke hearts, and simmer for 10 more minutes.

8. Dissolve cornstarch in a small amount of vegetable stock, and add to cooked eggplant and artichoke hearts; bring back to a quick boil, and reduce to a simmer for 5 minutes.

9. Place marinated lamb cubes on bamboo skewers, and grill to desired doneness.

10. Serve grilled lamb on a bed of the cooked vegetables and sauce.

Approximate values per serving: **Calories** 383, **Carbohydrates (grams)** 24.5, **Protein (grams)** 46.4, **Fat (grams)** 10.7, **Cholesterol (milligrams)** 133. Carbohydrates = 26% calories, Protein = 49% calories, Fat = 25% calories.

Pork Pot Roast and Cider

Although pork was once considered a fatty food, it is becoming a healthier food today. Farmers are carefully monitoring their animals' diets to assure a more lean pork product.

The pork loin is one of the most lean sections of the hog, especially if all the exterior fat is trimmed away. To replace the flavors lost by removing this fat, use the braising method to help the other flavors penetrate deep into the flesh of the pork loin. The vegetables are blanched separately to help them retain their natural flavors. When combined with the braised pork, they offer contrasting tastes.

Makes 10 6-ounce portions

3½ pounds pork loin, boneless and well trimmed
1/2 teaspoon white pepper, coarsely ground
1 tablespoon fresh ginger, grated
1 tablespoon garlic, finely chopped
2 cups, or 16 ounces, onions, medium diced
2 quarts or 64 ounces, white vegetable stock
2 cinnamon sticks
1 teaspoon cloves, ground
4 cups, or 32 ounces, hard cider
1 cup, or 4.5 ounces, cornstarch
2 cups, or 16 ounces, white turnips, medium diced
2 cups, or 16 ounces, yellow turnips (rutabagas), medium diced
2 cups, or 16 ounces, carrots, medium diced
2 cups, or 16 ounces, red bliss potatoes, diced with skin left on

1. Grill whole pork loin just long enough to color the outsides.

2. Mix all other ingredients together except turnips, carrots, and potatoes.

3. Bring liquid to a boil, and add pork roast.

4. Place whole pan in 350°F oven for 1½ hours or until pork is done.

5. Remove pork from pan, and add cornstarch dissolved in vegetable stock; bring back to a boil.

6. Strain sauce.

7. Cook turnips, carrots, and potatoes separately in plain water.

8. Add cooked vegetables to sauce.

9. Slice pork loin, and serve with vegetables and sauce.

Approximate values per serving: **Calories** 424, **Carbohydrates (grams)** 34, **Protein (grams)** 47, **Fat (grams)** 11, **Cholesterol (milligrams)** 133. Carbohydrates = 32% calories, Protein = 44% calories, Fat = 23% calories.

◀══ Fresh Ham Ragoût and Fettucini with Liebfraumilch, Currant, and Plum Sauce

Fresh ham does not have the health concerns attributed to the use of salt, sugar, and nitrates to cure other hams and bacon. It is also a lean cut of meat when the exterior rind (skin) and fat are removed.

Currants, plums, and liebfraumilch are used to add three separate, yet related flavors to the finished dish. The blended flavors of the liebfraumilch (see Chapter 8) are enhanced by the use of the fruit and mace. When cooked with the grilled ham cubes, the sauce imparts its collective flavors to the dominant flavor of the pork. When made with the vegetable stock and served on the bed of fettuccini, this makes a complete meal rich in fiber, vitamins, and minerals.

Makes 10 8-ounce portions

1 cup, or 8 ounces, onions, medium diced
1 cup, or 8 ounces, celery root, shredded
1/2 teaspoon white pepper, coarsely ground
1/2 teaspoon salt
1 teaspoon mace, ground
2 cups, or 16 ounces, liebfraumilch
3½ pounds fresh ham, trimmed and cut into 1-inch cubes
1 gallon, or 128 ounces, white vegetable stock
1 cup, or 6 ounces, dried currants
2 cups, or 16 ounces, purple plums, peeled and cut into wedges
1 cup, or 4.5 ounces, cornstarch
32 ounces fresh fettuccini, or 24 ounces dried

1. Mix together the first six ingredients; mix well.

2. Add diced ham and marinate for 1 hour.

3. Remove ham and place on bamboo skewers.

4. Grill ham just long enough to color the outsides.

5. Mix 2 quarts of vegetable stock to marinate, and bring to a boil.

6. Add browned ham cubes and reduce to a simmer.

7. Simmer for 1 hour.

8. Add currants and plums; simmer for 15 minutes.

9. Add cornstarch dissolved in vegetable stock, and bring back to a boil.

10. Cook fettucini separately in 2 remaining quarts of vegetable stock; strain.

11. Serve ragoût on a bed of fettuccini with sauce.

Approximate values per serving: **Calories** 724, **Carbohydrates (grams)** 79, **Protein (grams)** 53.6, **Fat (grams)** 16.6, **Cholesterol (milligrams)** 136. Carbohydrates = 43% calories, Protein = 31% calories, Fat = 22% calories.

≈*Venison Pie with Cornbread Topping*

This recipe reflects a combination of different culinary techniques used to enhance the nutritional value of an otherwise simple meat pie.

The use of venison instead of beef provides a much leaner and more flavorful meat while contributing the all-important B vitamins and iron. The corn oil used in the bread topping is one of the richest sources of linoleic fatty acids. Linoleic is an essential fatty acid that the human body cannot make itself. Only the necessary amount of oil is used for the topping; therefore, calories are kept to a reasonable amount.

Squash, tomatoes, and potatoes are laden with potassium, which helps control high blood pressure. Even though salt is used in this recipe, it is an extremely small amount considering the entire volume of the finished recipe.

Makes 15 8-ounce portions

1 tablespoon garlic, chopped
2 teaspoons allspice, ground
1 tablespoon black pepper corns, cracked
2 cups, or 16 ounces, dry red wine
3½ pounds venison top round, cut into 1-inch cubes
1/2 cup, or 4 ounces, tomato paste
1 teaspoon fresh rosemary leaves
2 tablespoons fresh parsley, chopped
1½ quarts, or 48 ounces, venison stock (use red vegetable or beef stock if venison stock is not available)
3/4 cup, or 3 ounces, cornstarch
1 pint, or 16 ounces, pearl onions, peeled and halved
1 pound yellow turnips, large diced
1 pound butternut squash, large diced
1 pound red bliss potatoes, skin on, large diced
1 cup, or 4.5 ounces, cornstarch

Cornbread Topping

2 cups, or 14 ounces, cornmeal
2 cups, or 9 ounces, flour
2 tablespoons sugar, granulated
2 tablespoons baking powder
1/2 teaspoon salt
2 cups, or 16 ounces, low-fat milk
4, or 4 ounces, egg whites, lightly beaten
1 tablespoon corn oil

1. Mix together garlic, allspice, black pepper corns, and red wine.

2. Add cubed venison to marinade, and marinate for 1 hour.

3. Remove venison, reserving marinade, and place on bamboo skewers.

4. Grill venison to just below desired degree of doneness. The venison will cook slightly when placed in the oven to finish.

5. Add tomato paste, rosemary, parsley, and venison stock to marinade; bring to a boil.

6. Reduce to a simmer and add pearl onions, turnips, butternut squash, and potatoes; cook for 20 minutes or until vegetables are tender.

7. When vegetables are tender, adjust the seasoning.

8. Dissolve cornstarch in some stock, and add to sauce.

9. Bring sauce back to a boil to thicken.

10. Add cooked venison to sauce.

11. Ladle the stew into oven crocks, making sure to distribute the venison and vegetables.

12. To make topping, sift together all dry ingredients, and gently stir in milk, egg whites, and corn oil.

13. Spoon cornbread topping on top of crocks, and spread evenly with the back of a spoon.

14. Bake crocks in a 400°F oven until cornbread topping is done (about 15 to 20 minutes).

Approximate values per serving: **Calories** 681, **Carbohydrates (grams)** 76.2, **Protein (grams)** 54.4, **Fat (grams)** 13.3, **Cholesterol (milligrams)** 135. Carbohydrates = 47% calories, Protein = 34% calories, Fat = 19% calories.

Venison Stir Fry

Stir fries can be a healthy way of preparing foods. Be careful when measuring the amount of oil used, however, and use a well-seasoned wok. Cut everything into thin strips, bias cuts, or slices. The thinner the ingredients, the faster they will cook (thus eliminating the need to use a lot of extra oil).

Cabbage makes this dish a nutritious choice. Cabbage is one of the cruciferous vegetables recommended by the American Cancer Society for the prevention of cancer. Cabbage also contains an unusually high amount of vitamin C. If cooked quickly with little or no water, as in this recipe, and if not shredded too soon before cooking, cabbage can provide between 33 and 48 milligrams of vitamin C per cup. This amount goes a long way toward supplying the daily allowance of 60 milligrams vitamin C.

Makes 20 8-ounce portions

3½ pounds venison steak cut into finger-length strips
2 tablespoons peanut oil
1 teaspoon sesame oil
1 tablespoon garlic, chopped
1 tablespoon fresh ginger, grated
2 teaspoons black pepper, coarsely ground
1/4 teaspoon red pepper, crushed
3 cups, or 1½ pounds, carrots, cut on the bias
3 cups, or 1½ pounds, celery, peeled and cut on the bias
2 cups, or 1 pound, red bliss potatoes, cut into thin slices
2 quarts, or 24 ounces, Chinese cabbage, shredded
2 cups, or 16 ounces, spring onions, whites and tender greens, thinly sliced
2 cups, or 16 ounces, tomatoes, flesh only, julienne
1 cup, or 8 ounces, sherry wine, dry
1/2 cup, or 2.25 ounces, cornstarch

1. Combine peanut and sesame oils, and sear venison strips until lightly browned; remove from pan.

2. Add garlic, ginger, and peppers to the pan, and stir fry for a few seconds.

3. Add carrots, celery, and potatoes and cook until almost tender (should still have a slight "bite").

4. Add cabbage, and continue to stir fry until cabbage is tender.

5. Return venison to pan; add sliced onions and tomatoes; stir well.

6. Dissolve cornstarch in the sherry and add to the pan; cook for 2 additional minutes.

Approximate values per serving: **Calories** 464, **Carbohydrates (grams)** 31, **Protein (grams)** 47, **Fat (grams)** 15.1, **Cholesterol (milligrams)** 134. Carbohydrates = 27% calories, Protein = 42% calories, Fat = 30% calories.

Poultry

Poultry has gained in popularity among people who are concerned about health and diet. Poultry is generally leaner and, consequently, contains less fat and cholesterol than other meats. It has long been considered a healthy alternative to red- and pink-fleshed meats.

Different species of poultry, from chickens to quail, partridge, and pheasants, are now available throughout the year. Cooks and chefs can purchase specific types and specific parts of almost every kind of commercially raised poultry. Boneless breasts, leg and thigh quarters, turkey breasts, wings, and market ground turkey, pigeon, and pheasant breasts are commonly available. This availability allows full utilization of the products as determined by recipe specifications.

Poultry contributes protein, vitamin A, thiamin, riboflavin, niacin, phosphorous, potassium, sodium, calcium, and trace amounts of other vitamins and minerals to the human diet. All forms of poultry are generally lower in calories, total fat, and saturated fat than red meats.

Most of the fat in poultry is found just beneath the skin. Removing the skin before or after cooking decreases the overall amount of fat by as much as 60% in breasts and 40% in legs and thighs.

According to the USDA white, uncooked chicken meat, with skin, contains only 65 milligrams of sodium per 3.5-ounce edible portion. The same amount of uncooked dark meat, with skin, contains slightly more, at 73 milligrams for the same size portion.

Chicken, turkey, game hen, and other lean birds lend themselves to almost any recipe or cooking procedure known to the modern cook or chef. Whether it's poaching, braising, grilling, or roasting, all healthy cooking applications can be used on poultry and poultry parts with great success.

Poultry (especially chicken and turkey) does present some safety and health issues. Chicken and turkey are naturally susceptible to salmonella infestation. Strict handling, preparation, and cooking guidelines must be followed to protect the health of consumers:

- Thaw frozen poultry properly (under refrigeration, under cold running water, or during the cooking process, never at room temperature).
- Always wash poultry thoroughly before preparation.
- Clean and sanitize knives and cutting boards after preparing poultry and before preparing any other ingredients.
- Never store raw poultry above other ingredients in the refrigerator.
- Cook poultry thoroughly, to a minimum internal temperature of 165°F.
- Cook poultry from beginning to end; partially cooking poultry to finish at a later time can have hazardous results.
- To serve already cooked poultry hot, reheat to an internal temperature of 165°F as quickly as possible.

Poultry is a healthy and safe food when prepared properly. It is easy to achieve variety in menus by offering more types and more forms of poultry.

⟿ *Grilled Sesame Chicken Breast with Basil Marinade*

In this recipe, sesame oil is used much like a seasoning. It has been added to enhance the taste of the product without overpowering the other flavors.

By cooking the vegetables in the same stock that is used to make the sauce all water soluble vitamins are retained for the final dish. The sauce thickened by cornstarch should be only slightly thick; poured over the chicken breast you should still be able to see the grill marks through the sauce.

Makes 10 8-ounce portions

10 chicken breasts, 4 to 6 ounces, boneless and skinless
1 tablespoon, or 1/2 ounce, sesame oil
1 cup, or 8 ounces, onions, finely chopped
1 tablespoon garlic, chopped
2 tablespoons, or 1 ounce, lemon juice
1 teaspoon black pepper, coarsely ground
2 tablespoons fresh basil, chopped, or 2 teaspoons dried basil

1 cup, or 8 ounces, dry white wine
1 quart, or 32 ounces, lean chicken stock
2 cups, or 16 ounces, zucchini, julienne
2 cups, or 16 ounces, yellow squash, julienne
2 cups, or 16 ounces, carrots, julienne
1/2 teaspoon salt
1 cup, or 4.5 ounces, cornstarch
1/4 cup, or 1 ounce, sesame seeds, dry roasted

1. Whisk together sesame oil, onions, garlic, 1 tablespoon lemon juice, pepper, basil, and white wine.

2. Place chicken into this marinade and refrigerate for a minimum of 1 hour.

3. Simmer julienned vegetables in chicken stock until tender; strain and reserve stock.

4. Add the other 1 tablespoon lemon juice and salt to vegetables; keep warm.

5. Remove chicken breasts from marinade and grill until well marked and cooked through.

6. Dissolve cornstarch in chicken stock and bring to a quick boil.

7. Strain sauce.

8. Serve cooked chicken breast on a bed of julienned vegetables with a little sauce on top.

9. Garnish with toasted sesame seeds.

Approximate values per serving: **Calories** 316, **Carbohydrates (grams)** 20, **Protein (grams)** 38, **Fat (grams)** 7.4, **Cholesterol (grams)** 96.2. Carbohydrates = 27% calories, Protein = 51% calories, Fat = 22% calories.

➤ *Roasted Sage Chicken*

The addition of garlic to this recipe may enhance the healthfulness of the dish as well as the flavor of the filling. Garlic contains the chemicals allium, diallyl sulfide, and ajoene. Allium is responsible for the odor of garlic and kills the bacteria staphylococcus, salmonella, and mycobacteria. It also kills fungi and yeast. Diallyl sulfide inhibits colon, lung, and esophageal cancer in mice and may have similar results in humans. Ajoene causes blood platelets to become less sticky and slows clotting in test-tube experiments.

Makes 6 6-ounce portions

1 whole roasting chicken
1 tablespoon, or 1/2 ounce, olive oil
1 cup, or 8 ounces, celery, peeled and finely diced
1/2 cup, or 4 ounces, onions, finely diced
2 teaspoons garlic, chopped
1 tablespoon sage
1/4 teaspoon white pepper, ground
1/2 teaspoon black pepper, coarsely ground
2 cups, or 10 ounces, cornbread crumbs
1 cup, or 4.5 ounces, cornstarch
3 pints, or 48 ounces, lean chicken stock
1 cup, or 8 ounces, low-fat sour cream

1. Completely debone the chicken, reserving the skin for wrapping; remove excess fat from the meat and skin.

2. Sauté celery and onions in oil until tender.

3. Add garlic, sage, and peppers, and sauté for an additional minute.

4. Remove from heat and stir in cornbread crumbs and 1 cup of chicken stock.

5. Lay the chicken skin flat on the table, and lay the meat back onto the skin, covering as much area of the skin as possible.

6. Spoon the cornbread into the center of the chicken skin, and roll the whole chicken into a cylinder shape.

7. Tie the rolled chicken together with butcher's twine, if possible, to help retain its shape during cooking.

8. Roast seam side down on a rack in a roasting pan at 375°F for approximately 90 minutes or until the chicken reaches an internal temperature of 165°F.

9. Slice into 12 even slices.

10. Dissolve cornstarch in some stock, and add to the rest of the chicken stock; bring to a boil.

11. Reduce to a simmer for 10 to 15 minutes.

12. Stir in low-fat sour cream just before serving.

13. Serve 2 slices on top of sauce.

Approximate values per serving: **Calories** 247, **Carbohydrates (grams)** 11.8, **Protein (grams)** 36, **Fat (grams)** 5.4, **Cholesterol (milligrams)** 88. Carbohydrates = 17% calories, Protein = 63% calories, Fat = 19% calories.

⟭ Chicken Paprika

This simple recipe creates an unforgettable flavor using a blend of light-flavored ingredients, that is, chicken breasts, onion, red bell pepper, and dry white wine, accentuated by the smokiness from cooking on the grill and spiced with the use of the black and red peppers and Spanish paprika. Using fresh diced tomatoes will give a sweet flavor to the finished sauce, as well as added color and consistency to the sauce when pureed together.

Makes 4 6-ounce portions

4 chicken breasts, boneless, skinless
2 teaspoons garlic, chopped
1/2 cup, or 4 ounces, onions, finely diced
1/2 cup, or 4 ounces, red bell peppers, medium diced
1 cup, or 8 ounces, dry white wine
1/2 cup, or 4 ounces, tomatoes, peeled, seeded, and diced
1 teaspoon black pepper, coarsely ground
1/8 teaspoon red pepper, crushed
1 bay leaf
2 tablespoons Spanish paprika

1. Grill chicken breasts until well browned on both sides.

2. Place garlic, onions, and bell peppers in a sauce pot with the white wine.

3. Cook until wine is almost evaporated and vegetables are tender.

4. Add tomatoes, peppers, bay leaf, and paprika to pan; heat through.

5. Add par-cooked chicken breasts to pan and cover.

6. Bake in 375°F oven for 45 minutes or until chicken reaches an internal temperature of 165°F.

7. Remove chicken and bay leaf from pan.

8. Puree sauce and strain.

9. Serve sauce over chicken.

Approximate values per serving: **Calories** 165, **Carbohydrates (grams)** 2.9, **Protein (grams)** 27, **Fat (grams)** 5.3, **Cholesterol (milligrams)** 70. Carbohydrates = 8% calories, Protein = 73% calories, Fat = 21% calories.

⤳ *Cajun Chicken Burgers with Jack Cheese Pockets*

Chicken is a perfect meat for making specialty burgers. It's naturally lower in fats (including saturated fats) than beef and works well with many herb and spice combinations.

A plain chicken burger, on the other hand, would be a poor substitution for a beef burger. A well-seasoned chicken burger, however, served with or without cheese and with many varieties of condiment sauces, can be found on some of the more upscale restaurant and bistro menus. Tarragon, thyme, basil, garlic, cumin, and even cinnamon can be used to add variety to these low-fat burger alternatives.

Makes 12 6-ounce portions

3 pounds chicken breast meat, ground
1½ cups, or 12 ounces, onions, finely diced
1/2 cup, or 4 ounces, coarsely prepared mustard or Dijon mustard
1 tablespoon fresh thyme, chopped, or 2 teaspoons dried leaf thyme
1 tablespoon fresh marjoram, chopped, or 2 teaspoons dried leaf marjoram
2 tablespoons fresh parsley, chopped
1 tablespoon cumin, ground
1 tablespoon paprika

1 teaspoon black pepper, coarsely ground
1/2 teaspoon white pepper, ground
1/4 teaspoon red pepper, crushed
2 cups, or 10 ounces, dry bread crumbs
1 cup, or 5 ounces, Monterey Jack cheese, shredded
10 hamburger or Kaiser rolls
1 head leaf lettuce
4 tomatoes, sliced
1 medium onion, thinly sliced
1/2 cup, or 4 ounces, pickle slices

1. Mix together all ingredients except cheese.

2. Measure chicken mix into 6-ounce and cheese into 1/2-ounce portions.

3. Form the cheese into small balls, and wrap chicken meat around each ball.

4. Flatten chicken and cheese balls into flat burgers.

5. Cook burgers on grill until well marked on both sides (about 4 minutes each side).

6. Finish cooking chicken burgers in 400°F oven for 20 minutes or until they reach an internal temperature of 165°F.

7. Serve on toasted buns with lettuce, tomato, sliced onion, and pickles.

Approximate values per serving: **Calories** 536, **Carbohydrates (grams)** 43.7, **Protein (grams)** 55.3, **Fat (grams)** 14.3, **Cholesterol (milligrams)** 138. Carbohydrates = 33% calories, Protein = 42% calories, Fat = 24% calories.

Smothered Chicken and Onions

Because chicken has a delicate flavor, it can be used in combination with many other flavors in the creation of excellent dishes. The onions, leeks, garlic, and white wine used in this recipe make a simple food taste great.

To reduce the fat content, remove the chicken skin before grilling the quarters.

Makes 8 6-ounce portions

2 whole chickens, quartered
1 tablespoon, or 1/2 ounce, olive oil
2 cups, or 16 ounces, onions, thinly sliced
2 cups, or 16 ounces, leeks, thinly sliced
1 tablespoon garlic, finely chopped
1/2 teaspoon white pepper, ground
1/2 teaspoon salt
2 tablespoons fresh marjoram, chopped, or 1 tablespoon dried leaf marjoram
2 bay leaves
2 cups, or 16 ounces, dry white wine

1. Grill chicken quarters until well colored on both sides.

2. Sauté onions and leeks in olive oil until lightly browned.

3. Add garlic and spices to sautéed onions; continue to cook for 2 additional minutes.

4. Add wine and chicken quarters.

5. Cover the pan, and cook in 350°F oven for 1 hour or until chicken reaches an internal temperature of 165°F.

6. Serve with sauce.

Approximate values per serving: **Calories** 280, **Carbohydrates (grams)** 11.8, **Protein (grams)** 36.8, **Fat (grams)** 5.9, **Cholesterol (milligrams)** 96. Carbohydrates = 19% calories, Protein = 60% calories, Fat = 21% calories.

Farmer's Style Chicken Marsala

A traditionally prepared chicken or veal marsala would call for dredging in seasoned flour, sautéing in butter, and finishing off with sliced mushrooms, Marsala wine, and demiglace. In this recipe, everything is cooked together in the same pan, with the rice. This allows you to maximize nutrient retention, with little added fats or salt, and serve a healthy portion of chicken, vegetable, and grain in a single dish.

Removing the skin from the chicken before or after cooking will also significantly reduce the overall fat in the finished recipe.

Makes 10 8-ounce portions

10 chicken breasts, boneless, 4 to 6 ounces each
1 tablespoon, or 1/2 ounce, olive oil
1 tablespoon garlic, chopped
1 cup, or 8 ounces, onions, finely diced
1 cup, or 8 ounces, bell peppers, finely diced
1 tablespoon fresh thyme, chopped, or 2 teaspoons dried leaf thyme
2 tablespoons Spanish paprika
1 teaspoon black pepper, coarsely ground

1/2 teaspoon white pepper, ground
2½ cups, or 20 ounces, long grain rice
2 cups, or 10 ounces, button mushrooms
1 cup, or 8 ounces, sweet peas
2 cups, or 16 ounces, tomatoes, peeled, seeded, and diced
3 cups, or 24 ounces, lean chicken stock
1 cup, or 8 ounces, dry Marsala wine

1. Grill chicken breasts until well colored on all sides.

2. Sauté garlic, onions, and bell peppers in olive oil until tender.

3. Stir in thyme, paprika, peppers, and rice; stir well.

4. Add mushrooms, peas, tomatoes, stock, and wine; bring the whole mixture to a full boil.

5. Pour into a shallow pan, and lay chicken breasts on top.

6. Cover and bake at 350°F for 45 minutes or until chicken reaches an internal temperature of 165°F.

Approximate values per serving: **Calories** 481. **Carbohydrates (grams)** 58, **Protein (grams)** 42, **Fat (grams)** 6.2, **Cholesterol (milligrams)** 96.3. Carbohydrates = 51% calories, Protein = 37% calories, Fat = 12% calories.

Tzimmes (Jewish-Style Chicken Stew)

Prunes are a refreshing change in this traditional Jewish-style poultry dish. They are a good source of iron and vitamin A and are known for their function in digestive tract regulation. Prunes and other dried fruits add extraordinary flavors to many stews and sauces.

Makes 20 10-ounce portions

1 cup, or 8 ounces, leeks, white only, thinly sliced
1 cup, or 8 ounces, celery, peeled, medium diced
1 cup, or 8 ounces, carrots, peeled, medium diced
2 tablespoons, or 1/2 ounce, olive oil
10 chicken breasts, skinned, deboned, large diced
1 tablespoon cinnamon, ground
1 teaspoon white pepper, ground
1/2 cup, or 2.25 ounces, all-purpose flour
2 quarts, or 64 ounces, lean chicken stock
2 cups, or 16 ounces, sweet potatoes, peeled, medium diced
2 cups, or 16 ounces, red bliss potatoes, peeled, medium diced
1½ cups, or 9 ounces, dried pitted prunes

1. In large, straight-sided pot (rondo) sauté leeks, celery, and carrots in hot oil until leeks are tender (about 5 minutes).

2. Add diced chicken breast meat, cinnamon, and white pepper; stir well.

3. Cook until chicken is firm but not brown.

4. Add flour and stir.

5. Reduce heat and cook for 5 minutes, stirring frequently.

6. Add chicken stock and stir well; bring to a full boil.

7. Add raw potatoes and dried prunes. Reduce to a simmer, and cook for 1 hour or until vegetables are tender.

8. Adjust seasonings.

Approximate values per serving: **Calories** 413, **Carbohydrates (grams)** 51, **Protein (grams)** 39, **Fat (grams)** 6.1, **Cholesterol (milligrams)** 96.2. Carbohydrates = 49% calories, Protein = 38% calories, Fat = 13% calories.

⬛ *Chicken Piedmont*

This northern Italian recipe illustrates how basic preparations can produce delicious and healthy dishes. With the help of the fennel bulb, the herbs, and the wine, this recipe has a lot of flavor with little fat or salt. The small amount of salt called for in this recipe is just enough to help blend the delicate flavors of the other ingredients and conforms to low-sodium standards (less than 2400 milligrams).

Makes 10 8-ounce portions

10 chicken breasts, with rib cage, 4 to 6 ounces each
4 fresh fennel bulbs, cut into wedges
2 tablespoons shallots, finely chopped
2 tablespoons fresh basil, finely chopped, or 4 teaspoons dried leaf basil
2 tablespoons coriander leaves, finely chopped
1 teaspoon black pepper, coarsely ground
2 cups, or 16 ounces, dry white wine (perhaps a nebbiolo d'Alba or pinot grigio)
1/2 teaspoon salt
1 quart, or 32 ounces, lean chicken stock
2 cups, or 16 ounces, frozen chopped spinach
1 quart, or 32 ounces, new potatoes, peeled, thinly sliced
1 cup, or 8 ounces, black olives, sliced
1 cup, or 4.5 ounces, cornstarch

1. Grill chicken breasts and fennel bulb until well colored.

2. Cook shallots, basil, and coriander leaves in wine, and cook until the liquid is reduced by half.

3. Add stock, pepper, and salt, and bring to a boil.

4. In the bottom of a shallow baking pan, lay the chopped spinach, and cover with the sliced potatoes.

5. Layer chicken pieces and fennel bulb on top of the potatoes.

6. Pour seasoned stock and wine over the entire dish, and sprinkle with sliced black olives.

7. Cover and bake in 325°F oven for 1½ hours.

Approximate values per serving: **Calories** 291, **Carbohydrates (grams)** 12.8, **Protein (grams)** 37.2, **Fat (grams)** 6.4, **Cholesterol (milligrams)** 96.2. Carbohydrates = 20% calories, Protein = 58% calories, Fat = 22% calories.

Maryland's Chicken Succotash

The small amount of oil used in this recipe does not add up to many fat calories when used with the boneless, skinless chicken breasts, onions, white vegetable stock, new potatoes, corn, and lima beans. Using corn oil adds another level of corn flavor in addition to the whole kernel. Succotash is traditionally a vegetable accompaniment of corn and lima beans. Adding the chicken and potatoes makes this dish a complete meal.

Makes 10 8-ounce portions

10 chicken breasts, 4 to 6 ounces each, skinned, deboned, large diced
1 tablespoon, or 1/2 ounce, corn oil
1 cup, or 8 ounces, onions, small diced
2 tablespoons fresh lemon thyme, chopped
1 teaspoon white pepper, ground
1/2 teaspoon salt
3 pints, or 48 ounces, white vegetable stock
2 cups, or 16 ounces, new potatoes, peeled, medium diced
3 cups, or 24 ounces, whole kernel corn
2 cups, or 16 ounces, baby lima beans

1. Brown chicken breasts in hot corn oil.

2. Add onions, lemon thyme, and white peppers, and salt, and cook until onion is tender.

3. Add stock, potatoes, corn, and lima beans.

4. Bring to a quick boil.

5. Cover pan and cook in a 350°F oven for 1 hour; when potatoes are fully cooked, dish is done.

Approximate values per serving: **Calories** 347, **Carbohydrates (grams)** 31.8, **Protein (grams)** 40.3, **Fat (grams)** 6.6, **Cholesterol (milligrams)** 96.2. Carbohydrates = 37% calories, Protein = 46% calories, Fat = 17% calories.

Sicilian Chicken Stew

Sicily is well known for its peasant style of cooking, and also for its heavy use of wines and vegetables to flavor main dish entrees. This recipe takes simple ingredients that, when combined together and seasoned well, can make a great-tasting dish. Cooked pasta, of any shape, gives body to the dish and contributes to a complete meal of protein, vegetables, and grain products. The dusting of parmesan cheese over the dish when it is served gives a slight saltiness to the bite and a fragrant aroma to the dish without adding too many fat calories.

Makes 20 8-ounce portions

10 chicken breasts, 4 to 6 ounces each, skinned, deboned, large diced
1 tablespoon, or 1/2 ounce, virgin olive oil
2 tablespoons fresh marjoram, chopped, or 4 teaspoons dried leaf marjoram
2 teaspoons sage
2 teaspoons black pepper, coarsely ground
1 tablespoon garlic, finely chopped
1 cup, or 8 ounces, onions, small diced
1 cup, or 8 ounces, fresh fennel, medium diced
2 cups, or 16 ounces, dry white Sicilian wine (Etna bianco is one type)

4 cups, or 32 ounces, zucchini, medium diced
2 cups, or 12 ounces, white button mushrooms, halved
1 quart, or 32 ounces, tomatoes, peeled, seeded, and diced
10, or 16 ounces, artichoke hearts, cut into quarters
1 quart, or 32 ounces, lean chicken stock
1 cup, or 4 ounces, cornstarch
16 ounces dry pasta, any shape
1/4 cup, or 2 ounces, parmesan cheese, grated

1. Using a nonstick or well-seasoned pan, heat the olive oil and cook diced chicken until well browned.

2. Add spices, garlic, onions, and fennel; cook until vegetables are tender.

3. Add white wine and reduce to half its volume.

4. Add zucchini, mushrooms, tomatoes, artichoke hearts, and stock; bring to a quick boil and reduce to a simmer.

5. Dissolve the cornstarch in some stock and add to the stew; simmer stew for at least 40 minutes to marry the flavors.

6. In the meantime, cook the pasta in plain, unsalted water until just tender.

7. Serve stew on a bed of cooked pasta, and sprinkle with parmesan cheese.

Approximate values per serving: **Calories** 465, **Carbohydrates (grams)** 51, **Protein (grams)** 47, **Fat (grams)** 8.3, **Cholesterol (milligrams)** 100.7. Carbohydrates = 43% calories, Protein = 41% calories, Fat = 16% calories.

⚝ *Raspberry Duck and Pinto Beans and Braised Romaine*

Although duck is considered a fatty bird, the breast is less fatty overall. Removing the skin and fat before grilling also helps reduce the fat content and makes this recipe a nutritious choice.

Raspberries and Chambord make the pinto beans more than just a usual accompaniment. Beans cooked this way make their own sauce, which covers the pasta evenly without watering it down.

The Chambord, raspberries, and braised romaine add color, vitamins, minerals, and a great amount of contrasting flavors to complement the duck and the beans.

Makes 10 8-ounce portions

1½ cups, or 12 ounces, pinto beans, dried

2 quarts, or 64 ounces, white vegetable stock

1 cup, or 8 ounces, onions, small diced

1 cup, or 8 ounces, celery, peeled, small diced

1 tablespoon fresh rosemary leaves, or 1 teaspoon dried rosemary leaves

2 teaspoons sage

1 teaspoon black pepper, coarsely ground

1/4 teaspoon white pepper, coarsely ground

1 pint, or 16 ounces, fresh raspberries

1/4 cup, or 2 ounces, Chambord liqueur

10 duck breasts, 4 to 6 ounces each, boneless and skinless

1½ pounds dry pasta, any shape

1 head romaine lettuce

1 cup, or 8 ounces, white vegetable stock

1 tablespoon, or 1/2 ounce, fresh lemon juice

1. Soak pinto beans in cold water overnight.

2. Drain beans and cook in 2 quarts of white vegetable stock until tender (about 2 hours).

3. Add onions, celery, and spices and cook together for 15 more minutes.

4. Add whole raspberries and Chambord to cooked beans.

5. Grill duck breasts until well marked (duck may be safely served at a lower internal temperature than other forms of poultry; some people even like it served rare).

6. Simmer shredded romaine lettuce in 1 cup of white vegetable stock and lemon juice; simmer for 10 minutes.

7. Cook pasta separately in plain, unsalted water.

8. Serve pinto beans on a bed of cooked pasta with grilled duck breast on top; serve lettuce on the side.

Approximate values per serving: **Calories** 254, **Carbohydrates (grams)** 23.9, **Protein (grams)** 27.5, **Fat (grams)** 5.6, **Cholesterol (milligrams)** 87.2. Carbohydrates = 37% calories, Protein = 43% calories, Fat = 20% calories.

⟨Turkey Breast with Bulgur Clam Stuffing

This turkey breast recipe, a complete, lean protein choice, is enhanced by the rich minerals of the clams. Clams are an important source of iodine, which is necessary for proper function of the thyroid gland. Without iodine, the thyroid gland cannot produce thyroxin, a hormone that directly affects our metabolism (a lack of thyroxin causes us to be sluggish and to gain weight more easily). Severe deficiencies of iodine can cause goiter, a disease of the thyroid gland that causes the gland to malfunction and swell to enormous sizes.

People on reduced-sodium diets also reduce the amount of iodine in their diets, which is supplied by iodized table salt. Clams and oysters are important, in these instances, for their natural iodine content.

Bulgur is a wheat berry that is first parboiled to crack the germ, dried, and ground in many grades and sizes. When coarse ground, it can be cooked and treated like rice in many dishes. It is one of the main ingredients in the Middle Eastern appetizer *tabbouleh*.

Makes 10 8-ounce portions

2 quarts, or 64 ounces, turkey stock
2 tablespoons fresh marjoram, chopped, or 4 teaspoons dried leaf marjoram
1 tablespoon fresh thyme, chopped, or 2 teaspoons dried leaf thyme
1 teaspoon white pepper, ground
1 teaspoon mace, ground
1 tablespoon garlic, chopped
1/2 cup, or 4 ounces, shallots, small diced
1 cup, or 8 ounces, celery, peeled, finely diced
1/2 cup, or 4 ounces, pimentos, small diced

1½ cups, or 14 ounces, bulgur
4 dozen cherrystone clams, chopped
1, or 3 pounds, split turkey breast, deboned and skinless
2 cups, or 9 ounces, all-purpose flour
4, or 4 ounces, egg whites, lightly beaten
2 cups plain bread crumbs
1 cup, or 4.5 ounces, cornstarch
1 cup, or 8 ounces, low-fat sour cream

1. Add all spices, garlic, shallots, celery, and pimentos to 3 cups of turkey stock; bring to a full boil.

2. Add the bulgur and chopped clams and stir completely.

3. Bring to a quick boil; reduce to a simmer and cook in a covered pot until liquid is completely absorbed (about 20 minutes).

4. Cool cooked bulgur and clam stuffing for easier handling.

5. Slice turkey breast into 1/2-inch slices and flatten them using a meat tenderizer or mallet.

6. Place 1/4 cup, or 2 ounces, of stuffing on each piece of turkey and roll the turkey like a cigar.

7. Dredge turkey roll in flour, whipped egg whites (with 2 tablespoons water), and dried bread crumbs.

8. Roast turkey rolls in hot oven (375°F) until golden brown and stuffing has reached an internal temperature of 165°F.

9. Dissolve cornstarch in some turkey stock and add to remainder of the stock; bring to a boil.

10. Stir in sour cream just before serving.

11. Serve turkey rolls sliced over the sauce.

Approximate values per serving: **Calories** 448, **Carbohydrates (grams)** 46.4, **Protein (grams)** 43, **Fat (grams)** 9.5, **Cholesterol (milligrams)** 107.7. Carbohydrates = 42% calories, Protein = 39% calories, Fat = 19% calories.

Seafood

Over the past 10 to 15 years, the popularity of seafood has risen to record heights in the United States. Concerns about the negative effects of red meat consumption led to the popularity of poultry and then seafood, both of which are vying for a greater share of American eating choices—and winning.

From meager, almost obligatory offerings on restaurant menus to spotlighted specials, seafood now appears in interesting and stylistic ways on menus across the nation. From grilled flounder on breakfast menus to tuna carpaccio on luncheon menus, seafood has found a permanent place on the American table.

Continued research proves that seafood can be one of the healthiest protein choices. Its generally low-fat, high-protein content is the perfect combination for proper nutrition. With the healthful benefits of omega 3 fatty acids, which all seafood contains and which appear to aid in the prevention of coronary heart disease, seafood is a good choice for a variety of reasons.

Seafood has become such a popular menu item that new harvesting and raising techniques continue to be perfected. Farm raising is now seen as a viable resource to ensure a good supply of seafood and shellfish in the future. As natural habitats become exhausted, farm-raised species and less-known species will begin to dominate the American culinary scene.

Seafood choices used to be regionally oriented, but this is no longer true. A continually shrinking global market means that salmon is now available in Florida, conch in Seattle, Maryland crab meat in Denver, and Maine lobsters in Kentucky. Cooks are enjoying many healthful seafood choices. There are only a few guidelines to keep in mind in selecting seafood for nutritional menus:

- Buy only the freshest seafood possible.
- Be flexible to allow for seafood substitutions based on availability.
- Keep fresh seafood on ice, and frozen seafood frozen, until ready for use.

- Fresh seafood has a short shelf life; buy only what is needed right away.
- Most varieties of seafood can be cooked using low-fat cooking techniques: poaching, grilling, baking, and en papillote (in paper).

The fat content of fish varies according to each species used. Cod, haddock, whiting, rockfish, flounder, and sole have less than 1% fat by weight; salmon, mackerel, lake trout, and blue fish all have considerably higher amounts of fat, with some as much as 25% of body weight. Even though this fat is considered a "healthy" fat, it is advisable to use leaner varieties more often for total caloric control in the diet.

The vitamin content of fish also varies. Fatty fish are good sources of vitamins A and D, whereas all fish contain good amounts of thiamin, riboflavin, niacin, calcium, phosphorous, and iron. Saltwater fish and shellfish species are also good sources of iodine. These types of fish do not contain noticeably more salt than other species of fish or shellfish, and only slightly more than other meats.)

The delicate flesh of seafood, although highly perishable, is the perfect medium for a variety of taste and flavor combinations. Even fatty fish with stronger fish flavors, like salmon, mackerel, and blue fish, lend themselves well to many varieties of herbs, spices, and other natural flavoring agents.

Oven Poached Salmon with Leek and Fennel Sauce

This recipe combines the no-fat cooking of poaching with the ease of baking. In this way all the flavors of the poaching liquid are absorbed by the fish, and the infusion of fish essence into the liquid forms the basis of a great sauce. The salmon filets rest flat on the bottom of the pan and can be lifted out easily when done.

Salmon is a cold water fish and therefore has a higher than average amount of omega 3 fatty acids in its flesh. Omega 3 fatty acids help prevent blood clots, thus lessening the possibility of strokes and some forms of heart disease.

Makes 10 8-ounce portions

1 bay leaf
1 teaspoon cardamom seeds, crushed
1 teaspoon fennel seeds, crushed
1/2 teaspoon white pepper corns, crushed
6 nails of clove
2 teaspoons shallots, finely diced
1/2 teaspoon salt
1 quart, or 32 ounces, lean fish stock, preferably salmon
1 tablespoon lemon juice
2 salmon filets cut into 10 4- to 6-ounce portions
2 cups, or 16 ounces, leeks, julienne, white only
2 cups, or 16 ounces, fennel bulbs, julienne
1/4 cup, or 2 ounces, fresh orange juice
1 cup, or 4.5 ounces, cornstarch

1. Make a sachet of spices, using a piece of cheese cloth and butcher's twine, for the bay leaf, cardamom, fennel seeds, white pepper corns, and cloves.

2. Mix together all other ingredients except salmon, leeks, fennel bulbs, orange juice, and cornstarch.

3. Add sachet, and bring entire mix to a full boil; simmer for 10 minutes.

4. Lay salmon filets on the bottom of a shallow baking dish, and pour hot mixture over top.

5. Top fillets with julienne vegetables.

6. Cover pan first with parchment paper and then with aluminum foil or metal lid.

7. Bake in 350°F oven for 40 minutes or until fish is done.

8. Gently remove salmon filets and keep hot.

9. Dissolve cornstarch in orange juice and add to remaining liquid; bring to a boil to thicken; remove sachet, and discard when done.

10. Serve salmon with sauce and vegetables.

Approximate values per serving: **Calories** 209, **Carbohydrates (grams)** 17.4, **Protein (grams)** 23.9, **Fat (grams)** 4.6, **Cholesterol (milligrams)** 39.6. Carbohydrates = 34% calories, Protein = 46% calories, Fat = 20% calories.

Steamed Salmon with Tomatoes and Artichoke Hearts

Pan steaming is a no-fat cooking technique that allows for the flavors of the main ingredients, in this case the salmon, to blend with the ingredients that will later become the accompanying sauce.

Serve this dish with a vegetarian rice pilaf or angel hair pasta for a full and complete menu item.

Makes 10 8-ounce portions

1 tablespoon shallots, finely chopped
4 cups, or 32 ounces, tomatoes, peeled, seeded, and cut into wedges
1½ cups, or 12 ounces, artichoke hearts, canned, cut into quarters
2 tablespoons Cynar (arromatized wine flavored with artichokes)
2 tablespoons fresh basil, chopped, or 4 teaspoons dried leaf basil
1/2 teaspoon white pepper, ground
1 tablespoon lemon juice, fresh
1/2 teaspoon salt
1 cup, or 4 ounces, dried bread crumbs
2 salmon filets, cut into 10 4- to 6-ounce ounce portions

1. Gently mix together everything except salmon and bread crumbs.

2. Pour into a shallow roasting pan, and sprinkle dry bread crumbs over mix.

3. Lay cut salmon filets on top of tomatoes; cover the pan, and bake in 400°F oven for 1 hour or until salmon is done.

4. Serve each filet with some tomato and artichoke sauce.

Approximate values per serving: **Calories** 219, **Carbohydrates (grams)** 16.7, **Protein (grams)** 25.8, **Fat (grams)** 4.9, **Cholesterol (milligrams)** 40. Carbohydrates = 31% calories, Protein = 48% calories, Fat = 21% calories.

Oven Poached Sea Trout

This recipe reiterates the ease and diversity of combining poaching and baking in a single recipe; this time whole, dressed fish are used. Substitute any variety of small whole fish for the sea trout and any variety of fresh herbs to create a myriad of other flavorful and nutritional choices.

In procedures such as this one, root vegetables, like carrots, should be blanched first. The slow-cooking method does not allow for many vegetables to cook before the fish is overdone. Vegetables that are first julienned will have a better chance of cooking to the al dente stage than vegetables that are cut in larger shapes or sizes.

Although sea trout is a relatively fatty fish, the amount of omega 3 fatty acids that it contains render it a healthy choice. Served with the angel hair pasta, the overall fat percentage of this dish is within recommended guidelines.

Makes 10 8-ounce portions

2 whole, dressed sea trout, approximately 1½ to 2 pounds each
2 sprigs fresh thyme, or other fresh herb
1/2 teaspoon white pepper, ground
1/2 teaspoon salt
2 tablespoons shallots, chopped
1½ cups, or 12 ounces, white Zinfandel wine
2 cups, or 16 ounces, white vegetable stock
2 tablespoons parsley, chopped
2 tablespoons lemon juice, fresh
2 cups, or 16 ounces, onions, thinly sliced
1 cup, or 8 ounces, carrots, sliced, blanched
16 ounces angel hair pasta

1. Clean sea trout thoroughly.

2. Place herbs inside of trout and sprinkle with white pepper and salt combination.

3. In shallow roasting pan, place shallots, wine, and stock.

4. Lay whole fish in liquid.

5. Top with remainder of pepper and salt combination, parsley, and lemon juice.

6. Top with sliced onions and blanched carrots.

7. Cover with parchment paper and metal lid and bake in hot oven (350°F) for 40 minutes or until fish is done.

8. Cook angel hair pasta separately in plain water.

9. Serve sea trout with onions, carrots, and pasta, using some of the poaching liquid as a thin sauce.

Approximate values per serving: **Calories** 450, **Carbohydrates (grams)** 49.9, **Protein (grams)** 28.6, **Fat (grams)** 12.3, **Cholesterol (milligrams)** 62. Carbohydrates = 47% calories, Protein = 27% calories, Fat = 26% calories.

⚞Broiled Tuna with Chili Garlic Sauce and Polenta

Our Western diet is rich in saturated fat and omega 6 polyunsaturated fatty acids. Much of the omega 6 polyunsaturated fat comes from grains, nuts, and seeds. Corn oil is used in many processed foods because it is inexpensive and reduces cholesterol, and cattle are fed large amounts of grains in their diets. Too much omega 6 fatty acid, however, converts to an overload of thromboxane, the prostaglandin that causes platelet aggregation and vasoconstriction, which can lead to blood clots and decreased blood flow to the heart. Omega 3 fatty acid competes in the cell membrane with omega 6 fatty acid and produces a prostaglandin that decreases platelet aggregation and increases vasodilation. Fish (including tuna) is the best source of this valuable omega 3 fatty acid.

Makes 10 8-ounce portions

1 whole bulb of garlic, broken into peeled cloves
1 cup, or 8 ounces, dry white wine
2 tablespoons, or 1 ounce, fresh lemon juice
1/2 teaspoon white pepper, ground
1 tablespoon paprika
10 tuna steaks, 4 to 6 ounces each
1 cup, or 8 ounces, bell peppers, small diced
1 cup, or 8 ounces, Spanish onions, small diced
1 cup, or 8 ounces, celery, peeled and small diced

3 cups, or 24 ounces, tomatoes, peeled, seeded, and diced
1 tablespoon chili powder
2 teaspoons cumin, ground
2 teaspoons celery seed
1 teaspoon black pepper, coarsely ground
1/8 teaspoon red pepper, crushed
2 cups, or 14 ounces, cornmeal
1 cup, or 8 ounces, low-fat milk
2 teaspoons jalapeños, seeded and chopped
1/2 teaspoon salt

1. Place peeled garlic cloves in small roasting pan; roast in 400°F oven until dark brown (about 20 minutes).

2. Remove from oven and add wine, lemon juice, white pepper, and paprika; bring to a boil; remove and chill.

3. Place tuna steaks in cold marinade for 30 minutes to 1 hour.

4. Add celery, onions, bell peppers, spices, and tomatoes and simmer for 1½ hours.

5. Remove tuna from the marinade and reserve until sauce is almost finished.

6. Add remaining marinade to sauce and bring back to a full boil; simmer for another 30 minutes.

7. Mix cornmeal with milk, jalapeños, and salt; bring to a boil, and reduce to a simmer until thick. This becomes polenta.

8. Pour polenta onto a flat pan lined with paper, and allow to cool.

9. Cut cold polenta into desired shapes (rounds, diamonds, etc.), and grill to reheat for service.

10. Grill tuna until desired degree of doneness; fresh tuna steaks can be safely served rare to well done; do not overcook or tuna will be dry.

11. Strain sauce, and adjust seasonings.

12. Serve grilled tuna on top of sauce, with side of grilled polenta.

Approximate values per serving: **Calories** 407, **Carbohydrates (grams)** 40.5, **Protein (grams)** 34, **Fat (grams)** 9.9, **Cholesterol (milligrams)** 63. Carbohydrates = 42% calories, Protein = 35% calories, Fat = 23% calories.

⚞Broiled Cajun Catfish

Catfish is becoming more popular since farm raising has continued to yield good-size and good-tasting fish consistently. This simple procedure prepares an item that meets the 30% calories from fat rule and still creates an exciting and appetizing dish. Frying the catfish, which is more traditional, will increase the fat calories dramatically.

Makes 10 6-ounce portions

1 cup, or 8 ounces, dry white wine
1 tablespoon fresh thyme, chopped, or 2 teaspoons dried leaf thyme
1 tablespoon fresh marjoram, chopped, or 2 teaspoons dried leaf marjoram
1 tablespoon Hungarian paprika
2 teaspoons garlic powder
2 tablespoons shallots, finely chopped
1 teaspoon black pepper, coarsely ground
1/2 teaspoon white pepper, ground
1/8 teaspoon red pepper, ground
1 tablespoon, or 1/2 ounce, lemon juice
10 catfish filets, approximately 6 ounces each

1. Mix together all ingredients except catfish filets.

2. Brush seasoned liquid onto both sides of each filet, and place in shallow pan.

3. Pour remaining liquid over filets to marinate.

4. Marinate for 1 hour.

5. Grill catfish filets for 3 to 4 minutes on both sides or until done.

6. You may also use the blackening technique, without fat, to create blackened catfish. For blackening, heat a griswald to the smoking point; place filets one at a time in the skillet for 3 minutes on each side.

Approximate values per serving: **Calories** 195, **Carbohydrates (grams)** 1.2, **Protein (grams)** 30.1, **Fat (grams)** 5.3, **Cholesterol (milligrams)** 93.4. Carbohydrates = 3% calories, Protein = 69% calories, Fat = 28% calories.

Hazelnut Snapper

The mild flavor of canola oil makes it a versatile cooking medium. The benefits of canola oil are similar to those of olive oil (without the pronounced olive taste that some people find objectionable). Canola oil comes from the rapeseed plant, a relative of the mustard family.

One of the fats in rapeseed is euric acid, which contains a toxic substance. The FDA would not allow rapeseed to be used in this country until recently, when the euric acid levels were lowered.

Monounsaturated oleic acid is also found in canola oil. Oleic acid lowers LDL cholesterol in humans without affecting the HDL (good) cholesterol.
For nutritional analysis, assume that half the oil is absorbed during cooking.

Makes 10 8-ounce portions

1 cup, or 4.5 ounces, corn flour
1/2 cup, or 4 ounces, roasted hazelnuts, finely ground
1/2 teaspoon white pepper, ground
10 6-ounce snapper filet portions
4, or 4 ounces, egg whites, lightly beaten
1/2 cup, or 4 ounces, canola oil
1/2 cup, or 4 ounces, Frangelica liqueur
1 tablespoon fresh lemon juice
2 cups, or 16 ounces, brown rice
4 cups, or 32 ounces, vegetable stock
2 cups, or 10 ounces, shitake mushrooms, chopped
1 cup, or 8 ounces, early peas
1/2 teaspoon white pepper, ground

1. Mix together corn flour, ground hazelnuts, and first 1/2 teaspoon white pepper.

2. Dip fish filets first in lightly beaten egg whites; then dredge in flour and ground nuts.

3. Sauté filets in hot canola oil.

4. Drain off extra oil, and add Frangelica and lemon juice to sauté pan.

5. In the meantime, simmer brown rice in vegetable stock with chopped mushrooms, peas, and second 1/2 teaspoon white pepper, until done.

6. Serve snapper with brown rice.

Approximate values per serving: **Calories** 641, **Carbohydrates (grams)** 60.7, **Protein (grams)** 45, **Fat (grams)** 23, **Cholesterol (milligrams)** 93. Carbohydrates = 27% calories, Protein = 41% calories, Fat = 32% calories.

Flounder en Papillote

En papillote can be a totally fat-free cooking technique. It is a simple procedure that can be prepared in advance and cooked as needed.

The liquid placed in the paper with the fish helps to create the steam that cooks the fish and makes a light sauce for the finished dish.

Any assortment of vegetables can be added for flavor, color, texture, and garnish. Vegetables should be cut very thin (julienne is one way) to assure that they are cooked in the same amount of time it takes to cook the fish.

Choose a leaner fish than flounder, like snapper, grouper, redfish, or cod, and produce an even lower-fat recipe.

Makes 10 6-ounce portions

10 4- to 6-ounce flounder filets
5 heart-shaped pieces of parchment paper
1 cup, or 8 ounces, white Zinfandel wine
1 tablespoon fresh lemon juice
1 tablespoon shallots, finely chopped
1/2 teaspoon salt
1/2 teaspoon white pepper, ground
2 teaspoons fresh tarragon, chopped, or 1 teaspoon dried leaf tarragon
2 teaspoons fresh parsley, chopped
1 cup, or 16 ounces, carrots, julienne
1 cup, or 8 ounces, celery, julienne
1 cup, or 5 ounces, Enoki mushrooms

1. Place flounder filets on one side of heart-shaped paper.

2. Sprinkle wine, lemon juice, shallots, spices, tarragon, and parsley on top of filets.

3. Layer tops of filets with carrots, celery, and mushrooms.

4. Wrap filets and fold edges to make a complete seal.

5. Bake in 400°F oven until bags expand; cook for 2 additional minutes after they have expanded.

6. Remove from oven and place directly on the plate. Cut open paper just before service.

Approximate values per serving: **Calories** 271, **Carbohydrates (grams)** 6.3, **Protein (grams)** 35, **Fat (grams)** 9.5, **Cholesterol (milligrams)** 101. Carbohydrates = 10% calories, Protein = 56% calories, Fat = 34% calories.

Grouper Florentine with Sesame Sauce

Any fish can be substituted for the grouper in this recipe. Shrimp, oysters, mussels, and crab meat make exciting variations.

Makes 10 8-ounce portions

3 pounds cooked, chopped spinach
1 tablespoon shallots, finely chopped
1 teaspoon fresh garlic, chopped
1½ cups, or 12 ounces, dry white wine
1/4 teaspoon nutmeg, ground
1/2 teaspoon white pepper, ground
1/2 teaspoon salt
2 cups, or 16 ounces, plain, low-fat yogurt
1/2 teaspoon sesame oil
10 grouper filets, 4 to 6 ounces each
3/4 cup, or 3 ounces, dry bread crumbs
1/4 cup, or 2 ounces, dry roasted sesame seeds

1. Mix together spinach, shallots, garlic, white wine, nutmeg, pepper, and salt.

2. Spread mixture on the bottom of a shallow roasting pan.

3. Mix together yogurt and sesame oil.

4. Lay grouper filets on bed of chopped spinach, and spoon yogurt sauce on top of each filet.

5. Cover the pan and bake at 400°F for 30 minutes or until grouper is done.

6. Remove cover and sprinkle bread crumbs on top; place under a salamander, or broiler, until bread crumbs begin to brown.

7. Garnish with dry roasted sesame seeds.

Approximate values per serving: **Calories** 238, **Carbohydrates (grams)** 11, **Protein (grams)** 34.6, **Fat (grams)** 4.3, **Cholesterol (milligrams)** 75.5. Carbohydrates = 20% calories, Protein = 63% calories, Fat = 18% calories.

Madeira Shrimp Kabobs

Although fatty forms of seafood contain generous amounts of omega 3 fatty acid, which prevents clotting in the arteries, these species are also more likely to pick up dangerous toxins when harvested from the wild. Therefore, you must heed any State Health Department warnings on specific fish species that have been found to contain toxins.

Lean seafood, like shrimp, is generally less likely to contain harmful toxins. Lean seafood will also help keep the total fat in the diet down to 30% of calories. Shrimp are low in total fat and are a good source of protein, iron, and zinc.

Makes 10 8-ounce portions

40, or 3 pounds, U-12 shrimp (less than 12 to a pound), peeled and deveined
20 pearl onions, peeled
4 tomatoes, peeled, seeded, and cut into wedges
4 zucchini, large diced
1 tablespoon shallots, finely chopped
2 teaspoons garlic, chopped
2 teaspoons fresh ginger, grated
1½ cups, or 12 ounces, Madeira wine
2 tablespoons fresh basil, chopped, or 2 teaspoons dried leaf basil
1 teaspoon white pepper, ground
1/4 teaspoon liquid red pepper
2 cups, or 16 ounces, pearl barley
2 cups, or 16 ounces, yellow squash, shredded
1 cup, or 8 ounces, Jerusalem artichoke, shredded
4 cups, or 32 ounces, white vegetable stock
1/2 teaspoon salt

1. Put kabobs together, alternating shrimp with vegetables (4 shrimp per kabob).

2. For marinade, mix together shallots, garlic, ginger, Madeira wine, basil, pepper, and pepper sauce.

3. Place kabobs in marinade for 1 hour.

4. Mix together barley, yellow squash, Jerusalem artichoke, vegetable stock, and salt.

5. Bring to boil; cover and let simmer for 20 minutes or until barley is tender.

6. Broil kabobs for approximately 3 minutes each side or until shrimp are done.

7. Serve kabobs on a bed of cooked barley.

Approximate values per serving: **Calories** 380, **Carbohydrates (grams)** 55, **Protein (grams)** 31, **Fat (grams)** 1.9, **Cholesterol (milligrams)** 203. Carbohydrates = 60% calories, Protein = 35% calories, Fat = 5% calories.

Calamari and Eggplant Stew

This recipe is a fine example of how a combination of flavors can create an over-all impression of taste rather than a contrast of dominant flavors. Eggplant and squid (calamari) both have distinct yet delicate flavors that might be lost or overpowered in other preparations. The tomatoes, herbs, and wine add to the overall flavors of this recipe without detracting from the flavors of the main ingredients.

Squid is a natural source of fluorine, which has been shown to inhibit tooth decay in humans.

Makes 10 10-ounce portions

2 eggplants, peeled, diced in 1-inch cubes
1 cup, or 8 ounces, onions, finely diced
1 cup, or 8 ounces, green bell peppers, small diced
2 teaspoons garlic, chopped
1 teaspoon black pepper, coarsely ground
1/2 teaspoon white pepper, ground
2 tablespoons fresh basil, chopped, or 4 teaspoons dried leaf basil
1 tablespoon fresh marjoram, chopped, or 2 teaspoons dried leaf marjoram
2 tablespoons parsley, chopped
2 bay leaves
1½ cups, or 12 ounces, dry red wine
4 cups, or 32 ounces, tomatoes, peeled, seeded, diced
3 pounds squid, cleaned, cut in 1/2-inch slices
16 ounces shell macaroni

1. Mix together eggplant, onions, bell peppers, garlic, and all other spices.

2. Place mixture in shallow roasting pan, and bake in 450°F oven for 30 minutes.

3. Remove pan from oven and place on stovetop on medium heat.

4. Add wine to pan and allow to cook until reduced by half.

5. Add tomatoes and cut squid to pan; simmer for 20 minutes.

6. Cook shell macaroni separately in lightly salted water.

7. Remove bay leaves from stew before serving; adjust seasonings.

8. Serve stew on a bed of cooked shells.

Approximate values per serving: **Calories** 326, **Carbohydrates (grams)** 46.4, **Protein (grams)** 29.8, **Fat (grams)** 2.2, **Cholesterol (milligrams)** 75. Carbohydrates = 57% calories, Protein = 37% calories, Fat = 6% calories.

⚘*Veal and Shrimp Country Gumbo*

Naturally lean veal and shrimp form the basis of this tasty and healthy dish. Whereas gumbos are traditionally thickened by a roux, this recipe relies on the fresh okra, gumbo file powder, and cooked rice for thick and rich texture.

Makes 10 10-ounce portions

1 cup, or 8 ounces, onions, small diced
1/2 cup, or 4 ounces, red bell peppers or pimientos, small diced
2 teaspoons garlic, finely chopped
2 bay leaves
1 tablespoon fresh thyme, chopped, or 2 teaspoons dried leaf thyme
1 tablespoon fresh marjoram, chopped, or 2 teaspoons dried leaf marjoram
1 tablespoon gumbo file powder
1 teaspoon black pepper, coarsely ground
1/2 teaspoon white pepper, coarsely ground
1/8 teaspoon red pepper, crushed
1½ cups, or 12 ounces, fresh okra, sliced
1 quart, or 32 ounces, tomatoes, peeled, seeded, and diced
2 cups, or 16 ounces, yellow turnips, peeled, medium diced
2 quarts, or 64 ounces, red vegetable stock
1½ pounds veal chuck, boned, medium diced
2 cups, or 10 ounces, oyster mushrooms, cut into 1-inch pieces
1 pint, or 16 ounces, brown rice
1 cup, or 8 ounces, fresh sweet peas
1½ pound shrimp, 36 to 40 count, or similar count, peeled and deveined

1. Mix together everything except mushrooms, rice, peas, shrimp, and veal.

2. Bring to a boil, and simmer for 20 minutes.

3. Place veal cubes on a wooden skewer, and grill until well browned on all sides.

4. Add veal to stew, and simmer for 1 hour.

5. Add raw rice and mushrooms to stew, and cook together for an additional 20 minutes or until rice is done.

6. Add peas and shrimp; cook everything together for 10 minutes or until shrimp are done.

Approximate values per serving: **Calories** 436, **Carbohydrates (grams)** 52, **Protein (grams)** 35, **Fat (grams)** 9.2, **Cholesterol (milligrams)** 159. Carbohydrates = 48% calories, Protein = 33% calories, Fat = 19% calories.

Scallops and Pineapple Shell Macaroni

Scallops are a sweet-tasting mollusk, a sea animal that lives inside a pair of hard, hinged shells, and are available in two sizes: sea scallops and bay scallops. Sea scallops are larger and may be as large as 2 to 3 inches in diameter, whereas bay scallops are smaller and usually do not grow more than 1/2 to 1 inch in diameter. The larger scallops, sea scallops, make an attractive presentation when combined with the large diced pineapple and cooked shell macaroni. This recipe creates a dish fruity in flavor with the use of orange and lemon zest, allspice, pimentoes, and pineapple. The fresh chopped mint used at the end gives this dish a signature flavor that complements the other flavors without being overpowering.

Makes 10 8-ounce portions

1 cup, or 8 ounces, leeks, white only, thinly sliced
1 cup, or 8 ounces, celery, peeled, small diced
1 teaspoon allspice, ground
1 teaspoon orange zest, grated
1/2 teaspoon lemon zest, grated
1 cup, or 8 ounces, pimentos, small diced
3 cups, or 1/2 pineapple, peeled, cored, large diced
2 cups, or 16 ounces, white vegetable stock
1 cup, or 8 ounces, dry white wine
1 cup, or 8 ounces, pineapple juice
1/2 cup, or 2.25 ounces, cornstarch
3 pounds sea scallops
16 ounces shell macaroni, dry
2 tablespoons fresh mint, chopped

1. Mix together everything except scallops, pineapple juice, macaroni, cornstarch, and mint; place in a large sauté pan and bring to a boil; reduce to a simmer for 20 minutes.

2. Dissolve cornstarch in pineapple juice and add to mixture; bring back to a boil, and simmer for an additional 10 minutes.

3. Add scallops, and cook gently until scallops are done: Do not overcook.

4. Precook macaroni in plain, unsalted water until just tender; cool quickly to stop cooking.

5. Adjust seasonings.

6. Serve scallops on a bed of cooked macaroni; garnish each serving with fresh chopped mint.

Approximate values per serving: **Calories** 368, **Carbohydrates (grams)** 56.7, **Protein (grams)** 28, **Fat (grams)** 1.3, **Cholesterol (milligrams)** 47.5 Carbohydrates = 59% calories, Protein = 18% calories, Fat = 29% calories.

⟪Cornbread Oyster Florentine

The folk tale about sex and oysters may stem from the fact that oysters are the best natural source of zinc. The main function of zinc is sperm production in human males. An overconsumption of oysters might speed up this production system.

Zinc is also important in the senses of taste and smell. Therefore, diets that are rich in oysters can help reduce dependency on chemical flavor enhancers and excessive salt (four oysters fulfill the daily zinc requirement). In addition, oysters supply iron, iodine, and copper.

Notice that the natural salt in the oysters and the feta cheese is adequate for flavoring this recipe. No added salt is used.

Some customers may like to melt whole butter over the pie before eating it, but it is perfectly good without butter.

Makes 10 6-ounce portions

2 cups, or 14 ounces, yellow cornmeal
1 cup, or 4.5 ounces, corn flour
2 tablespoons baking powder
1/2 teaspoon white pepper, ground
1/8 teaspoon red pepper, crushed
2 tablespoons corn oil
4, or 4 ounces, egg whites
1½ cups, or 12 ounces, low-fat milk
1 cup, or 8 ounces, Spanish onions, finely diced
2 teaspoons garlic, chopped
2 tablespoons fresh oregano, chopped, or 4 teaspoons dried leaf oregano
2 pounds fresh spinach
1 cup, or 8 ounces, dry white wine
40 select whole oysters
1½ cups, or 10 ounces, Feta cheese, grated

1. Place cornmeal, corn flour, baking powder, white and red pepper, 2 tablespoons corn oil, egg whites, and milk in a bowl and mix thoroughly; set aside.

2. Mix together onion, garlic, oregano, spinach, and wine in a sauté pan and heat through; drain off excess liquid.

3. In lightly oiled casserole dish, layer cooked spinach, raw oysters, and cheese; repeat the process until all the ingredients are used.

4. Pour cornbread mix over entire casserole and bake in 375°F oven until cornbread is done.

5. Cut and serve like a pie.

Approximate values per serving: **Calories** 446, **Carbohydrates (grams)** 55.6, **Protein (grams)** 27.7, **Fat (grams)** 10.6, **Cholesterol (milligrams)** 111. Carbohydrates = 52% calories, Protein = 26% calories, Fat = 22% calories.

✒ *Maryland Blue Fish Cakes*

Blue fish is a relatively inexpensive fish. Many people are not accustomed to the pronounced fishy taste of blue fish and therefore shy away from using this versatile fish. The strong taste of blue fish is primarily found in the fatty strip, almost black in color, that runs along the back of each filet. Removing this fat strip before cooking reduces the overall fat content and makes the flavor more acceptable.

This recipe takes into account blue fish's strong flavor by combining it with other pronounced flavors, such as onion, mustard, and spices. The blue fish is poached first, to reduce further the fishy flavor, and then mixed with the other recipe ingredients. Guests will find it hard to distinguish the flavors of the blue fish from other flaky fish and even crab meat.

Makes 15 4-ounce portions

1 quart, or 32 ounces, white vegetable stock
1 cup, or 8 ounces, dry white wine
1 tablespoon fresh lemon juice
3 pounds blue fish filets, fat strip removed
1 cup, or 8 ounces, onions, finely diced
1 cup, or 8 ounces, red bell peppers, finely diced, or pimentos
1/2 cup, or 4 ounces, coarsely prepared mustard
8, or 8 ounces, egg whites, lightly beaten
2 teaspoons Worcestershire sauce
2 teaspoons fresh garlic, chopped
4 tablespoons Old Bay seasoning
1 teaspoon black pepper, coarsely ground
1/8 teaspoon red pepper, ground
2 cups dried bread crumbs

1. Mix together vegetable stock, white wine, and lemon juice to make a poaching liquid.

2. Bring to a boil, and reduce to a simmer.

3. Poach blue fish filets until tender; remove and cool.

4. Mix together all other ingredients.

5. Break apart blue fish filets into small pieces.

6. Gently fold fish into mustard, egg whites, and bread crumb mix.

7. Shape into 4-ounce patties; place on parchment paper–lined steel pan and bake at 450°F for 15 minutes. The patties can also be broiled on lightly oiled sizzling platters.

Approximate values per serving: **Calories** 330, **Carbohydrates (grams)** 27.9, **Protein (grams)** 35, **Fat (grams)** 6.5, **Cholesterol (milligrams)** 75.8. Carbohydrates = 36% calories, Protein = 45% calories, Fat = 19% calories.

Vegetarian Entrees

The topic of vegetarianism and its effect on a person's diet was covered in the protein section of Chapter 3 and all of Chapter 12. The recipes that follow address some of the culinary implications in the preparation of vegetarian cuisine.

Not everyone who chooses vegetarian entrees is a practicing vegetarian. Many people just like to experiment with new and exciting dishes; others believe the low-fat mystique surrounding vegetarian cooking and occasionally choose vegetarian entrees as part of an overall controlled diet plan. Still others may try a well-prepared and satisfying vegetarian entree at the recommendation of vegetarian friends and family. Whatever the reason, the prevalence of vegetarian selections on restaurant menus continues to increase.

Vegetarian entrees go far beyond mere plates of vegetables and grain-rich foods. A plate of broccoli and green beans with a side of rice cannot excite many appetites; why would a vegetarian choose to buy such an entree? Cooks must be ingenious in creating vegetarian entrees with taste and visual appeal.

Although the food components in a vegetarian diet come from a limited number of food groups, the numbers of food types within each group are astounding. Technological advances in horticulture and farming mean that those choices continue to expand.

A well-planned and well-executed vegetarian entree should include a variety of items from the acceptable food groups: vegetables, fruits, nuts, seeds, legumes, and grain-rich foods for all vegetarians and vegans; dairy for lacto vegetarians; and eggs for lacto-ovo vegetarians. Three to five major ingredients, including two or three vegetables, one grain product, one seed or nut product, and a choice of legumes, can supply balanced nutrition, good visual and taste appeal, and a controlled calorie count.

Strict vegans have to take extra steps to guarantee proper protein intake in their diets. For other vegetarians, the dairy products and/or eggs that they consume can provide adequate protein. Vegans, who choose not to eat dairy or eggs, have a greater risk of protein deficiency (particularly in the essential amino acids) than any other group of people.

Soybeans contain the closest elements to animal proteins in the vegetable kingdom. Asians have long taken advantage of the healthy properties and versatility of soybeans in their cuisine. Recently, in light of increased interest in vegetarian foods, soybean consumption has spread across the globe.

Soybeans are legumes but are the only ones known to contain all essential amino acids. They are also naturally rich in fiber, calcium, iron, folate, and potassium. Soybeans are lower in starch than many other legumes; they are cholesterol free and low in saturated fat and sodium.

Soybeans are also versatile. They can be eaten as a vegetable, turned into a type of milk and cheese, fermented into a rich sauce (soy sauce), and mashed or ground into many other marketable forms. The following are some of the more common forms of soybeans used in professional kitchens:

- *Miso:* fermented soybeans made into a paste ground with grains; used to season soups, sauces, dressings, and dips
- *Soy milk:* made by soaking and pressing whole soybeans
- *Soy flour:* ground from roasted soybeans
- *Soy grits:* a coarsely ground soybean
- *Soybean oil:* pressed from soybeans; contains good amounts of oleic, linoleic, and linolenic acids; oleic is a monounsaturated fat, and linoleic and linolenic are polyunsaturated fats
- *Hydrolyzed vegetable protein (HVP):* soybean protein broken down by acid
- *Textured soy protein (TSP):* used as a meat substitute or meat extender in traditionally meat-based items like sausage, hot dogs, hams, and ground beef
- *Tofu:* soybean curd made from curdled soy milk and pressed like cheese; available in soft and firm varieties

Vegetarianism is not necessarily a low-fat diet. Care must be taken not to fill vegetarian entrees with fatty beans, nuts, and seeds or overuse vegetable oils in frying, baking, dressing, and marinating foods. A vegetable kabob that has been marinated in an oil-rich dressing and served with a peanut, almond, or walnut sauce is not a low-fat item. Stir-fried vegetables are not necessarily low-fat items either. Care must be taken to measure only the proper amount of oil required to do the cooking and cut the vegetables in thin and small pieces to assure fast cooking.

Offer vegetarian entrees that embody the healthy properties of nonmeat items, using the same guidelines of counting the calorie content of fats and mixing vegetables, grains, and vegetable protein foods to assure a balance of vitamins and minerals.

Vegetable and Wild Rice Stir Fry with Water Chestnuts

Water chestnuts and wild rice both contribute protein to this vegan recipe. Diets that lack all animal proteins become dependent on grains and nuts to supply the proteins needed for building and renewing body tissues.

Although it is not necessary to consume grains and nuts in the same meal, both supply protein, so it is beneficial to do so whenever possible. The proteins are necessary, and the combination of nuts and grains adds texture, flavor, and sustenance to the final dish.

Makes 15 8-ounce portions

2 pints, or 32 ounces, vegetable stock
2 cups, or 16 ounces, wild rice
2 tablespoons fresh marjoram, chopped, or 4 teaspoons dried leaf marjoram
1/2 teaspoon salt
1/2 teaspoon white pepper, coarsely ground
2 tablespoons, or 1 ounce, peanut oil
1 teaspoon sesame oil
1 tablespoon fresh ginger, grated
2 teaspoons fresh garlic, chopped
2 cups, or 16 ounces, spring onions, white and tender green, diced

1 cup, or 8 ounces, celery, bias cut
2 cups, or 16 ounces, carrots, julienne
1 cup, or 8 ounces, red bell peppers, julienne
2 cups, or 16 ounces, broccoli flowers
2 cups, or 10 ounces, shitake mushrooms, sliced
1 cup, or 8 ounces, tomatoes, peeled, seeded, and diced
1 cup, or 8 ounces, water chestnuts, sliced
1/2 cup, or 4 ounces, vegetable stock
1/4 cup, or 1 ounce, cornstarch

1. Bring 2 pints of vegetable stock to a boil and add wild rice, marjoram, salt, and pepper.

2. Reduce rice to a simmer, and cook covered for 20 minutes or until rice is tender.

3. Heat peanut and sesame oil together in a wok or a nonstick or well-seasoned frying pan.

4. Stir fry ginger, garlic, and spring onions for 2 minutes.

5. Add all vegetables except mushrooms and tomatoes, and stir fry for an additional 5 minutes.

6. Add mushrooms, water chestnuts, and tomatoes; stir fry for a final 4 minutes.

7. Dissolve cornstarch in 1/2 cup vegetable stock and add to stir fry; heat through for 2 minutes at low simmer.

8. Serve stir fry on a bed of cooked wild rice.

Approximate values per serving: **Calories** 315, **Carbohydrates (grams)** 62.8, **Protein (grams)** 11.2, **Fat (grams)** 4.1, **Cholesterol (milligrams)** 0. Carbohydrates = 75% calories, Protein = 14% calories, Fat = 11% calories.

◄═══Herbed Black-Eyed Peas with Almonds and Raisins

Raisins are a concentrated source of all the nutritional elements available in grapes. Their most valuable nutritional feature is iron (5.1 milligrams of iron in 1 cup of raisins; the daily iron requirement for a man is 10 milligrams). Black-eyed peas also contain a lot of iron—3.3 milligrams per 1 cup (cooked).

To get the most iron absorption from the raisins and the peas, a food rich in vitamin C should also be part of the meal. In this recipe, the bell peppers provide the vitamin C.

Makes 15 8-ounce portions

2 cups, or 16 ounces, black-eyed peas
1½ quarts, or 48 ounces, white vegetable stock
1 cup, or 8 ounces, onions, medium diced
1 cup, or 8 ounces, bell peppers, medium diced
1 cup, or 8 ounces, celery, peeled, small diced
1 cup, or 6 ounces, raisins
1 tablespoon fresh thyme, chopped, or 2 teaspoons dried leaf thyme
2 teaspoons garlic, finely chopped
2 teaspoons cumin, ground
1 teaspoon fresh rosemary, or 1/2 teaspoon dried leaf rosemary
1 teaspoon cloves, ground
2 teaspoons black pepper, coarsely ground
1/8 teaspoon red pepper, crushed
1 quart, or 32 ounces, red vegetable stock
1/4 teaspoon salt
1/2 teaspoon white pepper, ground
16 ounces couscous
1 cup, or 5 ounces, almonds, sliced, dry roasted

1. Soak peas overnight in cold water.

2. Drain water from peas and cook in vegetable stock until almost tender (about 2 hours).

3. Add onions, bell peppers, celery, raisins, herbs, and all spices except salt and white pepper; cook for an additional 30 minutes. The raisins will plump and the celery will still have a slight crunch when done.

4. Bring red vegetable stock, salt, and white pepper to a boil.

5. Stir in couscous, cover and remove from heat; let stand for 5 minutes.

6. Make a ring on the plate using the cooked couscous.

7. Using a slotted spoon, spoon peas into the center of the ring.

8. Garnish each serving with dry roasted almonds.

Approximate values per serving: **Calories** 411, **Carbohydrates (grams)** 72.6, **Protein (grams)** 14, **Fat (grams)** 8.6, **Cholesterol (milligrams)** 0. Carbohydrates = 68% calories, Protein = 13% calories, Fat = 18% calories.

✒ *Millet Pilaf with Dates, Apples, and Pistachio Nuts (Lacto Vegetarian)*

Millet is a staple grain in Africa, China, and Japan. It has a bland taste but lends itself to a variety of other flavors when cooked with vegetables and spices. A whole grain, millet contains more iron than many other grains along with a good supply of magnesium (a nutrient that is removed from processed grains).

Dates contain five of the B vitamins, including B_6 and folacin, and are a source of potassium, calcium, phosphorus, magnesium, iron, zinc, copper, and manganese (10 dates contain 228 calories).

All nuts supply protein, but pistachios provide one of the highest amounts, exceeded only by black walnuts. Three ounces of pistachio nuts have the same amount of calcium as a whole cup of cottage cheese and more phosphorus than 3 ounces of liver. Pistachio nuts also contain vitamin A, which is usually not found in nuts, and vitamins B_1, B_3, and E.

Makes 15 8-ounce portions

2 cups, or 16 ounces, millet
1 cup, or 8 ounces, onions, small diced
2 teaspoons garlic, finely chopped
1 teaspoon fresh ginger, grated
2 tablespoons, or 1 ounce, virgin olive oil
1/2 teaspoon allspice, ground
2 teaspoons black pepper, coarsely ground
4 cups, or 32 ounces, white vegetable stock
2 cups, or 16 ounces, carrots, julienne

2 cups, or 16 ounces, yellow squash, julienne
2 cups, or 10 ounces, snap peas
1 cup, or 8 ounces, leeks, julienne
1 cup, or 8 ounces, vegetable stock
2 teaspoons fresh mint, chopped
1/4 cup, or 2 ounces, plain, low-fat yogurt
3 cups, or 24 ounces, red delicious apples, small diced
1/2 cup, or 4 ounces, pistachio nuts, dry roasted

1. In a large, oven-proof pan, sauté millet, onions, garlic, and ginger in oil until millet begins to brown and gives off a slightly nutty aroma.

2. Add 32 ounces of stock and spices and stir well.

3. Bring the stock to a full boil.

4. Cover the pan and bake in a 350°F oven for 20 minutes.

5. Place stock in large sauté pan and bring to a boil.

6. Add carrots, squash, snap peas, and leeks; reduce to simmer and cook for 10 minutes.

7. Strain excess stock from vegetables and add yogurt and mint leaves; heat through.

8. Stir the apples and pistachio nuts into millet just before service; apples should stay crunchy.

9. Spoon a portion of millet into the center of a plate, and spoon cooked vegetables and sauce into a circle surrounding the millet.

Approximate values per serving: **Calories** 356, **Carbohydrates (grams)** 59.4, **Protein (grams)** 9, **Fat (grams)** 10.4, **Cholesterol (milligrams)** 2.8. Carbohydrates = 65% calories, Protein = 10% calories, Fat = 25% calories.

Southeast Indian Bean and Cabbage Pie (Lacto Vegetarian)

Southeast Indian cuisine is known for its vegetarian entrees. Its creative use of flavoring ingredients, herbs, and spices makes these vegetarian dishes full of flavor and substance. This recipe uses Indian ground spices like cumin, coriander, and turmeric to give color and flavor to a traditional bean recipe. The beans are full of protein and fiber, with little fat. When this bean stew is baked in a pie crust, the finished dish represents a complete meal. The cornmeal-based crust used here would not have been used in traditional East Indian recipes. We borrow something from the Americas (cornmeal) to give a traditional vegetarian dish more flavor, texture, fiber, and protein.

Makes 10 10-ounce portions

1 cup, or 8 ounces, dried pinto beans	1 teaspoon cumin, ground
1 cup, or 8 ounces, dried white beans	1 teaspoon coriander, ground
3 pints, or 48 ounces, white vegetable stock	1 teaspoon turmeric, ground
1 cup, or 8 ounces, celery, peeled, finely diced	1 teaspoon fresh ginger, grated
	3 cups, or 18 ounces, white cornmeal
1/2 cup, or 4 ounces, leeks, white only, finely diced	2 tablespoons baking powder
	6, or 6 ounces, egg whites, slightly beaten
2 cups, or 12 ounces, green cabbage, finely shredded	1½ cups, or 12 ounces, low-fat milk
2 teaspoons garlic, finely chopped	1/2 teaspoon salt
	1/2 teaspoon white pepper, ground

1. Soak beans in cold water overnight.

2. Drain the beans and simmer them in the vegetable stock until tender (about 2 to 3 hours).

3. Add celery, cabbage, leeks, garlic, and spices to the beans and stock; cook together for 30 minutes.

4. Mix together the cornmeal and baking powder in a separate bowl; then add the egg whites, milk, salt, and white pepper.

5. Stir the cornbread ingredients together to the consistency of a heavy batter; if too thick, add a little more milk.

6. Ladle bean mixture into individual portion–sized oven crockery or a similar type of dish or terrine.

7. Spoon cornbread mixture on top and smooth evenly up to the rim.

8. Bake in 400°F oven for 30 to 45 minutes or until cornbread is lightly browned.

Approximate values per serving: **Calories** 414, **Carbohydrates (grams)** 81.7, **Protein (grams)** 18.7, **Fat (grams)** 1.8, **Cholesterol (milligrams)** 1.3. Carbohydrates = 78% calories, Protein = 18% calories, Fat = 4% calories.

Creole Vegetables with Aromatic Rice

Aromatic rice is a special variety of rice grown in the southeastern United States, particularly in Louisiana, Georgia, and Mississippi. It is a long grain rice with a natural aromatic taste. If aromatic rice is not available, use brown rice and increase the amounts of herbs during cooking.

Makes 15 10-ounce portions

2 cups, or 16 ounces, red vegetable stock
1 cup, or 8 ounces, onions, small diced
1/2 cup, or 4 ounces, bell peppers, small diced
1/2 cup, or 4 ounces, celery, peeled, finely diced
2 teaspoons garlic, finely chopped
1/4 cup, or 2 ounces, tomato paste
1 teaspoon black pepper, coarsely ground
1/8 teaspoon cayenne pepper, ground
1 cup, or 8 ounces, dry sherry
2 cups, or 16 ounces, tomatoes, peeled, seeded, and diced
2 cups, or 16 ounces, yellow squash, thinly sliced
2 cups, or 16 ounces, okra, sliced
1 tablespoon lemon juice, fresh
2 cups, or 12 ounces, button mushrooms, whole
2 cups, or 16 ounces, green beans, French cut
3 cups, or 24 ounces, white vegetable stock
1½ cups, or 12 ounces, aromatic rice
2 teaspoons fresh thyme, chopped, or 1 teaspoon dried leaf thyme
1 teaspoon coriander seeds, ground
2 tablespoons fresh parsley, chopped

1. Place 2 cups red vegetable stock in large saucepan and bring to a boil.

2. Add onions, bell peppers, celery, and garlic; cook until tender.

3. Add tomato paste and peppers and cook for 2 additional minutes.

4. Add sherry wine, tomatoes, squash, okra, and lemon juice and simmer everything together for 1 hour.

5. Add mushrooms and green beans for the last 15 minutes of cooking.

6. Bring white vegetable stock to a boil and add rice, thyme, coriander, and parsley.

7. Reduce rice to a simmer; cover and cook for 20 minutes.

8. Serve the Creole vegetables over the cooked rice.

Approximate values per serving: **Calories** 228, **Carbohydrates (grams)** 49.5, **Protein (grams)** 7.4, **Fat (grams)** 1.3, **Cholesterol (milligrams)** 0. Carbohydrates = 82% calories, Protein = 12% calories, Fat = 5% calories.

Spaghetti Squash with Red Bean Goulash

This vegetarian dish borrows its flavors from traditional Hungarian Goulash. Red beans are used instead of the meat that is traditionally used. In place of beef stock, vegetable stock is used. The resulting flavors resemble traditional goulash, with the caraway seeds and paprika, but with no meat or meat products. If you want more protein alternatives in the final dish, you can use tofu. Add the diced tofu during the last 10 minutes of cooking. Tofu has to simmer only briefly with the other ingredients to warm through.

Makes 15 8-ounce portions

2 cups, or 16 ounces, dry red beans
3 pints, or 48 ounces, red vegetable stock
1 cup, or 8 ounces, celery, peeled, finely diced
1 cup, or 8 ounces, onions, small diced
1 tablespoon peanut oil
2 teaspoons garlic, finely chopped
1 teaspoon caraway seeds
1 tablespoon fresh thyme, chopped, or 2 teaspoons dried leaf thyme

2 teaspoons black pepper, coarsely ground
1/2 teaspoon salt
2 tablespoons Hungarian paprika
2 bay leaves
1/2 cup, or 4 ounces, tomato paste
24 ounces boiling potatoes, peeled, medium diced
2 cups, or 16 ounces, tomatoes, peeled, seeded, and diced
2 spaghetti squash

1. Soak dry beans in cold water overnight.

2. Cook drained beans in vegetable stock until tender (about 2 hours).

3. In the meantime, sauté celery and onions in oil until onions are tender but not brown.

4. Add garlic, caraway seeds, thyme, pepper, paprika, salt, and bay leaves and sauté together for 2 minutes.

5. Stir in tomato paste and reduce heat to low for an additional 20 minutes.

6. Cook potatoes separately in plain water.

7. When the beans are tender, drain most of the liquid and save.

8. Add fresh tomatoes to the cooked beans and stir well.

9. To the same pot, add cooked potatoes and just enough of the bean juices to make a light sauce.

10. Simmer together for 20 minutes before serving.

11. Cut spaghetti squash in halves.

12. Place squash flesh side down in a pan with 1/4 inch of water and bake in 375°F oven for 45 minutes to an hour or until flesh is soft.

13. When squash is tender, remove from the pans and scoop the flesh onto the serving plate (will resemble strings of spaghetti).

14. Serve bean goulash over squash. (Make sure to remove the bay leaves first.)

Approximate values per serving: **Calories** 189, **Carbohydrates (grams)** 38.1, **Protein (grams)** 5.7, **Fat (grams)** 2.5, **Cholesterol (milligrams)** 0. Carbohydrates = 77% calories, Protein = 12% calories, Fat = 11% calories.

Fennel Seed Noodles with Cabbage and Yellow Split Peas (Lacto-Ovo-Vegetarian)

The use of fettucini noodles (eggs and flour) and the parmesan cheese makes this a lacto-ovo-vegetarian recipe. Eliminate the fettucini and cheese and you would have a vegan recipe.

The yellow split peas are a good source of calcium, phosphorus, and potassium. Together with the cabbage, brussels sprouts, leeks, and Pernod, split peas add color and nutrients to a rich flavored sauce.

Makes 15 10-ounce portions

1½ cups, or 12 ounces, yellow split peas, dry
1 cup, or 8 ounces, leeks, white only, sliced
2 teaspoons garlic, finely chopped
1 teaspoon white pepper, ground
1/8 teaspoon cayenne pepper, ground
4 cups, or 32 ounces, white vegetable stock
2 pounds green cabbage, shredded
2 cups, or 16 ounces, brussels sprouts, sliced
2 tablespoons fresh basil, chopped, or 4 teaspoons dried leaf basil
16 ounces dry fettucini noodles
1 tablespoon, or 1/2 ounce, virgin olive oil
1 teaspoon fennel seeds
1/2 cup, or 4 ounces, Pernod (optional)
2 tablespoons, or 1 ounce, parmesan cheese
2 tablespoons fresh parsley, chopped

1. Place split peas, leeks, garlic, peppers, and stock in saucepan and cook until peas are tender (about 1 hour).

2. Add cabbage, sliced brussels sprouts, and basil; simmer uncovered for an additional 30 minutes.

3. Cook the fettucini noodles in lightly salted boiling water until tender.

4. In a sauté pan, heat the oil with the fennel seeds (crush seeds first using a rolling pin or flat side of a knife).

5. Add drained noodles to sauté pan, then Pernod, and toss all ingredients together.

6. Plate noodles and spoon cabbage and split bean sauce on top.

7. Sprinkle each serving with parmesan cheese and then parsley.

Approximate values per serving: **Calories** 396, **Carbohydrates (grams)** 74.7, **Protein (grams)** 19, **Fat (grams)** 3.6, **Cholesterol (milligrams)** 2.2. Carbohydrates = 73% calories, Protein = 19% calories, Fat = 8% calories.

⤙ *Vegetable Lasagna (Lacto-Ovo-Vegetarian)*

In layered dishes, such as a lasagna, the overall flavor comes from the taste combinations in each layer. Therefore, it is extremely important to make each layer as evenly distributed with the ingredients as possible. The lasagna noodles will absorb some of the excess moisture in the sauce and vegetables, making the final product firm and easy to cut into portions.

The eggplant gives the sauce a unique flavor without overpowering the total taste. The addition of any other vegetables in the layered sections would give excellent results.

Makes 20 8-ounce portions

1 large eggplant, peel on, cut into
1/2-inch cubes
2 cups, or 16 ounces, zucchini, medium diced
2 cups, or 10 ounces, crimini mushrooms, sliced
1 cup, or 8 ounces, onions, small diced
1/2 cup, or 4 ounces, green bell peppers, small diced
2 teaspoons garlic, finely chopped
2 tablespoons fresh basil, chopped, or 4 teaspoons dried leaf basil
1 tablespoon fresh oregano, chopped, or 2 teaspoons dried leaf oregano
2 tablespoons fresh parsley, chopped

2 teaspoons black pepper, coarsely ground
1/8 teaspoon cayenne pepper, ground
3 pints, or 48 ounces, plum tomatoes, peeled, seeded, and diced
1/4 cup, or 2 ounces, tomato paste
2 cups, or 16 ounces, red vegetable stock
1½ pounds dry lasagna noodles
2 cups, or 16 ounces, part skim mozzarella cheese, shredded
1/4 cup, or 2 ounces, parmesan cheese, grated
2 cups, or 16 ounces, part skim ricotta cheese

1. Place everything, except noodles and cheeses, in a large sauce pot and bring to a boil; reduce to a simmer and cook for 1 hour.

2. Cook lasagna noodles in plain water until tender; drain and set aside.

3. Mix together mozzarella and ricotta cheese.

4. In large roasting pan, spoon enough eggplant sauce to coat the bottom.

5. Place one layer of cooked lasagna noodles over sauce (all noodles should be laid in one direction).

6. Spoon on more sauce to cover noodles.

7. Spoon one-third combined cheeses over sauce and spread thinly to cover entire layer.

8. Repeat procedure three times with noodles (layered in the opposite direction from the previous layers), sauce, and cheese.

9. Cover the last layer of sauce and cheese with a final layer of noodles and sauce.

10. Sprinkle entire dish with the parmesan cheese.

11. Bake in 350°F oven for 45 minutes or until sauce is bubbly hot and cheese is melted.

Approximate values per serving: **Calories** 444, **Carbohydrates (grams)** 51.5, **Protein (grams)** 28.8, **Fat (grams)** 14.1, **Cholesterol (milligrams)** 42.8. Carbohydrates = 46% calories, Protein = 26% calories, Fat = 28% calories.

⚘ *Vegetable Pizza (Lacto-Vegetarian)*

This complete meal demonstrates how a few ingredient substitutions can transform a traditionally high-calorie, high-fat dish into a nutritionally balanced vegetarian meal. Substituting oat and whole wheat flours for the usual amounts of plain white flour in the dough increases the flavor of the crust and adds bran for nutrition and fiber. Substituting fresh flavoring vegetables for high-fat meat toppings keeps the percentage of fat in line with recommended levels.
As always, use the freshest ingredients possible for the best results.

Makes 2 pies, or 16 portions

1 teaspoon sugar
2 teaspoons dry yeast
2 cups, or 16 ounces, warm water (about 80°F)
1/4 teaspoon salt
2 tablespoons, or 1 ounce, virgin olive oil
1½ cups, or 7 ounces, oat flour
1½ cups, or 7 ounces, whole wheat flour
1½ cups, or 7 ounces, bread flour
1/2 cup, or 4 ounces, onions, small diced
1/2 cup, or 4 ounces, bell peppers, small diced
1 cup, or 8 ounces, zucchini, small diced
1 tablespoon garlic, finely chopped
2 tablespoons fresh basil, chopped, or 4 teaspoons dried leaf basil
1 tablespoon fresh oregano, chopped, or 2 teaspoons dried leaf oregano
2 tablespoons fresh parsley, chopped
1/2 teaspoon black pepper, coarsely ground
1½ quarts, or 48 ounces, tomatoes, peeled, seeded, and diced
2 cups, or 16 ounces, part skim mozzarella cheese, shredded
1 cup, or 8 ounces, onions, thinly sliced
1 cup, or 8 ounces, zucchini, thinly sliced
1 cup, or 6 ounces, mushrooms, thinly sliced

1. To make the dough, add sugar and yeast to warm water and stir to dissolve.

2. Allow the yeast and water to set for a few minutes until a foamlike substance begins to form on the top.

3. Add salt, oil, oat flour, and whole wheat flour and mix until smooth; if using a mixing machine, run at first speed for only a few seconds.

4. Add bread flour, a little at a time, until a good dough consistency is reached.

5. Hand knead the dough for 15 minutes, or with mixer at second speed for 5 minutes. The finished dough should roll freely on a lightly floured table without sticking to the fingers.

6. Cover dough with plastic wrap and place in refrigerator for at least 2 hours.

7. Combine next nine ingredients together; bring to a boil; reduce to a simmer; and cook for 1 hour.

8. After dough has rested for 2 hours, divide it into 2 portions (recipe makes 2 pies).

9. Roll out dough to 1/4-inch thickness and place in shallow pan (the shape is unimportant).

10. Cover the dough generously with the sauce and spread evenly.

11. Cover entire pizza with cheese, and distribute vegetable toppings on top.

12. Sprinkle basil over entire pie.

13. Bake in 500°F oven for 30 minutes or until crust is well browned and cheese is melted.

Approximate values per serving: **Calories** 262, **Carbohydrates (grams)** 36.4, **Protein (grams)** 12, **Fat (grams)** 7.9, **Cholesterol (milligrams)** 15.2. Carbohydrates = 55% calories, Protein = 18% calories, Fat = 27% calories.

Portuguese-Style Beans with Pasta

This full-bodied dish utilizes three different beans, fresh herbs, fresh diced tomatoes, and Madeira wine to present a complete balanced meal when served on top of cooked pasta. You could substitute Marsala, port, or sherry for the Madeira to create relative and still distinctively different dishes.

Makes 15 10-ounce portions

1 cup, or 6 ounces, red kidney beans, dry
1 cup, or 6 ounces, baby lima beans, dry
1½ quarts, or 48 ounces, red vegetable stock
1½ cups, or 12 ounces, tomatoes, crushed
1 teaspoon rosemary leaves
1 tablespoon fresh thyme, chopped, or 2 teaspoons dried leaf thyme
1 teaspoon black pepper, coarsely ground
1/8 teaspoon red pepper, crushed
1/2 teaspoon salt
1 cup, or 8 ounces, Madeira wine
2 cups, or 16 ounces, cut green beans
1/2 cup, or 4 ounces, red bell peppers, julienne
16 ounces dry pasta, any shape

1. Soak kidney and lima beans in cold water overnight.

2. Drain the beans and add vegetable stock, tomatoes, and spices; cook together until beans are tender.

3. Add Madeira wine, green beans, and bell peppers to cooked beans and allow to cook for 20 more minutes.

4. Cook pasta in separate pot with lightly salted water.

5. Serve beans on a bed of cooked pasta.

Approximate values per serving: **Calories** 305, **Carbohydrates (grams)** 59.3, **Protein (grams)** 11.7, **Fat (grams)** 1.1, **Cholesterol (milligrams)** 0. Carbohydrates = 81% calories, Protein = 16% calories, Fat = 3% calories.

Desserts

Does the notion of healthy desserts seem like an illusion? We are so used to the mousse cakes and cheesecakes that fill pastry carts that it is hard to imagine that low-fat and less caloric desserts could taste as good as traditional desserts. Most people do not believe that nutritionally prepared desserts can satisfy cravings or provide dining pleasure.

Successful healthy baking can be achieved when the same principles of flavor manipulation used in preparing nutritious appetizers and entrees are applied to baking formulas and dessert presentations. Knowledge of the ingredients, their use in the baking process, and the flavors they impart, as well as skill in manipulating ingredients according to the science of baking, are tools needed for the production of healthy desserts.

The choice of baking ingredients depends on the desired final results. Baking follows a strict chemistry, and when one ingredient is substituted for another or eliminated, there may be drastic physical changes. Therefore, we must look for baking and serving strategies instead of simple substitutions when designing low-fat, healthy desserts.

Trying to make low-fat, low-calorie, high-fiber mirror images of traditional desserts may be asking too much of bakers. Is a pound cake without eggs, butter, refined flour, or milk still a pound cake? Or should it be called something different?

New desserts can be designed that contain less fat, more vitamins, minerals, and fiber, and less calories with just as much flavor, plate presentation, and dining appeal as traditional desserts. Consider the parts that make up a dessert—the base, fillings, icings, sauce, and garnish—all subject to nutritional concerns and each contributing to the appeal of the final product.

Concern about nutrition and desserts is centered around the fat-laden icings and fillings and the heavy use of refined sugars and flours in the majority of baking formulas. Cholesterol rich, laden in saturated fats, and high in empty calories, traditional desserts are far from being healthy. With proper planning, however, even a génoise can be used as the base of many healthy desserts designed to fit nutritional guidelines.

The following guidelines will help you prepare nutritious and tasty desserts:

- Substitute skim milk for whole or low-fat milk.
- Use low-fat, mock sour cream, or low-fat yogurt for sour cream.
- Try egg substitutes for whole eggs.
- Replace all or part of the egg requirement with egg whites only.
- Add whole wheat, rye, buckwheat, or oat flours to basic formulas.
- Use low-fat condensed milk or soft tofu instead of cream.
- Substitute cocoa for baking chocolate.
- Use natural condensed fruit juices for refined sugars.

When an ingredient is substituted for or eliminated because of fat content, flavor is also sacrificed. The prudent cook will understand this and make adjustments through the selection and use of other flavorful ingredients. Extracts, real fruit, fruit juices, fruit zest, honey, molasses, wines, liqueurs, and brandies are important flavor ingredients in healthful baking. A dessert with reduced fat and calories but no flavor will not be a success. The goal of nutritional baking is to follow dietary guidelines yet still create desserts that people will savor and enjoy.

Oat Bran Muffins with Maple-Glazed Bananas

This recipe was a simple muffin formula transformed into a healthy alternative and enhanced by the addition of a flavorful fruit accompaniment. The combination of the low-fat, high-fiber muffin with the sweetness of the bananas and flavor of the maple syrup makes this a unique and satisfying dessert.

To make this recipe more nutritional, the normal amount of eggs is reduced by half and supplemented with extra egg whites. Canola oil substitutes for butter or margarine.

Makes 24 2-ounce muffins

1¾ cups, or 14 ounces, skim milk
2 cups, or 4 ounces, oat bran cereal, uncooked
1, or 2 ounces, whole egg
2, or 2 ounces, egg whites
1/2 cup, or 8 ounces, honey
1½ teaspoons cinnamon, ground
1 teaspoon pure vanilla extract
1 tablespoon canola oil
2 cups, or 9 ounces, pastry flour
2 teaspoons baking powder
1½ cups, or 12 ounces, pure maple syrup
1 teaspoon lemon juice, fresh
1 dozen semiripe bananas
1/2 cup, or 2 ounces, powdered sugar

1. Combine milk and cereal.

2. Add egg, egg whites, sugar, cinnamon, vanilla, and oil; mix well.

3. Combine baking powder and flour and add to mixture.

4. Lightly mix until dry ingredients are moistened.

5. Fill paper-lined muffin cups two-thirds full and bake at 400°F for 20 minutes.

6. Mix lemon juice with maple syrup and heat slowly on top of the stove.

7. Add bananas sliced into 1-inch rings; heat through.

8. Split one muffin in half, per order, and spoon banana mixture over the top.

9. Dust with powdered sugar and serve while sauce is warm.

Approximate values per serving: **Calories** 211, **Carbohydrates (grams)** 49.5, **Protein (grams)** 2.7, **Fat (grams)** 2, **Cholesterol (milligrams)** 13.2. Carbohydrates = 90% calories, Protein = 8% calories, Fat = 2% calories.

Orange and Pineapple Tea Muffins with Marmalade Citrus Sections

The simplicity of the muffin formula, transformed by healthful substitutions, is enhanced by the complex framework of this dessert. The fruit in the muffin counterbalances and complements the taste of the marmalade and the freshness of the citrus sections. Loaded with flavor, vitamins, and fiber, fruits add nutritional value to a standard dessert.

Makes 24 2-ounce muffins

2 cups, or 8 ounces, pastry flour, sifted
2 teaspoons baking soda
1/2 teaspoon cinnamon, ground
2 cups, or 4 ounces, bran flakes
1½ cups, or 12 ounces, orange juice
1, or 2 ounces, whole egg
2, or 2 ounces, egg whites
1 teaspoon orange zest, grated
1 tablespoon safflower oil
1 teaspoon sugar substitute
1/2 cup, or 4 ounces, pineapple, crushed
1 cup, or 8 ounces, orange marmalade
1 teaspoon lemon juice, fresh
3 cups, or 24 ounces, orange sections
1 pint, or 16 ounces, low-fat plain yogurt
1 tablespoon orange zest, grated

1. Sift together the dry ingredients, except for sugar substitute.

2. Add bran flakes.

3. Beat together orange juice, egg, egg whites, orange zest, oil, and sugar substitute until well blended.

4. Stir in crushed pineapple; mix well.

5. Gently stir the dry ingredients into the orange juice and pineapple mixture.

6. Fill paper-lined muffin cups two-thirds full, and bake at 400°F for 20 minutes.

7. Mix the marmalade with the lemon juice and heat slowly in a pan on top of the stove.

8. Add orange sections, and simmer for 2 to 3 minutes only.

9. Spoon glazed orange sections into a shallow bowl, and place one muffin in the center.

10. Garnish with a dab of yogurt sprinkled with grated orange zest.

Approximate values per serving: **Calories** 117, **Carbohydrates (grams)** 25.8, **Protein (grams)** 2.8, **Fat (grams)** 1, **Cholesterol (milligrams)** 0.9. Carbohydrates = 83% calories, Protein = 9% calories, Fat = 7% calories.

⟪⟫ Lemon and Spice Cupcakes with Lime Sorbet and Whipped Meringue

Cupcakes, by themselves, may not constitue a very exciting dessert. But when presented with lime sorbet and whipped meringue, they too can become exotic enough for the most exclusive restaurants. Neither the sorbet nor the meringue contain fat. Therefore, their additional use in the presentation of the lemon and spice cupcakes reduces the percentage of fat calories to total calories to below 10%.

Makes 24 2-ounce cupcakes

1½ cups, or 12 ounces, pastry flour, sifted
1 cup, or 4½ ounces, whole wheat flour
2 teaspoons baking soda
1/2 teaspoon cinnamon, ground
1/4 teaspoon allspice, ground
1/4 teaspoon nutmeg, ground
1/4 teaspoon ginger, ground
1, or 2 ounces, whole egg
2, or 2 ounces, egg whites
2 tablespoons, or 1 ounce, lemon juice, fresh
1 teaspoon lemon zest, grated
1 tablespoon, or 1/2 ounce, vegetable oil
1½ cups, or 12 ounces, buttermilk
8, or 8 ounces, egg whites
1/2 cup, or 3 ounces, granulated sugar
3 pints, or 48 ounces, lime sorbet

1. Sift together dry ingredients.

2. Whip egg, egg whites, lemon juice, lemon zest, oil, and buttermilk together.

3. Gently stir dry ingredients into the wet mix.

4. Fill paper-lined muffin pans two-thirds full; bake at 400°F oven for 20 minutes.

5. Whip egg whites until frothy; add sugar and continue to whip until soft peaks form. This makes the meringue.

6. Place 1/4 cup, or 2 ounces, of sorbet into shallow bowls.

7. Slice one cupcake, and place the slices around the sorbet.

8. Use a pastry bag to pipe whipped meringue decoratively where the cupcake slices touch the sorbet.

Approximate values per serving: **Calories** 157, **Carbohydrates (grams)** 33.2, **Protein (grams)** 3.4, **Fat (grams)** 1.4, **Cholesterol (milligrams)** 13. Carbohydrates = 84% calories, Protein = 9% calories, Fat = 8% calories.

Yogurt and Banana Mousse

This dessert can be served by itself or used as a topping for muffins, cakes, and pies. Other yogurt fruit mousses can be made simply by substituting equal parts of fresh fruit for the bananas.

Makes 10 4-ounce portions

2 cups, or 16 ounces, skim milk
1 ounce unflavored gelatin
6 ripe bananas
2 teaspoons pure vanilla extract
6, or 6 ounces, egg whites
1/3 cup, or 2 ounces, sugar, finely granulated
2 cups, or 16 ounces, plain, low-fat yogurt
2 tablespoons almonds, sliced, dry roasted

1. Combine gelatin and skim milk to soften the gelatin granules, and place in saucepan.

2. Heat mixture until milk begins to simmer.

3. Add 4 sliced bananas and continue to cook for 2 additional minutes.

4. Puree bananas and milk mixture until very smooth; set aside to cool, but not set.

5. Beat egg whites until soft peaks form.

6. Add sugar and vanilla to egg whites and mix for 30 more seconds.

7. Fold whipped egg whites into cooled banana mixture.

8. Fold in yogurt and remaining sliced bananas.

9. Garnish with more yogurt and dry roasted almonds.

Approximate values per serving: **Calories** 186, **Carbohydrates (grams)** 38.4, **Protein (grams)** 6.7, **Fat (grams)** 1.8, **Cholesterol (milligrams)** 3. Carbohydrates = 78% calories, Protein = 14% calories, Fat = 9% calories.

Meringue Pie Crust Fruit Tarts

Meringue pie shells can take the place of more traditional flour pie crusts in many presentations. The meringue shells contain no fat and only enough sugar to give them solid structure. The rest of the sweetness and flavors come from the fruit.

Makes 10 4-ounce portions

10, or 10 ounces, egg whites
1/2 teaspoon cream of tartar
1½ cups, or 9 ounces, sugar, finely granulated
1/2 pint, or 4 ounces, fresh strawberries
1/2 pint, or 4 ounces, fresh raspberries
1/2 pint, or 4 ounces, fresh blueberries
1 quart, or 32 ounces, plain, low-fat yogurt

1. Whip egg whites and cream of tartar together until very fluffy.

2. Slowly add sugar while continuing to whip egg whites.

3. Continue to whip egg whites until soft peaks are formed.

4. Using a pastry bag with a star tip, pipe 4-inch-diameter plates with high decorative edges on a parchment paper–lined sheet pan.

5. Bake in 200°F oven for 2 hours or until well dried but not browned.

6. Reserve one-quarter of the fruit, sliced for garnishes.

7. Puree the rest of the berries with the plain yogurt in a blender until smooth.

8. Spoon fruited yogurt into dry meringue shells and cover with fresh, sliced berries.

Approximate values per serving: **Calories** 199, **Carbohydrates (grams)** 40.5, **Protein (grams)** 7.5, **Fat (grams)** 1.3, **Cholesterol (milligrams)** 4.4. Carbohydrates = 80% calories, Protein = 15% calories, Fat = 6% calories.

Apple and Oatmeal Crisp

Pies that do not have bottom crusts can be just as satisfying as traditional pies when served with this interesting oatmeal topping. The oats supply fiber, vitamins, and minerals. This dessert can be served hot or cold, by itself or with low-fat yogurt.

Makes 10 4-ounce portions

10, or 50 ounces, Granny Smith apples, peeled, cored, and sliced
1/4 cup, or 2 ounces, apple juice concentrate
1 tablespoon cornstarch
1 teaspoon cinnamon, ground
1/4 teaspoon nutmeg, ground
1/2 teaspoon pure vanilla extract
1 cup, or 3½ ounces, rolled oats
1/4 cup, or 1 ounce, all-purpose flour
1/4 cup, or 2 ounces, light brown sugar
1/4 cup, or 2 ounces, pecans, chopped
2 tablespoons, or 1 ounce, butter

1. Dissolve cornstarch in apple juice and pour over sliced apples.

2. Add spices and stir well.

3. Mix together oats, flour, sugar, and pecans.

4. Melt butter and add to oat mixture; stir until mixture crumbles in the hand.

5. Place apples in baking dish.

6. Cover with topping, spreading evenly on top and on the sides of the pan.

7. Bake in 350°F oven until crust is brown and apple juice bubbles through the sides.

Approximate values per serving: **Calories** 236, **Carbohydrates (grams)** 41.9, **Protein (grams)** 2.1, **Fat (grams)** 8.5, **Cholesterol (milligrams)** 7.8. Carbohydrates = 67% calories, Protein = 3% calories, Fat = 30% calories.

White Fluffy Cake with Peaches and Nectar

This reduced-fat cake formula achieves only partial rise from the small amount of creamed butter and sugar; the rest of the rise, in baking, comes from the whipped egg whites. The sliced peaches, nectar, and brandy serve as an icing to replace more traditional butter cream icings. Other fruits, fruit juices, and fruit-flavored brandies can be substituted for the peaches to create more varieties of the same dessert.

Makes 1 12-inch tube cake or 12 portions

1/4 cup, or 2 ounces, butter
1/2 cup, or 3 ounces, sugar, granulated
1 cup, or 8 ounces, skim milk
1 teaspoon pure vanilla extract
1/2 teaspoon almond extract
2½ cups, or 12 ounces, pastry flour, sifted
1 tablespoon baking powder
4, or 4 ounces, egg whites
1/4 cup, or 1 ounce sugar, finely granulated
1 quart, or 32 ounces, fresh peaches, peeled and thinly sliced
1 cup, or 8 ounces, peach nectar
1/4 cup, or 2 ounces, peach brandy

1. Cream butter and sugar together until very light and fluffy.

2. Mix together all other wet ingredients, and stir into mix.

3. Sift together all dry ingredients and fold into combined mixture.

4. Beat egg whites until light and fluffy; add finely granulated sugar slowly while continuing to whip until soft peaks form; fold gently into mix.

5. Pour mixture into lightly greased tube cake pan and bake at 350°F for 45 to 60 minutes. (Cake is done when sides pull away from the pan and cake springs back when pressed with a finger.)

6. In a sauté pan, heat the peaches with the nectar, and simmer together for 10 minutes.

7. Remove from heat and add brandy; cool sauce.

8. Sauce can be served cold or warm over the sliced cake. Sorbet or low-fat yogurt could also be served with the cake.

Approximate values per serving: **Calories** 218, **Carbohydrates (grams)** 40.6, **Protein (grams)** 5.1, **Fat (grams)** 4.2, **Cholesterol (milligrams)** 10.1. Carbohydrates = 73% calories, Protein = 9% calories, Fat = 17% calories.

Date, Applesauce, and Black Walnut Torte

In this recipe the apple juice takes the place of refined sugar and is better utilized by the body. It also helps us reduce the amount of oil in this recipe, since the apple juice adds moisture, one of the attributes of using fat in baking, to the finished product. Black walnuts were selected because they have less fat than English walnuts, as well as a more distinctive flavor.

Makes 1 8-inch torte, or 12 portions

1 cup, or 6 ounces, dry dates, pitted, chopped
1 teaspoon baking soda
1 cup, or 8 ounces, boiling water
1/2 cup, or 4 ounces, apple juice concentrate
1½ cups, or 12 ounces, applesauce
2 tablespoons, or 1 ounce, vegetable oil
2, or 2 ounces, egg whites
2 cups, or 9 ounces, pastry flour, sifted
1/2 cup, or 2 ounces, black walnuts, chopped

1. Place dates in saucepan and sprinkle with baking soda.

2. Pour boiling water over dates and put aside.

3. In a large bowl, mix apple juice, applesauce, oil, and egg whites until well blended.

4. Add the dates and water and stir well.

5. Add flour and walnuts; stir until smooth.

6. Bake in a paper-lined cake pan at 375°F for 30 to 35 minutes or until toothpick comes out clean and sides of the cake pull away form the pan.

7. Slice into 12 equal portions; serve plain or with sliced fresh fruit.

Approximate values per serving: **Calories** 184, **Carbohydrates (grams)** 31.3, **Protein (grams)** 4.2, **Fat (grams)** 5.3, **Cholesterol (milligrams)** 0. Carbohydrates = 66% calories, Protein = 9% calories, Fat = 25% calories.

✒ *Fresh Berry Streusel*

This recipe takes advantage of fresh berries, when in season, to make a tasty and attractive dessert. The brown sugar, rolled oats, and spices make a great streusel-like topping that nicely complements the sweet freshness of the berries. Any berries, or other cut fruits, can work as well in this preparation.

Makes 12 2-ounce portions

1 teaspoon lemon juice, fresh
1/4 cup, or 2 ounces, Anisette liqueur
5 cups, or 32 ounces, fresh blueberries
5 cups, or 32 ounces, fresh strawberries, sliced
1/2 cup, or 3½ ounces, light brown sugar
2 cups, or 7 ounces, rolled oats
1 teaspoon cinnamon, ground
1/2 teaspoon mace, ground
1/4 cup, or 2 ounces, butter, melted
2 tablespoons cornstarch
1 cup, or 8 ounces, apple juice concentrate

1. Add lemon juice and Anisette to berries and allow to sit for 15 minutes.

2. Blend together sugar, rolled oats, spices, and melted butter in a separate container; the mixture should be crumbly but will hold together when pressed.

3. Dissolve cornstarch in apple juice and pour over berries; stir gently.

4. Place berries in baking dish, and top with oatmeal topping.

5. Bake in 400°F oven for 20 minutes.

Approximate values per serving: **Calories** 178, **Carbohydrates (grams)** 33, **Protein (grams)** 1.8, **Fat (grams)** 4.7, **Cholesterol (milligrams)** 10.3. Carbohydrates = 73% calories, Protein = 4% calories, Fat = 24% calories.

Champagne Poached Pineapple and Plums with Chocolate Meringue Dots

This simple poaching recipe can be used on most fruits to create many variations. Fruits can be served by themselves or as a sauce for cakes, muffins, and brownies.

Makes 10 4-ounce portions

1 ripe pineapple, peeled, cut into 1-inch cubes
12, or 36 ounces, red plums, peeled, seeded, and sliced
1/2 teaspoon cloves, ground
1/2 teaspoon mace, ground
1 cup, or 8 ounces, unsweetened pineapple juice
1 cup, or 8 ounces, dry champagne
6, or 6 ounces, egg whites
1/4 teaspoon cream of tartar
1½ cups, or 12 ounces, sugar, granulated
1 tablespoon cocoa powder

1. Place pineapple, plums, spices, pineapple juice, and champagne in a large saucepan.

2. Bring the liquid and fruit slowly up to a simmer by cooking over low to medium heat; do not boil.

3. Poach fruit in the champagne and pineapple juice for 20 minutes after it comes to a simmer.

4. Whip egg whites and cream of tartar together to soft peaks.

5. Mix together sugar and cocoa powder and pour into egg whites while still mixing; mix only to blend. This makes chocolate-flavored meringue.

6. Using a pastry bag and a plain tube, pipe out tiny drops of chocolate meringue on a parchment paper–lined sheet pan.

7. Bake meringue dots at 200°F for 2 hours or until dry.

8. Serve poached fruit, hot or cold, with several chocolate meringue dots sprinkled on top as garnish.

Approximate values per serving: **Calories** 256, **Carbohydrates (grams)** 58.9, **Protein (grams)** 2.8, **Fat (grams)** 0.9, **Cholesterol (milligrams)** 0. Carbohydrates = 92% calories, Protein = 5% calories, Fat = 3% calories.

Broken Meringue Parfait with Black Currants and Yogurt

Parfaits are traditionally made with ice cream, liqeurs, whipped cream, and other high-fat ingredients. This procedure eliminates practically all of the fat and still presents a satisfying dessert choice. The broken meringue (whipped dried egg whites and sugar) adds a unique texture, or crunch, to the parfait. Plain low-fat yogurt or fruit-flavored low-fat yogurt can be used.

Makes 10 6-ounce portions

10, or 10 ounces, egg whites
1/2 teaspoon cream of tartar
3 cups, or 20 ounces, sugar, granulated
2 cups, or 12 ounces, black currants, dried
1/2 cup, or 4 ounces, water
2 tablespoons, or 1 ounce, peppermint Schnapps
1 quart, or 32 ounces, low-fat yogurt, plain
12 mint leaves
2, or 2 ounces, egg whites, slightly beaten
1/3 cup, or 2 ounces, sugar, finely granulated

1. Whip first amount of egg whites and cream of tartar together until soft peaks form.

2. Gradually add the first amount of sugar while continuing to whip.

3. Pipe whipped meringue onto parchment-lined sheet pan in long, narrow strips; bake in 200°F oven for 2 hours; when dry, break into small pieces (any leftover broken pieces of meringue from other desserts can also be used).

4. Heat currants with water until they come to a quick boil.

5. Remove from heat and add peppermint Schnapps.

6. Allow to cool completely.

7. Fold currants and sauce into the low-fat plain yogurt.

8. Place some of the currant and yogurt mixture into the bottom of parfait glasses and cover with broken meringue.

9. Cover with more yogurt and more meringue.

10. Make at least four layers, topping the last layer off with yogurt; chill completely.

11. Dip mint leaves in lightly whipped egg whites and then in finely granulated sugar; serve as garnish.

Approximate values per serving: **Calories** 333, **Carbohydrates (grams)** 74.4, **Protein (grams)** 8.3, **Fat (grams)** 1.3, **Cholesterol (milligrams)** 4.4. Carbohydrates = 87% calories, Protein = 10% calories, Fat = 3% calories.

Vegetarian Mincemeat Pie

Mincemeat pies take their name from the minced, chopped meat and beef suet (fat) used in the original recipes. In medieval England (ninth to eleventh centuries), sweet meat pies were served as a main entree, as a way of hiding the old, smelly meats that resulted from poor preservation techniques. Honey would be used to sweeten mixtures of chopped meat, meat fat, herbs, and spices, which would be encrusted in dough to make an appetizing dish. As years progressed, mincemeat pies became more of a dessert item than a main course meal. Meat was partially replaced with apples and raisins, and the fat, or suet, barely used.

This recipe duplicates the flavor of the modern mincemeat pie without any meat or suet. Extra apples and raisins are added to give the finished pie body and substance. The heavy use of spices, orange, and lemon zests gives this a very satisfying taste that can accompany light or heavy meals.

Makes 2 10-inch pies, or 16 portions

2 tablespoons, or 1 ounce, dry sherry
1 cup, or 6 ounces, dried raisins or currants
3 cups, or 12 ounces, pastry flour
3/4 cup, or 6 ounces, butter
3/4 cup, or 6 ounces, cold water
2 tablespoons cornstarch
3/4 cup, or 6 ounces, unsweetened apple juice, condensed
1 cup, or 6 ounces, sweet cherries, pitted and halved
3 pints, or 2 pounds, Macintosh apples, peeled, cored, small diced

1 teaspoon pure vanilla extract
1/2 teaspoon almond extract
1 tablespoon orange zest, grated
2 teaspoons lemon zest, grated
1½ cups, or 9 ounces, sugar, finely granulated
1 teaspoon cinnamon, ground
1/2 teaspoon allspice, ground
1/2 teaspoon cloves, ground
1/4 teaspoon nutmeg, ground

1. Pour sherry over raisins and allow to sit for 15 minutes.

2. Using a pastry knife, cut butter into flour until the butter is pea sized.

3. Add cold water to make a pastry dough.

4. Dissolve cornstarch in apple juice, and add cherries, apples, extracts, fruit zest, sugar, and spices; mix well.

5. Measure dough into four equal balls; roll each out to 1/4-inch thickness.

6. Line two pie pans with 2 pieces of the pie dough.

7. Divide ingredients equally between the two shells.

8. Cover pies with the other two pieces of dough rolled out to the same thickness.

9. Crimp edges of crust together to seal in the pans, and make 3 or 4 slits in the top of the dough to allow steam to escape during baking.

10. Bake at 400°F for 35 to 40 minutes or until apples are tender and the juice begins to bubble.

Approximate values per serving: **Calories** 277, **Carbohydrates (grams)** 47.8, **Protein (grams)** 3.1, **Fat (grams)** 9.2, **Cholesterol (milligrams)** 23. Carbohydrates = 67% calories, Protein = 4% calories, Fat = 29% calories.

Bibliography

Journal Articles

Addes, P. 1990. "Coronary Heart Disease, An Update with Emphasis on Dietary Lipid Oxidation Products," *Food and Nutrition News*, Vol. 62, No. 2. Chicago, IL: National Live Stock and Meat Board.

Allegrini, M., Pennington, J., and Tanner, J. 1983. "Total Diet Study: 'Determination of Iodine Intake by Neutron Activation Analyses.'" *Journal of American Dietetic Association*, Vol. 83, No. 1, 18–23.

Alpers, Linda, and Sawyer-Morse, Mary K., MS, RD. 1996. "Eating Quality of Banana-Nut Muffins and Oatmeal Cookies Made with Ground Flaxseed." *Journal of the American Dietetics Association*, Vol. 96, No. 8, 794–796.

Anderson, A. 1988. "Chromium in Human Health and Disease." *Nutrition and the M.D.*, Vol. 14, No. 3.

Anonymous. 1980. "Atherosclerosis and Auto Oxidation of Cholesterol." *Lancet*, Vol. 1, 946–965.

Beaudette, Theresa, MS, RD, ed. 1997. "Health Benefits of Diet and Exercise." *Seminars in Nutrition*, Vol. 16, No. 3, 1–14.

Beaudette, Theresa, MS, RD, ed. 1996. "Healthy Weight Maintenance, A Challenge for Dietitians." *Seminars in Nutrition*, Vol. 16, No. 2, 1–14.

Call, D. L. 1988. "Animal Product Options in the Marketplace." *Food and Nutritional News*, Vol. 60, No. 4.

Chandra, R. 1986. "Nutrition and Immunity." *Contemporary Nutrition*, Minneapolis, MN: General Mills, Vol. 11, No. 11 and Vol. 11, No. 12.

"Clinical Assessment of Mild Iron-Deficiency Anemia." 1987. *Nutrition and the M.D.*, Vol. 13, No. 3.

Cook, J. 1983. "Nutritional Anemia." *Contemporary Nutrition*, Vol. 8, No. 4. Minneapolis, MN: General Mills.

Council on Scientific Affairs, American Medical Association. 1988. *Contemporary Nutrition*. Minneapolis, MN: General Mills, Vol. 13, Nos. 3, 4.

"Diet and Exercise in the Prevention and Control of Chronic Disease." 1989. Littleton, CO: *Seminars in Nutrition*, pp. 2–12.

"Dietary Beans, a Risk Factor for Cholesterol Gallstones." 1989. *Nutrition Reviews*, Vol. 47, 369.

"Dietary Boron and Osteoporosis." 1987. *Nutrition and the M.D.*, Vol. 13, No. 3.

"Dietary Guidelines for Individuals with Diabetes." 1989. *Nutrition and the M.D.*, Vol. 15, No. 9, 4.

"Enhancing Calcium Absorption." 1988. *Nutrition and the M.D.*, Vol. 15, No. 1, 8.

"Estimating Adult Energy Needs." 1987. *Nutrition and the M.D.*, Vol. 13, No. 12.

Etherton, P. M., Krummel, D., Dreon, D., Mackey, S., and Wood, P. 1988. "The Effect of Diet on Plasma Lipids, Lipoproteins, and Coronary Heart Disease," *American Dietetics Association*, Vol. 88, No. 11.

"Fish Oil Supplements and Hypertriglyceridemia." 1989. *Nutrition and the M.D.*, Vol. 15, No. 9, 3–4.

Food and Drug Administration, U.S. Department of Agriculture Food Safety and Inspection Service. Oct. 1993. *An Introduction to the New Food Label*. Department of Health and Human Services Publication No. (FDA) 94-2271.

Friedman, R. 1987. "Calcium Supplements: Don't Depend on Them." University of California, *Berkeley Wellness Letter*, Vol. 3, No. 6.

Gorring, J. 1986. "Why Blame Butter: Discussion Paper." *The Royal Society of Medicine*, Vol. 78, 661–663.

Greenwald, Peter, MD, DrPh, Sherwood, Karen, MS, RD, and McDonald, Sharon S., MS. July 1997. "Fat, Caloric Intake, and Obesity: Lifestyle Risk Factors for Breast Cancer." Supplement to *Journal of the American Dietetic Association*, p. S24.

Grosvenor, M. 1989. "Diet and Colon Cancer." *Nutrition and the M.D.*, Vol. 15, No. 4, 1–2.

Grundy, S. M. 1989. "Recent Research on Dietary Fatty Acids: Implications for Future Dietary Recommendations," *Food and Nutrition News*, Vol. 61, No. 5.

Guthries, A. 1980. "Atherosclerosis and Auto-Oxidation of Cholesterol," *Lancet*, Vol. 1, 964–965.

Halberg, F. 1983. "Chronobiology and Nutrition," *Contemporary Nutrition*, Vol. 8, No. 9. Minneapolis, MN: General Mills.

Harris, W. S. 1985. "Health Effects of Omega 3 Fatty Acids." *Contemporary Nutrition*, Vol. 10, No. 8, 1–2.

Hartmann, P., and Bell, E. 1984. "Nutrition for the Athlete." *Sports Medicine for the Primary Care Physician*. East Norwalk, CT: Appleton-Century-Crofts, pp. 105–121.

Heaney, R. 1986. "Calcium Bioavailability." *Contemporary Nutrition*, Vol. 11, No. 8. Minneapolis, MN: General Mills.

Hideshige, I., Werthessen, N., and Taylor, B. 1976. "Angiotoxicity and Atherosclerosis due to Contaminants of USP-Grade Cholesterol." *Archives Pathological Laboratory Medicine*, Vol. 100, 565–572.

Hine, R. Jean, PhD, RD. 1996. "What Practitioners Need to Know about Folic Acid." *Journal of the American Dietetics Association*, Vol. 96, No. 5, 451–452.

Hoeg, J. M. 1987. "Managing the Patient with Hypercholesterolemia." *Nutrition and the M.D.*, Vol. 13, No. 9.

Holly, H. 1982. "Diet and Hypertension, An Update on Recent Research." *Contemporary Nutrition*, Vol. 7, No. 11. Minneapolis, MN: General Mills.

Hulley, S., Cohen, R., and Widdowson, G. 1977. "Plasma High Density Lipoprotein Cholesterol Level." *Journal of the American Medical Association*, Vol. 238, No. 2, 2269–2271.

"Hypervitaminosis A." 1988. *Nutrition and the M.D.*, Vol. 14, No. 19, 1.

Imai, H., et al. 1976. "Angiotoxicity and Arteriosclerosis due to Oxidized Cholesterol." *Arch. Path. Lab. Med.,* Vol. 100, 565–572.

Kinsella, J. 1989. "Dietary Polyunsaturated Fatty Acids, Eicosanoids, and Chronic Diseases." *Contemporary Nutrition,* Vol. 14, No. 2. Minneapolis, MN: General Mills.

Kurtz, T., Hamoudi, A., Al-Bander, M., and Curtis, R. 1987. "Salt Sensitive Hypertension in Men—'Is the Sodium Ion Alone Important?.'" *New England Journal of Medicine,* Vol. 317, 1043.

Kwiterovitch, Peter O., Jr., MD. July 1997. "The Effect of Dietary Fat Antioxidants, and Pro-Oxidants on Blood Lipids, Lipoproteins, and Atherosclerosis." Supplement to *Journal of the American Dietetic Association,* p. S31.

Liebman, Bonnie. 1995. "Heart Disease, How to Lower Your Risk." *Nutrition Action Health Letter,* Vol. 22, No. 8, 1–10.

Liebman, Bonnie. 1995. "Folic Acid—For the Young at Heart." *Nutrition Action Health Letter,* Vol. 22, No. 7, 1–7.

Liebman, Bonnie, and Schardt, David. 1995. "Vitamin Smarts." *Nutrition Action Health Letter,* Vol. 22, No. 9, 1–10.

Liebman, Bonnie, Wootan, Margo, and Rosofsky, Wendy. 1996. "Trans: The Phantom Fact." *Nutrition Action Health Letter,* Vol. 23, No. 7, 10–11.

Lipkin, Richard. 1995. "Vitamin K—Physiological Aspects." *Science News,* Vol. 148, No. 13, 199.

Lukaski, H., Johnson, P., Bolonchuk, W., and Lykken, G. 1985. "Assessment of Fat-Free Mass Using Bioelectrical Impedance Measurements of the Human Body." *American Journal of Clinical Nutrition,* Vol. 41, 810.

Lyons, P., Truswell, A., Mira, M., Vizzard, J., and Abraham, J. 1989. "Reduction of Food Intake in the Ovulatory Phase of the Menstrual Cycle." *American Journal of Clinical Nutrition,* Vol. 49, No. 6.

Maryland Dietetic Association. 1987. "The Omega Families." *Chesapeake Dietetic Lines,* Vol. 40, No. 4. Lutherville, MD: Maryland Dietetic Association.

Mayer, J. 1988. "Vitamin E Has as Many Mysteries as It Does Unsubstantiated Claims." Baltimore, MD: *Sun Paper.*

Monsen, E. 1988. "Iron Nutrition and Absorption: Dietary Factors Which Impact Iron Bioavailability." *Journal of the American Dietetic Association,* Vol. 88, 786.

Monson, Elaine, R., PhD, RD. 1996. "New Dietary Reference Intakes Proposed to Replace the Recommended Dietary Allowances." *Journal of the American Dietetics Association,* Vol. 96, No. 8, 754–755.

"More on Meal Frequency." 1989. *Nutrition and the M.D.,* Vol. 15, No. 12.

"Nutrition Close-Up: Dietary Guidelines: Recent Developments in Information." 1998. Washington, DC: Egg Nutrition Center, Vol. 5, No. 2.

"Nutrition Close-Up: Surgeon General's Report on Nutrition and Health—Recommendations on Dietary Fat and Cholesterol." 1988. Washington, DC: Egg Nutrition Center, Vol. 5, No. 3.

"Nutrition Close-Up: The Role of Abnormal Apoproteins in Atherosclerosis." 1989. Washington, DC: Egg Nutrition Center, Vol. 6, No. 2.

"Nutrition Close-Up: Exercise, Weight Loss, and Heart Disease." 1989. Washington, DC: Egg Nutrition Center, Vol. 6, No. 1.

"Nutrition Close-Up: LDL Metabolism and Incorporation into Atherosclerotic Plaques." 1989. Washington, DC: Egg Nutrition Center, Vol. 6, No. 2.

"Nutrition Close-Up: Today's Egg Contains 25% Less Cholesterol." 1989. Washington, DC: Egg Nutrition Center, Vol. 6, No. 2.

"Nutrition Close-Up: Hydrogenated Vegetable Fats Shown to Increase Serum Cholesterol." 1990. Washington, DC: Egg Nutrition Center, Vol. 7, No. 3.

"Nutrition Close-Up: Lipid Metabolism and Heart Disease." 1989. Washington, DC: Egg Nutrition Center, Vol. 6, No. 1.

Offenbacher, E., and Xavier, F. 1983. "Temperature and pH Effects on the Release of Chromium from Stainless Steel into Water and Fruit Juices." *Journal of Agriculture and Food Chemistry,* Vol. 31, Nos. 89–92.

"Palm Oil." 1989. *Nutrition and the M.D.,* Vol. 15, No. 9, 4–5.

"Pharmacologic Management of Hyperlipidemia." 1989. *Nutrition and the M.D.,* Vol. 15, No. 9, 2.

Pozefsky, T. 1986. "Concepts and Controversy in Management of Obesity"—Lecture, Baltimore, MD, Union Memorial Hospital.

Rajagopalan, K. 1987. "Molybdenum—An Essential Element," *Nutrition Reviews,* Vol. 45, No. 11, 321.

Raloff, Janet. 1996. "Vitamin E Slows Artery 'Aging.'" *Science News,* Vol. 149, No. 18.

Randal, J. 1990. "Fluoride in the Water—A New Animal Study Suggests It Can Cause Cancer." Washington, DC: *Washington Post.*

Rankin, C. 1990. "Eating Disorders"—Lecture. Baltimore, MD, Mercy Hospital.

Recher, R. 1983. "Osteoporosis." *Contemporary Nutrition,* Vol. 8, No. 5. Minneapolis, MN: General Mills.

Savaiano, D., and Kotz, C. 1988. "Recent Advances in the Management of Lactose Intolerance." *Contemporary Nutrition,* Vol. 13, Nos. 9, 10. Minneapolis, MN: General Mills Nutrition Department.

Sherwin, R. 1982. "Obesity as a Risk Factor,"—Lecture to staff, Baltimore, MD, University of Maryland Department of Epidemiology.

Simonson, M. 1982. "Advances in Research and Treatment of Obesity." *Food and Nutrition News,* Vol. 53, No. 4, 1–4.

Smith, R. "Nutrition, Brain and Behavior." *Sierra Pacific Seminars.* Baltimore, MD: The New England Center for Nutrition Education.

Solomons, N., Guerrero, A., and Torun, B. 1985. "Dietary Manipulation of Postprandial Colonic Lactose Fermentation: Effect of Solid Food in a Meal." *Clinical Nutrition,* Vol. 41, 199.

Stamler, J. "Cutting Cholesterol." *Nutrition Action Health Letter,* Vol. 16, No. 7, 5–7. Washington, DC: Center for Science in the Public Interest.

Tolstoi, L. G. 1989. "The Role of Pharmacotherapy in Anorexia Nervosa and Bulimia." *Journal of the American Dietetic Association,* Vol. 89, No. 11.

U.S. Department of Agriculture, Dietary Guidelines Advisory Committee, Agricultural Research Service. 1995. *Report of Dietary Guidelines Advisory Committee on the Dietary Guidelines for Americans,* pp. 1–58.

U.S. Department of Agriculture, U.S. Department of Health and Human Services. 1995. *Nutrition and Your Health; Dietary Guidelines for Americans,* 4th ed., pp. 1–44.

U.S. Department of Health and Human Services, Public Health Service. 1998. *Summary and Recommendations, the Surgeon General's Report on Nutrition and Health,* publication DHHS (PTTS) No. 88-50211, pp. 1–78.

"Use of the Harris/Benedict Equation in Determining Energy Expenditure." 1987. *Nutrition and the M.D.,* Vol. 13, No. 3.

"Vitamin A and Photoaged Skin." 1987. *Nutrition and the M.D.,* Vol. 13, No. 10.

Wasan, Harpreet S., and Goodlad, Robert A. 1996. "Fiber—Supplemental Foods May Damage Your Health." *The Lancet,* Vol. 348, No. 9023, 319–321.

Watson, R. 1989. "Nutrition and Cancer." *Food and Nutrition News,* Vol. 63, No. 3. Chicago, IL: National Live Stock and Meat Board.

Weisburger, John H., MD(HON), PhD. July 1997. "Dietary Fat and Risk of Chronic Disease: Mechanistic Insights from Experimental Studies." Supplement to *Journal of the American Dietetic Association,* pp. S16–23.

Williams, Peter G., PhD, Drp Nutr Diet, MHP, APD. 1996. "Vitamin Retention in Cook/Chill and Cook/Hot Hold Hospital Food Services." *Journal of the American Dietetics Association,* Vol. 96, No. 5, 490–496.

Wootan, Margo, Liebman, Bonnie, and Rosofsky, Wendy. 1996. "Trans: The Phantom Fat." *Nutrition Action Health Letter,* Vol. 23, No. 7, 10–11.

Books

Adams, C. 1986. *Handbook of the Nutritional Value of Foods in Common Units, U.S.D.A.* New York: Dover Publications.

Alpers, D., Clouse, R., and Stenson, W. 1983. *Manual of Nutritional Therapeutics.* Boston, MA: Little, Brown.

Bosco, D. 1980. *The People's Guide to Vitamins and Minerals from A to Zinc.* Chicago, IL: Contemporary Books.

Brillat-Savarin, Jean-Anthelme. 1984. *The Philosopher in the Kitchen.* Middlesex, England: Penguin Books, Ltd.

Brown, Elizabeth Burton. 1977. *Grains, an Illustrated History.* Englewood Cliffs, NJ: Prentice Hall.

Chalmers, Irena. 1988. *Good Old Food.* New York: Barron's.

Committee on Diet and Health, Food and Nutrition Board, Commission on Life Sciences, National Research Council. 1989. *Diet and Health Implications for Reducing Chronic Disease Risk.* Washington, DC: National Academy Press.

Coyle, L. Patrick, Jr. 1982. *The World Encyclopedia of Food.* New York: Facts on File, Inc.

Davis, Frank. 1983. *The Frank Davis Seafood Notebook.* Gretna, LA: Pelican Pub.

De Selincourt, Aubrey, trans. 1959. *Herodotus, The Histories.* Baltimore, MD: The Penguin Press.

Duyff, Roberta Larson, MS, RD, CFCS. 1996. *The American Dietetic Association's Complete Food and Nutrition Guide.* Minneapolis, MN: Chronimed Publishing.

The Education Foundation of the National Restaurant Association. 1995. *Applied Foodservice, Sanitation, a Certification Coursebook,* 4th ed. Chicago, IL: Educational Foodservice, National Restaurant Association.

The Encyclopedia of Organic Gardening. 1978. Emmaus, PA: Rodale Press.

Freeman, Margaret. 1948. *Herbs for the Medieval Household,* 2nd ed. New York: Huxley House.

Furnas, C. C., and Furnas, S. M. 1937. *The Story of Man and His Food.* New York: The New Home Library.

Johnson, J. 1980. "The Molybdenum Cofactor Common to Nitrite Reductions, Xanthine Dehydrogenase and Sulfite Oxidase." In *Molybdenum and Molybdenum Containing Enzymes.* Elmsford, NY: Pergamon Press.

Hartbarger, Janie Coulter, and Hartbarger, Neil J. 1983. *Eating for the Eighties, A Complete Guide to Vegetarian Nutrition.* New York: Berkley Publication Group.

Hillman, Howard. 1981. *Kitchen Science.* Boston: Houghton Mifflin.

Hodges, A. 1989. *Culinary Nutrition for Foodservice Professionals.* New York: Van Nostrand Reinhold.

Howard, R., and Herbold, N., 1978. *Nutrition in Clinical Care.* New York: McGraw-Hill.

Hunter, Beatrice Trum. 1972. *The Natural Foods Primer.* New York: Simon & Schuster.

Hunter, Beatrice Trum. 1978. *The Great Nutritional Robbery.* New York: Charles Scribner's Sons.

Levinson, Yaakov. 1995. *The Jewish Guide to Natural Nutrition.* Jerusalem and New York: Feldheim Publishing.

MacNeil, Karen. 1981. *The Book of Whole Foods Nutrition and Cuisine.* New York: Vintage Books.

Martin, D., Mayes, P., and Rodwell, V. 1983. *Harpers Review of Biochemistry,* 19th ed. Los Altos, CA: Lange Medical Publication.

Martin, Ethel Austin. 1963. *Nutrition in Action,* 3rd ed. New York: Holt, Rinehart and Winston.

McCormick and Co. 1984. *Spices of the World Cookbook.* New York: McGraw-Hill.

Mitchell, M. 1990. Instructors Manual and Test Bank to Accompany Wardlaw, G., and Insel, P., *Perspectives in Nutrition.* Boston: Times Mirror, Mosby College Publishing.

Null, Gary. 1987. *The Vegetarian Handbook.* New York: St. Martin's Press.

Parry, J. W. 1953. *The Story of Spices.* New York: Chemical Publishing Co.

Pike, R., and Brown, M. L. 1975. *Nutrition, An Integrated Approach,* 2nd ed. New York: John Wiley.

Proudfit, F., and Robinson, C. 1958. *Nutrition and Diet Therapy.* New York: Macmillan.

Ritchie, Carson, I. A. 1981. *Food in Civilization.* New York: Beaufort Books.

Rondale Press Editors. 1985. *Nuts and Seeds, The Natural Snacks.* Emmaus, PA: Rodale Press.

Smith, T. 1989. *Nutrition, Hypertension and Cardiovascular Disease.* Portland, OR: The Lyncean Press.

Stare, Fredrick, J., MD, Olson, Robert, MD, and Whelan, Elizabeth M., ScD. 1989. *Balanced Nutrition Beyond the Cholesterol Scare.* Holbrook, MA: Bob Adams.

Stobart, Tom. 1982. *Herbs, Spices and Flavorings.* New York: Overlook Press.

Tannahill, Reay. 1973. *Food in History.* New York: Stein and Day.

Wenk, D., Baren, M., and Dewan, S. 1983. *Nutrition.* Englewood Cliffs, NJ: Prentice Hall.

Whiteside, L. 1984. *The Carob Cookbook.* Wellingborough, Northamptonshire, Great Britain: Thorsons Publishers Limited.

Whitney, E., and Hamilton, E. 1977. *Understanding Nutrition,* St. Paul, MN: West Publishing.

Wilson, E., Fisher, K., and Pilar, At. 1979. *Principals of Nutrition,* 4th ed. New York: John Wiley.

Zeman, F. 1983. *Clinical Nutrition and Dietetics.* Lexington, MA: Collamore Press.

𝒫amphlets

Agricultural Research Service. 1977. "Fat in Food and Diet." U.S.D.A., Bulletin No. 361. Washington, DC: U.S. Government Printing Office, p. 5.

American Institute for Cancer Research Newsletter. 1988. "Good Grades for Lean Beef Update," Vol. 21, 10.

Ballentine, C. 1985. "The Essential Guide to Amino Acids." FDA Consumer, HHS Publication Number 86-1124, Rockville, MD: Department of Health and Human Services.

Department of Health and Human Services. 1983. "Potassium—Keeping a Delicate Balance." FDA Consumer, HHS Publication 83-2170, Rockville, MD: U.S. Government Printing Office.

Division of Agricultural and Food Chemistry of the American Chemical Society. 1982. "Symposium: Unconventional Sources of Dietary Fiber." Washington, DC: American Chemical Society.

Food and Drug Administration, U.S. Department of Agriculture, Food Safety and Inspection Service. 1993. "An Introduction to the New Food Label." Department of Health and Human Services (DHHS) Publication No. 94-2271.

"Food Fats and Oils." 1988. Washington, DC. Institute of Shortening and Edible Oils, Inc.

Grant, A. 1979. "Nutritional Assessment Guidelines." Seattle, WA: Author.

"Guide to Good Eating—A Recommended Daily Pattern" 1977. Rosemont, IL: National Dairy Council.

Heinz International Research Center and Heinz Research Fellowship of Mellon Institute. 1963. "Nutritional Data." Pittsburgh, PA: H.J. Heinz Company.

Mead Johnson Laboratories. 1975. "Cow's Milk Allergy. A Review of Current Scientific and Clinical Findings." Evansville, IN: Mead Johnson and Company.

Monty, K., and McElroy, W. 1959. *Food, the Yearbook of Agriculture.* Washington, D.C., U.S. Government Printing Office, pp. 122–129.

Rapp, Doris J., M.D. 1987. "Recognize and Manage Your Allergies." New Canaan, CT: Keats Publishing Inc.

Rogers, Marc. 1978. "Vegetable Seeds." Prownal, VT: Garden Way Publishing.

Taylor, F. 1978. "Iodine—Going from Hypo to Hyper." FDA Consumer, HHS (FDA) 81-2153. Rockville, MD: U.S. Government Printing Office.

U.S. Department of Agriculture, Dietary Guidelines Advisory Committee, Agricultural Research Service. 1995. "Report of the Dietary Guidelines, Advisory Committee on the Dietary Guidelines for Americans, 1995." Washington, DC: U.S. Government Printing Office, pp. 1–58.

U.S. Department of Agriculture, U.S. Department of Health and Human Services. 1995. "Nutrition and Your Health: Dietary Guidelines for Americans," 14th ed. Washington, DC: U.S. Government Printing Office, pp. 1–44.

U.S. Department of Health and Human Services, Public Health Service. 1988. "Summary and Recommendations: The Surgeon General's Report on Nutrition and Health." DHHS Publication No. 88-50211, pp. 1–78.

"What You Should Know About Allergies." Wayne, NJ: Cooper Laborites Inc.

Index

A

Acidophilus, 23
Acids, 142–143, 156
Adrenal glands, 63
Adrenaline, 22, 35
Acid/base balance, 80
Agaricus mushrooms, 136
À la Grecque, 241
Albuminoids, 13
Alcohol, 62
Ale, 151
Alkaline, 57, 106, 156
Allergies, food, *see* Food allergies
Allspice, 117
Aluminum, 92
    cookware, 92
Alzheimer's disease, 92
Amaretto, 152
American Culinary Federation, 128
American Diabetes Association, 32
American Indian
    Cree Indians, 10
    foods of, 9
    pemmican, 9–10
Amines, 56
Amino acids, 35–38, 89, 220, 302
    complementary proteins, 38, 186
    essential, 35–36, 358
    formation of, 21
    limiting, 35

lysine, 38
    methionine, 38
    nonessential, 35–36, 38
Amylopectin, 20
Amylose, 20
Anaheim peppers, 135
Ancho pepper, 135
Anemia, 87, 259
Anise, 118, *see also* Anisette
Anisette, 152
Anosmia, 107–108
Antacids, 59
Antioxidants, 41, 51, 100
    vitamin E, 56
Appert, Nicholas, 10
Appetite, 98
    suppressants, 176
Appetizers, 227–245
Apple and Oatmeal Crisp, 378
Apple Blintzes, 221
Apple Pickles, 244
Apple Syrup, 217
Arachidonic acid, 51
Aromatized wines, 150–151
Arsenic, 93
Arthritis, 33, 101
Ascorbic acid, 51, 264
Asparagus with Port Wine Vinaigrette, 267
Athletes
    and protein, 39
Avidin, 59

B

Banana peppers, 135
Barbecue Fruit with Honey and Poppyseed
    Dressing, 245
Barley Salad with Sweet Yellow and Red
    Peppers, 266
Barley wine, 151
Basil, 118
Bay, 118
Beef Tenderloin Tips in Wild Mushroom
    and Cherry Sauce, 310
Beer, 145–146, 151–152, 161
Bell peppers, 135
Benedictine, 152
Beriberi, 62
Beta carotene, 51, 55–56, 100, 249
Bile, 58, 249
Biotin, 59
Biscuits, 224
Blackened, 158
Blintzes, 220–221
Blood pressure, 101–102
Blue Fish, 353
Blueberry Oatmeal Crunch, 218
Boron, 91
Botulism, *see Clostridium botulinum*
Boyarsky, Victor, 10
Braised Beef Eye Round Sicilian, 307
Braised Beef Sirloin with Ginger-Orange
    Sauce, 309
Braised Beef Tips au Poivre with Rice Pilaf
    and Roasted Plum Tomatoes, 304
Braised Cabbages and Bell Peppers, 283
Braised Mixed Greens with Roasted Garlic,
    297
Braised Red Cabbage with Apple Cider and
    Sauterne, 300
Braising, 157
Bran, 26–27, 29–30, 100, 212, 290, 367
Brandy, 146, 152, 161
Breakfast foods, 209–226
Brillat-Savarin, Jean-Anthelme, 5, 104, 106
Broccoli and Cauliflower Coleslaw, 272
Broccoli-Pasta Salad with Fresh Tuna, 268
Broiled Cajun Catfish, 346
Broiled Tuna with Chili Garlic Sauce, 344
Broiling, 158, 160
Broken Meringue Parfait with Black Cur-
    rants and Yogurt, 383
Brown Rice Pilaf with Chick Peas and
    Pecans, 290
Brown Vegetable Stock, 139
Browning, 131

Brunoise Salad, 231
Brussels sprouts, 298
Buckwheat, 35–36
Bulgur, 336
Butter, 141
    clarified, 159

C

Cabbage and Broccoli Soup with Chick
    Peas, 253
Cadmium, 93
Cajun, 239, 264, 328, 346
Cajun Bean Salad, 264
Cajun Chicken Burgers with Jack Cheese
    Pockets, 328
Cajun Chicken Tenders, 239
Calamari and Eggplant Stew, 351
Calcium, 41, 72–75, 85, 224, 250, 263, 315,
    323, 340, 358, 361, 365
    absorption of, 23
    caseinate, 43
    stearate, 43
Calorie reduction, 171
Cancer, 41, 70–71, 101, 269, 328
    colon, 28
    from fatty fish, 48
    lung, 56
    protection against, 31
    selenium and, 86–87
    skin, 58
Capsaicin, 101, 106,
Capsicum peppers, 101, 119, 123, 134–135
Caramel, 26
Caraway, 118
Caraway Beef with Pearl Onions, 306
Carbohydrates, 17–20, 35, 59, 228
    calories of, 9
    discovery, 13
    for energy, 18–19, 21, 24, 63
    from protein, 39
    metabolism, 74
    monocarbohydrate, 28
Carcinogens, 56, 158
Cardamom, 118–119
Carmine, 43
Carotenoids, 70
Carrot, 133
Casein, 43
Cassia, 119
Catfish, 346
Cauldrons, 11, 114
Cauliflower Creole, 291

Cayenne, 119, 135
Celeriac, 133
Celery, 133–134
Celery seed, 119
Celiac disease, 202
Cellulose, 24–25, 28–29
Champagne Poached Pineapple and Plums
    with Chocolate Meringue Dots, 382
Chanterelle, 136
Cherry peppers, 135
Chervil, 119
Chick Pea Dip and Vegetables, 243
Chicken, 238–239, 258, 270, 278, 325–334
Chicken and the Sea, 258
Chicken Fingers with Sauce Anisette, 238
Chicken Paprika, 327
Chicken Piedmont, 332
Chili garlic sauce, 344
Chili sauce, 233
Chitterlings, 5
Chloride, 76, 79–81
Chlorophyll, 75
Cholesterol, 44–48, 51–52, 89, 162, 180,
    191, 207, 209, 228, 259, 295, 371
    diets high in, 24
    HDL, 46–47, 52, 89, 146, 166, 263, 347
    LDL, 28, 46–47, 52, 263, 347
    lowering levels, 249
    recommended dietary intake, 41
    regulation of nerve tissue, 63
    risk factor for elevated blood levels, 50
    use in synthesizing vitamin D, 58
    VLDL, 28, 46, 63
Cholestyramine, 57
Choline, 68
Chromium, 89–90, 254
Chutney, 235
Chyme, 20
Cinnamon, 119
Cinnamon sauce, 228
Clams, 336
Clostridium botulinum, 140
Cloves, 120
Cobalamin, 59, 67
    and vegetarians, 67
    see also Vitamin B
Cochineal, 43
Coconut oil, 46, 220
Coffee liqueur, 152
Collagen, 40, 68
Columbus, Christopher, 113, 119
Copper, 87, 230, 250, 354
Coriander, 120
Coriander Turkey Chili, 252

Cornbread Biscuits and Tomato Gravy, 224
Cornbread Oyster Florentine, 354
Cornbread Pizza, 237
Country Slaw, 273
Country Waffles with Hazelnut Yogurt, 215
Crab, 240
Crab Coins Maryland, 240
Cranberry Rice Pilaf with Peanuts, 289
Cream de cacao, 152
Creme de cassis, 152
Creme de menthe, 152
Creme de noyaux, 152
Creole, 291, 363
Creole Vegetables and Aromatic Rice, 363
Crimini, 136
Cruciferous vegetables, 272, 283
Cumin, 120
Curacao, 152
Curried Corn and Lima Beans, 296
Curried Rice Salad, 265
Cysteine, 132

D

da Gamma, Vasco, 113, 119
Dahe, Qin, 10
Daikon, 134
Date, Applesauce, and Black Walnut Torte,
    380
Deep frying, 157
Department of Agriculture, U.S., 2, 17–18,
    38, 179
Department of Health and Human Services,
    U.S., 2, 89, 181
Desserts, 192, 371–384
Dextrin, 20
Diabetes, 22, 33, 98–100
    blood sugar control, 29
    insulin dependent, 99–100
    noninsulin dependent, 31, 48, 99–100
Diallyl disulfide, 132
Diaz, Bartholomew, 113
Diet
    and aging, 98
    behavior modification, 169
    books, 3, 166
    effect on metabolism, 167
    fad, 3, 165
    health problems, 4
    health and diet, 97
    skipping meals, 209
    variety and flexibility, 174
Dietary goals, U.S., 33

Dietary guidelines, 2, 5
Dietary Guidelines for Americans, 17
Dietician, 2–5, 100
    creation of special diets, 2
Dill, 120, 288
Dill and Shallot Hashbrowns, 288
Disaccharide, 20
Diverticulosis, 31
Donkin, Bryan, 10
Drambule, 152
Dressings, 192, 262
Duck, 335

E

Elastin, 40
Endosperm, 28, 30
Entremets, 261–281
Eggplant, 230, 242, 271, 316, 351, 366
Eggplant Pate, 230
Eggplant Salsa, 271
Eggs
    benefits of, 220
    cholesterol and, 45–46, 220
    cooking choices, 225
Egypt
    Nile Valley, 9
    use of salt, 10
Elephant garlic, 132
Enoki, 136
En papillote, 158, 348
Estrogen, 99
Etienne, Jean-Louis, 10
European Renaissance, time of, 9, 11
Evidence, empirical, 3
Exercise and weight control, 177

F

Farmer's Style Chicken Marsala, 330
Fats, 17, 43–53, 216
    calories of, 9
    discovery, 13
    for energy, 63
    and flavor, 2, 140–142
    flavor based on traditions, 3
    natural need for, 8
    palatability of, 9
    monounsaturated, 44, 47–48, 180, 258
    omega 3, see Omega 3
    omega 6, see Omega 6
    oxidation, 51
    polyunsaturated, 44, 47–48, 56, 181

    reducing total content in traditional
        recipes, 235
    saturated, 44, 162
    transfat, see Transfat
    trans fatty acid, see Trans fatty acid
    unsaturated, 50
    vegetarian concerns, 185
Fennel, 120, 134
Fennel and Artichoke Hearts: À La
    Grecque, 241
Fennel Seed Noodles with Cabbage and Yel-
    low Split Peas, 365
FenPhen, 176–177
Fiber, 24–31, 208, 212, 215, 248, 287, 290,
        317, 358, 367
    dietary, 73
    insoluble, 24–25
    laxative, 41
    soluble, 24–25, 251
Flavor
    collaboration of taste, 4
    harmony of, 5
    natural flavors of foods, 8
Flaxseed, 28
Flounder en Papillote, 348
Fluoride, 88–89
Fluorine, 230, 351
Foccacia, 120
Folacin, 59, 251
Folate, 64–67, 264
    for DNA, RNA, 65
    see also Vitamin B
Folic acid, 26, 59, 64–66, 295. See also
        Vitamin B
Food allergies, 200–205
Food and Drug Administration, 48, 179, 199
Food Guide Pyramid, 17–18, 42, 173, 281
    as a model, 2
Food intolerances, 201–206
Food label, 179, 197
Food preservation
    canning, 11, 13
    drying, 10–11
    refrigeration and freezing, 11
    smoking, 10–11, 269
Forester Chicken Soup, 254
Fortified, 99
French onion soup, 131
French wines, 147–148
Fresh Berry Streusel, 381
Fresh Ham Ragoût and Fettucini with Lieb-
    fraumilch, Currant, and Plum Sauce, 320
Fritters, 226, 235
Fructose, 21, 24
Fruit Salad with Honey-Orange Dressing, 279

Fruit wines, 151
Funatsu, Keizo, 10

G

Galliano, 152
Garlic, 121, 132, 328
    roasted, 297
Gelatin, 35, 43, 202, 376
Germ, 26, 30
German wines, 149
Ginger, 121, 284
Gingerbread Pancakes with Applesauce
    and Yogurt, 213
Ginger-Orange sauce, 309
Glazed Yellow Turnips with Figs, 285
Glucose
    carbohydrates converted into, 20
    hormone regulated, 22
    from proteins, 35
    testing, 69
Glycerol, 44
Glycogen, 168
Goals 2000, 179
Goncalves, Captain, 150
Grains, 281–300
Gran Marnier, 152
Granola, 218–219
Gravy, 224
Green Beans and Potato Salad with Interna-
    tional Greens and Walnut Vinaigrette,
    276
Green onions, 132–133
Grilled Chicken Breast with Spanish
    Sauce, 226
Grilled Chicken Salad, 280
Grilled Flank Steak with Braised Lentils
    and Chestnuts, 313
Grilled Lamb with Braised Eggplant and
    Port Wine, 316
Grilled Sesame Chicken Breast with Basil
    Marinade, 325
Grilling, 158, 160
Grits, 222
Grouper Florentine with Sesame Sauce,
    349
Gumbo, 352
Gums, 24
    guar gum, 25

H

Habañero peppers, 135
Ham, fresh, 320

Ham and Cheese Grits, 222
Hashbrowns, 288
Hazelnut Snapper, 347
Health and diet, 97
Heart disease, 66, 70–71, 98, 166
    ischemic, 84
Hemicellulose, 24–25, 28
Hemoglobin, 36, 41, 65, 263
Herbed Black-eyed Peas with Almonds and
    Raisins, 360
Herbs, 112–124
Herodotus, 119
High blood pressure, 78–79, 81, 102, 166,
    180, 285
Homefries, 287
Honey-Berry sauce, 312
Honey-Mustard dressing, 286
Honey-Orange dressing, 279
Horseradish, 121, 134
Horseradish sauce, 232
Human civilization, evolution of, 3
Hungarian goulash, 308, 364
Hungarian wax peppers, 135
Hydrochloric acid, 81
Hydrogen, 44
Hydrogenation of fats, 50
Hydrolysis, 39
Hydrolyzed vegetable protein, 358
Hypertension, *see* High blood pressure
Hypoglycemia, 22

I

Insulin, 22, 35, 168
Iodine, 85–86, 354
    salt, 85
    sanitizers, 85
Iron, 81–84, 253, 287, 340, 350, 354, 358,
    360
    component of myoglobin, 81
    heme iron, 41, 81–82
    invention of the metal, 11
    nonheme iron, 41, 81–82
    during pregnancy, 83
Italian Beef and Tomato, 259
Italian Vegetables with Tomato Basil Vinai-
    grette, 274
Italian wines, 148–149

J

Jalapeño peppers, 135
Jerusalem artichoke, 134
Juniper, 121

K

Kohlrabi, 134
Kummel, 152
Kwashiorkor, 39

L

Lactic acid, 22–23
Lactose, 20–22
    intolerance, 22–23, 99
Lamb, 314–316
Lamb Stew with Cranberries and Madeira,
    315
Lauric acid, 46, 302
Lead, 93
Lecithin, 74
Leek, 133
Leek and fennel sauce, 341
Legumes, 281–300
    cholesterol free, 358
Lemon and Spice Cupcakes with Lime
    Sorbet and Whipped Meringue,
    375
Lignin, 24–25, 28, 31
Limburger cheese, 5
Linoleic fatty acid, 47–48, 270, 319
Liqueurs, 146–147, 152–153
Locust bean gum, 28
Lypotropes, 68
Lysine, 35

M

Mace, 121
MacKenzie, Alexander, 9–10
Macrominerals, *see* Minerals
Macronutrients, 17
Madeira Shrimp Kabobs, 350
Magnesium, 74–75, 361
Maître d'Hôtel, 141
Maltose, 20–21
Manganese, 88
Maple Flavored Vegetable Blintzes, 220
Marbling, 301–302
Margarine, 141
Marinated Pinto Bean Salad, 263
Marjoram, 121
Maryland Blue Fish Cakes, 353
Maryland Chicken Succotash, 333
Meats, 301–321
    composition, 301

game, 161
grading, 302
Menus
    construction, 191–195
    marketing, 198–202
    planning, 189–195
    vegetarian, 186
Mercury, 92–93
Meringue, 375, 377, 382–383
Meringue Pie Crust Fruit Tarts, 377
Metabolic rate, 168–169
Mexican Lentil, 250
Mexican lime salsa, 238
Microminerals, *see* Minerals
Micronutrients, 17
Millet Pilaf with Dates, Apples, and Pista-
    chio Nuts, 361
Minerals, 71–93, 157, 210
    macrominerals, 72–80
    microminerals, 81–91
    unclassified minerals that may have
        health implications, 91–93
Mint, 122
Mirepoix, 130–131
Mise en place, 137
Miso, 42, 72, 358
Molybdenum, 90, 252
Monell Chemical Senses Center, 9, 105,
    107
Monosaccharides, 20–21
Monosodium glutamate (MSG), 76, 78, 105,
    140, 201, 204
Montmorency, 161
Morels, 136
Mousse, 376
Mucilage, 24
Muffins, 373–374
Mushrooms, 135–136
Mustard, 122
Myoglobin, 41, 81
Myristic acid, 46, 302

N

Nasal cavity, 104
National Restaurant Association, 184
Niacin, 62–63, 289, 315, 323, 340. *See also*
    Vitamin B
Nitrates, 106
Nitrites, 56
Nitrogen balance, 39
Nutmeg, 122
Nutritional awareness, 195

Nutritional cooking, 2, 3, 116, 155–163, 195, 207, 247
  absence of fats and salt, 5
  fad or trend, 190–191
  protein alternatives, 194
  substituting fats, 193–194
  substituting meats, 194–195
  for vegetarians, 185–186
Nutritional labeling, on convenience foods, 3
Nutritional menu nomenclature
  heart healthy, 2, 3
  light fare, 2, 3
Nutritional science, 1–5, 98
  affirmation of, 1
  awareness, 1, 4
  balance, 4–5,
  basic tenets, 4
  guidelines, 3–4, 195
Nutrition Labeling and Education Act (NLEA), 50, 179, 199

O

Oat Bran Muffins with Maple Glazed Bananas, 373
Obesity, 33, 52, 166, 175–176
  fashionable, 9
  risk factors, 22
  in women, 170
Occupational Safety and Health Administration (OSHA), 92
Odors, 107–108
Oils, 45–53
  for flavor, 140–142, 186
  in stir fries, 157
Okra, 5
Oleic acid, 47, 270, 347
Olfactory, 104, 106–109
  olfacere, 107
Olfactory lobes, 98, 107
Olfactory neurons, 98, 107
Omega 3 fatty acids, 41, 46, 48–49, 51, 100, 339, 341, 343, 352
  EPA, DHA, 48
Omega 6 fatty acids, 48–49, 51–52
Onions, 131–133
Orange and Pineapple Tea Muffins with Marmalade Citrus Sections, 376
Oregano, 122
Osmotic pressure, 80
Osteoporosis, 58, 70, 87, 98, 99, 180

Oven Poached Salmon with Leek and Fennel Sauce, 341
Oven Poached Sea Trout, 345
Oven Roasted Sweet Potato Homefries, 287
Oxalic acid, 73
Oxidation, 156
Oyster Fritters with Apple and Raisin Chutney, 233
Oyster mushrooms, 136
Oysters, 235, 354

P

Palate, 103
Palmitic acid, 46, 302
Palm oil, 46, 220
Palm kernel oil, 46
Pan frying, 157
Pancake, 211–214, 223, 232
Pancreas, 20, 22, 35
  amylose, 20
Pantothenic acid, 59, 63. *See also* Vitamin B
Paprika, 122, 327
Paratoid glands, 39
Parfaits, 161
Parsley, 122–123
Parsnip, 134
Pasteur, Louis, 13
Pasteurization, 13
Peach Granola, 217
Peach Syrup, 215
Pear and Pineapple Relish, 244
Pear liqueur, 153
Pearl onion, 133, 306
Pecan honey dressing, 275
Pectin, 24–25, 28
Pellagra, 62
Pemmican, *see* American Indian
Pepper, 123, 134–135
Peppered Cornsticks with Mexican Lime Salsa, 236
Peppercress, 123
Peppermint schnapps, 153
Phenolic acid, 29
Phosphates, 73, 79, 85
Phosphorus, 73–74, 315, 365
  for RNA, DNA, 74
Phytic acid, 27, 29, 73
Phytochemicals, 70–71
  sources of antioxidants, 101
  in vegetables, 31, 41
Pickles, 244

Pimento, 135
Piperine, 106
Pizza, 237, 367
Plum sauce, 318
Poaching, 158
Polenta, 344
Polypeptides, 34
Polysaccharides, 20, 25
Popcorn Shrimp with Chili Sauce, 233
Poppyseed Dressing, 245
Porcini, 136
Pork, 315, 317
Pork Pot Roast and Cider, 317
Portabella, 136
Portuguese Style Beans with Pasta, 369
Portuguese wines, 15
Potassium, 76, 78–80, 285, 288, 319, 323,
        358, 361, 365
Potatoes, 281–300
Pottage of Winter Squash, 256
Poultry, 323–337
Pregnancy, 83
Premenstrual syndrome, 59
Prince Henry, 113
Prostaglandin, 44, 344
Proteins, 17, 31–44, 59, 73, 228, 252
    alternatives, *see* Nutritional cooking
    calories of, 9
    complementary, *see* Amino acids
    complete proteins, 263
    digestion and absorption, 34–35
    discovery, 13
    effectiveness rating (PER), 38
    as energy, 36
    net utilization (NPU), 38
Prudhomme, Paul, 108, 158
Psyllium, 27–28
Pumpkin Soup, 257
Puree of Cauliflower and Yellow Split Peas,
        260
Pyridoxine, 64. *See also* Vitamin B
Pyruvic acid, 132

R

Radish, 134
Rapeseed, 48
Raspberry Duck and Pinto Beans and
        Braised Romaine, 335
RDA
    calcium, 73
    chlorine, 81
    fiber, 27

iron, 82
magnesium, 76
pyridoxine, 64
selenium, 86
thiamin, 62
riboflavin, 63
vitamin A, 56
vitamin C, 68
vitamin D, 57
vitamin E, 55
vitamin K, 57
zinc, 84
Redux, 177
Recipe, 193
Red Vegetable Stock, 138
Religion, Christian Lenten practices, 10
Relleño peppers, 135
Relish, 244
Restaurant styles
    fast food, 1, 3, 165
    convenience, 3
Riboflavin, 41. *See also* Vitamin B
Rickets, 58
Roast Leg of Lamb with Honey-Berry
        Sauce, 314
Roasted Rolled Pork Loin with Turkey
        Sausage, 313
Roasted Sage Chicken, 326
Roasted Sweet Peppers Vinaigrette, 242
Roasting, 158
Rosemary, 123

S

Saffron, 123
Sage, 123
Salads, 261–281
Salivary amylase, 20
Salmon, 341–342
Salsa, 236, 271
Salt
    flavor based on tradition, 3
    iodized, 86
    natural need for, 8
    substitutes, 79
    as taste enhancer, 2
Sambucca, 153
Sausage, 223, 315
Sautéing, 157
Savory, 123
Scallions, 132–133, 284
Scallops, 353
Scallops and Pineapple Shell Macaroni, 353

Scurvy, 11, 68
Sea trout, 343
Seafood, 339–353
Selenium, 41, 86–87, 255
Serraño peppers, 135
Sesame, 124, 234, 293, 325, 349
Sesame Carrots and Raisins, 293
Sesame sauce, 349
Senses, natural, 4
Shallot, 133
Shirred Eggs and Turkey Primavera, 225
Shitake, 136
Shrimp, 233–234, 258, 350, 352
Sicilian Chicken Stew, 334
Simplese, 43
Skewered Sesame Shrimp, 234
Skin, 98
Slaw, 273
Sloe gin, 153
Smell, 103, 107–109, 116–117
    collaboration of taste, 4
Smoked Turkey with Feta and Ziti, 269
Smothered Chicken and Onions, 329
Snapper, 347
Sodium, 76–78, 285, 323
    levels, 169
Sodium caseinate, 43
Sodium chloride, 106
Somers, Geoff, 10
Soups, 247–260
    as staple meals, 11
Southeast Indian Bean and Cabbage Pie, 362
Southern Greens with Honey Mustard
        Dressing, 286
Soy beans, 358
Soy flour, 358
Soy grits, 358
Soy milk, 358
Soy sauce, 295
Spaghetti Squash with Red Bean Goulash,
        364
Spanish Omelet, 214
Spanish onion, 133
Spanish Pancakes, 214
Spanish Sauce, 226
Spanish wines, 149–150
Spices, 112–124
Spring onions, *see* Scallions; Green onions
Starches, 20
Steamed Salmon with Tomatoes and Arti-
        choke Hearts, 342
Steaming, 158
Stearic acid, 47, 302
Steger, William, 10

Stew, 351
Stewing, 157
Stir frying, 157, 359
Straw mushrooms, 136
Strawberry Granola Parfait, 217
Streusel, 381
Stroke, 46
Succotash, 296, 333
Sucrose, 20–21, 43
Sugars, 20, 43
Sulfites, 200, 204
Sulfur, 81
Summer Squash with Ginger and Spring
        Onions, 286
Sunflower Seed Pancakes with Honey
        Roasted Figs, 209
Sweating of vegetables, 131
Sweet-and-Sour Brussels Sprouts, 298
Sweet Potato Salad with Pecan Honey
        Dressing, 275
Syrups, 210, 217

T

Tannin, 82
Tarragon, 124
Taste, 3–4, 103–106
    as complex sense, 4
    with herbs and spices, 111
    mouth feel, 231, 300
    personal preference, 5, 11
    physiological associations, 8
    pleasure of, 5
    as primal sense, 5
    psychological associations, 8
    as refined sense, 5
Teriyaki Peanut Pasta, 295
Texture, of food, 4
Textured soy protein (TSP), 358
Thiamin, *see* Vitamin B
Three Bean Soup with Kale, 251
Throxine, 85
Thyme, 124
Tofu, 42, 72, 358
Tomato gravy, 220
Tongue, 4, 104
    mechanisms of, 4
    taste buds, 4, 104–105, 115, 159
    taste pores, 105
Traguncanth, 29
Trans fatty acids, 50, 180
Transfat, 50
Transisomers, 50

Triglyceride, 44, 89

Triple sec, 153

Tropical Chicken Salad with Raspberry
    Vinaigrette, 270

Truffles, 136

Tryptophan, 62–64

Tuberculosis, 64

Tuna, 268, 344

Turkey, 338

Turkey Breast with Bulgur Clam Stuffing,
    338

Turkey Sausage, 223

Turmeric, 124

Tzimmes, 333

U

Umami, 105

V

Vanadium, 91

Vanilla, 124

Vanilla Bran Pancakes with Strawberry Yo-
    gurt, 212

Veal, 352

Veal and Shrimp Country Gumbo, 352

Vegetable and Wild Rice Stir Fry with Water
    Chestnuts, 359

Vegetable Barley Soup, 249

Vegetable Lasagna, 366

Vegetable Pancakes with Sour Cream
    Horseradish Sauce, 232

Vegetable Pizza, 367

Vegetables, Legumes, Potatoes, and Grains,
    281–300

Vegetable stock, 136–140

Vegetarian Mincemeat Pie, 384

Vegetarian Pilaf, 292

Vegetarianism, 3, 35, 40–44, 183–187, 192,
    302
    deterioration of spinal chord, 59
    entrees, 357–369
    fruitarian, 40
    lacto vegetarians, 40, 184, 357, 361–362,
      367
    lacto-ovo vegetarians, 40–41, 184, 357,
      365–366
    pesco vegetarians, 40
    protein choices, 40
    risk for zinc deficiency, 84
    vegan, 40, 184, 357–358
    vegetarians, 1

Venison Pie with Cornbread Topping, 319

Venison Stir-Fry, 321

Vidalia onion, 133

Vietnamese noodle soup, 247

Vinegars, 142–143, 186

Vitamins, 210
    affecting retention, 158
    discovery, 13
    fat soluble, 44, 54–59
    and oxidation, 156
    provitamin, 55
    pseudovitamins, 67
    supplements, 54
    vitamin A, 40, 54–56, 180, 220, 264, 287,
      315, 323, 331
    vitamin B, 27, 40, 42, 54–55, 59–68, 180,
      220, 259, 264, 286, 319
    vitamin C, 11, 41–42, 51, 54, 68–70, 180,
      266, 315, 321, 360
    vitamin D, 27, 41, 46, 54–55, 57–59, 73, 220
    vitamin E, 42, 54, 56–57, 264, 293
    vitamin K, 54–55, 57, 251, 253, 264
    water soluble, 54, 59–70, 156, 158

von Liebig, Justus, 13

W

Waffles, 215–216, 223

Walnut French Beans, 294

Walnut vinaigrette, 276

Wasabi, 124

Weight control, 165–177

Weight Watchers, 165

Whey, 43

White Bean Clam Chowder, 255

White Fluffy Cake with Peaches and Nectar,
    379

White Vegetable Stock, 138

Whole Wheat and Almond Waffles, 216

Wild Mushroom and Cherry Sauce, 310

Wild Rice Corn Fritters with Sour Cream,
    Cinnamon Sauce, 228

Wines, 145–151, 161

Winter Squash with Apples and Pears, 299

Wok, 157

World Association of Cooks Societies, 128

Y

Yellow onion, 133

Yogurt and Banana Mousse, 376

Z

Zinc, 41, 84–85, 99, 350, 354

Recipe Index

Breakfast Foods, 209–226

Sunflower Seed Pancakes with Honey Roasted Figs, 211
Vanilla Bran Pancakes with Strawberry Yogurt, 212
Gingerbread Pancakes with Applesauce and Yogurt, 213
Spanish Pancakes, 214
Country Waffles with Hazelnut Yogurt, 215
Whole Wheat and Almond Waffles, 216
Apple Syrup, 217
Peach Syrup, 217
Blueberry Oatmeal Crunch, 218
Peach Granola, 219
Strawberry Granola Parfait, 219
Maple Flavored Vegetable Blintzes, 220
Apple Blintzes, 221
Ham and Cheese Grits, 222
Turkey Breakfast Sausage, 223
Cornbread Biscuits and Tomato Gravy, 224
Shirred Eggs and Turkey Primavera, 225
Grilled Chicken Breast with Spanish Sauce, 226

Appetizers, 227–245

Wild Rice Corn Fritters with Sour Cream, Cinnamon
    Sauce, 228
Eggplant Pate, 230
Brunoise Salad, 231

Vegetable Pancakes with Sour Cream Horseradish Sauce, 232
Popcorn Shrimp with Chili Sauce, 233
Skewered Sesame Shrimp, 234
Oyster Fritters with Apple and Raisin Chutney, 235
Peppered Cornsticks with Mexican Lime Salsa, 236
Cornbread Pizza, 237
Chicken Fingers with Sauce Anisette, 238
Cajun Chicken Tenders, 239
Crab Coins Maryland, 240
Fennel and Artichoke Hearts: À la Grecque, 241
Roasted Sweet Peppers Vinaigrette, 242
Chick Pea Dip and Vegetables, 243
Pear and Pineapple Relish, 244
Apple Pickles, 244
Barbecue Fruit with Honey and Poppyseed Dressing, 245

Soups, 247–260

Vegetable Barley Soup, 249
Mexican Lentil, 250
Three Bean Soup with Kale, 251
Coriander Turkey Chili, 252
Cabbage and Broccoli Soup with Chick Peas, 253
Forester Chicken Soup, 254
White Bean Clam Chowder, 255
Pottage of Winter Squash, 256
Pumpkin Soup, 257
Chicken and the Sea, 258
Italian Beef and Tomato, 259
Puree of Cauliflower and Yellow Split Peas, 260

Salads and Entremets, 261–279

Marinated Pinto Bean Salad, 263
Cajun Bean Salad, 264
Curried Rice Salad, 265
Barley Salad with Sweet Yellow and Red Peppers, 266
Asparagus with Port Wine Vinaigrette, 267
Broccoli-Pasta Salad with Fresh Tuna, 268
Smoked Turkey with Feta and Ziti, 269
Tropical Chicken Salad with Raspberry Vinaigrette, 270
Eggplant Salsa, 271
Broccoli and Cauliflower Coleslaw, 272
Country Slaw, 273
Italian Vegetables with Tomato Basil Vinaigrette, 274

Sweet Potato Salad with Pecan Honey Dressing, 275

Green Beans and Potato Salad with International Greens and Walnut Vinaigrette, 276

Grilled Chicken Salad, 280

Fruit Salad with Honey-Orange Dressing, 279

Vegetables, Legumes, Potatoes, and Grains, 281–300

Braised Cabbages and Bell Peppers, 283

Summer Squash with Ginger and Spring Onions, 284

Glazed Yellow Turnips with Figs, 285

Southern Greens with Honey Mustard Dressing, 286

Oven Roasted Sweet Potato Homefries, 287

Dill and Shallot Hashbrowns, 288

Cranberry Rice Pilaf with Peanuts, 289

Brown Rice Pilaf with Chick Peas and Pecans, 290

Cauliflower Creole, 291

Vegetarian Pilaf, 292

Sesame Carrots and Raisins, 293

Walnut French Beans, 294

Teriyaki Peanut Pasta, 295

Curried Corn and Lima Beans, 296

Braised Mixed Greens with Roasted Garlic, 297

Sweet-and-Sour Brussels Sprouts, 298

Winter Squash with Apples and Pears, 299

Braised Red Cabbage with Apple Cider and Sauterne, 300

Meat, 301–321

Braised Beef Tips au Poivre with Rice Pilaf and Roasted Plum Tomatoes, 304

Caraway Beef with Pearl Onions, 306

Braised Beef Eye Round Sicilian, 307

Braised Beef Sirloin with Ginger-Orange Sauce, 309

Beef Tenderloin Tips with Wild Mushroom and Cherry Sauce, 310

Grilled Flank Steak with Braised Lentils and Chestnuts, 311

Roast Leg of Lamb with Honey Berry Sauce, 312

Roasted Rolled Pork Loin with Turkey Sausage, 313

Lamb Stew with Cranberries and Madeira, 315

Grilled Lamb with Braised Eggplant and Port Wine, 316

Pork Pot Roast and Cider, 317

Fresh Ham Ragoût and Fettucini, 318

Venison Pie with Cornbread Topping, 319

Venison Stir-Fry, 321

Poultry, 323–337

Grilled Sesame Chicken Breast with Basil Marinade, 325
Roasted Sage Chicken, 326
Chicken Paprika, 327
Cajun Chicken Burgers with Jack Cheese Pockets, 328
Smothered Chicken and Onions, 329
Farmer's Style Chicken Marsala, 332
Tzimmes (Jewish Style Chicken Stew), 331
Chicken Piedmont, 332
Maryland's Chicken Succotash, 333
Sicilian Chicken Stew, 334
Raspberry Duck and Pinto Beans, 335
Turkey Breast with Bulgur Clam Stuffing, 336

Seafood, 339–355

Oven Poached Salmon with Leek and Fennel Sauce, 341
Steamed Salmon with Tomatoes and Artichoke Hearts, 342
Oven Poached Sea Trout, 343
Broiled Tuna with Chili Garlic Sauce, 344
Broiled Cajun Catfish, 348
Hazelnut Snapper, 347
Flounder en Papillote, 348
Grouper Florentine with Sesame Sauce, 349
Madeira Shrimp Kabobs, 350
Calamari and Eggplant Stew, 351
Veal and Shrimp Country Gumbo, 352
Scallops and Pineapple Shell Macaroni, 353
Cornbread Oyster Florentine, 354
Maryland Bluefish Cakes, 355

Vegetarian Entrees, 357–369

Vegetable and Wild Rice Stir Fry with Water Chestnuts,
    359
Herbed Black-eyed Peas with Almonds and Raisins, 360
Millet Pilaf with Dates, Apples and Pistachio Nuts, 361
Southeast Indian Bean and Cabbage Pie, 362
Creole Vegetables and Aromatic Rice, 363
Spaghetti Squash with Red Bean Goulash, 364
Fennel Noodles with Cabbage and Yellow Split Peas, 365
Vegetable Lasagna, 366
Vegetable Pizza, 367
Portuguese Style Beans with Pasta, 369